THE EMERGENCY OF BEING

The Emergency of Being

On Heidegger's *Contributions to Philosophy*

RICHARD POLT

Cornell University Press

Ithaca and London

First published 2006 by Cornell University Press
First printing, Cornell Paperbacks, 2013

Library of Congress Cataloging-in-Publication Data

Polt, Richard F. H., 1964–
    The emergency of being : on Heidegger's Contributions to philosophy / Richard Polt.
      p. cm.
    Includes bibliographical references and index.
    ISBN-13: 978-0-8014-3732-8 (cloth : alk. paper)
    ISBN-13: 978-0-8014-7923-6 (paper : alk. paper)
    1. Heidegger, Martin, 1889–1976. Beiträge zur Philosophie. I. Title.
B3279.H48B4536 2006
193—dc22   2006001751

Cornell University Press strives to use environmentally responsible suppliers and materials to the fullest extent possible in the publishing of its books. Such materials include vegetable-based, low-VOC inks and acid-free papers that are recycled, totally chlorine-free, or partly composed of nonwood fibers. For further information, visit our website at www.cornellpress.cornell.edu.

Cloth printing   10 9 8 7 6 5 4 3 2 1
Paperback printing 10 9 8 7 6 5 4 3 2 1

Die Not, jenes Umtreibende, Wesende—wie, wenn es die Wahrheit des Seyns selbst wäre, wie, wenn mit der ursprünglicheren Gründung der Wahrheit zugleich das *Seyn wesender* würde—als das Ereignis?

Emergency—that urgency that assails us in its essential happening—what if it were the truth of be-ing itself? What if, with the more originary grounding of truth, *be-ing* would also come to *happen more essentially*—as the appropriating event?

— *Beiträge zur Philosophie (Vom Ereignis)*, §17

Contents

Acknowledgments

Work on this project was supported by a National Endowment for the Humanities Summer Stipend in 1998 and by sabbatical leaves from Xavier University in fall 1999 and spring 2004.

Earlier versions of portions of this book first appeared as "Metaphysical Liberalism in Heidegger's *Beiträge zur Philosophie*," *Political Theory* 25, no. 5 (October 1997): 655–79, © 1997 by Sage Publications, reprinted by permission of Sage Publications; and "The Event of Enthinking the Event," in *Companion to Heidegger's "Contributions to Philosophy,"* edited by Charles E. Scott, Susan M. Schoenbohm, Daniela Vallega-Neu, and Alejandro Vallega (Bloomington: Indiana University Press, 2001), reprinted by permission of Indiana University Press.

Earlier versions of other portions were presented as "What Is Inceptive Thinking?" at the 1998 meeting of the North American Heidegger Conference, and "Evoking the Momentous Site: Time-Space in the *Contributions to Philosophy*" at the 2003 meeting. I thank Martin Weatherston and Allen Scult for commenting on these papers, and the organizers and attendees for their support and reactions.

I am grateful to Charles Scott and John Sallis for inviting me to participate in the 2000 Collegium Phaenomenologicum in Città di Castello, Italy, which was devoted to the *Contributions*. I learned much from the other participants, including Miguel de Beistegui, Robert Bernasconi, Walter Brogan, Daniel Dahlstrom, Dominique Janicaud, Kenneth Maly, Michael Naas, Hans Ruin, Dennis Schmidt, Susan Schoenbohm, Daniela Vallega-Neu, and David Wood.

For their help in the writing process I thank Timothy Bagley, Duane H. Davis, Daniel J. Dwyer, Chad Engelland, Daniel Fidel Ferrer, Barbara Fiand, Gregory Fried, Charles Guignon, Bob Korth, William McNeill, Sidnie Reed, and Frank Schalow. Special thanks go to Theodore Kisiel for our cooperative archival research.

Abbreviations

GA   Martin Heidegger, *Gesamtausgabe* (Frankfurt am Main: Vittorio Klostermann, 1975–). Followed by volume number and page number(s). Complete information on these volumes is provided in the bibliography.

SZ   Martin Heidegger, *Sein und Zeit*, 8th ed. (Tübingen: Niemeyer, 1957). I provide the German pagination and quote the translation by John Macquarrie and Edward Robinson, *Being and Time* (New York: Harper and Row, 1962).

All references within parentheses in the main text are to GA 65, *Beiträge zur Philosophie (Vom Ereignis)*, edited by Friedrich-Wilhelm von Herrmann, second, revised edition (1994), unless otherwise indicated. The pagination of GA 65 is also provided in *Contributions to Philosophy (From Enowning)*, translated by Parvis Emad and Kenneth Maly (Bloomington: Indiana University Press, 1999). However, translations from GA 65 are my own, as are all other translations unless otherwise indicated. For consistency with my own translations, I have substituted "being" for "Being" and "being-there" for "Dasein" in all quotations from other translations; these substitutions have not been individually noted. Unless otherwise noted, all italics in quotations are from the original.

THE EMERGENCY OF BEING

Introduction: Thinking the Esoteric

The enigmatic manuscript titled *Beiträge zur Philosophie (Vom Ereignis)* was composed by Martin Heidegger in private during 1936–38. It sets the stage for all his later thought by shifting from *Being and Time*'s hermeneutic phenomenology of *Dasein* (the entity who understands being) to a meditation on "the event of appropriation" (*das Ereignis*) as the happening of "be-ing" (*Seyn*) itself.

The project seems crucial, but so far there is less consensus about this book than about nearly any other twentieth-century philosophical text. Is it "Heidegger's major work" or "metaphysical dadaism"?[1] An earthshaking achievement or laughable gibberish? Specialists do not even agree on how to translate *Ereignis*—much less on the value of the text. Even Heidegger himself was uncertain. By showing the manuscript to just a few friends during his lifetime, he gave it a special mystique—but his secretiveness was partly due to his misgivings. The text describes itself only as a premonition of a "work" that would be called *Das Ereignis* (77).[2] It itself is unsuited for publication as

1. Otto Pöggeler, *Martin Heidegger's Path of Thinking*, trans. Daniel Magurshak and Sigmund Barber (Atlantic Highlands, N.J.: Humanities Press, 1987), 286–87; Rüdiger Safranski, *Martin Heidegger: Between Good and Evil*, trans. Ewald Osers (Cambridge: Harvard University Press, 1998), 310. For two early assessments of the *Contributions* that cast doubt on Pöggeler's claims without simply dismissing Heidegger's book, see Jean Grondin's review in *Archives de Philosophie* 53, no. 3 (July–September 1990): 521–23, and Dieter Thomä, *Die Zeit des Selbst und die Zeit danach: Zur Kritik der Textgeschichte Martin Heideggers 1910–1976* (Frankfurt: Suhrkamp, 1990), 761–74.
2. The 1941–42 text by this title that is to be published as GA 71 should not be considered the great "work"; it is a thought-provoking compilation of sketches, much like the *Contributions*,

a "work," Heidegger notes shortly after its completion (GA 66, 427); it is "a framework but not a structure" (GA 69, 5). In fact, even at its inception he surely never expected it to take the form of a treatise to be presented to the public during his lifetime.[3] In 1948, he recalls that when he was working on the text in his cabin in the summer of 1936, he knew that it was an essential step, perhaps the "genuine" (*eigentlich*) step; yet he always understood the text as completely precursory, as its title implies.[4]

Whatever their worth as a work may be, the *Contributions to Philosophy* are forbiddingly strange. They are an arrangement of 281 opaque notes and fragmentary sketches. The language is hypnotically repetitive and dense, consisting of formula after formula in which Heidegger tries to say everything unsayable all at once. The style borrows from Nietzsche's *Zarathustra* and Hölderlin's hymns, without attaining the grace of either writer. The book's pronouncements on the present age offer the grotesque spectacle of a Hegelianized Kierkegaard, where world history is conceived in terms of decision and the moment of crisis, yet no individuals—or hardly any—are capable of making decisions. As an account of the "essential happening of be-ing," the text resembles a treatise; as an investigation of the roots of concepts, it resembles history of philosophy; as an analysis of a crisis, it resembles cultural critique; as an invocation of a moment of decision, it resembles prophecy; as a self-conscious deployment of language, it resembles poetry.

The book's tone is tense, almost desperate.[5] Even though its fundamental mood is said to be "restraint" (§13), it is full of sweeping judgments and im-

---

that describes itself from the start as an attempt that leads down a *Holzweg:* "Das Ereignis" (typescript), *Vorworte*, Loyola University of Chicago Archives, Martin Heidegger-Barbara Fiand Manuscript Collection, acc. no. 99–13, box 4, folder 1. Cf. Friedrich-Wilhelm von Herrmann, "*Contributions to Philosophy* and Enowning-Historical Thinking," in *Companion to Heidegger's "Contributions to Philosophy*," ed. Charles E. Scott et al. (Bloomington: Indiana University Press, 2001), 108.

3. "If in regards to *Being and Time* one may speak of a work that fails, in the case of the *Beiträge* we have to speak of something like a 'work' that from the start *knows that* it fails, and that consequently never considers itself a work at any moment": Felipe Martínez Marzoa, "A propósito de los 'Beiträge zur Philosophie' de Heidegger," *Daimon* 2 (1990): 242. Babette E. Babich suggests that "Heidegger composed his *Beiträge* as a 'posthumous' text," hoping to match the impact of Nietzsche's *Will to Power* while avoiding the editorial manipulations to which Nietzsche's *Nachlaß* was subjected: "Heidegger Against the Editors: Nietzsche, Science, and the *Beiträge* as Will to Power," *Philosophy Today* 47, no. 4 (winter 2003): 329.

4. Martin Heidegger, letter to Fritz Heidegger, June 26, 1948. I thank Barbara Fiand for kindly giving me this letter, which was given to her by Fritz Heidegger.

5. Alexander Schwan effectively describes the *Contributions'* "mixture of heightened emphasis and deepest fury, of ecstatic jubilation and pained infatuation with decline and abyss": "Heidegger's *Beiträge zur Philosophie* and Politics," trans. Elizabeth Brient, in *Martin Heidegger: Politics, Art, and Technology*, ed. Karsten Harries and Christoph Jamme (New York: Holmes and Meier, 1994), 86.

passioned denunciations, driven by an effort to set in motion a revolution comparable only to the beginnings of Greek philosophy—to sow the seeds of a question that might determine the style of thinking for centuries (19). The *Contributions* are arrogant and obsessive, stubborn and self-important, because they are the result of their author's decision to let himself give vent to intimations that were long held back in hesitation (xvii).

What are we to make of this? Many readings of the *Contributions* are either dismissive or imitative. The few analytic philosophers who have not ignored the book have mocked it; this was predictable enough, but the mockery is all the more gleeful thanks to the sheer silliness of the available English translation.[6] The interpretations on the other end of the spectrum tend to be faithful, all too faithful, so that when it comes to the central thoughts of the *Contributions* there is little difference between original and interpretation.[7] The problem here is that interpreting, as Heidegger insists, means working out a projected possibility (SZ 150). The projection opens an interpretive space, a context; to understand something is to put it into context. And it is strictly impossible for a text to state all the context for all its statements. It follows that in order to understand a book, we have to go beyond it. To use a non-Heideggerian metaphor: stereoscopic vision requires different perspectives. To reproduce the surface of a text, no matter how accurately, is not to see the depth, the source of its sayings. Without a perspective of our own on the matter at stake, our interpretation becomes a Potemkin village.[8] It is

---

6. Simon Blackburn, "Enquivering," *The New Republic*, October 30, 2000, 43–48.

7. This is the trend in the writings of Friedrich-Wilhelm von Herrmann, the editor of the *Contributions*, and his students' dissertations. See Friedrich-Wilhelm von Herrmann, *Wege ins Ereignis: zu Heideggers "Beiträgen zur Philosophie"* (Frankfurt am Main: Vittorio Klostermann, 1994) (a collection of essays directly and indirectly concerning the *Contributions*); Paola-Ludovica Coriando, *Der letzte Gott als Anfang: Zur ab-gründigen Zeit-Räumlichkeit des Übergangs in Heideggers "Beiträge zur Philosophie (Vom Ereignis)"* (Munich: Wilhelm Fink, 1998); Christian Müller, *Der Tod als Wandlungsmitte: Zur Frage nach Entscheidung, Tod und letztem Gott in Heideggers "Beiträgen zur Philosophie"* (Berlin: Duncker und Humblot, 1999); Daniela Neu, *Die Notwendigkeit der Gründung im Zeitalter der Dekonstruktion: Zur Gründung in Heideggers "Beiträgen zur Philosophie" unter Hinzuziehung der Derridaschen Dekonstruktion* (Berlin: Duncker und Humblot, 1997); Sang-Hie Shin, *Wahrheitsfrage und Kehre Martin Heideggers: Die Frage nach der Wahrheit in der Fundamentalontologie und im Ereignis-Denken* (Würzburg: Königshausen und Neumann, 1993). However, these authors do recognize the need for an independent grasp of the matters (e.g., Coriando, *Der letzte Gott als Anfang*, 23; Neu, *Die Notwendigkeit der Gründung*, 131), and they present a number of valuable thoughts.

8. Parvis Emad sets up a false dichotomy when he writes, "The notion of a more familiar, more intelligible, more traditional language is a notion with which metaphysics attempts to obfuscate *Ereignis* . . . we who come after Heidegger should stay with his words as words that come from and shelter . . . be-ing": "On 'Be-ing': The Last Part of *Contributions to Philosophy (From Enowning)*," in Scott et al., *Companion*, 243; cf. Parvis Emad, "On the Inception of Being-Historical Thinking and its Unfolding as Mindfulness," *Heidegger Studies* 16 (2000): 71. Instead of opposing familiar language to Heideggerian language, we should oppose imitation (of the tra-

equally true, however, that any interpretation that forces a text into its own preconceptions is reductive and shallow. The solution is to engage in a hermeneutic circle: the reader's own standpoint should illuminate the text, but the text, in turn, should be allowed to transform that standpoint. In a good interpretation, this circle reveals progressively more facets of both the text and the issues at hand. The goal is not to correspond to the words of the text, but to co-respond with the text to the issues.

This approach is exemplified by Reiner Schürmann's posthumous magnum opus, *Broken Hegemonies*,[9] and Miguel de Beistegui's *Truth and Genesis*.[10] Both authors present close but tendentious readings of the *Contributions* as part of their larger projects. Schürmann's project is a deconstructive account of the self-dissolution of principles; Beistegui's is a constructive, Deleuzian account of being as difference. Although I disagree with both interpretations, their very tendentiousness makes them the most thought-provoking to date.

I have tried, then, to provide perspective on the *Contributions*—neither in order to reduce the text to familiar concepts nor to refute it, but to engage with it in a confrontation about "the things themselves." A confrontation is not a polemic, but an encounter with a way of thinking that respects it and learns from it precisely by struggling with it.[11] In a confrontation, more must

---

dition or of Heidegger) to genuine thought. If Heidegger manages to "shelter be-ing," it is not by means of particular words but by finding a voice that is his *own*. This is what we must try to do as well. The point is to find our own resources for thinking about Heidegger's topics, and not to translate Heidegger into an "ontologically neutral language" (Emad rightly observes that there is no such thing): Parvis Emad, "The Place of the Presocratics in Heidegger's *Beiträge zur Philosophie*," in *The Presocratics after Heidegger*, ed. David C. Jacobs (Albany: State University of New York Press, 1999), 70.

9. Reiner Schürmann, *Broken Hegemonies*, trans. Reginald Lilly (Bloomington: Indiana University Press, 2003). This book incorporates and supersedes Schürmann's essays on the *Contributions*: "A Brutal Awakening to the Tragic Condition of Being: On Heidegger's *Beiträge zur Philosophie*," in Harries and Jamme, *Martin Heidegger*; "Riveted to a Monstrous Site," in *The Heidegger Case: On Philosophy and Politics*, ed. Joseph Margolis and Tom Rockmore (Philadelphia: Temple University Press, 1992); "Technicity, Topology, Tragedy: Heidegger on 'That Which Saves' in the Global Reach," in *Technology in the Western Political Tradition*, ed. Arthur M. Melzer, Jerry Weinberger, and M. Richard Zinman (Ithaca: Cornell University Press, 1993); "Ultimate Double Binds," in *Heidegger Toward the Turn: Essays on the Work of the 1930s*, ed. James Risser (Albany: State University of New York Press, 1999). For an introduction to *Broken Hegemonies* see Reginald Lilly, "The Topology of *Des Hégémonies brisées*," *Research in Phenomenology* 28 (1998): 226–42; for an overview of Schürmann's reading of the *Contributions* see Dominique Janicaud, "Back to a Monstrous Site: Reiner Schürmann's Reading of Heidegger's *Beiträge*," *Graduate Faculty Philosophy Journal* 19, no. 2/20, no. 1 (1997): 287–97.

10. Miguel de Beistegui, *Truth and Genesis: Philosophy as Differential Ontology* (Bloomington: Indiana University Press, 2004). This book incorporates and supersedes Beistegui's "The Transformation of the Sense of Dasein in Heidegger's *Beiträge zur Philosophie (Vom Ereignis)*," *Research in Phenomenology* 33 (2003): 221–46.

11. Confrontation (*Auseinandersetzung*) is essential to Heidegger's understanding of truth: see Gregory Fried, *Heidegger's Polemos: From Being to Politics* (New Haven: Yale University Press,

be at stake than competing sets of statements; the parties must remain focused on a shared concern. Accordingly, this book is not simply an introduction to the *Contributions*.[12] Although I seek various points of entry to the text, my main goal could be called an *extra*duction. I want to lead myself and my readers through the text and out of it in order to encounter the issues at stake. In fact, the very distinction between inside and outside is ultimately artificial: one cannot dwell "within" a text unless one interprets the theme that lies "outside" it.

The central theme in my confrontation with the *Contributions* is emergency. The *Contributions* venture the thought that being comes into its own in *Not*—emergency, urgency, exigency. Genuine encounters with beings (*das Seiende*)—the earth on which we dwell, the tools we use, the art we create, the communities in which we try to work out our goals—require a rare, urgent moment when we appropriate and are appropriated by the significance of beings as a whole. Heidegger usually calls this significance *Sein*, "being," while calling the event of appropriation, the event in which being emerges, *Seyn*—which I render as "be-ing." (I develop these concepts at length in chapter 1.) The heart of history, for Heidegger, is not a sequence of occurrences but the happening of be-ing—the eruption of significance at "inceptions," or critical junctures. Such a juncture decides the course of an epoch; it initiates a realm of truth and an order of representation. An inception would appropriate us, or bring us into our own, by making all being, including our being, into an urgent issue. Unlike a conventional emergency, such a moment may not call for immediate action; in fact, it may leave us at a loss and call for long reflection. Yet the word *emergency* appropriately describes how such an extraordinary event calls us into question. In emergency, being emerges.

Heidegger charges our tradition with oblivion to the emergency of being. In particular, the three political alternatives of the twentieth century—lib-

---

2000), 44–66; Gail Stenstad, "*Auseinandersetzung* in the Thinking of Be-ing," *Existentia* 10 (2000): 1–10.

12. I provide brief orientations in *Heidegger: An Introduction* (Ithaca: Cornell University Press, 1999), 140–52, and in "*Beiträge zur Philosophie (Vom Ereignis):* Ein Sprung in die Wesung des Seyns," in *Heidegger-Handbuch: Leben — Werk — Wirkung*, ed. Dieter Thomä (Stuttgart: J. B. Metzler, 2003). Daniela Vallega-Neu's *Heidegger's "Contributions to Philosophy": An Introduction* (Bloomington: Indiana University Press, 2003) skillfully discusses the *Contributions* in Heidegger's own language, improves on the Emad and Maly translation, and relates the *Contributions* to *Being and Time*. Two early but exceptionally lucid overviews are Jean Greisch, "Études heideggériennes: Les 'Contributions à la Philosophie (À Partir de l'*Ereignis*)' de Martin Heidegger," *Revue des sciences philosophiques et théologiques* 73, no. 4 (October 1989): 605–32, and the review by Walter Patt in *Philosophisches Jahrbuch* 98 (1991): 403–9. Another excellent survey is Hans Ruin, "Contributions to Philosophy," in *A Companion to Heidegger*, ed. Hubert L. Dreyfus and Mark A. Wrathall (Oxford: Blackwell, 2005).

eral democracy, communism, and fascism—all come under attack. Contemporary politics, along with science, philosophy, and religion, are part of a Western culture that Heidegger sees as estranged from the happening of history—dangerously so, because our oblivion brings with it the hubris of supposing that we can establish an absolute, ahistorical mode of representing and manipulating beings. This hubris is a betrayal of our unique role as *Dasein*—the guardians and cultivators of emergent being. The *Contributions*, then, attempt to shock us into an awareness of our current crisis—*die Not der Not-losigkeit*, the emergency of the lack of urgency—by exposing the oblivion of be-ing.[13] Heidegger tries to find a way beyond this crisis by reflecting on its ancient roots and developing a new way of thinking that is appropriate to the event of appropriation.

The central questions for my interpretation are: how would being emerge in an emergency? How would this emergency draw us into our own world, our own way of approaching all that is? And how would we properly think and speak of this event? In pursuing these questions, I interpret *das Ereignis* as a unique happening that is not in effect a priori or "always already." It is also a *possible* event that demands to be thought in a future-subjunctive tonality, as a "what if?" Such thinking is not a description of what is directly or indirectly given, but an experimental thinking that ventures into the possibility of the self-concealing event of giving. Against most interpreters, I choose this *difficilior lectio*—a reading that is more difficult, not at all because it contradicts Heidegger's text but because it upsets our received ways of conceiving. We tend to think of philosophy in a present-indicative tonality, as an account of present or quasi-present structures. In contrast, the *Contributions* invite us to risk a kind of thought that leaps into a singular possibility, a possibility that exceeds thought but also requires thought. In this sense, the event of thinking of appropriation "is" the very event that it thinks.

Although my confrontation with the *Contributions* requires a close interpretation of the text, it is not intended as an all-inclusive commentary. The sheer length and richness of Heidegger's book rule that out. I provide detailed readings of some particularly important passages, but in general I range freely through the text as I gather relevant references; and while I discuss all the main "positive" ideas in the *Contributions*, I say little about their "negative" ideas. Heidegger's critiques of traditional philosophy and the modern world cannot be judged properly until we have confronted their source—the

---

13. For another interpretation of the *Contributions* that takes this theme as its "thread of Ariadne" see Umberto Regina, "Phenomenology and the Salvation of Truth: Heidegger's Shift in the *Beiträge zur Philosophie*," in *Manifestations of Reason*, ed. Anna-Teresa Tymieniecka (Dordrecht: Kluwer, 1993).

thought of *Ereignis*.[14] In my final chapter, however, I engage with parts of Heidegger's critique—his attacks on liberalism and reason—in order to begin a reply to his characterization of the West.

One more task I have had to forego is an account of the *Contributions'* place in Heidegger's writings as a whole—not to mention their endless connections to other thinkers.[15] I draw on other Heideggerian texts and discuss the

14. As Massimo De Carolis observes, "the analysis of the present is not a simple 'application' . . . of theories advanced in the *Beiträge*," but spurs the central thoughts of the text by experiencing the present age as threatened by a lack of genuine history and be-ing: "La possibilità della decisione nei 'Beiträge,'" *Aut Aut* 248–49 (March–June 1992): 177. Nevertheless, such an experience presupposes some "positive" understanding of history and be-ing. In chapter 4 I investigate the relation between our experience of the present and the possibility of appropriation. For accounts of the "negative" dimension of the *Contributions*, see Babich, "Heidegger Against the Editors"; Stuart Elden, "Taking the Measure of the *Beiträge*: Heidegger, National Socialism and the Calculation of the Political," *European Journal of Political Theory* 2, no. 1 (January 2003): 35–56; Parvis Emad, "Mastery of Being and Coercive Force of Machination in Heidegger's *Beiträge zur Philosophie* and *Besinnung*," in *Vom Rätsel des Begriffs: Festschrift für Friedrich-Wilhelm v. Herrmann zum 65. Geburtstag*, ed. Paola-Ludovika Coriando (Berlin: Duncker und Humblot, 1999); Sigbert Gebert, "'Für die Wenigen—Für die Seltenen': Heideggers Zeitdiagnose, Technikkritik und der 'andere Anfang,'" *Perspektiven der Philosophie* 30 (2004): 209–38; Trish Glazebrook, "The Role of the *Beiträge* in Heidegger's Critique of Science," *Philosophy Today* 45, no. 1 (spring 2001): 24–32; Friedrich-Wilhelm von Herrmann, "Technology, Politics, and Art in Heidegger's *Beiträge zur Philosophie*," in Harries and Jamme, *Martin Heidegger*; Su-jeong Lee, "Zeitkritik bei Heidegger," in Coriando, *Vom Rätsel des Begriffs*; Paul Livingston, "Thinking and Being: Heidegger and Wittgenstein on Machination and Lived-Experience," *Inquiry* 46 (2003): 324–45; Theodorus C. W. Oudemans, "Echoes from the Abyss? Philosophy and 'Geopolitics' in Heidegger's *Beiträge* and *Besinnung*," *Existentia* 10 (2000): 69–88; Otto Pöggeler, *The Paths of Heidegger's Life and Thought*, trans. John Bailiff (Atlantic Highlands, N.J.: Humanities Press, 1997), 172–85; Tom Rockmore, *On Heidegger's Nazism and Philosophy* (Berkeley: University of California Press, 1992), chap. 5; Schwan, "Heidegger's *Beiträge zur Philosophie* and Politics"; Charles E. Scott, "Seyn's Physicality," *Existentia* 10 (2000): 21–27; Nicolas Tertulian, "The History of Being and Political Revolution: Reflections on a Posthumous Work of Heidegger," in Rockmore and Margolis, *The Heidegger Case*; Nicolas Tertulian, "Qui a peur du débat?" *Les temps modernes* 45, no. 529 (August–September 1990): 214–40; Silvio Vietta, *Heideggers Kritik am Nationalsozialismus und an der Technik* (Tübingen: Niemeyer, 1989), chap. 5. One should also be aware that Heidegger's interpretation of modernity owes much to his readings of Nietzsche (GA 43, GA 44, GA 46, GA 87) and Jünger (GA 90).

15. As an exploration of Heidegger's development in the context of broader intellectual history, with frequent references to the *Contributions*, Pöggeler's *Martin Heidegger's Path of Thinking* and *The Paths of Heidegger's Life and Thought* are unmatched. Quite a few studies connecting the *Contributions* to particular other thinkers are also available. For the surely unwitting parallels to Franz Rosenzweig's concept of *Ereignis*, see Bernhard Casper, "'Ereignis': Bemerkungen zu Franz Rosenzweig und Martin Heidegger," in *Jüdisches Denken in einer Welt ohne Gott: Festschrift für Stéphane Mosès*, ed. Jens Mattern (Berlin: Vorwerk, 2001). Going farther afield, one can compare the *Contributions* to neo-Platonism: Albert Peter Durigon, "Heidegger and the Greeks: Hermeneutical-Philosophical Sketches of Ignorance, Blindness and Not-Being in Heidegger's *Beiträge*, Plato, Plotinus and Proclus" (Ph.D. diss., Trinity College Dublin, 1998); Paul Edward Pedersen, "Martin Heidegger on the Homelessness of Modern Humanity and the Ultimate God" (Ph.D. diss., Cornell University, 2001). Or to Buddhism: Dieter Sinn, *Ereignis und Nirwana: Heidegger—Buddhismus—Mythos—Mystik; Zur Archäotypik des Denkens* (Bonn: Bou-

evolution from *Being and Time* in some detail, but my main focus is what I take to be distinctive about the *Contributions* themselves. There is a characteristic tone and approach in this text that fits its understanding of appropriation—an understanding that may not jibe with later works, which seem to dilute the urgency, uniqueness, and historicity of *Ereignis*.[16] Determining the precise relation between the *Contributions* and Heidegger's later writings would take much more textual and philosophical work than I have done; furthermore, we are still awaiting the publication of some of the private texts from the years immediately following the *Contributions*.[17] It is probably true that we could fit the *Contributions* into a unitarian interpretation of Heidegger's thought if we simply discarded their "apocalyptic language . . . the cosmic drama, the mystical metaphors, the Teutonic bombast."[18] Before we do

---

vier, 1991). On the more obvious and deliberate connections to Nietzsche, see Keith Ansell-Pearson, "The An-Economy of Time's Giving: Contributions to the Event of Heidegger," *Journal of the British Society for Phenomenology* 26, no. 3 (October 1995): 268–78; Babich, "Heidegger Against the Editors"; Ernst Behler, "The Nietzsche Image in Heidegger's *Beiträge, Contributions to Philosophy (On the Event)*," *International Studies in Philosophy* 27, no. 3 (1995): 85–94; Parvis Emad, "Nietzsche in Heideggers *Beiträge zur Philosophie*," in *"Verwechselt mich vor Allem nicht!": Heidegger und Nietzsche*, ed. Hans-Helmuth Gander (Frankfurt am Main: Vittorio Klostermann, 1994); Golfo Maggini, "Le 'style de l'homme à venir': Nietzsche dans les *Contributions à la Philosophie* de Martin Heidegger," *Symposium* 2, no. 2 (1998): 191–210.

16. See below, pp. 74–75, and Richard Polt, "*Ereignis*," in Dreyfus and Wrathall, *A Companion to Heidegger*. Most interpreters have assumed that the meaning of *Ereignis* is established in the *Contributions* and remains stable thereafter: e.g., Parvis Emad, "A Conversation with Friedrich-Wilhelm von Herrmann on Heidegger's *Beiträge zur Philosophie*," in *Phenomenology: Japanese and American Perspectives*, ed. Burt C. Hopkins (Dordrecht: Kluwer, 1999), 156; Friedrich-Wilhelm von Herrmann, "*Contributions to Philosophy* and Enowning-Historical Thinking," in Scott et al., *Companion*, 105, 125; Otto Pöggeler, "Being as Appropriation," trans. R. H. Grimm, in *Martin Heidegger: Critical Assessments*, ed. Christopher Macann, vol. 1 (London: Routledge, 1992). These interpreters follow Heidegger himself, who claims in 1962 that the essential structure (*Wesensbau*) of *Ereignis* was "worked out between 1936 and 1938": *On Time and Being*, trans. Joan Stambaugh (New York: Harper and Row, 1972), 43. (Pöggeler has subsequently modified his view: cf. *The Paths of Heidegger's Life and Thought*, 115.)

17. These texts include *Besinnung* (GA 66, written 1938–39, published 1997), *Die Geschichte des Seyns* (GA 69, written 1938–40, published 1998), *Über den Anfang* (GA 70, written 1941, published 2005), *Das Ereignis* (GA 71, forthcoming, written 1941–42), and *Die Stege des Anfangs* (GA 72, forthcoming, written 1944), as well as a series of notebooks titled *Überlegungen* (GA 94–96, forthcoming). English translations of GA 66 and GA 69 are in progress. I was able to consult typescripts of "Das Ereignis," "Überlegungen" VIII–XI, and "Der Anklang" (a text probably dating from the late 1930s) at the Loyola University of Chicago Archives, along with a typescript of the *Contributions* that includes handwritten annotations (all these papers belong to the Loyola University of Chicago Archives, Martin Heidegger-Barbara Fiand Manuscript Collection, acc. no. 99–13). I occasionally draw on these texts as well as on GA 66, GA 69, and GA 70 in this book. On the relation between the *Contributions* and their successors, see Beistegui, *Truth and Genesis*, chap. 5; Emad, "On the Inception of Being-Historical Thinking"; Jürgen Gedinat, "De l'un et de l'autre," *Heidegger Studies* 16 (2000): 73–86; Friedrich-Wilhelm von Herrmann, "Besinnung als seinsgeschichtliches Denken," *Heidegger Studies* 16 (2000): 37–53.

18. Thomas Sheehan, "A Paradigm Shift in Heidegger Research," *Continental Philosophy Review* 34 (2001): 201.

so, however, we should meditate on apocalypse. *Apo-calypsis* means exactly the same as *a-letheia:* unconcealment, revelation. Could it be that truth takes place in a moment of crisis?[19] Could it be that the *Contributions'* focus on emergency offers a distinctive and valuable understanding of truth and be-ing—including our own being?[20] Between *Being and Time*'s decisionistic ten-dencies and the later texts' nearly quietistic *Gelassenheit*, the *Contributions* may leave room for free action while thinking far beyond traditional concepts of subjectivity and will.

The first and closest interpretation of a foreign-language text is transla-tion. Parvis Emad and Kenneth Maly's translation of the *Contributions* rep-resents years of interpretive labor. However, I have presented my own translations and paraphrases here—first, so as not to spare myself the work of interpreting each word anew, and second, because it must be said that the existing translation is often peculiar, inconsistent, or misleading. Despite a number of felicitous coinages (such as "be-ing" for *Seyn*, which I gratefully adopt), and despite the fact that Heidegger himself invents words in the *Con-tributions*, the translators have resorted to neologisms too often. Their more bizarre constructions (such as "enswaying" and "charming-moving-unto") have made the fog surrounding Heidegger's text nearly impenetrable. This is the sort of esotericism that, as I will argue, is extrinsic and hinders readers from confronting the intrinsic mystery. I prefer to use established English words while allowing their connotations to adapt to a new context. Heideg-ger himself usually adopts normal words (such as *Ereignis* and *Wesen*), so that even though these words gain new meanings in his experiments, they retain a connection to the old. Language opens fresh horizons by drawing creatively on its own heritage—not by breaking with it.[21] In particular, I have not suc-

19. Cf. Mario Enrique Sacchi, *The Apocalypse of Being: The Esoteric Gnosis of Martin Heidegger*, trans. Gabriel Xavier Martinez (South Bend, Ind.: St. Augustine's Press, 2002), 13, 26, 110–11. Unfortunately, this book is a second-rate Thomist diatribe that does not take our question seriously.

20. "Are there fundamental shifts in the sense of be-ing that accompany the shift from *Con-tributions'* mood of anticipation, ambivalently suspended between awe and alarm, to the postwar quiet sense of releasement to what gives itself?" David Crownfield, "The Last God," in Scott et al., *Companion*, 226.

21. As Dennis J. Schmidt puts it, the ideal would be "a translation which operates in English in the same manner that Heidegger's language worked upon German": "Strategies for a Possi-ble Reading," in Scott et al., *Companion*, 45. What Heidegger does is "inscribe this common (and philosophically traditional) German word [*Wesen*] in a discourse so originary as to transform the sense of the word": John Sallis, "Grounders of the Abyss," in Scott et al., *Companion*, 196. In other words, the meaning cannot be captured by a recondite English expression, but must emerge from the context. By avoiding familiar renditions of words, Emad and Maly try to em-ulate Heidegger's own practice of "essential translation": see Parvis Emad, "Thinking More Deeply into the Question of Translation: Essential Translation and the Unfolding of Language," in *Reading Heidegger: Commemorations*, ed. John Sallis (Bloomington: Indiana University Press, 1993). But Heidegger's daring "translations" of Greek passages are meant for audiences who al-

ceeded in employing "enowning" as a meaningful English counterpart to *Ereignis*. The translators' cases against "event" and "appropriation" are less than convincing, as I will show—so I translate *Ereignis* by the more traditional "appropriation," "appropriating event," and "event of appropriation," expressions whose worst fault is their length.[22]

I have also decided to translate *Da-sein* (which is usually hyphenated in the *Contributions*) as "being-there." Since the publication of Macquarrie and Robinson's version of *Being and Time* in 1962, most Anglophone Heidegger scholars have left *Dasein* untranslated (with the notable exception of William J. Richardson, who uses "There-being" in his 1963 *Heidegger: Through Phenomenology to Thought*). I am persuaded by Daniel Dahlstrom that it is high time we found ways of speaking about the matter in English.[23] *Dasein* runs the risk of serving as a bit of jargon that is so familiar that we no longer pause to consider what it means. Dahlstrom recommends "being-here." For my purposes, "being-there" is best, because the *Contributions* suggest that we are not yet *Da-sein*, or not fully so. The child's backseat refrain is a good question: are we there yet? The "there" is not necessarily here, and being-there is not necessarily being human. In "being-there" we must hear several meanings. First, being-there is being *situated in* a "there," inhabiting a place or world. Second, it is a way of *being* the "there"—existing as a site (SZ 133). Third, it is the "there" *for* being—the site where the meaning of beings as such can be manifested, cultivated, and transformed. In short: if we attain being-there, we will dwell in our world in such a way that we become the arena where it is decided what it means to be.[24]

---

ready know the accepted sense of the original. A translation of an entire book meant for an audience that may never read the original has to be held to more conventional standards of accuracy. For a model of a more straightforward and responsible translation cf. Martin Heidegger, *Aportes a la filosofía: Acerca del evento*, trans. Dina V. Picotti C. (Buenos Aires: Editorial Almagesto and Editorial Biblos, 2003).

22. As opposed to "enowning," Karin de Boer's "the occurrence of own-ing" has the advantage of being actual (if hyphenated) English: *Thinking in the Light of Time: Heidegger's Encounter with Hegel* (Albany: State University of New York Press, 2000), 347. Other apt renditions of Ereignis would be "eventuation" (Susan Schoenbohm, "Reading Heidegger's Contributions to Philosophy," in Scott et al., *Companion*, 18; David Wood, *Thinking after Heidegger* [Cambridge, UK: Polity, 2002], chapter 10), "emergence" (John Bailiff's translation in Pöggeler, *The Paths of Heidegger's Life and Thought*, viii), or "befitting" (Gail Stenstad, following a suggestion by Kenneth Maly: Stenstad, "The Last God—A Reading," *Research in Phenomenology* 23 [1993]: 183). I choose "appropriation" partly for the sake of extending some established conversations in English-language secondary literature, and partly in order to preserve the sense of ownness. It should be noted that "appropriation" is more obviously abstract than *das Ereignis*, which suggests a singular happening.

23. Daniel O. Dahlstrom, *Heidegger's Concept of Truth* (Cambridge: Cambridge University Press, 2001), xxii–xxvi.

24. Against the translation "being-there" see Sheehan, "A Paradigm Shift," 193–94. Sheehan

The Esoteric Turbulence of the *Contributions*

So far, we have not confronted the *Contributions* but only announced the confrontation. The confrontation itself needs to begin with the book's style. How does it resist our desire for a straightforward and consistent doctrine? Why is it so turbulent and esoteric? What does it demand from its interpreters?

Heidegger claims that the pursuit of his single philosophical "way" *necessitates* a change in standpoints (84). If philosophy is a doctrine—a system of assertions—then this claim is a paradox: a change in the assertions is a change in the philosophy. But Heidegger always insists that truth is not a matter of assertions. Assertions rest on a more primordial unconcealment, an openness for beings and being. A thoughtful text should let its statements spring anew every time from an experience of an issue (21) and try to evoke an analogous experience in the reader. Such a text does not prove anything—if proving means establishing that an assertion is indubitably correct. Philosophy proves itself only by proving successful in *displaying* the issue to which its assertions are pointing. The effort of displaying has to involve both the writer and the reader. The process is faltering—"collapsing and climbing" (84)—because revelation is never total. Presence is always situated, display is always limited.

But why would a persistent focus on the same issue lead to a change of standpoints? We must look more closely at the limitations of display. *Being and Time* tries to show that presence requires the interplay of past and future (SZ 350). Our past, our habits and heritage, is the source from which we draw future possibilities. Thanks to these possibilities, we are able to deal with things—we understand them. Interpreting, then, is an intrinsically finite event: it can never abolish either the uncontrollable thrownness that comes with having a past or the prejudicial anticipations that come with having a future. Interpretation can never vouch for its completeness and permanence by securing an immediate and pure access to its object. But although we cannot eliminate the limits of interpretation, we can work with them and challenge them in an ongoing disclosure. Our past can be critiqued and retrieved; our prejudices can be altered in an attempt to do justice to the thing we are interpreting (SZ 153). This is the meaning of *Sachlichkeit*—devotion to the *Sachen*, the things themselves. It is a willingness to wrestle with the issues and with oneself in an interpretation that acknowledges its own temporality.[25]

---

prefers "openness," but the word "there" provides a needed sense of particularity and finitude, and I do not think it is right to interpret *-sein* as an abstract "-ness."

25. Richard Polt, "Heidegger's Topical Hermeneutics: The *Sophist* Lectures," *Journal of the British Society for Phenomenology* 37, no. 1 (1996): 53–76.

Unconcealment is not contained in any particular assertion generated by this interpreting. It occurs in the interpretive motion itself, as long as we continue to confront the issue at hand and the limits of our understanding. Consequently, a statement that participates in the event of truth at one moment may at a later moment be stuck in a stagnant understanding that is no longer actively interpreting.[26] Interpretations of the same thing must stay in motion in order to remain loyal to the thing.

Motion is not identical with alteration. Interpreting may remain in motion even if it simply consists of repeated efforts to grasp something with the same words and concepts. In fact, this repetitive style is common in the *Contributions* and Heidegger's other private manuscripts. Our task is to avoid mouthing his statements as mantras, and think through them anew on each occasion. In this way our understanding remains in motion, even if it is only moving in a circle. However, alteration can and should be part of the motion of interpreting. The circle can become a truly hermeneutic circle—or a helix that deepens its approach to its theme with each new turn. As we discover our limitations, our words and thoughts can change. Such progress is not upward progress, the construction of a cathedral of thought. It is downward progress, the excavation of our own foundations, the discovery of elusive bedrock that always threatens to be covered up again by the rubble we generate in uncovering it. This is quarry work. The turbulence of the *Contributions*—their sometimes rushing, sometimes halting search for new approaches to the same topic—is not due to the fact that the text is a set of notes rather than a finished work; turbulence is an essential aspect of interpretation as Heidegger sees it.[27]

But the book is not just hermeneutic; it is hermetic. Not only is it engaged in a constant struggle, but it also seems to refuse us access to its inner sanctum. At crucial points, it frustrates the desire for clarity. What is the source of this esotericism? An esoteric text keeps its meaning on the "inside," where only some are privileged to enter. But what does it mean to be inside or outside a text? And may one write about an esoteric text without being esoteric oneself?

---

26. Heidegger calls this degenerate understanding "a free-floating naming": *History of the Concept of Time: Prolegomena*, trans. Theodore Kisiel (Bloomington: Indiana University Press, 1985), 87. Cf. SZ 19, 36.

27. Parvis Emad has repeatedly objected to the view of the *Contributions* as "a compilation of a series of notes": "The Echo of Being in *Beiträge zur Philosophie — Der Anklang:* Directives for its Interpretation," *Heidegger Studies* 7 (1991): 28; cf. Emad, "A Conversation," 165. But the book obviously *is* a compilation of notes, albeit thoughtful notes carefully compiled. To deny this is to risk stilling the turbulence of thinking and establishing an overly schematic interpretation. On "the restlessness of beings" and "the uniqueness of be-ing," which call for a "re-inceptive struggle," see GA 65, 314.

To be admitted into a text is to be admitted into an experience of the issue of the text. An esoteric text maintains watch over who is admitted into the vicinity of its issue. It has a policy of restricted admissions. How do the *Contributions* enforce this policy? Whom do they admit and exclude? Why are they exclusive in the first place?

For decades, the *Contributions* were private in an obvious sense: they were unpublished, and their very existence was a matter for connoisseurs. Heidegger showed the text only to a few confidants who communicated brief selections to other scholars.[28] In Heidegger's last years, he specified that the *Contributions* and other private texts could be published only after all his lecture courses (513).[29] This makes a good deal of sense. The *Contributions* are written in such a condensed and allusive style that they are guaranteed to send a novice away in despair, while the lecture courses usually begin with the tradition and common sense, and are primarily devoted to challenging our presuppositions.

Do the lectures, then, provide the key that unlocks the *Contributions* and admits us to an experience of the issue at stake? The *Contributions* often assume familiarity with the lectures and *Being and Time*—so there is no reason to argue with Heidegger's recommendation that we read other texts first. However, this will not erase the esotericism of the *Contributions* themselves. "The lecture courses always remain superficial; within the fundamental mood, they begin at an apparently arbitrary stretch of the path, and from this point they offer views of the whole" (GA 66, 421). In order to grasp why the starting points of the lectures are not really arbitrary, one must already share the fundamental mood: one must already be initiated into the experience of the topic of Heidegger's thinking. "Maybe at some later time, some will succeed in experiencing what is kept silent [in the lectures] . . . and will then be able to set what is explicitly said within its [proper] limits" (GA 66, 421). The lectures, then, always "come from outside" (GA 69, 173). As exoteric texts, they cannot be fully understood unless one already understands the position from which Heidegger is speaking—so one must grapple with the esoteric *Contributions*.

---

28. Pöggeler, in particular, repeatedly refers to the text in his 1963 study *Martin Heidegger's Path of Thinking*.

29. Heidegger's directive was interpreted loosely, for at the publication of the *Contributions* in 1989, some lecture courses had not yet been published, although editors had been assigned to them. A second, revised edition of the *Contributions* appeared in 1994, and a third edition with no changes appeared in 2003. For the record, the second edition makes the following small corrections: p. 43, line 3: "der letzten" changed to "die letzte"; p. 407, line 2 from bottom: "dem zugehörigen" changed to "dem Zugehörigen"; p. 479, line 17: "seine" changed to "ihre." The photocopied typescript at Loyola University of Chicago includes the following handwritten corrections: GA 65, p. 120, line 20: "*Anspruchs*" changed to "*Aufbruchs*" (consistent with point 3 on page 121); p. 377, line 7 from bottom: "auch in einem" changed to "auch nicht in einem."

When we turn to the *Contributions* themselves, no matter how well we may know the lectures, we find that the style of the book enforces its esotericism—so much that although the text has now been published, its meaning can hardly be said to be public. Consider the second paragraph of §1. It warns us from the start that the text is "not yet able to join [*fügen*] the free juncture [*Fuge*] of the truth of be-ing from be-ing itself"; its center of gravity does not yet lie in the heart of its topic (4). So in order to understand the text, we must already have built our own way to an issue that is not successfully addressed in the text itself. When Heidegger does try to say something about the heart of the matter, in the conclusion of the paragraph we are considering, he resorts to an emphatic but highly obscure sentence, couched in idiosyncratic terms: the "essence of be-ing in its trembling . . . then strengthens into the power of the released mildness of an *intimacy* of that *godding* of the god of gods, from which the *assignment* of being-there to be-ing, as the grounding of truth for be-ing, comes into its own" (4). The words are like emissaries from the inner sanctum, tokens sent out from the hidden center. Like an oracle's words, they seem to speak a private language. This paragraph uses plays on words, repeated sounds, and neologisms: *fügen, Fuge, Gefüge; Götterung des Gottes der Götter. Er-eignis* is echoed in *sich ereignet* ("comes into its own" or, in its usual sense, "takes place"). The odd expression "trembling" (*Erzitterung*) is applied to be-ing, with no explanation. In fact, none of the key words is explained or defined. Some of them are stressed, but because we are not privy to their meaning the stress only heightens the mystery. This passage from the opening of the book shows us that the book has no opening; the beginning presupposes a vocabulary that will never be defined in familiar terms. There is no royal road to the meaning of the text. Instead, Heidegger experiments with families of words, sketching and unsketching connections, straining to say what he knows he is failing to say. The effect of this style is that no single passage is intelligible on its own; instead, we must thrash about and learn to swim.

Who will sink and who will stay afloat? Heidegger's style excludes those who are unfamiliar with his previous writings; those who are unfamiliar with the history of philosophy or too entrenched in some phase of it; and above all, those who are unwilling to experience a transformation. Those who are admitted are those who have followed much of Heidegger's path up to now and who are willing to go further—not because it is his path but because it is also part of their own path. We must experience his attempt as both coming from far away and belonging intimately to us (8).[30]

30. In this sense, Simon Blackburn's gibe is correct. "Heidegger's mantras are not expressions of some achieved vision or experience or emotion. They are instructions to work one up. They are not the records of a pilgrimage, but a prospectus into which you can inscribe your own detail. The orchestra is only tuning up": Blackburn, "Enquivering," 45.

Maybe this can be said of any text: only those with the necessary background and tenacity will be admitted to an experience of the issue that the text is about. But a nonesoteric text presents no deliberate barriers to the unqualified, and may even try to overcome the barriers that these readers carry with themselves. An esoteric text, in contrast, actively fends off the unqualified. It either prevents them from seeing anything at all or points them toward a public (exoteric) message that conceals and protects the true message. The *Contributions* are the former type: to the unqualified, they present not a misleading message, but no message at all—they are unintelligible.

Why write esoterically? One motive can be personal protection from political or religious persecution.[31] This motive might seem to apply to Heidegger. The *Contributions* often attack Nazi ideology, and they certainly could not have been published in the late thirties without exposing Heidegger to serious danger. In fact, the text is at odds not only with Nazism but with all current forms of political organization. And Heidegger was concerned about his political position (witness his stipulation that his 1966 interview with *Der Spiegel* could be published only after his death). But an author's caution does not, per se, make a text esoteric. A manuscript that is treated secretively, that is not published during the author's lifetime, is not necessarily an esoteric manuscript. In fact, the *Contributions* are rather direct in their political criticisms, even if they rarely get into specifics.[32] The political dimension of this book is not the root of its esotericism.

In a writer like Plato we find deeper motives for esoteric writing. Not only is Plato politically cautious (as a follower of Socrates might well be), but he also represents human beings as belonging to different ranks. The true rhetorician must be an expert psychologist who tailors his speech to the soul of his audience (*Phaedrus* 271d, 277b–c). Books—ordinary ones, that is— speak to everyone in the same voice, so they are clumsy and often harmful (*Phaedrus* 275e). Plato seems to have designed his dialogues in such a way that different audiences will be affected differently by them, but each effect will be beneficial for the particular audience affected. For instance, the *Phaedo* presents a number of arguments for the immortality of the soul, all of which are flawed, as well as a series of myths. Those who accept the myths or the arguments will come away with a salutary belief. Those who challenge the

---

31. Leo Strauss holds that philosophers will always have such a motive, since the very nature of what they do challenges the conventional order: *Persecution and the Art of Writing* (Westport, Conn.: Greenwood Press, 1973). We need hardly add that some orders are more dangerous to challenge than others. Cf. Heidegger, *The Essence of Truth: On Plato's Cave Allegory and "Theaetetus,"* trans. Ted Sadler (London: Continuum, 2002), 61–63.

32. Other texts are more direct: in *Besinnung*, Hitler is named, quoted, and criticized severely (GA 66, 122–23).

arguments and recognize the myths as myths will come away with something better: they will become participants in the examined life.

In the *Contributions*, Heidegger does not write in this Platonic way. His is the type of esoteric text that is simply opaque to outsiders, instead of offering them a salutary alternative to the esoteric message. However, he shares Plato's insistence on ranking human beings (§5, §45, §§248–52), and like Plato, he uses the capacity for philosophy as his main criterion. For Heidegger (and arguably for Plato), philosophy means a self-transforming engagement in questioning, not the argumentative construction of theories (13–14). His sentences are elusive, evocative, interrelated yet unsystematic, so that anyone who wants to extract a theory from the text will be frustrated. He thus excludes the philosophical establishment. Those who proceed beyond the bland, empty "public title" *Contributions to Philosophy* and who succeed in thinking *Of Appropriation* will be "the few and the rare" who are capable of solitary questioning (11). Heidegger claims not to care about the misunderstandings that may beset his project among the many: if a decision on behalf of be-ing ever expresses itself, it is inevitably misinterpreted, and this very misinterpretation protects it from "vulgar groping" (92).

Elitism runs deep in the *Contributions*. Heidegger often expresses contempt for the average understanding, which he associates with rationality. He claims reason destroys truth by ignoring differences in rank and treating unconcealment as if it were equally accessible to all (343, cf. 65). We may ask whether he has done justice to reason—but this critical assessment will have to wait. For now, we must see that his distaste for accessibility and rational clarity is linked to his understanding of truth and be-ing. The happening of be-ing is not something that can be represented at any time, however one likes, to whomever one chooses (251).

We are approaching the deepest sense in which this text is esoteric. The types of esotericism we have considered so far are based on prudence: it would be incautious to state certain views directly, because this could be damaging to the author (if the views are controversial), to the audience (if they are not prepared to grasp the views properly), or to the meaning of the text (if it falls into the hands of interpreters who would judge it by an alien standard). All these types of esotericism are extrinsic: the mystery of the philosophical thoughts is not crucial to the thoughts themselves, but is imposed by the cautious style of the author. However, there may also be an *intrinsic* esotericism, as Schelling suggests: "Philosophy is necessarily esoteric, by its very nature. There is no need to try to keep it secret, for, instead, it is essentially mysterious."[33]

33. F. W. J. Schelling, *Bruno: Or On the Natural and the Divine Principle of Things*, trans. and ed. Michael G. Vater (Albany: State University of New York Press, 1984), 133.

Even if we have qualified as genuine thinkers in Heidegger's sense and have grown familiar with his language, the *Contributions* cannot give us direct access to their topic, because this topic is *itself* intrinsically inaccessible to "direct" thought. The event of be-ing withholds itself in the very moment of granting being (the significance of beings). Being is born in the blinding flash of an inception that must remain inexplicable—for every explanation falls short of the inception and degrades it (188). The event of emergence is not itself something that has emerged; the source of openness is not itself open; the origin of givenness is not itself given. What is clear and distinct, then, can only be what is derivative. Heidegger puts this in the most histrionic terms when he declares that if philosophy makes itself understandable, it commits suicide (435). (In "Das Ereignis" he draws the conclusion that true philosophers never seek to understand other philosophers, but only to intensify the questioning.)

Many would object: isn't it the philosopher's mission precisely to clarify the unclear, to shed light on the mysterious? In response, Heidegger would insist that it is not just his text that is esoteric, but his topic itself that is dark. We have to wean ourselves from the notion that the dark is what is not yet illuminated, what would show itself fully if only we found the right access to it. When it comes to be-ing, the right access is partial and indirect. An obscure presentation of an obscure topic is, in a sense, clearer than a clear presentation of that topic. The obscure presentation does justice to the obscurity of the thing. When the topic of one's thought is self-concealing, then there is no difference between seeking and finding (80): the obscure question, the frustrated search, is itself the most appropriate response to the thing.

Heidegger's goal in the *Contributions* was "to say the truth of being simply."[34] Yet being proves to be enigmatic, not because it is too complex but precisely because it is so "simple"—so basic to everything we do and say. The simple saying of the simple topic of being becomes a saying that does not say, a telling silence (78–80). Telling silence makes the *Contributions* an intrinsically esoteric text. As a style of writing, it springs from "restraint" as a style of being-there (15, 33–34). Restrained existence and discourse is attuned to be-ing as what leaves us speechless—what cannot be explained propositionally but only named poetically (36). Restraint lets us respond to the strange without reducing it to the familiar.

Heideggerian restraint parallels Socratic irony. Irony is neither a personal quirk of Socrates that has nothing to do with his philosophical thought, nor a thesis that can be supported by a Socratic argument. It is a style of existing that pervades what Socrates does, says, and does not say—a style that is not

---

34. Heidegger, "Letter on 'Humanism,'" in *Pathmarks*, ed. William McNeill (Cambridge: Cambridge University Press, 1998), 239n (translation modified).

arbitrary but is based on Socrates' own experience of what is at stake in life. We do violence to Socratic irony, we differ from Socrates, as soon as we try to explain irony instead of participating in it. But we may say that Socrates' irony points to his experience of his own limits, an experience that makes him less limited than those who have not yet experienced their limits.

Heidegger, too, speaks from an experience of finitude—finitude as appropriation.[35] As we will see, on the basis of this experience he rejects the Socratic-Platonic postulate of the forms, the *ideai* that serve to orient a life lived in Socratic irony. We will have to ask whether this rejection is justified and whether Heidegger himself avoids postulating an *idea*.

Reading the *Contributions*

We will revisit the style of the *Contributions* in greater depth when we are ready to connect it more thoroughly to their content. But our preliminary look at the book's esoteric turbulence can already give us some guidelines for reading it.

First, if the point of a philosophical text is to reveal an issue, this revelation must depend on the reader at least as much as on the writer. The text demands that we think along with it: "to understand [a philosopher] always means . . . to run up against the same problems on one's own" (GA 28, 185). But how can we be sure that we and the writer are thinking about the same thing? We cannot. All we can do is let the writer's words resonate with our own thoughts and discover whether the insights we gain in this way lead us back productively to the text, showing us new facets of it. As long as this process continues, the reader and writer stand a good chance of being engaged in a dialogue about the same topic.

This is not to suggest that the reader should *agree* with the writer or use the same words. A shared focus brings with it the possibility and even the necessity of differing thoughts. Since our situation differs from Heidegger's, our presuppositions and expectations differ. In order to challenge these limits of our understanding, we need means that differ from his. Thinking the same as Heidegger does not mean being "Heideggerians" who recite his words and imitate his mannerisms. Strictly speaking, there is no such thing as a Heideggerian. Such a creature would have to accept all of Heidegger's assertions—including the assertion that thinking is not a matter of accept-

---

35. "The new concept of finitude is thought in this manner—that is, in terms of Appropriation itself, in terms of the concept of one's own [*Eigentum*]": "Summary of a Seminar on the Lecture 'Time and Being,'" in *On Time and Being*, 54.

ing or rejecting assertions. (Of course, there will always be those who call themselves or are called "Heideggerians," just as there are "Platonists" and "Nietzscheans.") An explanation of Heidegger in purely Heideggerian terms is useful only as a convenient collection of quotations, a reader's digest. It is a reference tool, not a work of interpretation.

How can we develop a vocabulary of our own that will differ from Heidegger's language without discarding it? If we are writing in English, this problem is especially acute: we are forced to "translate" Heidegger's thoughts into an alien tongue. And according to him, not only is it impossible to transfer a thought intact from one language into another, but Greek and German are uniquely suited to philosophical thought.[36] Before we dismiss this view as chauvinism, we have to reflect on certain disadvantages of English. In German, it is easier to transfer a meaning from one part of speech to another—say, to coin the gerund *Götterung* from the noun *Gott*. This helps one break free of certain metaphysical schemes that tend to get encoded by and in grammar. Furthermore, due to the Norman Conquest, most philosophical terms of art in English are based on French, Latin, or Greek rather than on the Anglo-Saxon words we use in everyday speech. But in German (at least until the postwar influx of American culture and vocabulary), most specialized words have been based on everyday words, in a way that makes their roots perspicuous and helps to provoke reflection. There are also certain German expressions that are perfectly suited to plays on words that have no English equivalent. The Hegelian *Aufhebung* is a famous example; a Heideggerian example is *Ur-sprung*, origin as "originary leap."[37]

The translator of Heidegger often has little recourse except to imitate his plays on words with Latinate puns that only some will understand, or to provide ample quotations from the original German. The commentator, however, can mine the extensive resources of English vocabulary, including everyday speech. The result will not be a translation of Heidegger, but an approach to his issue from our own language. It is impossible to make Heidegger speak English, but it is not impossible for English to speak of be-ing.

Of course, it is not enough to differ from Heidegger in our choice of words. We must be independent enough to consider alternative paths, and even to try to catch sight of the blind spot that accompanies him, making his thinking possible yet never itself coming into view. According to Heidegger, every thinker has such a blind spot—the gift of a rich "unthought."[38] In the *Contributions* he compares himself to the first runner in a relay race, who has

36. *Introduction to Metaphysics*, trans. Gregory Fried and Richard Polt (New Haven: Yale University Press, 2000), 60.
37. Ibid., 7.
38. *What Is Called Thinking?* trans. J. Glenn Gray (New York: Harper and Row, 1968), 76.

lit the torch and dared to begin to run. What he needs is not successors (*Nach-läufer*, after-runners) but "*fore*-runners" who will think even more simply, richly, and exclusively (415). Heidegger shudders at the thought of being digested and incorporated into an academic history of philosophy (8). He hopes for interpreters who can open a path to the future (83).

We are to grapple, then, in our own way with the issue of Heidegger's thought. But this issue, he insists, is intrinsically self-concealing—which brings us back to the question of the esoteric. Can a text *about* an esoteric text be any less esoteric than the original without spoiling the original mood and insight? Can we do anything at all in a secondary work that does not violate the darkness of what is at stake?

If we treat the subject of the *Contributions* as a matter to be explained systematically in crystal-clear propositions, we will have to differ violently from Heidegger. He would insist that we must not "explain" philosophy by reducing it to the established parameters of tradition, common sense, or science, because philosophy must preserve the fundamental ambiguity and uncertainty that belongs to its issue itself. Of course, there is no need for this warning to frighten off anyone who genuinely disagrees with Heidegger on this point. There is nothing necessarily wrong with trying to bring perfect clarity to his topic, as long as one recognizes that this attempt in itself is not a neutral method, but already constitutes a disagreement with him.

And if we agree with Heidegger that be-ing is intrinsically mysterious? Even then, we cannot rest satisfied with restating his mysterious words about the mystery. That would substitute his authority for an encounter with the problem itself—not to mention that it makes the very enterprise of secondary literature superfluous. However, we can bring out the grounds for some of his enigmatic statements without attempting to solve the ultimate mystery of be-ing. The *Contributions* are a quarry in which the rock-breaking tools remain invisible (436). But those tools can be made visible to a large extent, as Heidegger's own lecture courses show us. By filling in some gaps in his statements, we can better recognize the mysterious character of the mystery with which he is concerned. The mystery of be-ing may then prove to be not a confused and confusing unintelligibility, but a coherent happening that can show us how it does not show itself. A secondary work can also explore Heidegger's theme by new routes, finding new ways of indicating be-ing through "telling silence." Such a secondary work would itself be esoteric—but it would not abandon critical intelligence.

We should also recall that there is more than one level of esotericism in the *Contributions*. The deepest esotericism is a response to the mystery of be-ing itself. But a more extrinsic esotericism is found in the aspects of Heidegger's style that seem designed to foil the impure readers—those who are unwilling or unable to think along with him. It is possible to maintain the intrinsic esotericism without the extrinsic. In this case, our writing will reach out to readers rather than defend itself against them. It will be a writing designed to invite the reader to come face to face with the intrinsic obscurity of be-ing.

In this book, then, I try to think through Heidegger's text in the light of an independent reflection on its topic: the emergency of being. Hoping to make this topic accessible without imposing a false clarity, I try to avoid two extremes: attempting to capture Heidegger's thought in a propositional system, and complete capitulation to obscurity. The first extreme would be all too typical of an "analytic" approach, the second of a "continental" approach. But more important than these labels is the question of the grounds for esoteric writing. I agree with Heidegger that the topic of be-ing is not susceptible to perfect representation; an exposition of be-ing that aimed at total clarity would be misguided. However, I disagree with the extreme elitism of his understanding of truth. Common experience is capable of depth and transformation. Heidegger himself seems to have acknowledged this earlier: he begins with a respect for "life," for existence in its everyday concreteness, that he loses in his later thought. For early Heidegger, everydayness harbors a richness that is accessible even to the ordinary person, as long as one can resist the tendency to "fall" and can free oneself from some narrow traditional concepts. For later Heidegger, this richness seems to have slipped away. Ordinary existence is so overwhelmed by metaphysics that it is reduced, not just in theory but in fact, to an exercise in representation and manipulation. The encounter with mystery is reserved for "the few and the rare" who can encounter "the final god." In my view, this attitude is false and dangerous. Esotericism as a restricted admissions policy makes a comment on "the many" that does not do justice to the potential of most human beings and their experiences. I propose, then, that we can preserve Heidegger's insight into the self-concealing essence of his topic while avoiding the more elitist features of his style. Consequently, although I write with a limited audience in view, I do not, I hope, write in a way that repels or misleads the uninitiated. A book about one of Heidegger's most difficult texts is never going to appeal to most people, nor should it. But by relating our philosophical discussions to widely shared experiences and avoiding unnecessary jargon, we can produce texts that at least hold the door open to those who are curious and willing.

In keeping with the character of Heidegger's text, I am not presenting my interpretation of the emergency of being in terms of a single thesis or principle. Instead, I follow several avenues that lead to the heart of Heidegger's concerns, and then venture onto some paths of my own.

Chapter 1, "Toward Appropriation," reaches a basic interpretation of *Ereignis* by several routes. First I present a brief meditation on the problem of the given. How is it that beings and being are given to us? How can we understand the character of this giving? I then read Heidegger's early work, including *Being and Time*, as a response to this problem that anticipates the thought of appropriation by exploring modes of ownness or belonging that cannot be reduced to universals. Here I also consider Heidegger's reasons for abandoning the procedure of *Being and Time* and adopting the new approach that culminates in the *Contributions*. Finally, I explore *Ereignis* by way of a key formula from the *Contributions:* "be-ing essentially happens as appropriation."

Chapter 2, "The Event of Thinking the Event," looks more closely at Heidegger's distinctive thinking and writing in the *Contributions*. He tries to forge such a close link between the matter and the manner of his thought that this very distinction is called into question, so as we investigate "stylistic" and "methodological" issues we will be led deeper into the center of his concerns—as we were in this introductory chapter when we began to consider the style of the text. Various aspects of his way of thinking—"inceptive thinking," "bethinking," "sigetic"—reflect his attempt to think in a way that befits the emergency of being as the event of appropriation.

Chapter 3, "Straits of Appropriation," explores some ramifications of *Ereignis*. Appropriation does not have properties, but moments of its emergence as emergency; it has straits, not traits. Here I consider the self-concealment and "fissure" of be-ing, the main features of being-there, the question of "time-space," and be-ing's relations to beings and the gods.

Chapter 4, "Afterthoughts," concludes the book with a series of questions. Here I ask whether, in keeping with Heidegger's understanding of the finitude of philosophy, his own thought has its blind spots.

Are the *Contributions* a great work? When I first read the text, soon after its publication, I characterized it in my notes as "a fertile and infected symphony"—a mixed metaphor that may not be inappropriate for a book that is itself unwieldy and ambiguous. *Contributions to Philosophy* is a dissonant symphony that imperfectly weaves together its moments into a vast fugue, under the leitmotif of appropriation. This fugue is seeded with possibilities that are waiting for us, its listeners, to develop them. Some are dead ends—viruses that can lead only to a monolithic, monotonous misunderstanding of history. Others are embryonic insights that promise to deepen our thought, and perhaps our lives, if we find the right way to make them our own.

1

Toward Appropriation

The *Contributions to Philosophy* must be understood in the context of the basic question of Heidegger's thought. This question itself must be understood in the context of the Western philosophical tradition. Most important, in order to understand Heidegger and the tradition we have to reflect independently on the matters at stake.

All these preliminaries may seem redundant, since we presumably already know what is at stake in Heidegger's thinking and what, according to him, lies spoken or unspoken behind every philosophical problem: "the question of being." But what is this question asking? What topic does Heidegger's word *being* indicate, and why should this topic become a problem in the first place? Even experts on Heidegger often disagree about this most basic issue.[1] This is not a sign of our incompetence or his, but a sign that fundamental questions necessarily remain open to controversy and that we have to keep returning to them. The "preliminaries" often turn out to be the main event.

What we mean by the question of being is indicated by how we respond to it. One can go about answering it by establishing that certain beings exist, or by summing up the general characteristics of beings as such, or by defining what it means to be—yet none of these answers would be accepted by Heidegger as responses to what he means by *die Seinsfrage*. Perhaps we cannot fully understand the question until we have passed through his whole response to it in the *Contributions*. And in this case, a response will not be the

---

1. For an amusing account of the uncertainty see Sheehan, "A Paradigm Shift," 187–92. Sheehan himself proposes discarding the term *being* altogether as a name for the topic (192–93).

same as an answer. The question of being can never be answered as if it were a question about beings; all we can do is intensify the questioning (75).

Keeping these caveats in mind, we can try to broach the question of being in terms of *the problem of the given.* How is it that beings as a whole and as such are given to us? That is, how do we gain access to them and become capable of interpreting them? In addition, how is *being* given to us? That is, how can we come to understand what it means for beings to be? This chapter will first explore these questions independently and then interpret Heidegger's responses to them in his early work. We will then be ready for a basic interpretation of the *Contributions'* central thought: "be-ing essentially happens as appropriation."

The Giving of the Given

We can explore the problem of the given by considering its unfolding in a series of moments. These moments are not meant to correspond precisely to the development of this problem in Western philosophy; I am not suggesting, either, that this is a logically or psychologically necessary series. It is simply one possible sequence in which we can discover many ramifications of the problem.

Primal Familiarity

For most of us most of the time, the given as such is no problem at all. Things in general are simply available and present. We *take them for granted:* we do not recognize them either as something taken or as something granted. In ordinary experience we rely on beings, use them, and refer to them, without reflecting on the fact that they are accessible in the first place. Just as we automatically expect the ground to support us when we take a step, we count on the subsistence of the whole of beings in our every act. Plato's word for our relation to corporeal things is also the right word for our prephilosophical relation to all things: *pistis (Republic* 511e), which is best interpreted neither as belief nor as faith, but as trust.

Of course, *within* the sphere of things as a whole, there are problems and limits in abundance. Particulars are often untrustworthy or unavailable, painfully and importantly so. Our need for these nongiven things consumes our energy and our thought. We hunt, plan, communicate, and calculate as we try to secure the insecure. *Getting* beings can even become our main way to relate to them; we then treat action as a matter of getting and keeping objects, and knowledge as a matter of getting and keeping information. But while we are engaged in this attempt to get things, we take the whole for granted as reliable and thus *for-get* it. Strictly speaking, since we may never have recognized the whole in the first place, one can say that it lies in oblivion.

We are primally familiar with the whole; we inhabit it. It is our own in the sense that we are comfortable in it, as a fish is comfortable in the sea. But this is why we cannot recognize it *as* our own, any more than a fish can recognize that it belongs in the sea and not on land. Precisely because we trust the whole, we cannot experience it *as* a whole. As long as we are immersed in it, it is impossible for us to encounter it as such.

In terms of philosophical positions, this moment corresponds to a naive empiricism. In order to find the truth we are simply supposed to perceive what is there, get the facts about it, and generalize. This concept of knowledge will always be the most popular, because within our everyday immersion in the whole it functions perfectly well as a way of accumulating information. This attitude can pervade the most advanced scientific research no less than it pervades the most thoughtless, routine behavior; the questions and techniques may differ while the basic relation to the whole remains the same.

The experience of a whole as such requires a space that, paradoxically, is not contained within the whole. The verge of this space is the boundary that defines the whole, that allows it to be a "well-rounded sphere" (Parmenides, frag. 8). This limit divides what is from what is not. But in ordinary experience, nothingness is nothing; absence is absent. Particulars may be lacking and desired, but a radical other to beings as a whole is unsuspected. Things in general are present so thoroughly, so reliably, so inexhaustibly that they do not come into question.

Emergency as a Break in Familiarity

How do we emerge from this immersion in the whole? Somehow, some of us sometimes draw back from everything and feel the breath of nothingness that makes it possible to encounter beings as a whole. From the everyday perspective, this event must remain not just mysterious but impossible: a relation to nothing is no relation at all. But from the perspective of this transformed relation to the whole, the everyday attitude has lost its authority.

The break in everydayness can be provoked by many events—an error in judgment, an illness, a surprise, an experience of beauty. Sometimes the provocation is trivial; but even when it is important, it cannot fully account for the occurrence of the break. The break can also take many forms. In the opening of *Introduction to Metaphysics*, Heidegger expresses it in the question,

"Why are there beings at all instead of nothing?"[2] This question can arise in various moods: in despair, everything seems futile; in joy, it seems wondrous; in ennui, it seems unappetizing. The crisis can also take the form of _Angst_. At moments of anxiety, the sense of one's life becomes a problem. With the loss of this guiding light—which one may never have explicitly considered or chosen before—every detail of one's experience seems strange. One becomes uncomfortable not only in one's own skin but in the world as a whole, which was formerly a comfortable, transparent medium for one's perceptions and activities. One more way in which everydayness can be broken is through a sense of profound ignorance. We come to feel that, despite whatever expertise or facility we may have, there is nothing that we truly _know_. Knowing is no longer simply perceiving the given; the givenness of everything has come into question. This experience can then take different courses (consider Socrates and Descartes).

In these various ways, we can stop dwelling comfortably in the whole. Beings are then revealed as a whole and as such. Their difference from nothing comes into question; it emerges in an emergency. In reaction to such an experience, we may turn to myth, religion, art, or philosophy—or simply wait for it to pass. But what is revealed in the experience itself, before we manage to ignore it or incorporate it into our lives?

First, _the whole_ is displayed as such. We have gained that paradoxical distance from the whole, that foothold in nothingness, that makes the entirety of beings an issue for us.

Our _dwelling_ is also displayed as such. We realize that we have been living in our own, familiar home; we are now capable of experiencing and perhaps appreciating that home as such, precisely because we are now alienated from it, because we are fish out of water.

Furthermore, _beings_ are displayed as such. We can now experience what _is_ as other than what is _not_. If we are wondering why there are beings instead of nothing, then the difference between the two has somehow become apparent. Even if the spell of everydayness has been broken by radical doubt, by a deep sense of one's own ignorance, this implies an experience of separation from what _is_, and thus a sense of the "is" as such. Similarly, in the experience of anxiety, the very fact that things _are_ becomes distressing. None of this means that we can now articulate and explain what it means to be; but we sense this sense that formerly stayed in the background.

Finally, _the given_ is displayed as such. The fact that something is available

---

2. _Introduction to Metaphysics_, 1. On the sense of "nothing" in this text see Richard Polt, "The Question of Nothing," in _A Companion to Heidegger's "Introduction to Metaphysics,"_ ed. Richard Polt and Gregory Fried (New Haven: Yale University Press, 2001).

to us has become obtrusive and unmistakable. We may not experience what is *given* as equivalent to what *is;* in radical doubt, the question is precisely whether *beings* are given to us at all. But even then, something is given, something appears; we now conceive of it as "perceptions" or "phenomena." We then ask what, precisely, is given, and whether beings are given to us indirectly, within or by means of the phenomena. In contrast, in anxiety, whether the given *is* is not in question; the question is how to live with it. Joy or boredom have their own ways of experiencing the given. But in all these situations, whether we resent what is given or appreciate it, try to move beyond it or try to dwell with it, what we can no longer do is take it for granted. We now recognize that we are receiving a gift.

Unfor-getting the Prior

When everydayness breaks down in an emergency, the givenness of the familiar emerges. But this givenness does not appear as something new; it is revealed as having already been in effect. We recognize that while we were dwelling within the whole, the whole was there—it was simply in the background. Our experience is like remembering: it is not getting new information but unfor-getting what was established, rescuing it from oblivion.

In this an-amnesia, this re-collection, we gather up what we already had— but only now do we truly "get it." Before, we for-got it as soon as we got it; now, in unfor-getting, we knowingly appropriate it for the first time. To recollect the givenness of the given is not to relive an old experience of something, but to become aware of a sense of the whole that must be in place before anything can be experienced. (We cannot remember infancy because an infant's sense of the whole is still coming to be. Only after the whole is established can particular beings and happenings appear worthy or unworthy of remembrance. To "recollect" this fundamental sense of the whole is not to relive an inception—we never did have a lived experience of our inception, because there was no life-context for it yet—but to mature, to become "adult.")

We now recognize that our sense of givenness *had* to be in effect already, because it is a precondition for the first moment, the immersion in the whole. Now we have shattered the illusion of an immediate, automatic accessibility of beings (236). We could not have been pursuing and avoiding particular beings if beings as such had not already been granted to us. We could not have been seeking new and unfamiliar things if we had not already been familiar with the whole. It is not that without this prior familiarity we would be blind or paralyzed; we would not exist at all. Someone who has never had a sense of the whole is no one. Being someone requires a sense of one's own "there" within which things can be given, pursued, and avoided. In order to be someone, one must have been thrust into a there. Unfor-getting means finding that one is there in the there. All further explanations and articulations of the sense of givenness rest on this primal recognition of sheer thrownness.

The insight into the need for prior familiarity with the givenness of the whole often takes the form of a demotion of perception as a source of truth. To perceive, broadly speaking, is to get something new (a new sound or color, or in general, new "information"). But if in order to get something new, we must already have something old (givenness), then getting is neither the whole of knowledge nor its foundation. Knowledge that knows itself must include unfor-getting. Knowing as unfor-getting is what we traditionally call a priori knowledge, knowledge of what must already be in place before we can perceive. What is known in such knowledge is there in advance. We could simply call it "the prior."

Patterns of Givenness: The Question of Being

But is there some specific content to the prior? Now that it has been revealed as such, does it have any enduring patterns that we can describe? For instance, are all beings given in terms of a substance-attribute structure? Do we need a distinction between essence and existence? With such questions (which cannot be pursued further here) we enter the domain of what Heidegger calls being (*Sein*)—although we have not yet confronted be-ing (*Seyn*). The traditional inquiry into being investigates the structures of the prior. It thinks about that in terms of which particular beings are given to us, that which must already be in place in order for us to experience beings. Being is the givenness of beings as such and as a whole—that is, not the "mere fact" that something is given, but the background meaning that enables us to *recognize* anything as given. It is the difference it makes that there is something rather than nothing. (These descriptions are not *definitions* of being, since they require an understanding of the words *beings* and *is*, which in turn presuppose an understanding of being. The descriptions are just indications of something that, as Heidegger always insists, cannot be defined in the strict sense.)

The Source of Givenness: The Question of Be-ing

But there is a more fundamental question: what is the source of being itself? Beings are given to us thanks to being—but being itself is also given to us. It is available to us, since we can recognize it and attempt to describe it. How do we have access to it? We have now reached a more distinctively Heideggerian problematic. Heidegger's *Seyn*, I will argue, is best interpreted as the giving of being, that is, as the event in which beings as such and as a whole are enabled to make a difference to us.[3]

How is being given? Being (givenness) may be the result of repeated experiences of given beings. But this answer—the simplest and most plausible—raises the problem of how anything can be given in advance of a sense of givenness. Alternatively, one can hold that being is given through nonsensory perception (Husserl's "categorial intuition").[4] But perhaps what we grasp when we begin to "perceive" being is superficial. Being may be given, then, only through articulate discussion of some kind.[5]

If so, then being cannot be given without some activity on our part. In fact, there can be no giving without receiving, which is itself an activity. To put it most paradoxically, we could argue with Derrida that the gift is impossible. A gift must be free, gratuitous; it must also be received by its recipient. But the very act of receiving the gift is a basic form of acknowledgment, or gratitude; it thus constitutes some reciprocity, some payment for the gift. A gift paid for, however, is not a gift at all. The gift thus cancels itself out, because the gratitude it requires annuls the gratuity that defines it as a gift.[6] We can dissolve this paradox if we remove the assumption that a gift must be completely gratuitous, and think of it instead as involving a surplus or imbalance.

---

3. For a similar interpretation see Michael Lewis, "God and Politics in Later Heidegger," *Philosophy Today* 48, no. 4 (winter 2004): 386. As Sheehan puts it, "Heidegger's focal topic is not 'being' but *that which 'gives'* being": "A Paradigm Shift," 192. In Ernst Tugendhat's words, Heidegger asks not just about the ways in which beings are given, but about "the dimension of the ways of givenness themselves, that is, the happening of a 'cleared' encounter as such": *Der Wahrheitsbegriff bei Husserl und Heidegger,* 2nd ed. (Berlin: de Gruyter, 1970), 270. Although the *Contributions* drop the term *horizon* because of its transcendental connotations, I also essentially agree with Walter Patt's account of being as the concealed "horizon within which all beings are revealed and understandable to man," and *Ereignis* as the "happening" through which being "takes place" in the "there" of being-there: *Formen des Anti-Platonismus bei Kant, Nietzsche und Heidegger* (Frankfurt am Main: Vittorio Klostermann, 1997), 233–34.

4. Edmund Husserl, *Logical Investigations,* trans. A. J. Findlay (London: Routledge and Kegan Paul, 1970), Sixth Investigation. Descartes makes a similar suggestion in the Second Meditation (AT 30–31). For Heidegger on categorial intuition, see *History of the Concept of Time,* 47–72; "My Way to Phenomenology," in *On Time and Being,* 78–79; "Seminar in Zähringen 1973," in *Four Seminars,* trans. Andrew Mitchell and François Raffoul (Bloomington: Indiana University Press, 2003).

5. Plato suggests this in the *Theaetetus* (184b–186e). For Heidegger's commentary, see *The Essence of Truth,* 121–75. On the link between the *Theaetetus* and categorial intuition, see GA 22, 123, 272–73. For Heidegger's own concept of being as a phenomenon that needs to be uncovered through interpretation, see SZ 35–37.

6. Jacques Derrida, *Given Time: I, Counterfeit Money,* trans. Peggy Kamuf (Chicago: University of Chicago Press, 1992), 14. Derrida's arguments are relevant both to the anthropological question of human gift-giving practices and to the Heideggerian problematic of the *es gibt* and appropriation; see e.g., 18–21 on Heidegger. Derrida is mistaken, however, when he claims that Heidegger "surreptitiously" thinks the proper in terms of the gift (21). The question of giving runs *explicitly* through many of Heidegger's thoughts on appropriation.

Still, the paradox teaches us that there is no such thing as a completely passive "getting" of the given.[7]

If the givenness of being requires human activity, we may suspect that being stems *exclusively* from our activity. This approach obviates the problem of how we can be given anything through nonsensory means. Being may not be given at all until we give it to ourselves. But if being is a human creation, it is not a creation of any ordinary sort. If being were not given to us, we would not even exist as human beings. Our creation of being, then, would be an act of *self*-creation; it would also be an activity that we would *have* to perform. This is a strange sort of "activity," but there are several possible models for it. There are cultural practices, such as language and tool use; if our understanding of being is like these (as Wittgensteinians might say), then it is culturally relative, but it is not subject to arbitrary individual choice. There are contingent psychological laws, such as preferring sweet to bitter; like these, the understanding of being might be universally human, or nearly so, but carry no necessity (as a Humean could argue). There is also the activity of mathematical thought, which carries necessity with it; perhaps (as a Kantian might hold) there is a similar necessity in our understanding of being.

Being, then, may be revealed by perception or discourse, or generated by our own activities, whether these activities are contingent or necessary. But whichever of these explanations we may choose, it was an *emergency* that first alerted us to givenness by bringing it into question. What if emergency were not only a stimulus for philosophical reflection, but also *crucial to the very giving of being*? Then moments of emergency would not only reveal a prior sense of givenness that we could now unfor-get, but would revitalize and transform this sense. Maybe we would never have a sense of givenness—and never be ourselves—if it were not for emergencies. Maybe without the opportunity to make being our *own* that is provided by ruptures in our familiar world, we could not return to that world and truly inhabit it. Maybe without emergency, we could never truly belong.

If so, then our starting point—immersion in a familiar whole—may be nothing but the effect of forgotten emergencies. Emergency generates being, opening a world—but then we lapse or relapse *into* this world. Once again, we take the given for granted. The un-settling emergency that made genuine settlement possible tends to be forgotten as we settle into our home and settle for the quotidian. Fighting against this lapse would mean allowing ourselves to be vulnerable to emergency—an emergency that is not simply

---

7. "Only in the mechanical sphere does one of the sides remain passive in the process of reception": Hegel, *Lectures on the Philosophy of Religion*, ed. Peter C. Hodgson, vol. 3 (Berkeley: University of California Press, 1985), 260.

handed to us but which we must also seize; an event in which all being, including our own, would become urgent; an event in which we would fully *be there*; an event that would found belonging.

The Primacy of Belonging

I will use the word *belonging* to suggest a range of related phenomena that ultimately, according to Heidegger, stem from the event of appropriation. We can indicate these phenomena by way of a contrast with traditional theoretical thought.

Theory seeks the universal, what is identical in the manifold particulars. By viewing the particulars *sub specie aeterni*, we decontextualize them and supposedly identify their aspects that are independent of time and place. For Platonic, Aristotelian, and medieval metaphysics, the universal is primarily the form (whether understood as separable or as inherent in individual substances). For modern natural science, the universal is the aspects of beings that are susceptible to mathematical measurement. Of course, the particular does not just dwindle away in the theoretical point of view; it comes to light in a special way. Theory makes it possible to classify, describe, and measure individual things with great precision; it uncovers an abundance of information. However, the particulars are seen as cases of the universal. They are *data*—the things that are "given" when experience is interrogated in the light of some universal. For example, we approach an experiment in physics with universal categories such as "mass," "distance," and "energy" firmly in place, and then use the experimental equipment to elicit some reaction that can be interpreted and measured in these terms. Data are, in this sense, manufactured. They are facts, *facta*, "things made." The greatest modern philosophers recognize this. Whereas the ancients sought a "nature" that was independent of human interference, the great insight of modernity is that certainty and accuracy can be found most reliably through our own intervention. In Vico's formula, *verum et factum convertuntur*—the true is equivalent to the made. In one of Heidegger's formulations, "Nature, as the object of human representation, is presented to representation, and in this sense pro-duced" (GA 77, 11).

Whether ancient or modern, the theoretical approach to beings treats them as data or facts that instantiate universals. This approach tends to deemphasize and dismiss certain phenomena. In particular, theory leaves behind the imprecise, pretheoretical fields of appropriateness and inappropriateness that are felt rather than known. These include the perceptions, attachments, traditions, and habits that constitute *one's own* (*das Eigene*: cf. GA 52, 131–32). Such phenomena are dismissed as "subjective," "relative" conditions that have nothing to do with truth. One's own is overcome by what is common to all.[8]

Attempts to resist this move are often compromised by assumptions that they borrow from the dominant theoretical scheme. Romanticism, for instance, celebrates the heart, but accepts the opposition between heart and head; it fails to connect reason and passion in a comprehensive understanding of truth. More recently, it has become fashionable to show that the categories of theoretical thought are "socially constructed." But such analyses fail to explain how "constructed" categories can reveal beings. The challenge is still to combine *one's own* with *truth*.[9]

Our thoughts on the given may point to a way out of this problem. We began with the primal familiarity of immersion in the whole. In this condition, the availability of things is not a matter for surprise or wonder. Nevertheless, things *are* available; beings are given to us, even if they may be given in superficial or incomplete ways. Could it be that *familiarity* itself is indispensable to this primal givenness?

What is familiarity, then? To be familiar with a place or situation is not to know facts about it, but to know one's way around it. One has a sense of where one *belongs* in it, where other things and people *belong*, what behavior is *appropriate* and *inappropriate* within this milieu, and how the whole *hangs together*. These phenomena of "belonging" are felt and handled, not cognized. Our sense of them is embodied in patterns of competence and comfort—and incompetence and discomfort. (For example, one is familiar with how to behave in a restaurant when appropriate restaurant behavior sets one at ease, and inappropriate behavior makes one uncomfortable.)

It is conceivable that behind this everyday dwelling in belonging there lie unspoken beliefs, implicit theoretical propositions; these propositions, if we could identify them, would redescribe "one's own" in terms of facts and universals. However, it is also possible that familiarity involves an essentially *pre-*

8. As Kierkegaard puts it, if there is no "residual incommensurability" between the individual and the universal, other than the sheer failure of the individual to attain the universal, "then no categories are needed other than what Greek philosophy had or what can be deduced from them by consistent thought": *Fear and Trembling*, in *Fear and Trembling; Repetition*, ed. and trans. Howard V. Hong and Edna H. Hong (Princeton: Princeton University Press, 1983), 55. With Kierkegaard's new category, the "instant" or "moment of vision," a new age begins in philosophy: Heidegger, *The Fundamental Concepts of Metaphysics: World, Finitude, Solitude*, trans. William McNeill and Nicholas Walker (Bloomington: Indiana University Press, 1995), 150.

9. For an attempt at a hermeneutic solution of the problem, see Richard J. Bernstein, *Beyond Objectivism and Relativism: Science, Hermeneutics, and Praxis* (Philadelphia: University of Pennsylvania Press, 1983). Aside from the hermeneutic approach, which is indelibly influenced by Heidegger, the most important attempts to overcome the opposition between truth and "one's own" have been made by pragmatists—who, of course, share some ground with the early Heidegger.

theoretical understanding, and that ownness is irreducible to facts and universals. In this case, belonging would be deeper than all theory. Theoretical observations, then, as correct as they might be, would be only derivative forms of truth—manifestations of beings that can arise legitimately on special occasions, but that are parasitic on primordial belonging. So-called "data" or facts, then, would not be what is primordially given. The theoretical attitude, which apparently abstracts from one's own, would prove to rely covertly on ownness and appropriateness.

If there is such a pretheoretical belonging, then thinking about it would have to be a nontheoretical thinking. This thinking would be an attention that dwelled in and on one's own, that accepted its own belonging to belonging. Such thought would have to search for the source of belonging itself—the event of the upsurge of the own and the alien, the appropriate and the inappropriate, coherence and incoherence. And such an event may be an emergency—a moment that founds belonging by unsettling us, that outlines the whole by exposing us to nothingness. These are the insights that set Heidegger on his path to the *Contributions to Philosophy*.

Givenness and Belonging in Early Heidegger

> Even "givenness" already represents a categorial determination.
> —GA 1, 318 (1915)

> Is there the "there is"? / Does it give the "it gives"?
> —*Towards the Definition of Philosophy*, 52 (1919)

> The It that gives in "It gives being," "It gives time," proves to be Appropriation.
> —"Time and Being," in *On Time and Being*, 19 (1962)

The question of the given haunts Heidegger's thought.

In 1915, he thinks of givenness as a basic "categorial determination." Merely by addressing something as given—as "there" for us—we presuppose a meaning of givenness. Following his teacher Heinrich Rickert, he views the search for the meaning of givenness as a *logical* problem—a problem about the structures that govern theoretical assertion.[10]

In 1919, Heidegger wonders about the source of the meaning of givenness itself. Logic can no longer serve as such a source; "lived experience" in its

---

10. "Logic," in Heidegger's earliest work, means "theory of theory"—the theoretical investigation of the conditions and structures of theoretical meaning: GA 1, 23.

concreteness must be the answer. "Lived experience does not pass in front of me like a thing, but I appropriate [*er-eigne*] it to myself, and it appropriates itself according to its essence."[11]

In 1962, he is still reflecting on the givenness of beings—that which makes them available as what *is*. He now calls this givenness *being*, and asks how being itself is given. He proposes that being is given together with time, and the "it" that gives them is appropriation.

Heidegger has taken many steps along this way. Our goal in this section is to follow some moves in his writings through *Being and Time* to see the roots of the concept of appropriation. Our guiding theme will be the question of the given. Even in some of his earliest writings, Heidegger is trying to understand the givenness of beings in terms of what we called *belonging*. These attempts at thinking of belonging will culminate in the thought of appropriation.

We can begin with a few early differences with Husserl that foreshadow the importance that the proper or the own was to assume in Heidegger's thinking. The basic project of Husserl's *Logical Investigations* is to describe how thought has meaning—how we intend objects. What structures characterize the process by which we can refer to things and things can be given to us? This phenomenological approach rejects the psychologistic conception of logic, which holds that logic is just the empirical study of the operations of the psyche. Psychologism destroys the meaningfulness of thought because it fails to distinguish between the "expression" of thought (the particular performance of a mental act) and the "meaning," or content, of this act. Husserl argues in the first of his *Logical Investigations* that, despite the fact that expression is subject to linguistic and historical conditions, it can *mean* propositions that transcend these conditions. (Here he assumes that "truth pertains to propositions.") A single thought can be expressed in many different ways, but all these expressions will have the same meaning. This search for the same suggests a Platonic quest for identical forms. In fact, Husserl argues quite generally that the identity of species is the only possible ground for "unitary mutual belongingness" among phenomena. He tries to bridge the gap between concrete, temporal expressions and atemporal, universally valid meanings by way of an appeal to the identity of species. Disparate acts of thinking or speaking can have the same meaning, just as disparate objects can be of the same kind.[12]

In a lecture course of 1925–26, Heidegger objects that this Platonic orientation "seduced Husserl into a fundamental error": "the content of judg-

---

11. *Towards the Definition of Philosophy*, trans. Ted Sadler (London: Continuum, 2000), 63.
12. Husserl, *Logical Investigations*, 172, 347, 330.

ments is [not] the universal, the *genos*. . . . The 'universal' as the content of judgments—meaning—specifies itself only into this and that meaning, but never into acts" (GA 21, 60, 61). The chasm between meanings and acts has not been spanned, and Husserl's notion of intentionality remains unclear. The scheme of particular and universal fails to understand how truth happens in a lived moment.

Heidegger's criticism of this particular early Husserlian notion is part of his general resistance to the traditional search for identical universals. He persistently explores ways to think of a coherence that is prior to identity. As early as 1915–16, in explaining the Aristotelian and Scholastic doctrine of analogy, he directly contradicts Husserl's claim that all unity must be based on identity. "What stands in analogy is neither totally different nor totally the same. . . . The order in the domain of the real is thus *not* one of pure generalization in terms of kinds" (GA 1, 257, 261). The nonunivocal coherence of beings is a "heterogeneous continuum."[13] Such a continuum *allows* abstraction and mathematization, but cannot be *reduced* to a set of universals.

What is at stake here is the relation between truth and "one's own"—including one's own situation, actions, and words. As soon as we conceive of one's own as the "particular," we implicitly oppose it to a universal in which truth and meaning reside. By conceiving of one's own as an "expression" for an ideal meaning, Husserl too separates truth from one's own. But psychologism also fails to do justice to one's own: it inspects the psyche from a theoretical perspective, looking for universal psychological truths, in such a way that the truth *within* one's own experiences becomes unintelligible. Heidegger's goal is to overcome the split between truth and one's own without falling back into psychologism. One's own is to be thought from one's own and as one's own—not as an *instance* of a universal but as a unique *instant* of insight.

This thought comes into its own at a moment of emergency—the "war emergency semester" of 1919.[14] Here Heidegger argues that meaning does not reside in atemporal propositions but occurs thanks to the very temporality and historicity of our existence. Openness is based not on theory at all, but on our rootedness in particular situations. Meaning can happen only for

13. GA 1, 253. Heidegger adopts this expression from Rickert: Heidegger, *Towards the Definition of Philosophy*, 145.
14. "The Idea of Philosophy and the Problem of Worldview," in *Towards the Definition of Philosophy*. For more extended accounts of this lecture course see Theodore Kisiel, *The Genesis of Heidegger's "Being and Time"* (Berkeley: University of California Press, 1993), 21–25, 38–59; George Kovacs, "Philosophy as Primordial Science in Heidegger's Courses of 1919," in *Reading Heidegger From the Start: Essays in his Earliest Thought*, ed. Theodore Kisiel and John Van Buren (Albany: State University of New York Press, 1994); Polt, *"Ereignis"*; John Van Buren, *The Young Heidegger: Rumor of the Hidden King* (Bloomington: Indiana University Press, 1994), chaps. 12 and 13.

a concrete person in a concrete, historical world. In this context Heidegger first introduces the word *Ereignis*, contrasting it with *Vorgang* in order to distinguish occurrences that are genuinely part of someone's experience from theoreticized occurrences. *Vor-gänge* are happenings from which I am detached and which I merely watch pass by before me, while *Er-eignisse* are events that are my own.[15] "The event of situation happens [*das Ereignis ereignet sich*] to *me*, I make it my own, it relates to me."[16] (Here and in the *Contributions*, this is a pun rather than an etymological connection: *Ereignis* is not related to *eigen*, "own," but derives from *eräugen*, to display or present to the eyes, *Augen*.[17] This etymological sense is also welcome, however, since it suggests that what is at stake is an event of *manifestation*.) In an *Ereignis*, beings find a significant place within my world.

According to Heidegger, theory obscures this "worlding" by conceiving of beings as isolated objects that are represented by some ideal, indeterminate subject.[18] This criticism takes aim at Husserl. As Heidegger puts it a few years later, Husserlian phenomenology "disregards the fact that the [mental] acts are mine or those of any other individual human being and regards them only in their *what*."[19] Acts of meaning always belong to an individual who exists in a context. Theorizing is oblivious to the belonging-together of beings within a world to which we belong. When theory takes hold, "the situational character disappears. The unity of the situation is exploded. The experiences . . . lose the unity which the situation gave to them."[20]

Theoretical truth is subordinate to a primordial belonging—a lived familiarity with one's own world. But this familiarity also needs to be regenerated and refreshed by emergencies—extraordinary moments such as "gliding from one world of experience to another genuine life-world, or . . . moments of especially intensive life."[21] The meaning of "there is" is rooted in these basic experiences of the primal "something."

In order to talk about such phenomena, we have to develop "a science that is . . . non-theoretical," a thinking that does not drain the phenomena of their belonging and reduce them to universals and facts, obliterating the unique texture of the lived world.[22] The struggle to find such a way of thought ac-

---

15. *Towards the Definition of Philosophy*, 62–64.
16. Gerda Walther's notes to Heidegger's lecture course "Die Idee der Philosophie und das Weltanschauungsproblem," quoted in Kisiel, *The Genesis of Heidegger's "Being and Time,"* 65.
17. Cf. *Deutsches Wörterbuch von Jacob Grimm und Wilhelm Grimm* (Leipzig: S. Hirzel, 1854–1954), s. vv. *eräugen, ereigen, ereignen, ereignis.*
18. *Towards the Definition of Philosophy*, 62.
19. *History of the Concept of Time*, 109.
20. *Towards the Definition of Philosophy*, 174.
21. Ibid., 115.
22. Ibid., 81.

counts for the often tortured language of Heidegger's early lectures and their constant innovations in terminology. He is trying to use words and concepts in a way that "formally indicates" the phenomena at stake. Formal indication gestures toward a phenomenon (hence "indication") without pretending to exhaust its content (hence "formal"). Formally indicative thinking does not capture the essence of a thing and explain it with perfect theoretical clarity; it *alludes* to a phenomenon in our lives and encourages us to live in such a way that we pay closer attention to it.[23]

I turn now to the great fragment that is the culmination of Heidegger's early period—*Being and Time*. I presuppose a general knowledge of this text; I discuss only those of its features that are most important for the questions of givenness and belonging, and that will be central to Heidegger's concerns in the *Contributions*. We will consider in what sense *Being and Time*'s approach is transcendental, and how its interpretation of being-there brings out various modes of belonging, affirming their priority over theory and universals as keys to the givenness of beings and being.

Above I developed a notion of being as the givenness of beings as such and as a whole. Being seems prior to beings: it must already be in place in order for us to experience particular entities. As we saw, this basic scheme invites two questions. First, what is the content of being? What does it mean for something to *be*? Second, what is the status of being itself? How is *it* given to us?

Heidegger's theme in *Being and Time* is the *"question of the meaning of being"* (SZ 19). This formula is ambiguous enough that it embraces both of the questions above. First, Heidegger wants to explain what it is to be. He does not expect a univocal answer; in the published portion of *Being and Time* he describes several different ways of being—readiness-to-hand, presence-at-hand, and our own existence. He asks how many "variations" of being there are (SZ 241, 333) and how these ways of being belong together (SZ 45). Second, the "meaning" of something is the context that enables it to be understandable or accessible; it is that "upon which" we "project" our understanding of something (SZ 151–52, 324–25). Thus, asking about the meaning of being involves not only trying to understand being itself, but asking within which "horizon" being is *given*. Heidegger's thesis is that time is that horizon (SZ 1, 39). "Time" here refers to the temporality of being-there, and most of *Being and Time* as it stands is devoted to interpreting being-there. Heidegger's accounts of the environment, worldhood, being-in, and extraordinary emergencies such as anxiety and the call of conscience bring out various dimensions of belonging that are obscured by the theoretical attitude.

---

23. Heidegger's clearest explanation of formal indication is found in *The Fundamental Concepts of Metaphysics*, 296–97.

First, theory treats beings as present-at-hand objects, which are represented in assertions that predicate certain properties of these objects. But in everyday experience within an environment, most beings are ready-to-hand: they are available or unavailable for our purposes, functional or broken. A ready-to-hand entity belongs within a totality of uses and purposes; it has a place determined by its "belonging to other equipment" (SZ 68, cf. 353). Equipment also belongs to certain tasks and moments for which it is suited; this "appropriateness" is prior to any "properties" that we may attribute to the equipment when we treat it as a present-at-hand thing (SZ 83).

Husserl's reaction to this analysis shows that his insistence on the identical and universal is an enduring part of his thought.

> Theoretical interest is concerned with what is; and that, everywhere, is what is identical through variation of subjects and their practical interests. . . . Anybody can verify (if he takes a theoretical attitude) that this thing here counts for subject A as such and such a piece of equipment, for B as quite a different one, that anything can be woven into equipmental nexus of many kinds, both for the same and for different subjects. . . . [But] a being is something identical, something identifiable again and again.[24]

Husserl understandably resists what he sees as Heidegger's relativism: Heidegger seems to disregard the independence of the things we encounter, and to dissolve them into the relations they have to us at particular times.

Heidegger might concede that theory reveals identical and (at least seemingly) noncontextual aspects of beings—their present-at-hand features. He would insist, however, that ready-to-hand beings, as revealed in practice, are beings "in themselves" too (SZ 71). More important, he would argue that we are able to encounter present-at-hand beings in their selfsameness and independence from us only because they present themselves within a coherent world that opens for us in a pretheoretical way. The self-identity of present-at-hand beings is a genuine phenomenon; but this identity is revealed to us only through our participation in a field of belonging, a realm of appropriateness and inappropriateness. The point of Heidegger's analysis is not to reduce everything to "cooking pots, pitchforks, and lampshades" (GA 49, 44), but to found the display of identity on a dwelling in the world that is more primordial than both theory and practice (SZ 193, 364).

---

24. Edmund Husserl, "das ist gegen Heidegger," manuscript quoted by Hubert L. Dreyfus in *Being-in-the-World: A Commentary on Heidegger's "Being and Time," Division I* (Cambridge: MIT Press, 1991), 65–66.

Heidegger claims, then, that the texture of belonging in the everyday world cannot be understood purely through predication and identification. He extends this view to worldhood in general. The world—the gathering of everything into a whole—is a "context of assignments or references" (SZ 87). Space and time, as dimensions of worldhood, are to be understood in terms of appropriateness, not as mathematical abstractions. Space is where things belong or do not belong (SZ 83, 102); it is a web of places, sites, and routes, not an empty framework. Time is the right or wrong time (SZ 414); it is not just a string of instants but a gathering of opportunities, junctures, and moments, both trivial and momentous. Consequently, beings are not simply what is "identifiable again and again," as Husserl would have it, but are always characterized by temporal uniqueness. Space and time, in a word, are *owned*.

We human beings inhabit this world of belonging in a way that enables being and beings to be given to us. Heidegger's interpretations of our existence, like his account of readiness-to-hand and worldhood, appeal to modes of belonging that resist characterization in terms of universals. First, human beings are in such a way that their being *belongs* to them: being-there is *mine* in each instance (SZ 41). "Existence" is Heidegger's name for this way of being in which one's own being "is an *issue*" for one (SZ 12): each of us has to grapple for himself with who he is. One's own being is implicitly or explicitly a *problem*. The formula "*The 'essence' of being-there lies in its existence*" (SZ 42) expresses the difference between this distinctively human way of being and the essence of a thing as a species. Being-human cannot be understood adequately in terms of exemplifying a universal. As Heidegger had written years earlier, "each time we attempt to give a regional definition of the 'I' . . . we thereby 'efface' the sense of the 'am' and turn the 'I' into an object that can be ascertained and *classified* by inserting it into a region."[25] Subordinating being-there to a universal would mean reducing it to a present-at-hand thing.

An entity whose own being is an issue for it has two main possibilities: either to evade its responsibility for its own being or to own up, so to speak, to this responsibility. Hence the concepts of authenticity and inauthenticity.[26] In inauthenticity, one allows one's choices to fall into the ruts established by the "they," the familiar norms of the community to which one belongs. When "one" acts, one's actions do not truly belong to one (SZ 127). This sham belonging creates a sham givenness of beings: truth becomes a matter

25. "Comments on Karl Jaspers's *Psychology of Worldviews*" (1919–21), trans. John van Buren, in *Pathmarks*, 25–26. Cf. *History of the Concept of Time*, 110.

26. One could also translate *Eigentlichkeit* and *Uneigentlichkeit* as "ownedness" and "disownedness": *Contributions to Philosophy*, 213 (GA 65, 302).

of hearsay and chatter, and being-there "understand[s] everything without previously making the thing one's own" (SZ 169, cf. 224). Despite its aura of "generality," the "they" is not meant to be a *class:* what "one" does is not equivalent to what everyone does but is a manner of existing. The "they," like being-there in general, cannot be understood in terms of species and types (SZ 128–29).

As for authenticity, it involves a distinctive relation to the future and the past. "'Future' here . . . means the coming in which being-there, in its own-most ability-to-be, comes towards itself" (SZ 325). I exist authentically only when I seize my possibilities as *mine* in the face of "death" (or more accurately, mortality—the possibility of the impossibility of existing: SZ 250, 262). The future is thus the dimension of temporality that lets me *belong* to myself. But temporality also involves "thrownness": I find that I have always already been plunged into a situation (SZ 135). We belong not only to our own possibilities but also to a place and an age; our possibilities are always drawn from a context that has already claimed us. There is no chance of abolishing the "they," for the world always involves a shared sense of the appropriate and the inappropriate.[27] This means that authenticity cannot mean doing something completely different from what "one" does; instead, it takes over the "they" and appropriates one's tradition (SZ 130, 267). True selfhood, then, is not the constant presence of an ego, but a way of responding to the claims of future and past through a "steadfastness" that takes a stance in the moment (SZ 322).

Our account of authenticity as genuine belonging should not obscure the phenomenon of anxiety, the limit-situation that reveals the fundamental "not-at-home" lurking behind comfortable dwelling (SZ 189). As Heidegger says in *Introduction to Metaphysics*, "we cannot wholly belong to any thing, not even to ourselves."[28] Anxiety cracks open everyday dwelling and prevents us from taking ourselves or the world for granted. It brings us from canniness to uncanniness, from immersion in one's own to expropriation. We then discover the contingency and fragility of meaning. Having faced this abyss, we can return to our world and appropriate it resolutely. Genuine ownness is not the becalmed comfort of everydayness, but an appropriation in response to expropriation.

We can now return to the overall project of *Being and Time* in order to understand the interdependence of being-there and being in this text. Being is not "given" at all except insofar as it enters into being-there's understanding.

27. This point is not immediately clear in Heidegger's discussion of the "they" (SZ §27); it emerges only when he distinguishes between the "they" (an *existentiale*) and the "they-self" (an existentiell possibility) on SZ 129.

28. *Introduction to Metaphysics*, 31.

In turn, without being, there is no being-there, for being-there is precisely the entity who has an understanding of being (SZ 183).

Temporality is essential to this nexus, because it forms the horizon for being-there's understanding of being (SZ 1). How is this supposed to work? Understanding is not primarily theoretical cognition but an "ability to be" (*Seinkönnen*, SZ 143–44). This means that being-there is constantly "projecting" available ways of acting (in a broad sense of "acting" that includes producing and observing). Such projection is not deliberate planning, but an entry into possibilities. In terms of these possibilities, we understand not only ourselves, but all beings in their being (SZ 144–47). Thus, because being-there's own being is an issue for it, it has an understanding of being (SZ 12–13). We need to seize some possible way of existing; we are faced with the need to appropriate our situation in some way, to make something of it and of ourselves. Since we do so in a context, in a world, we cannot define who we are without also grasping the possibilities of other entities in this world. (I cannot become a novelist, for instance, without understanding the possibilities that define books, writing implements, and readers.) The fact that my own being is at stake for me means that the being of everything in my world is at stake for me.

Temporality is ecstatic (SZ 329): being-there has a future, past, and present by being drawn into three ecstases that carry it "out" toward other beings. The present emerges thanks to the future and the past, in the interplay of possibility and situation. Thus the present must give up the priority that it has traditionally enjoyed; it is always situated and finite, because it is bounded by mortality and thrownness. Division 3 of Part 1, "Time and Being," was to elucidate the concept of the "horizonal schema," introduced in §69c; the expression refers to *that toward which* an ecstasis carries us off. Future, past, and present involve three horizonal schemata that disclose the world—the field within which entities as such can be given to us (SZ 365). Unfortunately, these first steps toward a presentation of time as the horizon for being are little more than a set of technical terms.[29]

The vicissitudes of the terms *transcendence* and *transcendental* in *Being and Time* reflect the difficulties of Heidegger's project, and the question of the transcendental will be crucial to the *Contributions'* interpretation of *Being and*

---

29. Heidegger says he wrote a draft of the crucial Division 3, but destroyed it because it was "inadequate": GA 66, 413. However, a substantial number of notes for Division 3 survive, only a few of which have been published: see Theodore Kisiel, "The Demise of *Being and Time*: 1927–1930," in *Heidegger's "Being and Time": Critical Essays*, ed. Richard Polt (Lanham, Md.: Rowman and Littlefield, 2005). For a discussion of the horizonal schema of the present, or *praesens*, see *The Basic Problems of Phenomenology*, trans. Albert Hofstadter (Bloomington: Indiana University Press, 1982), 305; on the horizonal schema of the future, see *The Metaphysical Foundations of Logic*, trans. Michael Heim (Bloomington: Indiana University Press, 1984), 208.

Time. "Every disclosure of being is *transcendental* knowledge" (SZ 38). Time is "the transcendental horizon for the question of being" (SZ 39). Such claims can be read in a broadly Kantian sense: time is the condition of possibility for our understanding of being, and in turn, this understanding is the condition of possibility for our experience of entities. Heidegger is investigating the prior—what is "always already" in place whenever beings are given. In addition, he applies the terms *transcendent* and *transcendence* to being (SZ 3, 38), the world (SZ 364–66), and being-there (SZ 364). In brief, being-there, as being-in-the-world, reaches *beyond* beings to their being. The potentially misleading aspect of this language is that it might invite us to think of being-there as something originally self-contained; instead, being-there is necessarily "out" among other beings.[30] (To use a phrase favored by the *Contributions*, being-there is "the between.") When Heidegger calls his thought transcendental, then, he means that he is investigating how being-there, thanks to its temporality, reaches out to a world and to being, making possible its experience of beings.

Despite the Kantian tone of this project, Heidegger does not usually take himself to be establishing necessary, a priori truths. Since all theory is rooted in belonging, "existential" insights into existence as such are based on "existentiell" truth—the illumination that is embedded in concrete, contingent existing (SZ 316; cf. 13, 38, 436). The temporality of existing also militates against any attempt to capture truth in a thesis. "Because being cannot be grasped except by taking time into consideration, the answer to the question of being cannot lie in any proposition that is blind and isolated" (SZ 19). If it is time that allows us to understand being, then this understanding cannot be static—not simply because we are changing, but because we are *ec-static*. Our understanding is always a particular appropriation of possibilities on the basis of a particular thrownness, so it is not absolute but situated. Furthermore, we are continually falling into the present and inauthentically taking established understandings for granted, instead of continuing the process of interpretation. A fixed concept of being would thus be inauthentic stagnation. Instead of trying to prove a proposition, then, Heidegger begins with some general theses and everyday phenomena, and then deepens the interpretation of these phenomena, generating new concepts along the way. Such an investigation embraces the hermeneutic circle (SZ 153, 315), and in principle there is no reason for this ever-deepening circle to come to an end. The end of interpreting marks not the completion of a theory, but the decay of understanding.

All the same, certain passages suggest that the project will culminate in a fully clear and fixed concept of being (SZ 3, 8, 19). *Being and Time* is not com-

---

30. *The Metaphysical Foundations of Logic*, 165; GA 65, 217. Cf. SZ 132.

pletely free from the assumptions of traditional theory. A sign of this is an ambiguity regarding the possible. On one hand, Heidegger insists that possibility has priority for being-there: "being-there is in every case what it can be, and in the way in which it is its possibility" (SZ 143). All characteristics of being-there "are in each case possible ways for it to be, and no more than that" (SZ 42). On the other hand, he claims we must not construe being-there "in terms of some concrete possible idea of existence" (SZ 43), and tries to find *existentialia* that are not merely possible but necessary (for example, being-in-the-world is "necessary *a priori*," SZ 53). Yet in the crucial section 63, Heidegger affirms that we must, after all, begin with "*ontical possibilities*" (SZ 312). The very distinction between the "existentiell" and the "existential" (SZ 12) seems unstable, probably because it is overly indebted to the traditional distinction between the particular and the ahistorical universal, the contingent and the ahistorically necessary. By thinking of being-there futurally, as a historical possibility for humanity, the *Contributions* will attempt to leave this tradition behind.

The *Contributions* on *Being and Time*

A decade after *Being and Time*, Heidegger produces a dramatically different kind of text. Instead of patiently following the hermeneutic circle in order to build new concepts and phenomenological descriptions, the *Contributions* hit us at once with a stream of poetic fragments and alarming pronouncements. Is this only a surface difference, or has there been a deep change in Heidegger's thought? The lectures and essays that come between the two texts shift from a somewhat technical phenomenology to a poetic, restless style. This stylistic change accompanies an increased attention to history—both the historicity of being and the historical situation of Heidegger's thought itself. He explicitly links the question of being to the need to decide who "we" are in the contemporary crisis of the West. All these trends are evident in the *Contributions*. However, my goal here is not to present a developmental study—which would have to be quite complex—but to explore how Heidegger interprets the project of *Being and Time* within the *Contributions* in order to judge how far apart the two books stand. It will become clear that for a full understanding of the *Contributions'* account of *Being and Time*, we need to consider the *Contributions'* own thoughts in depth; for now, we can present only a taste of these thoughts.[31]

First, Heidegger makes a number of comments on the unity of his thought

---

31. For a better understanding of the *Contributions'* interpretation of *Being and Time* we must await the publication of Heidegger's more detailed commentaries on his earlier text, "Laufende

that should be taken to heart by anyone considering the question of whether there is a "turn" in his thinking.[32] We have already encountered his statement that his standpoints are constantly different *because* his question remains the same (84). His goal is not to establish and defend propositions but to keep reinterpreting the issue indicated by the question of being. Histories of philosophy often resort to "isms" without appreciating the process of questioning and reinterpretation; this is why Heidegger rejects all historiographical (*historische*) construals of his development (85–86). *Being and Time* is not false; it was a revealing project, although it was not (and did not pretend to be) the last word. Neither should we say that *Being and Time* already includes what comes later (85); the movement toward the *Contributions* is not a deduction of what is implied by some previous propositions, but trailblazing. All this is consonant with Heidegger's understanding of truth as located not in correct assertions but in the happening of openness, a happening that is sometimes instantiated in thought.

What we *can* say is that *Being and Time* is a work of transition (48, 68, 76, 182, 205–6, 228–29, 305). It looks back to the history of metaphysics and grasps it in terms of the question that guides the "first inception": what are beings as such? It prepares the way for the leap into the "other inception" and the grounding question: how does be-ing essentially happen? (73, 75–76, 171). "Be-ing" (*Seyn*), in my reading, indicates the event in which the significance of beings as such—their being—is given to us. As Heidegger now sees it, the labor of *Being and Time* is a necessary part of the transition to the question of be-ing, and still deserves our attention (48). Now, however, he has grown impatient with the tradition and the transition out of it, and wants to speak more directly. *Being and Time*'s account of truth, for example, was too reactive, too focused on showing that truth is *not* a matter of correct assertion. The *Contributions* no longer refrain from speaking of the essential happening of be-ing (351–52, cf. xvii).

In order to make the transition, *Being and Time* inquires into being-there,

---

Anmerkungen zu *Sein und Zeit*" and "Eine Auseinandersetzung mit *Sein und Zeit*," both written in 1936 and scheduled to be published in GA 82. On the *Contributions*' relation to *Being and Time* see also von Herrmann, *Wege ins Ereignis*, chap. 1, secs. I and III; Vallega-Neu, *Heidegger's "Contributions*," Part 1.

32. As we will see, in the *Contributions*, *die Kehre* or "the turn" does not refer to a stage in Heidegger's own development but to the relation between be-ing and being-there. In order to avoid confusion, I will avoid speaking of "the turn" as a developmental issue. On the relation between the developmental issue and the "turn" between be-ing and being-there, see Parvis Emad, "'Heidegger I,' 'Heidegger II,' and *Beiträge zur Philosophie (Vom Ereignis)*," in *From Phenomenology to Thought, Errancy, and Desire: Essays in Honor of William J. Richardson, S.J.*, ed. Babette Babich (Dordrecht: Kluwer, 1995); Alberto Rosales, "Übergang zum anderen Anfang: Reflexionen zu Heideggers 'Beiträge zur Philosophie,'" *Recherches husserliennes* 3 (1995): 51–83; Sheehan, "A Paradigm Shift," 195–96.

or the entity who understands being. This can create the impression that *Being and Time* is simply anthropology or an exploration of subjectivity. Heidegger now claims that this is either an illusion or a merely transitional aspect of *Being and Time* (68, 295). For instance, "care" is not just an anthropological concept but points to human beings' possible role as the custodians of be-ing (240, 297). "Existence" refers to standing in the truth of be-ing, not to the psychological phenomena that are the concern of *Existenzphilosophie* (302–3). Even "decision" is a matter of be-ing, not individual choice (87–88).

Such statements, it could be argued, are overreactions to anthropological readings of *Being and Time*. It is true that the explicit intention of the "fundamental ontology" of *Being and Time* was to describe being-there *as the entity who understands being*, and not merely as one particular sort of entity that we happen to be (SZ 12–14). However, there is no reason why this should prevent Heidegger's descriptions of being-there from shedding light on the tensions and dramas of human life as it is lived and on questions considered by "existential" thinkers.

But there is a deeper issue here. Whereas *Being and Time* seemed to identify human beings and being-there (SZ 11), Heidegger now says the two are not equivalent. Being-there is the basis of a particular, future way of being human, and not of "man" as such (300–301, 488). Being-there is a possibility for us, a "goal" that Heidegger is setting (16). However, he also denounces the concept of goals as overly Platonic (138) and wants to pass beyond morality and ideals (243). The question, then, is how we are supposed to affirm the possibility of being-there without setting it up as a Platonic ideal. We will explore this problem further in chapters 3 and 4. But regardless of whether Heidegger can avoid thinking of being-there as a "goal" in an objectionable sense, his presentation of it as a *possibility* for human beings is faithful to the idea that the traits of being-there are nothing but "possible ways for it to be" (SZ 42). The *Contributions* no longer look like a search for necessary essences; they are devoted to leaping into being-there as a possibility.

Three main themes from *Being and Time* are given a new interpretation in the *Contributions:* temporality, the meaning of being, and the inquiry into our understanding of being as a *transcendental* inquiry. First, Heidegger now interprets temporality as an intimation of appropriation (74, 372) and of "time-space." Time is not the only basis for the "truth of being," because time ecstatically opens the "there" of being-there, a *space* in which being-there can be grounded (189, cf. 193, 257, 433). The *Contributions* consistently think of time together with space, as "time-space" or "the site of the moment" (e.g., 234). *Being and Time* provides only a glimpse of the relation of time and space to truth and the grounding of being-there (308). We will explore these ideas in chapter 3; for now, it is enough to note that Heidegger's claim that being-there has to be *grounded* fits his attempt to think of it as a *possibility*. We do not just happen to "be there" already; it is a condition that needs to be established—through a leap, as we will see. Be-ing and being-there happen only when a site is grounded in the event of appropriation.

This is why Heidegger now explains the phrase "the question of the 'meaning' [of being]" as "the question of the grounding of the domain of projection." This interpretation, he says, is consistent with *Being and Time* (10). However, the emphasis on grounding is new. *Being and Time* gave the impression that temporality simply *was* the ground or horizon for our understanding of being; it was the basis of the givenness of the given. We now discover that the projection (*Entwurf*) of being is a *possibility* that needs to be founded. Heidegger is not speaking here of the willful imposition of a point of view, but of the opening of a space within which we can encounter things. (Emad and Maly translate *Entwurf* as "projecting-open" in order to drive home this point.) Heidegger also replaces the phrase "the meaning of being" with "the truth of be-ing" (10). The truth of be-ing is the same as be-ing itself, its own essential happening (93). The question of the truth of be-ing does not seek a formula that would correctly capture what be-ing "really is," but instead tries to join in the happening of be-ing's display. How be-ing is displayed, and in what sense this display also involves concealment, will be central to the *Contributions*.[33]

In *Being and Time*, as we saw, the expression "*transcendental* knowledge" (SZ 38) has a complex sense, which I glossed as an investigation of how being-there reaches out to a world and to being, making possible its experience of beings. The *Contributions* point out that the expressions "transcendental" and "transcendence" are ambiguous and might suggest that being-there could be self-enclosed (217, 322). Heidegger now says that the transcendental way was merely preparatory and transitional (305). On one hand, it refers back to Kant's search for the conditions of the possibility of experience (250, 468). On the other hand, it points forward to a decision (in the special Heideggerian sense) that can ground the truth of be-ing (223, 455).

The *Contributions*' interpretation of traditional transcendentalism is an especially illuminating indication of Heidegger's project. The transcendental approach inherits the metaphysical concept of being as entityhood or beingness (*Seiendheit*)—the most general characteristics of beings as such. This concept stems from the Platonic search for universals, and more broadly, from the theoretical approach to beings. Once a theory of beingness has been

---

33. On the antisubjectivist intent of the terminological shift from "meaning of being" to "truth of be-ing," see "Seminar in Le Thor 1969," in *Four Seminars*, 41, 47. Heidegger's late expression "topology of be-ing" is an attempt to avoid a misinterpretation of "truth" as correctness and to stress the place-quality of the clearing (ibid., 41).

established, metaphysics typically interprets this beingness as an a priori structure. But in fact, this so-called a priori is an "appendix" or "supplement" (111–12, 183, 293, 425–26, 458): beings really have the priority, and beingness is just an abstraction from them.[34] In Kant, beingness becomes the transcendental: it is that which necessarily characterizes all representing of the objectivity of objects (89). This interpretation of beingness is profound, and it hints at a new approach to being altogether: Kant's doctrine of the schematism suggests that our temporality is essential to our exposure to the being of beings. In his writings on Kant, Heidegger tried to bring out this hidden potential.[35] But in the end, Kant is compromised by his traditional commitment to thinking (understood as propositional judgment) as the guideline to being (215, 254).[36] Propositional truth is only a surface phenomenon, made possible by a more basic unconcealment.

Being and Time was, to some extent, caught up in the metaphysical search for beingness (93). The "ontological difference" between beings and being, as presented there, could easily be misunderstood as nothing but the relation between beings and beingness (250).[37] Presumably Heidegger has this danger in mind when he writes that Division III of *Being and Time* ran the risk of objectifying be-ing and thus was held back (451). When be-ing is taken exclusively as beingness, it is degraded to the level of beings (93).

We can add that the Kantian overtones of the project of *Being and Time* were in danger of suggesting that being-there has priority over being: it might seem that being-there's temporal structure *dictates* what being can mean, just as the forms of subjectivity in Kant dictate the structure of experience. Furthermore, the parallels to Kant might make it seem that we can establish a fixed concept of being and demonstrate its necessity a priori. All of this would be untrue to the historicity of be-ing (451) and to the receptivity of being-there—its dependence on a happening of be-ing that is not its own creation (239).

---

34. Cf. Roberta Dreon, "La questione dell'*a priori* tra *Sein und Zeit* e i *Beiträge zur Philosophie (Vom Ereignis)* di Martin Heidegger," *Teoria* 8, no. 1 (1998): 19–40.

35. GA 65, 93–94, 176, 253, 279, 448, 468. Heidegger's positive readings of Kant can be found in GA 21; *Phenomenological Interpretation of Kant's "Critique of Pure Reason,"* trans. Parvis Emad and Kenneth Maly (Bloomington: Indiana University Press, 1997); *The Essence of Human Freedom: An Introduction to Philosophy*, trans. Ted Sadler (London: Continuum, 2002); *Kant and the Problem of Metaphysics*, 5th ed., trans. Richard Taft (Bloomington: Indiana University Press, 1997); and *What is a Thing?* trans. W. B. Barton Jr. and Vera Deutsch (Chicago: Henry Regnery, 1967).

36. Consider Kant's derivation of the categories from the logical forms of judgment (*Critique of Pure Reason*, A79–81/B104–7).

37. Cf. Heidegger's points about the ontological difference in *The Fundamental Concepts of Metaphysics*, 357–58. Most significant as an anticipation of *Ereignis* is the point that the distinction between being and beings "happens *to us* as the fundamental occurrence of our being-there" (357).

The *Contributions* propose two main means of overcoming transcendentalism. First, being-there is a "thrown thrower." The projections by which we understand being (if we enter the condition of being-there) are not carried out by our subjectivity as a self-contained base of operations; instead, we find ourselves situated in the midst of beings, whose being has already been obscurely given to us. We not only rise up into a world, but are also "rooted in the earth" (259). This thrownness implies that being-there is *appropriated* by be-ing (217, 252, 304). Being-there *belongs* to be-ing, for we cannot truly be ourselves unless we respond to the claim that be-ing makes on us.[38] Our being-there is needed as a participant in the happening of be-ing, but we can never control the happening because we ourselves depend on it. Of course, it was already clear in *Being and Time* that being-there is thrown, and the hermeneutic concept of understanding implies that all understanding is thrown (321). However, Heidegger fears that thrownness in *Being and Time* could be taken merely as "the accidental occurrence of man among other beings" (318) instead of as our belonging to be-ing (447–48). In a sense, by pointing to this belonging, Heidegger is radicalizing transcendental philosophy: he is digging even deeper than Kant into the conditions of the possibility of experience.[39] However, this project leads to the discovery that no project can establish an unshakable foundation: all our projects presuppose a thrownness that cannot be circumvented or explained. All our attempts to identify necessary transcendental structures must then fail—and it is by recognizing this inevitable failure that we can best pay homage to be-ing.[40]

Heidegger's second antitranscendental idea is the "simultaneity" of be-ing and beings. In the other inception that he is inaugurating, be-ing is neither earlier nor later than beings (223–24). We will explore this vague idea more closely when we consider the relation between be-ing and beings in chapter 3. It is a difficult thought, especially because elsewhere Heidegger claims that be-ing essentially happens (*west*) before all beings (303) and that be-ing has a certain "precedence" even if it is not a priori (428). What is clear for the moment, at least, is that he wants to avoid the traditional division between particular beings and a universal beingness that hovers above them or lies beneath them, serving as their ground or condition of possibility.

The *Contributions* do not reject *Being and Time;* they venture farther into

---

38. For von Herrmann, this is the *"primary experience"* that determines the "immanent change" from *Being and Time* to the *Contributions* and forms the heart of Heidegger's new thinking: *Wege ins Ereignis*, 18, cf. 30, 56, 347; von Herrmann, "Technology, Politics and Art," 58.

39. Robert E. Wood, "The Fugal Lines of Heidegger's *Beiträge*," *Existentia* 11, nos. 3–4 (2001), 259–60.

40. Cf. Jean Grondin, "Prolegomena to an Understanding of Heidegger's Turn," trans. Gail Soffer, *Graduate Faculty Philosophy Journal* 14, no. 2/15, no. 1 (1991): 92–94, 101–3.

the thought of belonging that was already at work in *Being and Time* but was not fully implemented in that text, due to its transcendental slant.[41] In its aspiration to find fundamental structures of "existentiality" (SZ 12–13) and universal features of "historicality" (SZ 382), *Being and Time* may seem like an anomaly in the larger course of Heidegger's thought, which stresses concretion and situatedness. But as we saw, *Being and Time* also insists that philosophical insight is based on the "existentiell." Theory remains rooted in one's own; being is given in belonging. In the *Contributions*, Heidegger tries to avoid all appearance of a theory that might float free of one's own, and thus tries to do justice to belonging.

Be-ing as Appropriation

The problem of the given starts by recognizing that every entity is given to us thanks to being—thanks to a background understanding of the givenness of entities as such and as a whole. But being itself is given to us, too. *How is being given?*

I have argued that in his attempt to understand the givenness of being, Heidegger consistently points to modes of "belonging" that are prior to theoretical propositions and universals. His thought is, so to speak, the revenge of one's own against the Idea.[42] He rejects the notion that we can understand the being of a thing by finding the identical aspect that is universal to a collection of such things. This theoretical approach to beings is parasitic on belonging; things present themselves to us only through our pre-theoretical involvement in the world, our selfhood, and our situatedness. We have seen this approach taking shape in his earliest writings, where he searches for modes of belonging that are irreducible to identity. The word *Ereignis* first comes into his thinking in 1919 to name an event of ownness, a happening in which the world is primally given to an existing individual. *Being and Time* tackles the task of describing what it means to *be* an existing individual. The modes of belonging it explores include the *belonging-together* of entities within a world of spatiotemporal *appropriateness,* and the *belonging-yet-not-belonging* of being-there to that world and to itself. This (not-) belonging is

41. In this sense, William J. Richardson's position on this vexed question that he was among the first to raise seems right. "Heidegger II is *more original than Heidegger I,* went before him along the way": *Heidegger: Through Phenomenology to Thought,* 4th ed. (New York: Fordham University Press, 2003), 632.

42. Although the search for one's own is not reducible to politics, it always has a possible political dimension, as is clear in Heidegger's nationalism of the mid-thirties. For evidence of his lifelong fascination with "the homeland," extending much farther than his temporary support for National Socialism, see the brief pieces collected in GA 13.

revealed in the event of anxiety as a radical *expropriation* that indicates the need to *appropriate* one's own existence and become authentic, or *self-owned*.

According to *Being and Time*, temporality, which makes it possible for us to exist as beings whose own existence is at issue for us, also makes it possible for us to understand being itself. Time is the "transcendental horizon" that enables being to be given to us. But Heidegger's comments on *Being and Time* in the *Contributions* indicate that this was a misstep. The transcendental approach is too indebted to the Idea—beingness as a universal; the approach suggests that our mode of understanding dictates a significance of being that serves as an a priori, universal form for beings. This misconception threatened to cover up the modes of belonging that Heidegger originally wanted to reveal. He turns back from this *Holzweg*, then, and takes up his earlier insight into the primal event of "worlding" as *Ereignis*.[43]

In short, the move from *Being and Time* to the *Contributions* can be called a move "*from the understanding of being to the happening of being*" (GA 40, 219). As Heidegger dramatically puts it, be-ing itself announced its historical essence (451). Be-ing is not determined by being-there's understanding; instead, it takes place, and brings being-there along with it in this happening.

How does be-ing happen, then? How can being be given to us in appropriation? We have seen that Heidegger wants to think of appropriation as an event in which the possibility of being-there is grounded. In this event, space and time would flare up into a "site of the moment." At this site, being-there would take up its thrownness as a belonging to be-ing, and be-ing would take place "simultaneously" with beings.

All these concepts call for closer interpretation, but we can already venture some independent thought on why one might be attracted to the "event of appropriation" as a way of approaching the givenness of being. Any case of givenness must involve an event of appropriation. A gift must first belong to the giver and then belong to its recipient. The recipient must acknowledge it, appropriate it, make it her own—and in turn, she is appropriated by the gift, in the sense that she becomes beholden to the giver. The question of giving, then, is necessarily a question of owning. Any question about how something is given to us could be approached as a question about how it becomes our own.

What is it to be one's own? In the case of material property, ownership is the legal right to control and use a thing. But in other cases, ownness is quite different. The word *my* has a different meaning each time when I say "my family," "my hometown," "my thoughts," "my body," "my enemies," "myself." Is "my" said in as many ways as "be"?

---

43. We can see this move as early as 1928, when Heidegger writes, "the event of the world-entry of beings is the primal event [*Urereignis*]": *The Metaphysical Foundations of Logic*, 212.

Some modes of owning are more fundamental than others. My personality rarely depends on my receiving a material gift; yet "gifts" as talents may well be important to who I am. My enemies may or may not concern me; but the ways in which I relate to (or "own") my home, my family, and my body are unavoidably part of how I interpret "my" self.

How fundamental is the gift of being? If I did not have being, I could have no entities at all. The owning here is so fundamental that we could not own *ourselves*, we could not be anyone, without this event of appropriation. Since this owning is so crucial to our own existence, we might say that, instead of our coming to own being, being is coming to own *us*. But it would be better to say that the owning is mutual: being and being-there appropriate *each other.* After all, they are interdependent, as Heidegger already claimed in *Being and Time* (SZ 183). Furthermore, some sort of reciprocity is likely if, as we proposed earlier, there is no purely passive reception; getting the gift of being, making it our own, cannot simply be a matter of having it handed to us. Similarly, if it is best to say that we are appropriated by be-ing and become owned by it, then this becoming-owned is unlikely to be passive either. However, if we are not "there" at all until the appropriation happens, then it would also be misleading to describe our role as active; this might suggest that be-ing is chosen by an already-formed subjectivity. What is at stake here is a happening that precedes the distinction between active and passive, a happening that enables both being-there and being to come into their own.[44]

But why do we speak of a "happening" here at all, or of *becoming* one's own? Would it be better to speak of a necessary relation that always obtains between being-there and being? Certainly metaphysics has preferred this way of thinking: it is possible to tell a story about how we come to unfor-get being, but there is no story about how being became our own to begin with. But what if the atemporal perspective of metaphysics depends on a more primordial belonging? What if all necessity is grounded in emergency? Then the bond between being and being-there would originate in an *event* of appropriation, and being-there would be a possibility, not an established essence. Maybe even the event of unfor-getting—the happening in which we wake up from our familiar immersion in the world and begin to *question* being—is also an event of appropriation. There would no longer be a sepa-

44. "To appropriate something does not mean to claim ownership of it, but to bring it to its proper, to let it happen. But to let being happen, a human being has to become what he is": Françoise Dastur, "The Critique of Anthropologism in Heidegger's Thought," in *Appropriating Heidegger*, ed. James E. Faulconer and Mark Wrathall (Cambridge: Cambridge University Press, 2000), 132. As Peter Trawny puts it, the human essence is our "dowry," and "where the dowry is affirmed, appropriation happens": *Martin Heideggers Phänomenologie der Welt* (Freiburg: Karl Alber, 1995), 65. In chapter 3 we will look more closely at the relation between humanity and being-there.

ration between a historical event of our thinking of being and a constant, necessary relation between us and being.[45]

If being is given to us in an event of appropriation, we can think of history as centered on, or springing from, moments when appropriation happens. "History" here does not mean occurrences as studied by historians, but the way our shared lives extend from our past to our future. This is not just a sequence like the flowing of a stream—the next moment following upon the heels of the last—but a happening in which, for the sake of the future, we appropriate the past to which we belong, opening the present. The notion of be-ing as appropriation suggests a semiotic understanding of history as a sending and receiving of messages that sustains and refreshes the significance of beings.[46] Such messages include not only texts and sayings, but all the practices that are handed down to us as our heritage. Even the most everyday, habitual act is arguably an event of appropriation, since it receives and interprets an inherited practice. However, events of *profound* appropriation must be rare. The interplay between past and future may light up the present most deeply and intensely at moments of crisis—moments when fundamental questions emerge, moments of emergency.

This movement of historical appropriation might unify the various forms of belonging we have considered. The belonging-together of entities within a meaningful world of spatiotemporal appropriateness is founded on our reception of inherited messages and practices. As soon as we sense that these patterns of appropriateness are founded, we sense that they are contingent; their historical foundation is not an absolute ground. The contingency of meaning makes it possible for us to be expropriated, or alienated from the world, in an emergency—a moment of defamiliarization. But if being can become our own only within history, then this moment must impel us to *re*-appropriate the familiar—making it more deeply our own. This response to our crisis will then found a new configuration of appropriateness.

Earlier I suggested three models for types of human "activity" that would lie beyond ordinary choice, and would be activities of self-creation as well as the creation of being: culture, psychological reactions, and mathematical thought. If being and being-there are in a reciprocal relation, it would be misleading to say that we "create" being. However, we could say that we make being our own at the same time as it makes us its own; this is what happens

45. I explore this possibility further in my discussion of "bethinking" in chapter 2, where I also distinguish Heidegger's approach from that of Hegel, who *could* be said to tell a story about how we come to appropriate being.

46. As Kenneth Maly puts it: "thinking that is *seynsgeschichtlich* thinks the handing-over or sending, gathering-throw, shaping-sending, carrying-forth that is be-ing as enowning": "Turnings in Essential Swaying and the Leap," in Scott et al., *Companion*, 164.

in the event of appropriation. If we may still refer to our three models, then it seems clear that *culture* is closest to appropriation. Like culture, appropriation is contingent and historical. By turning to appropriation, then, Heidegger may have rescued culture from its denigration by theory, which we considered at the beginning of this chapter. I am not claiming that appropriation is "really just culture"; to the contrary, what we ordinarily call culture may turn out to be appropriation. Appropriation may offer us a way to think of culture ("one's own") together with truth (the givenness of beings). If the thinking of appropriation succeeds, it may manage to resituate truth and being, to understand how be-ing takes place (and takes time) within what we call culture. Be-ing would then be *finite*—not a form, not a condition of possibility, not an intuited necessity, but a contingent happening of ownness that outstrips all theory and all universals.

With these proposals in mind, we can look more closely at the *Contributions* themselves and interpret some of their central statements about *Ereignis*. Heidegger rightly warns us that no formula can capture the essential (247), but if we are looking for a formula that *points* to the central thought of the *Contributions to Philosophy*, we can hardly do better than this one: *das Seyn west als das Ereignis*, "be-ing essentially happens as appropriation" (30, 256, 260). We can use each word in this sentence as an occasion for exploring the issue at the root of the *Contributions*. Each word provides a distinct perspective on the single theme for which "appropriation" is the primary name in this text. My interpretation of this sentence and a few other central sayings about *Ereignis* will inform all the readings that are to follow. I have already attempted some sketches of appropriation; I had to do so in order to interpret Heidegger's central philosophical problem and his development. But now we need to enter the heart of the matter.

As we do so, however, we must keep in mind some "methodological" issues—for at one point, Heidegger immediately follows the sentence "*be-ing essentially happens as appropriation*" with a warning: "That is not a proposition but the nonconceptual, silent telling of the essential happening that opens itself only to the full, historical enactment of inceptive thinking" (260). By way of a preview of chapter 2, we can elucidate this warning.

If Heidegger's sentence were a "proposition," it would correctly or incorrectly assign a predicate to a subject; the subject and predicate would consist of established concepts that indicated entities or aspects of them. But here, the topic of the sentence does not lie in the realm of entities at all; it concerns how *being* is given. This giving of being happens historically, through critical moments of inception. In order for us to think of this happening, it itself has to happen in our thinking; our thought cannot just be *about* historicity, but must be carried out historically, inceptively. If we simply apply set concepts when we write or utter Heidegger's sentence, then nothing will be happening inceptively. We will then be operating *within* an interpretation of the whole, a givenness of being, without doing justice to the giving.

The words in Heidegger's sentence, then, have to be "incepts," not concepts (cf. 64). We have to "bethink" them poetically or inventively, that is, in a way that discovers and enhances their coming-to-meaning as it happens (cf. §265). Each use of these words, while drawing on a linguistic heritage, must perform them in a way that pays renewed attention to the matter at stake. Each act of thinking must be singular—not in the sense that it thinks a thought different from every other, but in the sense that, like the calligraphic execution of a Chinese character, it renews the inherited meaning by appropriating it in a unique moment. This way of thinking cannot be "correct" or "incorrect" like a theoretical claim. These terms apply only to propositions, which deal with preexisting entities to which predefined concepts can correspond or fail to correspond. However, this does not mean we are free to think whatever we like about be-ing. It is as demanding to think of be-ing as it is to compose a successful poem. The challenge is to evoke and invite the happening of be-ing in a way that befits the moment.

Finally, we must remember that we are doomed to fail to name be-ing in a way that would fully reveal it, because no matter what we say, we must always rely on a giving that cannot be controlled and reproduced. Be-ing is not representable as if it were an entity. This is why our speech must be attuned to restraint and incorporate a telling silence (§§37–38). But as we fail in our efforts to say be-ing, maybe the texture of our failures will point, for a moment, to what cannot be said.

An interpretation of *das Seyn west als das Ereignis* will not yield a definition, doctrine, or system. If it succeeds, it will provide a series of occasions to engage in bethinking—occasions that may join with each other and with Heidegger's text to delineate a quarry, a field where bedrock is broken (187, 421, 436).

Das Seyn

To begin with the expression *das Seyn:* why does Heidegger spell the word this way? What does it mean? Why is he concerned with it?

Earlier I presented the problem of the given in terms of the following moments. (a) We begin by dealing with familiar beings, while taking beings as such and as a whole for granted. (b) In an emergency, a rupture in this familiarity, we come to notice that beings are given as such and as a whole; we receive them as a totality that is not nothing. (c) We recognize that this givenness of beings as such and as a whole had to be in effect already, even when we were oblivious to it. (d) We can then explore the patterns that character-ize this prior givenness. (e) We can also ask how this patterned givenness is itself given to us. (f) We may then find that this giving involves a primacy of belonging over universals.

Although Heidegger discusses all these moments at various points in his texts, the last three moments are the ones that concern "the question of be-ing" most directly. Moment (d) is the problem that has animated the tradi-tion of metaphysics. Moment (e) is the problem that Heidegger is trying to address in terms of appropriation or belonging (f). We need to reconsider these moments.

In moment (d), we investigate the patterns of the givenness of beings. By "patterns," I mean channels along which the sense of beings as beings tends to flow. (Most metaphysicians have assumed that the patterns are eternal, the channels are unshifting—but they may also be contingent and mutable. We can leave this question open.) When we encounter anything that *is*, we en-counter it as exemplifying certain ways of being, which are connected to other ways of being. We do not normally focus on these patterns, but simply allow them to operate in the background. They do not directly spring into our awareness, even after we have become aware—in moments (b) and (c)—that there is some kind of prior givenness of beings as such. In fact, it may seem that "to be" is something utterly nebulous, so general and simple that it cannot involve any patterns. However, if being had no characteristics at all, it would be indistinguishable from not-being. This is not the case, since we immediately recognize that it makes a difference whether something is or is not.[47] When we examine our understanding of beings as such more closely, we find that it does involve some patterns, and that much can be said about them. The Aristotelian patterns of being, for example, include substance and attribute; potentiality and actuality; form and matter; unity, quality, quantity, relation, time, place, and more. Aristotle's account of such patterns as "cate-gories" is definitive for Western philosophy (76). The task of metaphysics, as the study of beings *qua* beings, is to describe such patterns and the relations among them.

Heidegger uses the word *beingness* to refer to these patterns of the given-ness of beings as they are described by traditional metaphysics.[48] Meta-physics assumes that to describe the patterns is to find the most universal characteristics of that which is. Heidegger has four criticisms of this approach.

---

47. *Introduction to Metaphysics*, 85–86.

48. For more on beingness see Heidegger, *Nietzsche*, ed. David Farrell Krell, 4 vols. (San Francisco: Harper and Row, 1979, 1984, 1987, 1982), vol. 4, 41, 156–57, 166, 194, 206–7.

1. Metaphysics presupposes that beings are given to us primarily through theoretical assertions, so it is dominated by logic (the rules of theoretical discourse). But beings are actually given to us pre-theoretically through phenomena such as mood, action, and nontheoretical discourse. Assertion always depends on deeper modes of uncovering and interpreting beings (457, cf. SZ §33).

2. The seeming multiplicity of patterns uncovered by metaphysics reduces to (or is at least centered on) presence, and more specifically, presence at hand (*Vorhandenheit*). For example, for Aristotle, although being is not univocal (469), the focal meaning of beingness is the actuality of a substance, its presence at hand. But presence at hand is only one mode of being, the mode that is revealed by theoretical assertion (SZ §69b).[49]

3. There is a tendency to mingle the search for the patterns of beingness with the search for a supreme *entity*, the entity that most fully exemplifies what it means to be and also functions as a first cause for beings as a whole. Metaphysics thus becomes "ontotheology."[50] Here the very distinction between beings and being is in danger of obliteration.

4. As we have seen, even though metaphysics attempts to discover structures that are *prior* to particular beings, the metaphysical conception of beingness is in fact just an appendix to beings (111–12, 183, 293, 425–26, 458). Metaphysics takes beings for granted, and then tries to find their most universal characteristics. The supposedly a priori structures uncovered by this procedure actually depend on a prior givenness of beings. Even though metaphysics may have begun in wonder at this givenness of beings—what I called moment (b)—the wonder has long since been effaced,

---

49. Presence is broader than presence at hand: according to *The Basic Problems of Phenomenology*, 306, readiness to hand is also understood in terms of *praesens* as the "horizonal schema" of the ecstasis of the present. Readiness to hand is one mode of being that has been neglected by traditional metaphysics. But metaphysics has also overlooked modes of being that cannot be understood in terms of presence *at all*—notably, care as the being of being-there. When taken out of context, some of Heidegger's statements suggest that he himself understands being as presence; Taylor Carman patiently exposes this misunderstanding in "Heidegger's Concept of Presence," *Inquiry* 38, no. 4 (December 1995): 431–53. Unfortunately, the misunderstanding cannot be stamped out completely: Frederick A. Olafson, "Heidegger on Presence: A Reply," *Inquiry* 39, nos. 3–4 (December 1996): 421–26. It is also unfortunate that Carman interprets appropriation as the "essentially ahistorical . . . conditions of the possibility" of our understanding of the meaning of being: "Heidegger's Concept of Presence," 446. This interpretation fits the 1962 "Time and Being" (Carman's main source on appropriation), but not the *Contributions;* see Polt, "*Ereignis.*" The *Contributions* do support Carman's main point, however: "Without being grasped as such, essential happening [*Wesung*] is presencing [*Anwesung*]," but "essential happening [is] not limited to 'presence'" (GA 65, 189, 75).

50. See "The Onto-Theo-Logical Constitution of Metaphysics," in *Identity and Difference*, trans. Joan Stambaugh (New York: Harper and Row, 1969). Cf. also GA 65, 425, on beingness as "what *is* above all" (*das Seiendste*).

instead of being radicalized into wonder at the givenness of the sense of being—moment (e).

In saying that Western philosophy has turned being into a mere universal predicate of beings, Heidegger appears to be ignoring Kant, who explicitly claims that being is not a "real predicate," not a predicate that denotes a property of a thing.[51] Modern symbolic logic echoes Kant: Frege and his successors treat the "existential quantifier" quite differently from predicates. In analytic philosophy, it is a commonplace to point out that it is wrong to think of being as just another predicate.[52] But is it enough to reject an untenable view of being as an attribute of beings? Has the Kantian argument clarified in a positive way what it means to *be*? Heidegger would insist that Kant and analytic philosophers have merely failed to understand their own metaphysical roots; they still operate within a traditional notion of being as presence, but simply take this notion for granted.[53]

It would be possible to develop a nontraditional metaphysics—to explore the patterns of the givenness of beings while overcoming the first three criticisms above. We would have to interpret beings as we encounter them in nontheoretical as well as theoretical behavior, look for modes of being that extend beyond presence, and avoid confusing the search for the meaning of being with the question of a supreme entity. In fact, Heidegger does all this in the finished portions of *Being and Time*. He interprets the meaning of the being of various kinds of beings—equipment, present-at-hand entities, and being-there. It would even be fair to say that he interprets the *beingness* of these beings.[54]

The fourth criticism, however, is more radical. It implies that any investigation of beings and their being is superficial. There is a more fundamental question: how do beings become accessible to us as beings in the first place?[55] This corresponds to moment (e), when we ask how the patterned givenness of beings—their being—is itself given to us.

51. See Kant, "Der einzig mögliche Beweisgrund zu einer Demonstration des Daseins Gottes" (1763); *Critique of Pure Reason*, A592–602/B620–630.
52. The logical positivists are especially insistent on this point: A. J. Ayer, *Language, Truth, and Logic* (New York: Dover, 1952), 43; Rudolf Carnap, "The Elimination of Metaphysics through Logical Analysis of Language," in *Logical Positivism*, ed. A. J. Ayer (New York: The Free Press, 1959), 73–74; Bertrand Russell, "Logical Atomism," in Ayer, *Logical Positivism*, 36; Moritz Schlick, "Positivism and Realism," in Ayer, *Logical Positivism*, 96.
53. On Kant's doctrine see Heidegger, *The Basic Problems of Phenomenology*, 27–76; "Kant's Thesis about Being," in *Pathmarks*.
54. The search for beingness is not wholly illegitimate, then. Heidegger is also willing to acknowledge that traditional structures of beingness have some validity. In 1931–32 he grants that there are abstract "characteristics of being" that apply to all entities, such as identity, difference, equality, and countability; but he stresses that these general characteristics "do not exhaust what beings *are* to *us*": *The Essence of Truth*, 158.
55. Cf. Sheehan, "A Paradigm Shift," 189–92.

Of course, *Being and Time* was not oblivious to this problem. Its goal was not just to describe various modes of being, but to establish that time is the horizon for being—that is, temporality enables being to be *given* to being-there. In *Being and Time*, Heidegger is well aware that this issue is philosophically more fundamental than, say, the analysis of the being of equipment. However, *Being and Time* needs the search for beingness as an initial approach to its problematic (93). It begins with relatively familiar phenomena and ways of questioning so that it can build toward the more fundamental issues by embracing the hermeneutic circle. Unfortunately, the text never reaches its goal; it gets bogged down in the transcendental mode of thinking.

In the *Contributions*, then, Heidegger tries to leap directly into the question of how being is given. It is in this context that he uses the spelling *Seyn*. Emad and Maly's "be-ing" is an apt counterpart to this mildly old-fashioned spelling.[56] *Seyn* is phonetically identical to *Sein*, so it indicates a distinction that cannot be heard, a subtle yet all-important otherness. Perhaps it is in this sense that being and be-ing are "the same and yet fundamentally different" (171). The spelling *Seyn*, then, suggests something older or prior that lurks within the familiar and can easily be confused with the familiar. The rendition "be-ing" has a similar atmosphere, along with a welcome suggestion of dynamism.

Heidegger does not always distinguish "being" from "be-ing." He seems to be unwilling to relegate the spelling *Sein* to the metaphysical domain of beingness, and often uses it synonymously with *Seyn*. *Sein* seems flexible enough to indicate either the whole range of the multifaceted "question of being," or various particular issues within this domain. However, in order to focus as clearly as possible on the problems, we need a more precise usage. From now on, I will use the word *being* alone only when the context calls for a vague, general expression such as "the question of being." This involves both the question of what it means to be and the question of how this meaning is given. In order to designate *what it means to be*, I will speak of *the being of beings*. This refers to the multifarious ways in which beings as such can have significance for us, or make a difference to us. The being of beings is the patterned givenness of beings. *Beingness* (*Seiendheit*) will refer to the particular approach to the being of beings that has dominated the metaphysical tradition: the being of beings is interpreted as the universal characteristics of en-

---

56. Hölderlin and Nietzsche wrote *Seyn*, and this spelling became obsolete only in 1901. The medieval "beon," used by William J. Richardson, exaggerates the antiquity of the spelling: Richardson, *Heidegger*, 554. Heidegger refers, all too briefly, to the difference between the spellings *Sein* and *Seyn* in GA 65, 171, 209, 436.

tities. Finally, *be-ing* (*Seyn*) is neither the narrowly metaphysical beingness nor the broader being of beings, but rather the *giving* of the being of beings—the happening of the granting of the meaning of beings as such.

Heidegger often explains what be-ing is *not* instead of giving a positive account of it: the question of be-ing is no longer about the being of beings (182); we are longer thinking "metaphysically" (436); all ontotheology is avoided (GA 66, 254). But he does provide some positive accounts of what is at stake in the question of be-ing. We must ask "why beings are 'being' [*seiend*] for us, and in what sense" (231); in other words, what is the being of beings, and how is it given to us? The answer lies in be-ing as appropriation: "Appropriation lets beings as such come forth"; "This 'coming' into the clearing happens with *ap-propriation*" (GA 66, 203, 202). The question of be-ing thus considers the origin or ground of the truth of beings as such (58, 76–77). This source is not itself an entity. In fact, entities can be without ever having any meaning or truth, without ever being interpreted by anyone—in other words, without any be-ing at all (30). But if beings *are* revealed, then it is incumbent on us, as the ones to whom they are revealed, to think of the source of this revelation.[57]

Is be-ing equivalent to truth? It would seem so, if truth is the essential happening of be-ing (93, 346) and if the question of the truth of be-ing is the question of the be-ing of truth (95, 428).[58] But Heidegger also writes that the investigation of truth is only a "preliminary question" for the question of how be-ing essentially happens (387). Maybe there is room for a distinction between be-ing and truth. To put this in the terms we have been using: beings are given to us, and this givenness of beings is patterned. We can refer to the patterned givenness of beings as their being. "Be-ing" would name the giving of the being of beings. The question of be-ing, then, is partly the question of truth: how are beings given, that is, how are they accessible and understandable? But the question of be-ing also embraces the question of

---

57. Postwar texts sometimes state the issue very clearly: "The appropriating event is . . . the giving yield whose giving reach alone is what gives us such things as a 'there is'": "The Way to Language," in *On the Way to Language*, trans. Peter D. Hertz (San Francisco: Harper and Row, 1971), 127.

58. For reasons such as this, Thomas Sheehan argues that Heidegger's question is essentially the question of the origin of truth as unconcealment; that is, Heidegger seeks the source of "the givenness or availability or accessibility (hence the usability and understandability) of whatever is": "*Kehre* and *Ereignis*: A Prolegomenon to *Introduction to Metaphysics*," in Polt and Fried, *A Companion to Heidegger's "Introduction to Metaphysics*," 6. Hubert Dreyfus, too, views the question of being as the question of "intelligibility": e.g., *Being-in-the-World*, 3. For an investigation of truth contemporaneous with the *Contributions*, see *Basic Questions of Philosophy: Selected "Problems" of "Logic*," trans. Richard Rojcewicz and André Schuwer (Bloomington: Indiana University Press, 1994).

beings *as such:* how are beings given *as beings* rather than nonbeings—as other than nothing? In this sense be-ing is the basis of the distinction between beings and beingness (436): be-ing makes beings available *as beings*, and thus (as the tradition sees it) in their beingness. When we focus on this aspect of be-ing, we concentrate on the question of what it means to be, instead of on the question of accessibility.

However, hunting for definitions and distinctions may be an overly scholastic approach to Heidegger's language. We should keep in mind that he is underway, that he is groping for something that cannot fully be said. Instead of trying to formalize the *Contributions* into a doctrine, it is better to risk our own attempts to evoke what is at stake in fresh language.

Be-ing is the giving of the being of beings. We can begin to think through this by exploring the range of what can be involved in the being of beings. The givenness of beings is not patterned only according to the rigid, universal categories of metaphysics. Its patterns are also revealed by the semi-fluid, local habits that we ascribe to "culture," such as our reactions to people and foods as "pure" or "impure." The patterns are revealed by "bodily" dispositions, such as nervousness or calm, which also enable beings to present themselves to us in particular ways (say, as disturbing or agreeable). Most of these patterns are normally not articulated, but mingle obscurely in the background of our thoughts and actions. The being of beings includes all our ways of making sense of beings. In order to avoid a hint of subjectivism in this formulation, we might prefer "ways in which beings make sense to us"—or, to remain neutral with respect to both subjectivism and objectivism, we can invent the term "ways-of-sense." For example, beings make sense as people, as animals, as tools, as present-at-hand objects, as artworks, as gods, and as earth. These ways-of-sense are inseparable from our dwelling in a world, an open region within which we can encounter beings and distinguish them from nonbeings. None of these ways-of-sense is *a being;* none of them can simply be reduced to what is given as and in the entity itself. Instead, they are modes of *access* to beings. Together, interwoven in the web of experience, they give us access to beings as a whole and as such. They mark out all that is, as opposed to all that is not.

We might refer to the entire web of ways-of-sense as the *import* of beings. The word means both "importance" and "meaning." To say that something has meaning is also to say that it has some importance, even if it is almost negligible. An utterly unimportant thing goes utterly unnoticed; it is, for us, a nonbeing. If we notice something, then it shows up as having import—even if it has the minimal import of being "irrelevant" or "trivial." This consideration tends to forestall any crude distinction between an objectively ascertainable "mere existence" of things and the "meanings" or "values" that we supposedly give to them: "mere existence," insofar as it makes any sense to us at all, is itself always a kind of import—a way in which things matter to us.[59]

Perhaps the Greek *dynamis* could also suggest what is at issue here. This word for power or potential can also mean *significance*—the power to reveal. In Plato's *Parmenides* (135c), Parmenides claims that if there are no forms, then discourse will completely lose its *dynamis*—its significative force, its import. Heidegger would, of course, disagree. Before we isolate aspects of beings and fixate them in forms and concepts, beings as such already stand in a *dynamis*, an import. As speakers, our task is to seek the right relation to language as the dwelling-place of this dynamic.

I have used still another phrase to indicate the being of beings: the difference it makes that there is something instead of nothing. As a definition, this would be circular, since it uses the word *is*. The point of the phrase is to connect the question of being to the wonder of the question, "Why are there beings at all instead of nothing?"[60] The "why" in this question need not express a search for a first cause; it can express the initial shock of the discovery that there is a sense, an import, of beings as such—that it makes a difference to us that beings *are*. Here, "making a difference" must not be restricted to immediate practical effects. It includes every way of marking import—practical, theoretical, religious, artistic. Since there are many ways in which things can make a difference to us, the being of beings is not univocal; still, it seems that all these ways of making a difference tend to cohere, to function together as our "understanding of being."

With all these expressions—ways-of-sense, import, *dynamis*, the difference it makes that there is something instead of nothing—we have pointed to the being of beings. But the being of beings is still preliminary to the issue of *Seyn*. With the word *Seyn*, Heidegger asks about the source of this entire complex of ways in which beings are enabled to show themselves as "something." These ways-of-sense are not simply there to be described and categorized. Their very "thereness," their givenness, is an issue. It becomes a *burning* issue when we recognize that import is (at least largely) contingent—it can flourish, decay, and be reborn. It can threaten to collapse, or become entrenched for centuries—without ever becoming necessary and eternal. The question of *be-ing*, then, asks how import takes place, or comes into effect. Be-ing is the contingent happening of meaning, import, *dynamis*—the *making* of the difference between something and nothing—the *giving* of the being of beings.

59. Similarly, we can question the strict distinction between "existence" and "real predicates," as stated by Kant and codified in symbolic logic. To experience something as existing is already to discover some import, some significance that would tend to express itself in predicates.
60. *Introduction to Metaphysics*, 1; cf. "What is Metaphysics?" in *Pathmarks*, 96; GA 52, 64.

By drawing our attention to this giving, Heidegger is not implying an ontic *donor*. No entity—not a god, a mind, a body, or a thing—can serve as a ground for the being of beings, or cause the happening of be-ing. The question of be-ing does not begin with particular beings, or with beings as such and as a whole, but with a leap into be-ing itself (76). We must experience beings as pointing to be-ing as "their other," which must be approached purely on its own terms (264).

Heidegger speaks as if this should be self-evident to anyone who thinks properly. But is it? It seems obvious that we would not have any sense of the being of beings if it were not for our bodies and our cultural practices—but bodies and practices are beings. Why isn't the question of how the being of beings is given a question about bodies, cultures, and other such ontic factors? The question would then be placed in the hands of anthropology, sociology, psychology, physiology, and other empirical sciences. To deny that there are ontic causes of our understanding of the being of beings goes against common sense. Perhaps it is only a way of asserting the professional prerogatives of the philosopher class.

We should allow these objections to simmer—they may promote some healthy skepticism. However, if they become convictions, they will prevent us from appreciating Heidegger's project at all. I offer the following considerations, then, not as final replies but as a way of keeping these objections in abeyance; we will return to them in chapter 4.

The sciences take it for granted that there are beings, and presuppose an understanding of the being of beings; this seems to cut them off from the question of be-ing. If we tried to explain be-ing sociologically, for example, we would have to take society for granted as something with a self-evident way of being. We could then give a factually correct description of how people operate within society and how their behavior brings with it certain beliefs about what it means to be. In doing so, however, we would have to leave our *own* beliefs about what it means to be unquestioned, so that they could serve as the stable basis for our empirical research. The question of the status and origin of our own understanding of the being of beings would have to be left unaddressed. Similarly, we might be able to give a physiological explanation of the workings of the brain, "explaining" consciousness in terms of the various complex neural responses that are associated with it. But in order to do so, we have to assume that the brain and consciousness have a certain way of *being* that we understand. If all our observations depend on this understanding of the being of brains and consciousness, then our observations cannot provide a satisfactory explanation of how the understanding of the being of beings occurs. If these considerations are valid, then any scientific attempt to explain be-ing is circular: it must presuppose a given sense of the being of beings. Now, if we are willing to embrace the circle by revising this sense in the course of our investigation, the circle may not be vicious; this is what *Being and Time* does, after all (SZ 153, 315). But then we are engaging in philosophy, not just empirical science. We are struggling with the limits of our sense of the being of beings, and thus experiencing it as contingent and finite. This distinctively philosophical experience is needed in order for being to *trouble* us.

The ontic disciplines seem unable to deal with the phenomenon of *meaning*. Researchers must assume that they can refer meaningfully to beings, and that beings can be revealed as meaningful to them; but their accounts of beings never make it clear how a sphere of meaning can emerge in the first place.[61] The ontic disciplines do not retain the wonder that beings are given as meaningful, that the being of beings has a meaning. A sense of wonder and surprise may be necessary if we are ever to question what it means to be, and inquire into the giving of this meaning.

West

If we accept the separation of be-ing from beings, we must say that there *is* no be-ing. Be-ing is not. Instead, *das Seyn west*. "If beings *are*, be-ing must *wesen*. But how does be-ing *wesen*?" (7). The word Heidegger is using has no close counterpart in English. The archaic verb *wesen* is the root of the noun *das Wesen*, the usual German version of the Latin *essentia*. The verb *wesen* survives in words such as *gewesen* (been), *anwesend* (present) and *abwesend* (absent), and as a poetic expression meaning to be, live, dwell, or work—in short, to do what one fundamentally does.[62] I translate *wesen* as "essentially happen," which seems to be the most neutral and open-ended rendition; like *wesen*, it simply turns "essence" into a verb.

The standard notion of essence reflects key assumptions of the metaphysical tradition. *Essentia* is a Romanization of *ousia*, the Greek word that Heidegger Germanizes as *Seiendheit*, "beingness." The concept has its origin in the Platonic search for the *idea* as the *koinon*, what is common or universal.

61. My argument here is a generalized version of Husserl's attack on psychologism (*Logical Investigations*, Prolegomena). An empirical, psychologistic account of thinking cannot explain how thinking manages to be meaningful, to reveal things; thus the psychologist fails to explain the basis of his own thinking. Steven Crowell deploys this Husserlian pattern of argument against Heidegger's own concept of "metontology" (1928) in "Metaphysics, Metontology, and the End of *Being and Time*," in *Husserl, Heidegger, and the Space of Meaning: Paths toward Transcendental Phenomenology* (Evanston: Northwestern University Press, 2001).

62. The Grimm *Deutsches Wörterbuch* includes a seventy-five-column article on *wesen* that struggles to articulate the word's central meaning as follows: "'to live and move' [*leben und weben*], i.e., 'to exist, to be there' . . . in an intensified sense that vaguely includes the concept of a specific expression of life or effectiveness."

For Platonism, essentiality means generality (66). What is decisive is not one's own, but what is identical throughout a class.

Essence is also traditionally opposed to existence. This familiar distinction does not arise immediately in Greek thought. Platonism makes it possible to distinguish the "what" of a thing from the particular individual as "existing," or instantiating the "what" (209, 271); since the Middle Ages, the distinction has become a truism. Throughout his writings, however, Heidegger undercuts it.[63] He clearly associates his "question of being" with the fact that there is something instead of nothing—that is, existence. But he also routinely uses "the being of x" to refer to what one would usually call the essence or nature of x. He thus challenges the traditional concepts of "what-being" and "that-being," as he often calls them. Consider the claim that "*the 'essence' of being-there lies in its existence*" (SZ 42). What is distinctive about being-there is its very way of being, which Heidegger calls "existence" in a special sense—a way of being in which being-there's own being is "at issue" for it.[64]

Be-ing, truth, and essence must now be interrogated together (288, 429). Heidegger's use of *wesen* and *Wesung* (the verbal noun) contributes to this project in at least two ways. First, by usually reserving *wesen* for be-ing, instead of beings, he emphasizes be-ing's nonontic character: beings *are*, but be-ing *essentially happens* (30, 286, 289).[65] Second, by reviving the verbal *wesen* he avoids the assumption that in order to understand what is most important about a phenomenon, we have to identify a timeless abstraction or everlasting core. A matter can hinge not on a general aspect but on a happening—an event in which the matter comes to fruition and displays itself for a while.[66] Essence is traditionally opposed to individuality; ultimate individuality is unthinkable and ineffable, because it cannot be grasped in terms of an *eidos*. But for Heidegger, essential happening is determined by the

---

63. Cf. *The Basic Problems of Phenomenology*, 77–122, esp. 116. This lecture course proposes that the distinction between essence and existence is rooted in Greek thought, and that because Greek thought is determined by the phenomenon of production, its understanding of being is too narrow.

64. Heidegger was to accuse Sartre of misinterpreting this thought in terms of the Scholastic concepts of *essentia* and *existentia*: "Letter on 'Humanism,'" in *Pathmarks*, 250–51.

65. However, Heidegger frequently uses the expressions "be-ing is . . ." or "appropriation is . . . ," where "is" functions as a copula that is not meant to reduce be-ing to an *entity*. I follow his usage, but for cautions on this point see Beistegui, *Truth and Genesis*, 111–12. §267 of the *Contributions* even experiments with the paradoxical and potentially confusing saying that be-ing is, while beings are not (cf. GA 66, 89).

66. *Wesen* means *währen* (to endure), but not *fortwähren* (to endure permanently, as traditional essences do): "The Question Concerning Technology" (1955), in *The Question Concerning Technology and Other Essays*, trans. William Lovitt (New York: Harper and Row, 1977), 30. In *Nietzsche*, vol. 1, 147–48, Heidegger denies that the notion of a changing essence leads to relativism.

unique (66). In trying to speak of this uniqueness, he is trying to say the ineffable. The traditional search for universals is thus supplanted by an experience of a unique event (354–55). If we asked how poetry *west*, for example, we would not have to look for a universal essence that applies to all poets at all times. Instead, we would listen to a poem and focus on what was taking place in it. In asking about the *Wesung* of be-ing, we are not seeking a Platonic form "beyond being": the *Wesung* of be-ing is be-ing's own way of taking place (286, 288).

If *Wesung* affirms the unique moment over the necessary, eternal, and universal, it might seem that this notion anticipates the postmodern deconstruction of all fixed centers and boundaries. On Reiner Schürmann's reading, when the *koinon* loses its force, the *arche* or first principle is undone. Phenomena are now *"event-like and therefore anarchic."*[67] "No system of qualities except an illusory one ranks [beings], and the theticism that promotes one or the other among them has never been anything but an act of arch-violence that selects one representation and confers upon it an immutable value."[68] Schürmann recognizes that the *Contributions* are not a celebration of radical pluralism. He reads the text as torn—indeed, tragic.[69] Still, he overestimates the degree to which Heidegger's thinking supports a postmodern turn. Consider Heidegger's affirmation: "What is the *inception*, that it can become the highest of all beings? It is the essential happening of *being* itself" (58). Heidegger does not understand the uniqueness of *Wesung* negatively, as the an-archic, but in temporal terms: it is the momentaneity of the founding moment, which takes place for the first and last time. The unique is the instant of inception. If *Wesung* is centered on inception, it can hardly be opposed to all *archai*. To be sure, for Heidegger the inception is not a necessary principle but a contingent event, an unpredictable rupture in history. But this does not prevent it from serving as the *decisive* source of meaning for an epoch—a source that establishes "rank" within beings (66).[70] We should not think, either, that the question of inception is separate from the "event-

67. Schürmann, "A Brutal Awakening," 95. For a full account of Schürmann's "an-archic" reading of Heidegger, see his *Heidegger on Being and Acting: From Principles to Anarchy* (Bloomington: Indiana University Press, 1987). For a very different postmodern reading of Heidegger's *Wesen* as functioning to *promote* a traditional "essentialism," see John D. Caputo, *Demythologizing Heidegger* (Bloomington: Indiana University Press, 1993), esp. chap. 6.

68. Schürmann, *Broken Hegemonies*, 545.

69. This tragedy consists in the "double bind" of appropriation and expropriation: ibid., 134, 518, 560, 584.

70. As Derrida observes, what is properly historical is neither the completely predictable nor an absolute rupture: Jacques Derrida et al., "Conversazione con Jacques Derrida," *Aut Aut* 248–49 (March-June 1992), 14. An expropriating emergency is also appropriating; it inaugurates an order of belonging, so it is not at all free of what Schürmann calls "theticism."

like" character of what Heidegger is trying to name. What distinguishes the event as *Ereignis* from a reproduction of an Idea is precisely its inceptiveness.

As inceptive, *Wesung* is decisive. It restores "decided difference" to the question of essence (151). If an issue is open to decision, then from the traditional perspective it is nonessential—it is arbitrary, subject to *arbitrium* or free choice. But for Heidegger, decision, which emerges from emergency, is not opposed to necessity: in fact, urgency is the *origin* of necessity (45, 97). Furthermore, decision is not a matter of human will; it must be understood in terms of the reciprocal relation of being-there and be-ing. This thought does not exclude us from the realm of the "essential"; in fact, it requires our deep involvement. For although essential happening is never our product, it needs us; it requires us to leap into being-there (287).

As the unique happening of be-ing, *Wesung* lies at the root of the division between existence and essence (289). In the first inception, *Wesung* is experienced only as *Anwesung*—the realm of presenting and representing, producing and reproducing (31, 32, 189). Within this realm, one can focus on the distinctive present aspect of a present being (its *idea*) and contrast it with the individual thing as exemplifying the *idea;* the distinction between essence and existence follows almost as a matter of course. However, the sense of the being of beings as presence that dominates this domain is not *Wesung* itself, but is bestowed by *Wesung.* Presence is just a present, a gift from a deeper time-space (271–72).

Heidegger occasionally also speaks of the essential happening of *beings* (66). We will explore the relation between be-ing and beings in chapter 3. For now, we can say that although in one sense he wants to think of be-ing in isolation from beings, in another sense he takes be-ing and beings as "simultaneous." Be-ing is not derived from beings through abstraction, but it does need to be "sheltered" in beings. The uniqueness of be-ing enhances the uniqueness of beings—including ourselves, if we enter being-there. Essential happening does not hover "over" beings, but engages them in the happening of truth (287, cf. 269).

I close my consideration of *wesen* with some thoughts on translation. If "essence" inevitably means *essentia*, then, as Emad and Maly argue, it is an impossible translation for Heideggerian *Wesen*.[71] But "essence" may be flexible enough to sustain Heidegger's meaning, just as the German *Wesen* is.[72] This point raises a larger question: should translations try to capture the

---

71. *Contributions to Philosophy*, xxiv–xxv.

72. Emad and Maly admit that the adjective "essential" does have such a flexible meaning: ibid., xxv. I see no reason to insist that "essence" can *never* mean "condition of possibility" or "ground of enabling": Kenneth Maly, "Translating Heidegger's Works into English: The History and the Possibility," *Heidegger Studies* 16 (2000), 131.

sense of the original within each word—creating unconventional terms and even neologisms? Or should they use more conventional choices, trusting that readers will understand each word in terms of the many contexts in which it is used, and will thus transform the traditional meaning of the word in order to adapt it to the text as a whole? The first option will often lead to tortured prose—for if we "steer clear of all terms that belong to substance-metaphysics," we will have to carry out a radical purge of our language.[73] In fact, the very idea of steering clear of the past is un-Heideggerian; the other inception is a possibility to be discovered in confrontation with the first inception, not in isolation from it. As for the second option, it makes a translation more readable and maintains a connection to the tradition—although it also leaves the text more open to misinterpretation by irresponsible readers who may take a few sentences out of context.

We are still left with the problem of the verb *wesen*. "To essence" is clumsy, although possible. It is tempting to toy with "to escence" (using the Latin *-scen* to indicate becoming), but such an artificial word is not attractive either. The renditions of *wesen* as "to presence" or "to come to presence," which have sometimes been employed, are simply wrong, as Emad and Maly point out.[74] Be-ing is not *present* at all—only entities are or become present. It is not *presence* either, but rather the granting of presence, along with other senses of the being of beings. It would be desirable to find a word that suggests insight into the importance of something without suggesting static atemporality. This is the intention of Maly's "moving at the heart of x is y" (for "the *Wesen* of x is y").[75] Another possibility is the quasi-Taoist "way-ing."[76] Gregory Fried and I, among others, have used "essentially unfold" (in our version of the *Introduction to Metaphysics*). Maly suggests "root-unfolding."[77] Richardson prefers "emerge."[78] We might consider "transpire"; the word means "to be revealed," but also "to happen" (although this usage is considered incorrect). *Wesung* is how be-ing transpires, or obscurely reveals itself in happening. However, "unfold," "emerge," and "transpire" can be mis-

---

73. Emad, "'Heidegger I,' 'Heidegger II,' and *Beiträge*," 136. On *Wesen* cf. Emad, "Thinking More Deeply into the Question of Translation," 338.

74. *Contributions to Philosophy*, xxv.

75. Kenneth Maly, "Reticence and Resonance in the Work of Translating," in Babich, *From Phenomenology to Thought, Errancy, and Desire*, 153–55.

76. Ansell-Pearson, "The An-economy of Time's Giving," 272.

77. Kenneth Maly, "Imaging Hinting Showing Placing the Work of Art," in *Kunst und Technik: Gedächtnisschrift zum 100. Geburtstag von Martin Heidegger*, ed. Walter Biemel and Friedrich-Wilhelm von Herrmann (Frankfurt am Main: Vittorio Klostermann, 1989), 195. As Stenstad points out, "root" may misleadingly suggest a nonabyssal ground: "The Last God," 184; cf. Stenstad, "*Auseinandersetzung*," 8.

78. William J. Richardson, "Dasein and the Ground of Negativity: A Note on the Fourth Movement in the *Beiträge*-Symphony," *Heidegger Studies* 9 (1993): 35–36.

interpreted as suggesting that a thing that exists independently of us is coming out of hiding and showing itself to us—whereas be-ing needs us, and cannot occur at all without involving us in some way. Furthermore, we should not focus excessively on the *change* that is involved in *Wesung* as "a movement and an ongoing emerging unfolding."[79] While *wesen* is certainly temporal, Heidegger's time is not just a medium for change, but the scene of the drama of ownness. This suggests Emad and Maly's rendition of *Wesen* as "what is ownmost" to something.[80] Despite its wordiness, and despite the fact that it cannot be turned into a verb, this is an appealing option. The phrase "what is ownmost" encourages us to reflect on what it means to own or be owned.

Finally, Emad and Maly often use the expressions "essential sway" and "hold sway." To say that be-ing holds sway is much better than saying that it is present; instead, be-ing is in effect, it takes effect, it takes place. ("Taking place" is an especially felicitous expression, as we will see, given Heidegger's interest in the "site" of being-there.) Although "hold sway" sounds more gentle than "dominate" or "rule," one could still object that the language of power is a little more appropriate to 1935 than to the *Contributions*.[81]

I will use the simplest options—"essence" and "essentially happen"—to render *Wesen* and *wesen*. But no established word is going to work perfectly, because Heidegger is not relying on a concept that can be discovered in a dictionary. The difficulty of translating *wesen* teaches us that, with this word, he has hit bedrock. To think and speak in a way befitting *Wesung* may not require a transformation of our vocabulary, grammar, and syntax, but it does demand a new relation to language. Our ordinary use of language assumes that every word names a universal essence—except proper names, which name unique individuals. But what happens when the universal is subordinated to the unique, when the essence springs from the event of owning? Then naming takes priority over predication, proper names hold sway over concepts.[82] To allow this inversion to happen may be to discover the proper order—an order in which we let language use *us* as it . . . *west*.

---

79. Maly, "Reticence and Resonance," 154. Similarly, Schoenbohm writes that "being's temporality means that there is no meaning of being—nor any being—that is permanent, ever-lasting, or unchanging": "Reading Heidegger's *Contributions to Philosophy*," 16. She thus translates *Wesung* as "coming-passing" (ibid., 27). But to be temporal is not necessarily to be temporary; even eternity is a temporal qualification (SZ 18). On the difference between *Ereignis* and traditional "motion" or "becoming," see GA 65, 280, 472; GA 70, 17, 22.

80. *Contributions to Philosophy*, xxvi.

81. *Walten* ("sway") plays a prominent role in *Introduction to Metaphysics* (1935).

82. One could argue on this basis (though not wholly without tongue in cheek) that we should use a capitalized "Being," since it is not a concept but a *proper* name for a unique event—the *appropriating* event.

Als

To ask how be-ing essentially happens is to ask how the giving (and reception) of the import of beings takes place. Heidegger replies to the question with an "as": *als das Ereignis.* Before we face *das Ereignis*, we have to dwell on the *als.* After all, this tiny word receives extraordinary attention in Heidegger's thought. "As" is the inconspicuous sign that expresses the very movement of interpreting—and even the "essential happening of be-ing" (GA 70, 82). All understanding takes something *as* something; an "as"–free staring, devoid of interpretation, is just a failure to understand (SZ 149). Assertions, which codify an "as"–relation in a subject-predicate structure, are based on a deeper interpreting that pervades our existence.[83] The word *as*, then, signifies significance—the occurrence of revelation in all its ambiguity, including the possibility of concealment. To act *as* a father, for instance, can mean to act *in one's capacity as* a father (assuming the mantle of fatherhood, accepting the responsibilities of a father-child relationship, or following a preestablished model of what it is to be a father); it can mean to act *as if one were* a father (stepping in for an absent father, fulfilling a function analogous to that of a father, playing the role of a father in a drama, pretending deceitfully to be a father); or it can mean to act *in a way that defines* a father (setting the standard for paternal behavior, being a role model, deciding what it means to call oneself a father). When one acts as a father, fatherhood can be a dominating paradigm or a creative improvisation, an opportunity for self-discovery or a mode of self-concealment.

The question of the *as* in Heidegger's sentence, then, is nothing less than the question of the relation between be-ing and appropriation. Is appropriation fathered by be-ing, or is be-ing fathered by appropriation? Are be-ing and appropriation the same? Is appropriation the true face of be-ing, or only its mask?

Clearly it would be inadequate to take appropriation merely as a disguise for be-ing. For all his emphasis on the self-concealment of be-ing (which we will investigate in chapter 3), Heidegger does not represent be-ing as a hidden object that sends out appropriation as its emissary. Be-ing is not an Unknown that lurks behind all its manifestations. The essential happening of be-ing names "be-ing's innermost, appropriation" (286, cf. 288). Here appropriation and be-ing are not wholly identified (if be-ing has an "innermost" then it presumably has externals that are *not* appropriation). Still, appropriation is not other than be-ing but its very heart.

---

83. See the distinction between the theoretical and historical "as" in GA 58 (1919–20), 111–14; this becomes the distinction between the apophantic and hermeneutic "as" in SZ §33.

84. "Time and Being," in *On Time and Being*, 21, 22, 19.

For an explicit discussion of the "inconspicuous" but "treacherous" word *as* we have to turn to late essays such as "Time and Being" (1962). Here Heidegger says it would be wrong to take either being or appropriation as a "species" of the other. Instead, time and being are "appropriated in" appropriation; appropriation is the "it" that "gives" time and being.[84] According to "The Way to Language" (1959), appropriation is the "essential origin" of being and is "richer than any conceivable definition" of being.[85] Appropriation, then, is the source of being, but not a cause or an entity. It is not a thing that gives us another thing, but is more like the very event of giving. Can it be distinguished from being at all, then? Heidegger also allows us to say that the "it" that gives being is being itself.[86]

If these remarks are slippery and inconclusive, this may be because Heidegger is trying to avoid "logical classifications."[87] Questions of whether two items are identical, or whether one is a subset of the other, may be appropriate only to given entities and not to the question of the giving of their being. But another source of obscurity in the late essays is the lack of a clear distinction between the being of beings and the event of be-ing. Using this distinction, we could hazard a clearer explanation of the "as": be-ing (the event of the giving of the being of beings) takes place "as" the event of appropriation. This donation is an appropriation; to receive the being of beings is also to enter the domain of the own. Neither be-ing nor appropriation has priority, because appropriation is be-ing's own happening—the transpiring of be-ing in its mysterious display. We can even leave out the "as" and say that be-ing *is* appropriation (470). But be-ing as appropriation does have priority over the being of beings, which emerges from this event.

Das

Another treacherous and inconspicuous word should give us pause. Heidegger speaks of *das Ereignis*. Should we translate this as "*the* appropriation"? What is the force of the *das* here?[88]

Unlike English, German can use the definite article with an abstraction: *die Freiheit*, especially in a philosophical text, means "freedom," not "the free-

85. "The Way to Language," in *On the Way to Language*, 129.

86. "Summary of a Seminar," in *On Time and Being*, 43. Cf. "Letter on 'Humanism,'" in *Pathmarks*, 254–55.

87. "Time and Being," in *On Time and Being*, 21.

88. One eccentricity of Emad and Maly's translation is that they often seem averse to using any article, even in cases where Heidegger uses the definite article and standard English would also tend to use it. For example: "We move into the time-space of [the] decision of the flight and arrival of [the] gods" (*Contributions to Philosophy*, 285 = GA 65, 405, "the" inserted to reflect the German). It is true that Heidegger often uses *Ereignis* without the definite article (e.g., GA 65, 345); however, one could ascribe this to the terse, notelike syntax of much of the text.

dom." Is the matter as simple as this? Heidegger, it seems, is pointing to appropriation as a general pattern. What is under discussion is not this or that instance of appropriation, but the essence of appropriation in general. But this interpretation is obviously unfaithful to Heidegger's thought. With nearly any other philosopher, it would go without saying that he or she would be investigating a general essence. Heidegger, however, insists that he is doing nothing of the kind; he is participating in a unique, inceptive happening. Can we take him at his word? What would this mean, if his word is *das Ereignis*?

Although all words function as abstractions to some extent in everyday language, *Ereignis* is not an eminently abstract term, such as *Freiheit*. The suffix *-nis* is used to form a noun from a verb, but not necessarily to indicate a universal. Heidegger does use many "essentialized" words (*Wahrheit, Zugehörigkeit, Einzigkeit*); in these cases we can perhaps understand what is being said in terms of *Wesung*. But he never resorts to a manifestly abstract construction (say, *Ereignismäßigkeit*, "eventlikeness") in order to name the theme at the core of this book. He sticks with *das Ereignis*, which in ordinary German would mean "the event."

"The event" could indicate a crucial event, one that defines a situation. To take an extreme case, it could be used like "the Creation." For a believer, this expression does not mean an abstract universal (creating in general), but the first and greatest event of all. Is Heidegger discussing some particular, especially important event in this text? The answer is yes. "The essential moment, immeasurable in its breadth and depth, has been inaugurated"; this is the "fundamental 'fact' of our history" (309). The crucial moment is the transition from the first inception to the other inception, from the being of beings to the truth of be-ing, from established humanity to being-there. This is a momentous moment, not an incidental incident. The text as a whole is structured by the "junctures" (*Fugen*) of this unique moment (64).

One could object that although the transition to the other inception is crucial to Heidegger's understanding of Western history, what is grasped in the transition (appropriation) is not identical with the transition. Appropriation must *always* hold sway, as long there is any meaning of being at all.[89] In making the transition to the other inception we are not *initiating* appropriation but *acknowledging* it. This point of view fits well with some of Heidegger's sayings: for instance, be-ing as ap-propriating was the ground of the ontological difference in metaphysics, but it remained unknown (466).

However, consider Heidegger's claim that his discourse is not just *about* ap-

---

89. "What Heidegger is expressing in [the] language of *Ereignis* is that being-open is the ineluctable condition of our essence": Sheehan, "A Paradigm Shift," 194.

propriation, but "*is*" appropriation (4)—a claim we will explore more thoroughly in chapter 2. If we take it as radically as possible, the statement suggests that appropriation has never truly happened until we think of it and in it. The other inception would then be *the* (sole and unique) event of appropriation. To entertain this possibility, consider how a few passages would sound if we translated *das Ereignis* using the definite article. "The appropriation assigns the god to man by appropriating man to the god" (26). The endurance of the flight of the gods "grounds the most distant nearness to the appropriation" (27). "Be-ing essentially happens as the appropriation" (30, 256, 260). With their definite articles preserved, these sentences sound less like generalizations and more like attempts to name a singular happening. I selected two sentences that name the gods—a theme we have skirted until now—in order to bring out the parallel to Christian expressions such as "the Annunciation" or "the Crucifixion." It could be that the *Contributions to Philosophy* are closer to the Bible in their thinking than they are to philosophy; they do not describe a universal but name the unique emergency, the critical juncture—the *crux*.[90]

A third alternative is that Heidegger is pointing neither to a universal nor to a singular event, but is pointing to a wide-ranging possibility from *within* a singular event. While rooted in a unique site and moment, he may be attempting to think so deeply into the urgent event in which he stands that he may reach a broad insight, one that extends beyond his own time and place to illuminate the varieties of urgency that can characterize "the essential inceptions and transitions of human history" (46).

We now have to turn more directly to appropriation and ask whether it constitutes eventfulness in general, *an* event, *the* event, or nothing like an event at all.

Ereignis

The thought of appropriation, I have argued, is the culmination of Heidegger's attempts to do justice to the priority of "belonging" or "one's own" over the universal, and thus to think of truth as situated and finite. In the event of appropriation, the being of beings and being-there become each other's

90. For a far-fetched, but not wholly baseless interpretation of the *Contributions* as Heidegger's "Christology," see George J. Seidel, "A Key to Heidegger's *Beiträge*," *Gregorianum* 76, no. 2 (1995): 363–72. Seidel continues his Christianizing interpretation (translating *Seyn* as "Logos"!) in "Heidegger's Last God and the Schelling Connection," *Laval Théologique et Philosophique* 55, no. 1 (February 1999): 85–98, and "Musing with Kierkegaard: Heidegger's *Besinnung*," *Continental Philosophy Review* 34, no. 4 (December 2001): 403–18. On the anti-Christianism of the *Contributions*, which Seidel conveniently disregards, see Luigi Pareyson, "Heidegger: la libertà e il nulla," *Annuario filosofico* 5 (1989): 11–18.

"own," or are given to each other. Beings are then revealed as beings, and be-ing-there becomes itself. I suggested that history is punctuated by crucial events of appropriation and unified by a less radical, continual appropriation of inherited messages and practices. The happening of appropriation makes possible the coherence of our world, the expropriation of anxiety, and the owned selfhood of authenticity. All this assumes, however, that "appropria-tion" refers to something that *happens*, to a kind of *event*. But is this the case?

First we need to review the etymology of *Ereignis*. As we noted, *Ereignis* derives from *eräugen*, to bring into view or come into view.[91] The sense of revelation became a sense of an *event* of revealing, and then an event in gen-eral. There is no etymological relation to *eigen* (own), which is the root of words such as *Eigenschaft* (property), *geeignet* (appropriate), and *eigentlich* (authentic). But thanks to its similarity to *eigen* in sound, the word *Ereignis* provides a unique combination: it names happening, but also suggests un-concealment and belonging—or as Albert Hofstadter puts it, "light" and "right."[92]

The question, then, is how Heidegger draws on the word *Ereignis* and its cousins in his thinking, and whether we can fruitfully interpret his usage with the help of the notion of an event. Does *Ereignis* stand apart from all hap-pening? Or is it, in some sense, an event? What we are looking for here is not an English word that captures Heidegger's sense, or a neat definition of a concept. If the thought of *Ereignis* is truly "inceptive," and if the whole text really springs "from appropriation" (3), then this thinking asks us to trans-

91. This etymology is not mentioned in the *Contributions*, but Heidegger does draw atten-tion to it in other writings. In "Das Ereignis," he reviews the Grimms' etymology and glosses *sich ereignen* as *lichten* (clearing, opening): quoted in Sheehan, "A Paradigm Shift," 197–98. Shee-han makes a convincing case that *Ereignis* is what "opens up openness," or "the dynamics that bring together givenness and human being" ("*Kehre* and *Ereignis*," 11, 9). However, largely be-cause of the etymology of *Ereignis*, Sheehan denies that the word in Heidegger primarily refers either to an event or to appropriation. "If we can call *Ereignis* an event at all, it is the 'apriori event' of the opening up of the open": Sheehan, "A Paradigm Shift," 198. *Ereignis* is an "ulti-mate state of affairs" or "ultimate *praesuppositum*": Sheehan, "*Kehre* and *Ereignis*," 13. I find Sheehan's reading not "dynamic" enough, given Heidegger's questioning of the a priori (GA 65, 222–23). As for whether *Ereignis* has anything to do with ownness and happening, in his remarks on etymology Heidegger himself shows that he wants to keep these senses: *Er-eignen* involves "becoming one's own" (*Sich zu eigen werden*): "Das Ereignis," quoted in Sheehan, "A Paradigm Shift," 198. Even if the senses of "event" and "own" are later accretions to *eräugen*, they are serendipitous accretions from Heidegger's point of view. "Der Satz der Identität," in *Identity and Difference*, 100–101, sketches an essential connection between seeing, happening, and owning: "Ap-propriating [*Er-eignen*] originally means: *er-äugen*, i.e. to catch sight [*erblicken*], to call to oneself in looking, to ap-propriate."

92. Albert Hofstadter, introduction to Heidegger, *Poetry, Language, Thought*, trans. Albert Hofstadter (New York: Harper and Row, 1971), xx. Hofstadter is mistaken in thinking that Hei-degger first emphasized "light" and then "right" (xx–xxi). We have seen that belonging is al-ready presented as the basis of unconcealment in Heidegger's earliest lecture courses.

form our words and concepts in accordance with it, not to subject it to some prior conceptual scheme. We cannot grasp *Ereignis* simply by subsuming it under some everyday concept expressed in the word *event*. Everyday concepts are shallow, because they are suited only for everyday transactions with entities. Thinking about be-ing has to deepen and transform our concepts, not dismiss the problems by labeling them with ordinary words. However, if we let the word *Ereignis* (or "appropriation," or "enowning") stand by itself, without contact with other words, then it will lose all meaning for us, because we will have no perspective on it. And even though *Ereignis* is not an everyday event, perhaps we can start to build a bridge to *Ereignis* by paying unusually close attention to phenomena that we usually call "events."

Foremost among those who have claimed that appropriation is not an event—and this might seem to settle the question as soon as it has been raised—is Heidegger himself. In several postwar essays, he emphatically distinguishes appropriation from an "occurrence" (*Vorkommnis*) or "happening" (*Geschehen* or *Geschehnis*).[93] The ordinary concept of event fails to think "in terms of Appropriating as the extending and sending which opens and preserves."[94] Is this enough for us to conclude that appropriation does not "happen" as a particular event at all, but is a constant? Not necessarily. Heidegger may be implying that the ordinary way of thinking about events is too shallow; maybe we should ultimately think of eventfulness in terms of appropriating. Ordinary concepts of the event may miss appropriating not because appropriation has nothing to do with events, but because these ordinary concepts are tied to an ontology of present beings. In support of this hypothesis, we could point to the fact that, in the passage we just cited, Heidegger characterizes *Ereignis* by way of a series of verbs. Can extending, sending, opening, and preserving be anything other than *events*? Maybe so; maybe the verbs mislead us into picturing "something which is not temporal" as an event that takes place within time.[95] Yet Heidegger is still willing to say that "being takes place [*geschieht*]."[96] So perhaps even when he speaks in noneventful language, he is insinuating a radically eventful thinking.[97] And even if the late essays de-

---

93. "The Way to Language," in *On the Way to Language*, 127; "Summary of a Seminar," in *On Time and Being*, 20; "The Principle of Identity," in *Identity and Difference*, 36. Along similar lines, Heidegger proposes in a seminar that appropriation is not caught up in historical destiny, precisely because it is the sending of this destiny. "There is no destinal epoch of enowning. Sending is from enowning": "Seminar in Le Thor 1969," in *Four Seminars*, 61.

94. "Summary of a Seminar," in *On Time and Being*, 20.

95. Ibid., 47.

96. "Time and Being," in *On Time and Being*, 8.

97. Heidegger says that, with the exception of "The Thing," his published work is nothing but "a first attempt to make my thought understandable on the basis of the tradition . . . [this work] always still speaks the language of metaphysics to some extent, or uses its language with a different meaning": letter to Dieter Sinn, August 24, 1964, cited in Sinn, *Ereignis und Nirwana*, 172.

finitively rejected the interpretation of *Ereignis* as an event, they would be at odds with the prewar writings, where Heidegger seems much less wary of "happening."[98] After all, why would he take up the word *Ereignis* if what he meant by it had nothing to do with its meaning in ordinary German?

None of these initial considerations proves anything, but they do suggest that we need a more substantive argument if we are to conclude that appropriation is not an event—or as Emad and Maly put it, that the word *event* "does not even remotely approximate *Ereignis.*" Their translation goes to some lengths to avoid associating *Ereignis* with events; for instance, it renders the reflexive verb *sich ereignen*, which in normal German means "happen" or "take place," as the passive "to be enowned." In support of these decisions, Emad and Maly claim that "'event' immediately evokes the metaphysical notions of the unprecedented and the precedent that are totally alien to *Ereignis.*"[99] I take this to mean that an event fits into a linear chain of events, either as its beginning or as one link within it; *Ereignis*, however, lies apart from any timeline. This is a plausible position, but it bears further investigation. Does "event" imply a linear sequence? Probably so. It is certainly difficult to conceive of an event that is not preceded and followed by other events. If we then link these events causally and place them within a flux of "nows," we are on the familiar ground of traditional metaphysics. Alternatively, we may try to posit a first event; then again, we easily fall into thinking of it in metaphysical terms, as a *causa sui.* But do we *have* to apply these metaphysical schemes to all events, or are there more promising ways of thinking about some events?

-Does *Ereignis* stand apart from all relations of before and after? One might think so, since Heidegger repeatedly says that *Ereignis* and be-ing are unique, *einzig* (66, 97, 252, 255, 371, 385, 460, 471). What is truly unique cannot be assimilated into the customary sequence of run-of-the-mill events. But he also favors the word *einmalig*, "singular" or "happening one time only" (55, 151, 228, 385, 463). This suggests that the uniqueness of appropriation is a *historical* uniqueness, a uniqueness that *happens.* Such a "unique moment" (97) could be unprecedented in its meaning or character, yet still be preceded and followed by other, lesser events.

---

98. For a discussion of the differences see Polt, "*Ereignis*"; Pöggeler, *The Paths of Heidegger's Life and Thought*, 115; Rudolf Wansing, "Im Denken erfahren: Ereignis und Geschichte bei Heidegger," in *Ereignis auf Französisch: Von Bergson bis Deleuze*, ed. Marc Rölli (Munich: Wilhelm Fink, 2004). One should also note that *Being and Time* uses the verb *geschehen* to indicate *Geschichtlichkeit* itself—a kind of happening that cannot be reduced to a vulgar concept of becoming as a sequence of "nows," but which is nevertheless the very opposite of an atemporal eternity (SZ 375).

99. *Contributions to Philosophy*, xx–xxi. Yet the translators themselves use the word *unprecedented* when they refer to the "unprecedented and monumental unfolding in the thinking of being that *is* the first beginning" (xxiv).

The problem forces us into a broader interpretation of Heidegger's understanding of time and appropriation. In fact, Emad and Maly rely on such an interpretation: "as born out by sections 238–242 of the *Contributions*, 'event' cannot live up to the demands put on it by *Ereignis* because 'event' emerges from within 'time-space' and as such is *itself* enowned by *Ereignis*."[100] Appropriation is not an event, but the precondition for the emergence of all events; it is the basis of time-space and is thus what first allows events, along with other beings, to become apparent *within* time-space.[101] Something here must be correct. *Ereignis* is not an entity, but what enables beings to appear. It follows that it is not just an occurrence within the domain of beings—an occurrence that itself *is*, such as a sunrise or a battle. Furthermore, *Ereignis* and time, or rather time-space, are inseparable (372)—and it would be strange to try to think of time itself in terms of some event *within* time. All the same, we might be able to distinguish ontic events within time from events that happen on the level of time and be-ing themselves. Time itself may "happen" or "take place." *Being and Time* thus refers to the *Zeitigung* of time (SZ 304)—its "maturation," "temporalizing," or "timing." The term is taken up again in the *Contributions*, along with *Räumung*, "spacing" (383). Heidegger speaks of time-space using verbs of motion: *Entrückung* and *Berückung* (384). We should not rule out the possibility that time-space—and thus *Ereignis*—can, in some sense, happen as an event.[102]

We can also approach the problem indirectly: if appropriation is not an event, and if it has priority over all events, then how can we think of this priority itself in a way that avoids metaphysics? Appropriation cannot be an essence or a universal, if we take seriously Heidegger's critique of the Platonic *idea* and all its avatars (e.g., §110). Appropriation cannot be an a priori condition of the possibility of experience, if we take seriously his rejection of

---

100. *Contributions to Philosophy*, xxi.

101. "*Ereignis* . . . cannot be thought as an event *in* the course of serial time, since it is the *source* of any kind of time as well as of everything else": Joan Stambaugh, *The Finitude of Being* (Albany: State University of New York Press, 1992), 154. Stambaugh adds, "This was precisely Heidegger's own reservation about my initial translation of *Ereignis* as 'event of appropriation'": ibid., 196. This report is consistent with Heidegger's statements in his postwar essays.

102. Hans Ruin writes, "The *Ereignis* does not signify an event in time; on the contrary, it is one of a series of fundamental concepts through which time itself is thematized": *Enigmatic Origins: Tracing the Theme of Historicity through Heidegger's Works* (Stockholm: Almqvist and Wiksell, 1994), 203. But Ruin adds, "To understand being historically . . . is to understand it as that which happens in a passage of thrownness and projection, of disappropriation and appropriation" (ibid., 205). So being is an event ("that which happens") after all. Similarly, Gail Stenstad writes that "be-ing *is* not, but *does*" ("The Last God," 180), yet claims "*Ereignis* is not an event or a series of events" (ibid., 183). The challenge, then, is to investigate a "happening" or "doing" deeper than what we ordinarily call events. In French one could speak of the *évenir* at the source of every *événement*: François Fédier, "Traduire les *Beiträge zur Philosophie (Vom Ereignis)*," *Heidegger Studies* 9 (1993): 32.

transcendental thinking (e.g., §122, §184). If it is difficult to think of time-space as happening, it is at least as difficult to think of it as a *non*-event without resorting to some variant of traditional metaphysics and representing appropriation as something quasi-present.

Let us look more closely at the sections on time-space that the translators cite (§§238–42). Here Heidegger does give time-space (and thus *Ereignis*) priority over traditional representations of time and space (372), over the fact that every historical occurrence happens at some place and time (377), and over the temporal succession that seems to flow past the present-at-hand (371, 382). However, all this evidence is inconclusive. Is Heidegger claiming that *Ereignis* is deeper than any event, or simply that it is deeper than the customary *picture* of events as present-at-hand occurrences that flow from not-yet-present to present to no-longer-present?[103]

We need to step outside the text in order to reflect on events. When we pay attention to what we normally label an event, can we find any phenomena that exceed traditional metaphysical notions—notions such as the chain of causes and effects or the flux of "nows"?

An event involves change; the happening of an event makes a difference, at least temporarily. But the difference can be made on various levels. Some levels of event are easiest to describe in terms of the traditional Aristotelian categories. For example, most events are alterations in the accidents of individual substances and in the relations among these substances. The sun comes over the horizon; the air is heated; a person gets thirsty and takes a drink. The beings here remain the beings that they are, but their qualities, positions, and other attributes change. In more radical events, an entity comes to be or passes away: a mouse is conceived and born, only to be killed by a hawk. Modern thinking (and much Greek thinking as well) tends to reduce this level of events to the first. Nothing is ultimately created or destroyed; the sum of what *is* is supposedly conserved. However, there is a vast difference between a live mouse and a dead one. The dead mouse is not, strictly speaking, a mouse; it is a heap of substances that formerly served as matter for a mouse (cf. *De Anima* 2.1). This Aristotelian description does justice to experience. There is a coherence to an entity—or at least, an organism—that can genuinely be created and destroyed. Coming to be and passing away happen at a level of event that presupposes the lower level (alteration) but cannot be reduced to it.

Now consider a further kind of event, an event that can happen only for

---

103. The thought of *Ereignis* is not "an interpretation of being as 'becoming'" (GA 65, 472). The seemingly obvious notions of becoming and change are embroiled in metaphysics (193–94, 280). But this does not rule out the possibility that appropriation "happens" in a nonmetaphysical sense.

an entity that makes sense of itself and its surroundings by way of its actions, and that can also change its way of acting and thus its understanding. A deep change in such an entity's way of acting could be called a *reinterpretive* event. Such an event alters the agent's own being as well as the agent's interpretation of the world. For instance, a shy girl takes part in a school play, learns to present herself in an outgoing way, and thus becomes outgoing; she comes to approach herself and her world more decisively and fearlessly, and thus experiences the world differently. A man fails to stand up to a challenge to his honor, and thus becomes a coward in his own eyes and those of others. A reinterpretive event heightens or resolves a tension that affects its protagonist's way of being someone in the world, and thus the course of his or her life. Such events are properly recounted in stories.

Because a reinterpretive event affects how beings are *revealed* to the actor, it happens on a different level from events in which beings are changed or destroyed while the mode in which they are manifest remains the same. Reinterpretive events are not just entities, but critical junctures in the emergence of the *appearing* of entities. They open and close our ways of being-in-the-world, and hence our ways of access to beings as a whole. Such an event cannot be reduced to a theoretical description of changes within a mathematicized space-time continuum, because it concerns meaning and truth. It is an e-vent not merely as the "outcome" of a process, but as a coming-out, as an emergence. Reinterpretive events clearly depend on other sorts of events: they involve alterations and presuppose the coming-to-be of certain things. However, they cannot be reduced to these other types of event, because they essentially involve unconcealment. Reinterpretive events are not the earliest in a timeline, but they are prior to other levels of event, in two senses: they cannot be understood in terms of these other levels, and they are presupposed by any understanding of the other levels, because such understanding is carried out by beings like us, whose interpretations bear the marks of many reinterpretive events.

When it comes to reinterpretive events, traditional metaphysics is largely silent. The Aristotelian categories become clumsy and opaque (unless we introduce some concepts from Aristotle's *Poetics*, which could be read as the first philosophical account of reinterpretive events).[104] Heidegger offers us fruitful concepts for such an account. Reinterpretive events can happen only for

---

104. See especially *Poetics*, 10–11, on reversal and recognition. For an analogous contemporary project informed by Heidegger, see Paul Ricoeur, *Time and Narrative*, trans. Kathleen McLaughlin and David Pellauer, 3 vols. (Chicago: University of Chicago Press, 1984, 1985, 1988). A summary of Ricoeur's account of the narrative "refiguration" of time can be found in his "Narrated Time," in *A Ricoeur Reader: Reflection and Imagination*, ed. Mario J. Valdés (Toronto: University of Toronto Press, 1991), 338–54.

being-there—an entity whose own being is "at issue" for it and who works out its being by existing as someone within a world, thus interpreting itself and its surroundings (SZ §4, §9). We could take reinterpretive events as turning points in the development of the hermeneutic "as" (SZ §33). Such points are *crises*—moments that decide the course of a life and its meaning. They are emergencies in which meaning emerges. For this reason, a reinterpretive event is unpredictable; the former order of meanings cannot account for it. As Françoise Dastur puts it, such an event "dislocates time and gives a new form to it . . . the event, as such, is upsetting."[105]

We have not yet reached appropriation. Clearly appropriation in the *Contributions* is extraordinary, not something that happens in a school play. But imagine the ultimate reinterpretive, or rather interpretive event—an event that makes possible interpretation and meaning themselves, that allows the hermeneutic "as" to come forth, not just for an individual but for a community and for an age. Such an event would be the emergency in which this shared being-there and the "there" itself first emerged. This happening would belong to an order higher than that of ordinary reinterpretive events, which must take place within an established site and age. It would be the establishing of time, space, and unconcealment themselves for this people and this epoch.[106]

A radical interpretive event fits some requirements for *Ereignis*. First, it is not a mere entity, because it concerns the appearing of beings as beings. Fur-

---

105. Françoise Dastur, "Phenomenology of the Event: Waiting and Surprise," *Hypatia* 15, no. 4 (fall 2000): 182. Material for a more extensive philosophy of events—particularly in their singularity and unpredictability—is provided by a number of French thinkers, not all congenial to Heidegger. See Alain Badiou, *Being and Event*, trans. Oliver Feltham (London: Continuum, 2006); Alain Badiou, *Manifesto for Philosophy*, trans. Norman Madarasz (Albany: State University of New York Press, 1999), chap. 8; Geoffrey Bennington, *Lyotard: Writing the Event* (New York: Columbia University Press, 1988); Gilles Deleuze, *The Fold: Leibniz and the Baroque*, trans. Tom Conley (Minneapolis: University of Minnesota Press, 1993), chap. 6; Gilles Deleuze, *The Logic of Sense*, trans. Mark Lester with Charles Stivale (New York: Columbia University Press, 1990); Jean-Luc Marion, *In Excess: Studies of Saturated Phenomena*, trans. Robyn Horner and Vincent Berraud (New York: Fordham University Press, 2002), chap. 2; Rölli, *Ereignis auf Französisch*; Claude Romano, *L'événement et le monde* (Paris: Presses Universitaires de France, 1998). Throughout *Truth and Genesis*, Beistegui employs "event" in a Deleuzian sense that he tends to assimilate to Heidegger's *Ereignis*: "event" here means a spatiotemporal field of virtuality and difference from which actual, particular beings emerge.

106. "History means . . . *the happening [Ereignis] of a decision about the essence of truth*. The manner in which the whole of beings is revealed, in which man is allowed to stand in the midst of this revelation, is grounded and transformed in such a decision. Such a happening is exceptional": *Basic Concepts*, trans. Gary E. Aylesworth (Bloomington: Indiana University Press, 1993), 17. Cf. *Introduction to Metaphysics*, 139: "appearing in the first and authentic sense . . . takes space in; it first conquers space; as standing there, it creates space for itself; it brings about everything that belongs to it, while it itself is not imitated. Appearing in the second sense merely steps forth from an already prepared space."

thermore, even though this event presupposes previous events and involves lower levels of event, it has an irreducible character of its own. It cannot be understood in terms of any other event, because it itself is the origin of all intelligibility; in this sense it is ultimate and "earliest." Finally, such an event would elude the categories of traditional metaphysics, which describes beings in their being but does not recognize the originary giving of the being of beings. This giving, I propose, happens in an ultimate interpretive event.

A number of passages in the *Contributions* support this proposal. First, unlike some of Heidegger's postwar essays, this text freely uses words such as *happening* in close connection with *Ereignis:* "only the greatest happening [*Geschehen*], the innermost *Ereignis,* can still save us" (57). Appropriation is said to become: "*Das Ereignis ereignet* means nothing other than: *Ereignis* and only *Ereignis becomes* truth" (349). Truth, too, is an event: "openness . . . is not a state but a happening [*Geschehnis*]" (333). Appropriation involves *Wesung* as the "happening of the truth of be-ing" (287). *Ereignis* is the "happening of owndom [*Eigentum*]" (320) in "happenings of owning [*Eignung*]" (310).

These passages might still leave room to argue that appropriation "happens" continually, as it were—it is a permanent fixture, not a particular event.[107] However, this argument becomes unworkable when we recall the connection between *Ereignis* and inception (*Anfang*). "The greatest *Ereignis* is always the inception" (57). "The inception—inceptively conceived—is be-ing itself . . . as *Ereignis*" (58). Lest we think that Heidegger is using the word *Anfang* in a nontemporal sense, to mean a first principle, he explicitly says that inceptions elude historical study not because they are supratemporally eternal, but because they are greater than eternity; they are "the *shocks* of time" (17).[108] The scheme of the "first inception" and "other inception,"

---

107. Parvis Emad seems to maintain such a position: "In contrast to the death-bound and finite occurrence of projection, being's appropriating forth-throw is *ewig,* i.e., ongoing self-sustaining and is not eliminated by *Dasein's* passing": "'Heidegger I', 'Heidegger II', and *Beiträge*," 144. But if be-ing *needs* being-there, as Heidegger often claims (e.g., GA 65, last sentence on page 265), then death cannot simply be a limitation that affects being-there and leaves be-ing untouched (GA 65, §§160–62). Being is not given except *to* mortal being-there. This is why "the eternal" (*das Ewige*) is precisely *not* the "ongoing" (*das Fort-währende*) but the unique, which may withdraw in a moment and return transformed (GA 65, 371). Heideggerian "eternity" is not atemporal, but is a creative inception that cannot be reduced to an established chronological sequence and that demands to be rediscovered and reinterpreted. According to "Überlegungen" VIII, §19, the essence of the eternal can be nothing but the deepest sweep (*Durchschwingung*) of time in its refusal and donation, preservation and loss. Cf. GA 65, 17, 55; GA 39, 54–55, 111; *Schelling's Treatise on the Essence of Human Freedom,* trans. Joan Stambaugh (Athens: Ohio University Press, 1985), 113; Jean Greisch, "The Eschatology of Being and the God of Time in Heidegger," trans. Dermot Moran, *International Journal of Philosophical Studies* 4, no. 1 (March 1996): 17–42; Gerd Haeffner, "Heidegger über Zeit und Ewigkeit," *Theologie und Philosophie* 64 (1989): 481–517.

108. Heidegger speaks of the "shocks" or "jolts" (*Stöße*) not only of time, but also of appropriation (GA 65, 463) and be-ing (242, 432, 464, 485–86). The word *Stoß* suggests the impact

then, does not refer to moments in which human beings recognize or fail to recognize a given state of affairs. Be-ing itself takes place *only* as an inception. To seek the other inception, then, is not just to hope for a new relation to be-ing, but to prepare for the essential happening of be-ing itself. The happening of be-ing is the primal "that" that forces itself upon us intermittently and unpredictably; the challenge is to experience "the nonderivable shock of be-ing itself, which is to be seized in its purest 'that'" (464, cf. 463).[109] Be-ing must strike us with the strangeness and obscurity of "what happens only once, only this time" (463). It is the rarest because it is the most unique, and it happens only at a few, inconspicuous moments (255). In short, be-ing is not a constant; "be-ing is at times" (*das Seyn ist zuzeiten:* GA 70, 15).

It hardly seems tenable now to deny that appropriation *happens*, and not just as an a priori structure but as an event.[110] "Event" here cannot indicate the sort of occurrence that is usually chronicled by physicists, historians, or journalists—this, I take it, is what Heidegger is trying to distinguish from *Ereignis* in his late remarks. Furthermore, by calling *Ereignis* an event, we do not just mean that appropriation is temporary (although it is true that it does not last forever), but that it inaugurates a unique epoch. Our task is to characterize this happening.

What occurs in the event of appropriation? Consider some key statements. First, "be-ing essentially happens as *the appropriating event of the grounding of the there*" (183). *Ereignis* is an abbreviation for *das Ereignis der Dagründung*, the event in which "the there . . . is ap-propriated [*er-eignet*]" (247). Appropriation is the event in which be-ing literally *takes place* (in German one could say *das Seyn findet statt*, "be-ing finds its site"). A site is staked out where interpreting can happen, where being-there can take root. Time and space then happen together as the "site of the moment" (323, 384). Such a site can be grounded only in an inception—an origin that founds an open realm. From the inceptive event of appropriation springs an order of unconcealment—a world in which the givenness of beings can be cultivated by a people (97).

Heidegger also writes that appropriation is "history" (32, 494). This does

---

of a transformative event (e.g., the call of conscience, SZ 271). (Throughout *Der Tod als Wandlungsmitte*, Müller speaks of "degrees" of *Ereignis* and its aspects, including emergency: e.g., 84, 264, 295–96, 323. This locution helps us avoid thinking of appropriation as a rigid structure; however, it does not do justice to the transformative suddenness of a *Stoß*.)

109. According to "Das Ereignis," what-being (essence) is just a stilling of the "that" of the event of appropriation, which has yet to be grasped and which was already lost when it was interpreted as *physis*. On the "that," cf. GA 70, 46.

110. Beistegui tries to have it both ways when he calls "the event of being" "the event of all events, or, more accurately perhaps, the eventness or eventuality of all events": *Truth and Genesis*, 113; cf. 114, 142, 338–39. Being as *Ereignis* is then a "primordial and forever recurring event": ibid., 112. But a constant "eventness" is precisely *not* an event, particularly not a historical event. Cf. Miguel de Beistegui, *The New Heidegger* (London: Continuum, 2005), 83.

not mean that it can be studied by historians, or that it is fleeting, but that it is the happening of be-ing. To think in tune with the history of be-ing, or "be-ing-historically," is not to tell a story about the ways be-ing has been conceived, but to grasp how be-ing itself takes place. History here must be understood not merely in terms of change (280, 472) but in terms of how we belong (or fail to belong) to a unique dispensation of meaning.[111] History (*Geschichte*) is the happening (*Geschehnis*) in which our fate and destiny (*Schicksal* and *Geschick*) are drawn into the sending (*Schickung*) of the being of beings to us.[112] The history of be-ing is thus the happening of the giving of the being of beings—it is a "history of donation" (GA 66, 68). Appropriation as history initiates a drama into which we are thrown, and in which the being of beings is thrown to us, so that we may catch it and in turn cast it forward into the future. It is our responsibility to question the inherited meaning of the being of beings and keep it alive by keeping it open to further unfolding. Then, through the interplay of remembrance and readiness, the present can flare up as a moment whose uniqueness cannot be reduced to mere evanescence (257).

"The god" plays an essential role in this event: "be-ing essentially happens as appropriation, the momentous site of the decision about the nearness and distance of the final god" (230). Our relation to the divine is essential to our participation in be-ing (34, 398–99, 470–71), so the "passing of the final god" will be central to the other inception (17, 27, 228, 331, 414). This "passing" is neither a direct revelation nor a disappearance, but a moment in which the problem of god (or gods, 437) *matters* to us once again—it becomes an issue calling for decision (405).

Precisely because be-ing happens as *event*—not as a present-at-hand process, but as a sending—be-ing involves *ownness*. Be-ing is not universal and eternal, but instead is *ours*, as the destiny of our own community. Our destiny lays claim to us, and we can succeed or fail in laying claim to it; this dynamic of claiming, or appropriating, is crucial to the happening of be-ing.[113] The founding of the there would be the crystallization of one's own, the appropriation of being-there (256). A unique place and age would be brought into a configuration that claims human beings as its own; the place and age would become a home where human beings could be there—could own and

---

111. See Charles Guignon, "The History of Being," in Dreyfus and Wrathall, *A Companion to Heidegger*, esp. 398–405.

112. "Time and Being," 8–9.

113. Emad and Maly raise some legitimate concerns about the term *appropriation*. The word is not nearly as elegant and flexible as *Ereignis*, and sometimes connotes "seizing, ruling, and hegemony": *Contributions to Philosophy*, xxi. However, one can appropriately appropriate a style of dressing or cooking, for example, without injustice or violence. The sense of "appropriation" is broad enough that, given the right usage and context, it can work well as a parallel to *Ereignis*.

be owned by be-ing. Only then could we be *ourselves* (311, 320; GA 69, 123–26). Becoming ourselves does not mean returning to some fixed nature, but accepting our role as the beings to whom our own being, and being in general, makes a difference (245). This can happen only if we enter owndom—the there as the realm in which being is an urgent issue for us.

Heidegger distinguishes two aspects of this grounding event: the fundamental happening of be-ing, and the happening in which this foundation is "attained and taken over" by being-there, which builds upon it (307). But neither of these aspects can take place without the other. We are appropriated by be-ing: it draws us into being-there. In turn, we can appropriate be-ing: we can stop taking the being of beings for granted and allow it to come alive for us as a gift that deserves to be questioned.[114] Be-ing requires humanity in order to happen essentially, and humanity belongs to be-ing; this oscillation (*Gegenschwung*) of requiring and belonging constitutes appropriation (251, cf. 286–87). Be-ing *braucht*—both needs and uses—being-there as its seeker, preserver, and guardian (17, 294). In turn, we cannot "be there" unless be-ing takes place. Heidegger calls this reciprocal relation "the turn in appropriation" (407). Due to the turn, the grounding of the there is both the grounding of be-ing and the grounding of being-there. In less Heideggerian terms: if the givenness of things is to become a living issue for us, then we have to become alive to it—and only then can we reach our highest potential.[115]

In all this, we should not forget the *non*-belonging that haunts the event of appropriation. Appropriation is not simply the triumph of the proper and the local. As we have seen, *Being and Time* suggests that our existence is a belonging-yet-not-belonging. We belong to a coherent world in which beings belong together, yet we cannot be claimed *inexorably* by this belonging because the world is contingent. Genuine selfhood (authenticity) requires a confrontation with nonbelonging (anxiety). Similarly, according to the *Con-*

114. Objecting to my formulations, Thomas Kalary rightly points out that Heidegger himself never says that being-there "appropriates" be-ing: "Hermeneutic Pre-conditions for Interpreting Heidegger: A Look at Recent Literature," pt. 1, *Heidegger Studies* 18 (2002): 170; pt. 2, *Heidegger Studies* 19 (2003): 144. Similarly, Walter A. Brogan nicely observes that *Ereignis* is "belonging itself, and never something that belongs": "Da-sein and the Leap of Being," in Scott et al., *Companion*, 171. In other words, we cannot master and possess be-ing. However, we can still make it more deeply our "own," much as we can appropriate "our" language: speakers of English will never control the meaning of all English words, but they can develop an appreciation for the language that is "theirs" and learn to draw on it tactfully. This is the sense in which I use the locution that we can "appropriate" be-ing. For a similar usage see Emad, "The Echo of Being," 22.

115. On the relation between the "appropriating throw" of be-ing and the "appropriated projection" of being-there, cf. von Herrmann, *Wege ins Ereignis*, 30–31, 56, 92–93. For von Herrmann and his students, this relation is the key to appropriation.

tributions, be-ing essentially happens as "estrangement" (*Befremdung:* 283, 347). *Ereignis* involves *Ent-eignung*—ex-propriation, dis-owning (GA 66, 312). The "away" belongs to the "there," as attested by the ever-looming nothingness of death (§202). In a different sense, we can say that being-there is "away" in everydayness, alienated from both be-ing and the nothing; in this sense, "being-away" is the *Contributions'* counterpart to inauthenticity (§177, §201). True ownness requires us to face the contingency of our site, instead of getting so comfortable in our routes that they become ruts. We must acknowledge homelessness for the sake of genuine dwelling in a home. If appropriation were only ownness, it would not be appropriation at all. Without a *tension* between belonging and estrangement, there could be no appropriation, no interpretive event, no opening of the there as a *question*—a condition that makes ownness an *issue*. If we were fully "appropriated," absorbed into our site, we would not be-there, but would be mere animals.[116]

We must learn to recognize our everyday complacency as a crisis, so that the emergency of be-ing can strike. Our age suffers from *die Not der Notlosigkeit* (11, 107, 119, 125, 234–37): in a time that is indifferent to decision and urgency, the greatest danger is that be-ing will fail to happen, because we will fail to enter the condition of emergency that appropriation requires. All necessity is rooted in urgency (45, 97): beings emerge as meaningful only in emergencies, when what it means for beings to be comes into question. As a crisis, the moment of appropriation demands "decisions," in a sense that involves not only human choice but also the destiny of be-ing (87–91). These thoughts follow from Heidegger's crucial hypothesis about be-ing: "Emergency—that urgency that oppresses us in its essential happening—what if it were the truth of be-ing itself . . . as appropriation?" (46, cf. 154).

We asked whether appropriation is an event. Our answer is yes—if "event" is understood radically enough, as the grounding of the there, the inception of history as owning and estrangement. But—to return to an earlier question—should we go farther, and think of appropriation as *the* event? Is appropriation a trait common to many moments of inception, or is it a single such inception? Some passages certainly suggest that appropriation is a *single* event. For instance, the "hint" is said to open a distinctive future, past, and present (383). This hinting is "the inceptive essence of appropriation, inceptive in the other inception. This essence of be-ing [is] unique and happens only once [*einzig und einmalig*], and thus satisfies the innermost essence of be-ing; *physis* too [is] unique and happens only once" (385). This passage

116. Or mere human beings—for being-there is not equivalent to humanity. On animals as wrapped up in their environments, see *The Fundamental Concepts of Metaphysics,* 255. On the tension between appropriation and expropriation cf. Schürmann, *Broken Hegemonies,* e.g., 134, 518, 560, 584.

suggests that although the first inception was unique, it did not attain appropriation. The other inception, then, is not just a new relation to or recognition of appropriation, but the first and last happening of appropriation itself.[117]

As we try to think through the singularity and uniqueness of be-ing, Heidegger warns us that be-ing is neither the "most general" nor the "most concrete," nor a combination of both (256). Both the universal and the particular (understood as the individual "this something," the Aristotelian *tode ti*) are legacies of traditional metaphysics. This may be why it is difficult to decide whether *das Ereignis* can happen more than once: the event of appropriation is not an *entity* that can be identified, compared to similar items, and counted up. On one hand, Heidegger insists on the singularity of the history of be-ing: we are to let the stream of the unique take its singular course (430). On the other hand, he sometimes uses the plural *Ereignisse*. In some passages, this expression simply seems to mean the various aspects or dimensions of the (possibly singular) event of appropriation, including its "uniqueness" and "loneliness" (470–71).[118] But in other passages, *Ereignisse* seem to be rare events, unique turning points in history (227–28, 463). We can call them "peaks" of time and be-ing.[119] Heidegger will not allow us to count these peaks: "When and how long being 'is' cannot be asked" (GA 69, 145). What *Ereignis* indicates "happens [*ereignet sich*] only in the singular, no, not in any number, but uniquely."[120] If we could know how often appropriation has taken place, we would not need to think the uniqueness of be-ing (488). In other words, the uniqueness at stake here is not a question of identity and difference among entities; the uniqueness consists in the *urgency* with which the event would appropriate us, belonging to us as our own problem, bringing entities to light in a way that is assigned to us as our own.

---

117. Cf. GA 65, 405: "Or is the decision the opening of a completely different time-space for a grounded truth of be-ing—the *first* grounded truth of be-ing—for appropriation?" As Pöggeler puts it, *das Ereignis* is not "a constant essence," but "the experience of this truth which is possible for *us today*": *Martin Heidegger's Path of Thinking*, 148. It seems wrong, then, to say that Heidegger takes the word *physis* "to indicate the very *Wesung des Seyns*": Alejandro Vallega, "'Beyng-Historical Thinking' in *Contributions to Philosophy*," in Scott et al., *Companion*, 54. Vallega-Neu also claims that *physis* was already be-ing itself: *Heidegger's "Contributions*," 40, 60, 68–69, 83. But if the Greeks "were not able to think this original event" (ibid., 69), and if there "is no truth of be-ing out there, standing by itself, which we could then think" (31–32), because "enowning does not occur separately from thinking but in and as it" (33, cf. 73), then we should conclude that the event of be-ing did not yet happen among the Greeks.

118. Cf. Neu, *Die Notwendigkeit der Gründung*, 215.

119. GA 39, 52, 56, 109; *Basic Questions of Philosophy*, 50. Referring to GA 65, 563, Schürmann interprets *Er-eignung* as a constant, a priori condition for historical *Ereignisse*: *Broken Hegemonies*, 563. In contrast, I interpret "appropriating" here as a name for the happening of the events themselves, which is deeper than the superficial interpretation of these events by historians.

120. "The Principle of Identity," in *Identity and Difference*, 36.

I suggested above that appropriation might be neither general nor concrete in the traditional sense, but a wide-ranging possibility that can be discerned only by embracing a unique happening—the happening in which "we" (Westerners) cross from the first to the other inception. This happening is broad enough to embrace an entire age, an extensive juncture in Western history. Thinking of it could also shed light on other radical events, without aiming at a universal form or a transcendental condition. An interpretation of *das Ereignis* will not yield a conceptual scheme that can be used by historians or anthropologists. There is no essence of appropriation that will simply transfer, say, to an interpretation of ancient Taoism—or even to an interpretation of the Greek first inception. However, the essential happening of the appropriation may find *resonance* in other events. Although we cannot mediate between the first and the other inception by finding their common properties, they are in a dynamic relation, which Heidegger calls the *Zuspiel*—an interplay or "pass," as in a ball game (169). We may not find universals, but we can engage in an interpretive exchange with other singular places and times, *retrieving* their singularity. To say that (the) appropriation is unique is not to isolate it from all communication or meaning—in fact, "*Only the singular is re-trievable*" (55). And in this retrieval, we may find that what we share with others is precisely *ownness*.

Another question looms: has the event of appropriation happened at all, or is it reserved for the future? We cannot answer the question adequately until we look more closely at inception (chapter 2), consider being-there and time-space (chapter 3), and reflect on the idea of a futural philosophy (chapters 2 and 4). But consider these statements: "*be-ing as ap-propriation is history*" (494); "be-ing needs man in order to happen essentially" (251); and "so far, man has never yet *been* historical [or historically]" (492, cf. 454). We are syllogistically drawn to the surprising conclusion that be-ing has never taken place, at least not as appropriation. Heidegger's discourse here seems to lie between philosophy and prophecy. It evokes and awaits the crucial event.

This stance is highly puzzling. If appropriation is the giving of the being of beings, and if we already understand the being of beings, then surely appropriation must have already (or even "always already") happened. As Heidegger himself puts it at one point, as soon as we have thrown ourselves free of beings toward being, ap-propriation has already occurred, though in a concealed way (452–53). But *have* we truly thrown ourselves free? And has being truly been *given* to us if we have not actively received it—taken it up as a question, instead of taking it for granted? Perhaps true giving and true history would take place only as a problem, only as an emergency, when we truly experienced "the estrangement of the *open*" (454).

Das Seyn west als das Ereignis: this formula points to be-ing's intimate happening, to the event of the decisive donation of the being of beings. The donation would take place as a crisis in which the givenness of the given—including ourselves—would come into question for us. This happening would initiate a site and age with a unique relation to the divine. It would lay claim to us as we laid claim to it, in a mutual giving and possessing that would never be all-absorbing, but would remain exposed to estrangement. This emergency, this "storm of be-ing" (300), would tear open the clearing like a sudden bolt of lightning.[121]

But how can we think of the event of appropriation, if thinking has traditionally been a theoretical search for universals and for facts that are interpreted in the light of those universals? Have all our attempts to think of appropriation so far been anything but self-defeating abstractions? What would it mean for a thinking of the happening of appropriation to *happen*? Throughout his search for belonging, Heidegger has also searched for ways of thinking about belonging without reducing it to a universal—such as formal indication and hermeneutic phenomenology. In the *Contributions*, where he is trying to confront appropriation itself, the need for such a way of thinking is especially pressing. Our next topic is the *Contributions'* search for the finite thinking of the finite, the appropriate thinking of appropriation, the event of thinking the event.

121. On *Ereignis* as *Erblitzen* or *Aufblitzen* (lightning, lightening, en-lightning), see GA 65, 28, 409, 228; cf. GA 39, 30, 58, 242–43; GA 66, 64; "The Turn," in *The Question Concerning Technology*, 44–46; "The Way to Language," in *On the Way to Language*, 133; "Anaximander's Saying," in *Off the Beaten Track*, ed. and trans. Julian Young and Kenneth Haynes (Cambridge: Cambridge University Press, 2002), 255; "Logos (Heraclitus, Fragment B 50)," in *Early Greek Thinking*, trans. David Farrell Krell and Frank A. Capuzzi (San Francisco: Harper and Row, 1975), 78; Hannah Arendt and Martin Heidegger, *Letters 1925–1975*, trans. Andrew Shields (Orlando: Harcourt, 2004), 59, 62; "Seminar in Le Thor 1966," in *Four Seminars*, 9. Cf. Robert J. Dostal, "The Experience of Truth for Gadamer and Heidegger: Taking Time and Sudden Lightning," in *Hermeneutics and Truth*, ed. Brice R. Wachterhauser (Evanston: Northwestern University Press, 1994). (Miguel de Beistegui's difference from Heidegger is summed up in his project of "identifying the general system in which the phenomenon *flashes*" "like lightning": *Truth and Genesis*, 291, 265. This would amount to an explanation of the sudden event of unconcealment, whereas for Heidegger such an event is inexplicable and precedes all systems.)

2

The Event of Thinking the Event

We have come far enough to see that appropriation demands a unique way of thinking and writing. Ordinarily, to think is to represent entities; but Heidegger wants to think of a coming-to-ownness that could take place between being-there and be-ing. Our task in this chapter is a *Wegbesinnung*, a meditation on the way (77). This cannot simply be a meditation *about* the way, a discourse on method, as if we could determine the proper path before setting foot on it. To think about the thinking of appropriation is, at the same time, to think of appropriation itself—and even to allow appropriation to happen.[1] Still, a distinction between "substantive" issues and "methodological" or "stylistic" issues has some use; by exploring "formal" questions before we go into the details of Heidegger's thoughts, we may avoid taking them in the wrong spirit. It is all too easy to read his text as a theory, a doctrine, a set of claims about essences—when instead, the *Contributions* are repeated attempts to participate in an event of appropriation that is more fundamental than any theoretical truth.

Are these attempts successful? In an elucidation of Nietzsche, Heidegger writes, "the grand style prevails wherever abundance restrains itself in simplicity."[2] According to the *Contributions*, style is a mature "certainty" that per-

---

1. As Vallega-Neu puts it, "*Contributions* attempts to perform what it thinks": *Heidegger's "Contributions,"* 49. For an insightful discussion of this "performativity," with reference to selfhood and inceptive thinking among other topics, see Wood, *Thinking after Heidegger,* chapter 10.
2. Heidegger, *Nietzsche,* vol. 1, 134. On the Nietzschean element in the style of the *Contributions* see Maggini, "Le 'style de l'homme à venir.'"

vades the sheltering of the truth of be-ing in beings, such as works of art (69). This text is itself such a sheltering, insofar as it tries to say be-ing within the language of beings (78). But the attempt is hardly a complete success; the moments of certainty and simplicity are scattered among pages of turgid struggles. Heidegger admits that the *Contributions* have not yet managed to "join the free juncture of the truth of be-ing" (4). They only foreshadow a work whose "juncture" would be en-joined by be-ing itself (4, 77). If the *Contributions* had succeeded, we might be completely unable to distinguish between form and content; the saying of be-ing would itself "be" be-ing (4; cf. GA 66, 51, 64), and to speak *vom Ereignis* would not mean to speak *about* appropriation, but to allow thinking to be appropriated by appropriation (3). (This is not to suggest that a perfected "work" would fully and finally express the truth of be-ing, summing it up in a system. To the contrary, the time of systems has passed [5], and the challenge is to be attuned to the self-concealing and inceptive character of the truth of be-ing.) Since the *Contributions* are a partial failure, they are partly out of tune with be-ing. Still, we can glimpse their stylistic goals both in passages where Heidegger seems to have succeeded and in those where, despite his hopes to meld style and substance, he speaks about stylistic certainty rather than achieving it.

It is strange to see Heidegger hope for certainty. But this is not a Cartesian certainty, a clear and distinct representation; it is the kind of certainty found in a successful artwork—a creative confidence that has discovered an appropriate way of handling its theme. There are countless viable ways of treating a theme in art, but not just any way will be satisfying; there is no objective standard of accuracy, but there is a special kind of rigor, an assured touch developed over years of practice. To say that an artist or artwork has "style" is to say that this assurance pervades the work and helps its theme to shine through. Although one might think of style, in this sense, as less rigorous than scientific objectivity, Heidegger would argue that settling for the universally accessible and verifiable is less rigorous than opening oneself to the unique order required by a unique moment of revelation (65). This concept of style can be extended from art to thought, and even to being-there as a whole (33–34). To have a style of being-there is not just to adopt a "lifestyle" but to engage in history, to achieve a fundamental orientation and stance, to inhabit a site in a way that appropriately opens one to appropriation. Thinking and writing can be part of this happening of history.

Heidegger's goal, then, is to engage in *seynsgeschichtliches Denken* (e.g., 3)— a kind of thought that responds to and participates in the historical happening of be-ing. Even though such thinking can ultimately be understood only by engaging in it, we can make some preliminary observations that should clarify what Heidegger is not doing—and so leave open the proper space for understanding what he *is* doing. I begin, then, with his criticisms of traditional notions of truth and thought. After reviewing the limitations of these notions and considering what I call the future-subjunctive tonality of the *Contributions,* I explore several ways in which Heidegger tries to articulate his style, including "bethinking," "inceptive thinking," and "telling silence."[3] Finally, I consider some ways in which he thinks of the unity of his text—not as a system, but as a "quarry" and a "juncture."

Be-holding, Representing, and the Identity of Knower and Known

Why does Heidegger reject traditional conceptions of thinking and truth? These include the notion of truth as correspondence, or correct representation; the traditional conception of thought as representing particulars in terms of universals; and the view of truth as an identity of knower and known.

Thinking as an exercise in correspondence attempts to formulate and support judgments that correctly represent some object. Heidegger's objections to this mode of thought emerge most clearly when we review his genealogy of truth as correspondence, which is also his story of the degeneration of the relation between thinking and being. The story is laid out clearly in *Introduction to Metaphysics* (1935) and elaborated in many later texts, including the *Contributions.* According to Heidegger, thinking and being were united for the pre-Socratics: these thinkers were not trying to represent being, but were participating in a reciprocal relation between the self-manifestation of present entities (the being of beings as presencing) and the articulation of this manifestation (thinking). With Plato and Aristotle, however, thinking as the establishment of correct judgments seizes power and attempts to *determine* being.

Heidegger's readings of Parmenides and Heraclitus suggest an original unity of thought and the being of beings. In Parmenides, Heidegger finds a way of thinking that is "the same" as being (see Parmenides, frag. 3; frag. 8, ll. 34–36).[4] Thinking as "apprehension" (*Vernehmen*) and the being of beings

---

3. Other labels for the *Contributions'* way of thought include "transitional thinking" (e.g., GA 65, 5), "essential thinking" (e.g., 8), and even "philosophy" (e.g., §§14–17, §§258–59). On transitional thinking see Brogan, "Da-sein and the Leap of Being," 173–74. On essential thinking see George Kovacs, "The Power of Essential Thinking in Heidegger's *Beiträge zur Philosophie (Vom Ereignis),*" in Babich, *From Phenomenology to Thought, Errancy, and Desire.*

4. Cf. "The Principle of Identity," in *Identity and Difference,* 27. This essay rejects the usual notion of sameness as identity or equivalence, and the traditional claim that the fundamental law of thinking is "A = A." Heidegger tries to show that this law is a statement about *beings*— after all, "A" denotes some indeterminate *being*—and thus the statement presupposes that we

belong together and need each other: "Apprehension happens for the sake of being. Being essentially happens as appearing, as stepping into unconcealment, only if unconcealment happens, only if a self-opening happens."[5] This self-opening takes place as apprehension. Similarly, in Heraclitus, Heidegger finds a *logos* of thinking that responds to the primal *logos* of the being of beings. This primal *logos* is the happening of *legein*—"the originally gathering gatheredness that constantly holds sway in itself."[6] The cosmos arranges itself into a coherent articulation; the human activity of *legein* articulates this cosmic self-articulation in thought and speech—allowing cosmic *logos* to become manifest.

The pre-Socratic unity of thinking and the being of beings depends on an experience of the being of beings as coming to presence, or presencing (*Anwesen*).[7] *Physis*, which Heidegger takes as the early Greek word for being, means presencing, the self-display of beings as emerging and abiding. The "sway" of this self-display requires primal gathering; thus primal *logos* is the same as *physis*, or presencing.[8] Being as presencing requires the intimate participation of thinking, because in order for beings to present themselves, they must be "apprehended"—perceived, in a broad sense. In the first inception, thinking is this gathering perceiving in which beings are unconcealed. Thinking, we might say, is a *be-holding* in which thought holds and is held by the potent presencing of beings.

Heidegger's accounts of pre-Socratic thought are sometimes mistaken for accounts of what *he* considers to be authentic thinking. But because the being of beings as presencing is not equivalent to be-ing as appropriation, beholding is not bethinking; we cannot identify the thinking of the first inception with the thinking that Heidegger is pursuing in the other inception.[9] Nevertheless, his account of early Greek thought provides valuable

---

understand the being of beings. In this sense, identity presupposes the belonging-together of being and human beings. This can be seen as Heidegger's final response to Husserl's insistence that "alikeness" and "belongingness" must ultimately be reducible to identity (*Logical Investigations*, 343, 347). For more on the distinction between identity and Heideggerian "sameness," see " . . . Poetically Man Dwells . . ." (1951), in *Poetry, Language, Thought*, ed. and intro. Albert Hofstadter (New York: Harper and Row, 1971), 218–19.

5. *Introduction to Metaphysics*, 148 (translation modified).

6. Ibid., 135.

7. Ibid., 64, 75, 108, 132.

8. Ibid., 16, 138.

9. Thus with appropriation, we are no longer thinking in a Greek way at all: "Seminar in Le Thor 1969," in *Four Seminars*, 61. Greek man does not "stand gathered in the property [*Eigentum*] of being—he remains outside and watches it arise—*physis*": Heidegger, "Das Sein (Ereignis)" (1937), *Heidegger Studies* 15 (1999), 13. See also the comment on beholding or apprehension (*Vernehmen*) as pure intuition in SZ 171 (cf. SZ 147). On this question cf. Emad, "The Place of the Presocratics in Heidegger's *Beiträge zur Philosophie*."

hints of his own way of thinking (just as presencing can hint at appropriation). In an echo of pre-Socratic be-holding, bethinking will involve a reciprocity between be-ing and thinking.

But for now, let us follow Heidegger's story of the degeneration and loss of the original unity between the being of beings and thinking. The fatal step is Platonism (§110). With Platonism, emergence into presence (*physis*) fades into the background, while thought focuses on the beings that are present and on their distinctive, characteristic aspects (the *eidos* or *idea* of a being— its "form"). For instance, one might ask, "What is piety?" while neglecting to ask how things, happenings, and people first emerge as holy or unholy, or indeed, as beings altogether. It is as if one became preoccupied with classifying and describing the patterns of foam on waves, while forgetting about the waves themselves and the surging of the sea beneath them. The degeneration from *physis* to *idea* entails a degeneration from an understanding of *logos* and truth as originary gathering to a notion of *logos* and truth as correct representation. "Because the *idea* is what really is, and the *idea* is the prototype, all opening up of beings must be directed toward [correctly] equaling the prototype."[10]

Heidegger goes on to explain how thinking comes to concentrate on forming correct assertions or propositions. That which can be correct or incorrect is taken to be an assertion, a judgment that attributes a predicate to a subject accurately or inaccurately. Now "decisions about truth, and so about beings, are made on the basis of logos [as assertion] and with reference back to it—and not only decisions about beings, but even, and in advance, about being."[11] What decisions are these? First, philosophers now assume that in order for something to *be*, it must be representable in an assertion. This implies that logic, which governs what can consistently be asserted, governs the being of beings itself. Since being is now conceived as beingness, to think of being now means merely to establish correct propositions about beingness by means of logic.[12]

---

10. *Introduction to Metaphysics*, 197. Cf. Heidegger's more extended discussion in "Plato's Doctrine of Truth" (1940), in *Pathmarks*, especially 176–77. For the *Contributions'* account of the Platonic origin of truth as correctness, see GA 65, 206–22, 331–35. Heidegger eventually abandoned the view that Plato was the turning point in the Greek conception of truth: "The End of Philosophy and the Task of Thinking" (1964), in *On Time and Being*, 70. For our present purposes, it does not matter whether his account of Plato is right; the point is to grasp the distinction between thinking that belongs to being as presencing and thinking that is merely representational. I argue in chapter 4 that despite the merits of Heidegger's story as an interpretation of Platonism, it is inadequate as an interpretation of Plato.

11. *Introduction to Metaphysics*, 199.

12. Aristotle, for example, establishes the basic characteristics of beings by way of the structures of what can be "said." The categories (such as substance, quality, and quantity) are "things

In subsequent metaphysics, the saying of the sway of being is supplanted by a kind of thought that supervises being and dictates to it. Being is reduced to a few pallid, vacuous generalities that pretend to answer the question: What are beings as such? (6). These generalities (such as the categories) are then viewed as a priori structures, when in fact they are derivative—they are abstracted from beings that are taken for granted as present and that are represented propositionally (183–84, 293, 458).

This story is briefly reviewed in the first part of §265 of the *Contributions*, Heidegger's main discussion of bethinking. As Heidegger puts it here, philosophical thinking (inquiry into being) adopts, as its guideline, the propositional representation of beings (thinking in a narrow sense). Thinking even becomes interpreted *exclusively* in terms of propositional representation (457). The consequences for philosophy are disastrous: our thought becomes incapable of a fresh experience of the disclosure of beings. The consequences for our world are also disastrous: modern research and "machination" operate according to this restricted mode of thinking, and under their sway, all beings tend to be reduced to mere objects to be inspected, measured, and exploited (e.g., §58).

Heidegger's account of the decline from be-holding to representation adds weight to his resistance to universals, which we explored in chapter 1. In place of universals, he pursues "belonging" or "one's own"—a group of phenomena involved in our creative reception of inherited messages and practices. Things present themselves to theoretical inspection thanks to our pre-theoretical involvement in a culture, our situated selfhood. But we tend to forget about this historical belonging that allows us to be open to beings, and sim-

---

said without combination," such as "horse," "white," and so on. Things said in combination—such as "the horse is white"—constitute an affirmation, and it is only in affirmations that truth or falsehood is possible: *Categories*, chapter 4. Aristotle thus takes affirmations and their elements as indicators of the nature of beings as such, and assumes that truth primarily consists in the correctness of affirmations. A truth is "a statement of that which is that it is, or of that which is not that it is not": *Met.* Γ 7, 1011b26; *Aristotle's Metaphysics*, trans. Hippocrates G. Apostle (Grinnell, Iowa: Peripatetic Press, 1979), 70. Aristotle does, however, recognize a secondary sense of truth that retains a connection to unconcealment: in the case of noncombined things, such as "horse," "truth about each of these is to apprehend [*thigein*] it or to assert it (for affirmation [*kataphasis*] and assertion [*phasis*] are not the same), and ignorance of it is not to apprehend it": *Met.* Θ 10, 1051b24–25 (*Aristotle's Metaphysics*, 159). *Phasis* means the conceptual grasping of a being, rather than an affirmative or negative proposition (*kataphasis*). Aristotle adds, "the truth about each such [noncomposite] being is the conception [*noein*] of it, and there is neither falsity nor mistake about it but only ignorance": *Met.* Θ 10, 1052a2 (*Aristotle's Metaphysics*, 159). We could say that this sort of truth is a kind of unconcealment. However, Aristotle assumes that if noncomposite beings are unconcealed at all, they are fully and directly unconcealed according to their *eidos*. Heidegger would presumably object that the *eidos* emerges only within the context of the unconcealment of a world, and that the emergence of this world also always involves a dimension of concealment.

ply concentrate on beings as they show themselves to us. The characteristics that mark a being as belonging to a type can then be identified as its *idea* or "essence." The discovery of the *idea* is a genuine discovery, and the search for the universal or *koinon* is still creative in Plato and Aristotle. But in post-Aristotelian thought, the universal is simply taken for granted as the proper milieu for the representation of beings (63–64). This attitude conceals the historicity of presentation and representation. Truth (unconcealment) is essentially historical: our past and future cooperate to make beings accessible to us in a world and thus to enable us to speak and think. Truth seems to congeal into something "eternal" only because instead of truth we pursue the true—that is, correct theoretical propositions (342). Theory (generalization, explanation, and proof), which the tradition takes as the essence of thinking in general, is correct and rigorous only within a limited domain. It is appropriate only as one means of representing given beings; it cannot think of be-ing, which happens through historical belonging. Thinking of be-ing must not only think *about* history, but think *historically* (5). Thought must think its own historicity as it thinks the historicity of be-ing.

For Heidegger, reason fails to think historically because it deals only in universals (65, 91, 121–22, 155, 251, 343). Rational argument maintains fixed senses for the general concepts it uses, as if they reflected eternal Ideas; without such fixation, there could be no logical rules of consistency. (If "all men are mortal" and "Socrates is a man" are to be used as premises in a syllogism, then "man" must have a fixed sense.) Heidegger's point is not that rational arguments are incorrect, but that they are superficial: they depend on a happening of unconcealment whose historicity they cannot address. Rational proofs are compelling only if one is satisfied with an understanding of truth as correctness (65). In order to fathom the historicity of truth we have to become properly historical ourselves; so while deductive proof presupposes a rigid way of representing on the part of the one following the proof, Heidegger's way of thought calls on us to be transformed with every step (13–14).

This critique of universals and reason has a political dimension. Heidegger paints reason as the "destructive force of what is valid for all, which arbitrarily justifies everyman and provides the satisfaction of supposing that no one has any essential advantage over anyone else" (343). The elitism and esotericism typical of the *Contributions* are obvious here, as well as in the remark that we must get out of the habit of wanting to make be-ing representable for anyone, anytime one likes (251). Naturally, to call this position elitist is not to refute it; Heidegger's claims about reason do, however, raise some troubling questions that we will address in chapter 4.

Aside from its political implications, Heidegger's position has radical consequences for philosophy. "To represent universally what holds universally is, according to prevalent views, the basic feature of thought."[13] Philosophy is supposed to deal with the most general of generalities—what is common to all beings (63, 458–59). But if Heidegger is right, generalizing begins with what is already present and simply looks for its most universal aspects, the present aspects of a present thing that it shares with other present things. What is missed here is *presencing* itself. Attending to the presencing of beings is a way of thinking that is quite different from abstraction and much more unusual. How is it that we are presented with present beings as such? How is their presence given to us in a unique event? What would it mean to think uniquely about the unique? These questions point us to the happening of be-ing.

But we are not ready to explore Heidegger's own way of thinking until we briefly consider some reactions to traditional theorizing that are found in the tradition itself. Both empiricism and common sense urge us to focus on particulars instead of universals. Another alternative, urged by the German idealists, attempts to unify the particular and the universal by grasping the unity of subject and object. Can these non-Heideggerian approaches overcome the limitations of traditional representational thought?

Common sense criticizes philosophy for its abstractness. Philosophy supposedly deals with bleached-out generalities that have been emptied of concrete content—and the concrete is what is relevant to our lives as we live them. But we can retort that everyday thought and language are pervaded by generalities. Every word in the sentence "I'll have this cheese sandwich" is an abstraction. (The "I" purports to be something single that pervades all experiences at all times. The "this" is so general that it can be applied to anything, as Hegel argues in the "Sense-Certainty" chapter of the *Phenomenology of Spirit*.) Common sense, then, already deals in universals—at least, as soon as it tries to articulate itself, to put itself into words and concepts. Traditional philosophy merely radicalizes this everyday tendency, so it is impossible to articulate a coherent criticism of traditional philosophy from the everyday point of view.

A simple philosophical empiricism will not get us much farther. It is easy to say that we should begin with the particular and rise to the universal, but the particular always becomes accessible in terms of universals. "How are we supposed to be able even to *look for* such things as trees, unless the representation of what a tree is in general is already lighting our way in advance?"[14]

---

13. "Language" (1950), in *Poetry, Language, Thought*, 189. In other words, "Philosophy is the knitting together of abstract nouns": Rita Mae Brown, *Starting from Scratch: A Different Kind of Writers' Manual* (New York: Bantam, 1989), 107. In contrast, Heidegger needs to develop "a way of speaking and thinking which does not submit itself in advance to the logic and presumptions of the language of the idea": Schmidt, "Strategies for a Possible Reading," 36.

14. *Introduction to Metaphysics*, 84.

The very concept "particular" is itself a general representation. Empiricism must begin, then, by presupposing some universals, even if, in the course of empirical research, our concepts of those universals are transformed. So simple empiricism cannot give a satisfactory account of the origin of universals—much less of the origin of the being of beings, the source of the sense of what is.[15]

The problem with simple empiricism is that it simply reverses a traditional priority, ranking the particular over the universal; it does not investigate the roots of the distinction. Empirical science is no less "metaphysical," in this sense, than neo-Platonism; both presuppose the distinctions between the one and the many, the universal and the particular, being and becoming. We cannot escape the tradition simply by raising the subordinate members of these oppositions over the dominant ones (63, 459–60). Nietzsche, for example, in Heidegger's reading, fails to transcend metaphysics and is "the last metaphysician," despite the fact that he celebrates becoming, appearance, and plurality.[16] Thinking of the history of be-ing cannot simply mean thinking in terms of the changing manifold. For similar reasons, be-ing-historical thinking differs from historicism, if historicism means the position that correctness is only temporary. This is merely a "quantitative" restriction of universal validity, argues Heidegger, not a radical challenge to the traditional duality of universal and particular (343).[17]

The same cannot be said of Hegel, who may seem to have anticipated much of Heidegger's thought. Heidegger claims that the tradition focuses on universals and correct representation at the expense of the historical emergence of the givenness of beings. But for Hegel, reason does *not* deal in fixed universals—these are the tools of mere understanding—but participates in the dialectical movement of the concept. Both the universal and the particular are "abstract" (one-sided), and can come to their truth only by working themselves out in time, in history. History tends toward the reconciliation of universal and particular, as well as subject and object.

Hegel's project is the culmination of a strain in Western thought that has interpreted truth not as correct representation but as an *identity* of knower and known. Does this aspect of the tradition escape Heidegger's critique? If

15. I qualify this empiricism as "simple" because there are far more sophisticated forms of empiricism to which Heidegger pays no attention—for example, the semiotic and pragmatic empiricism of Peirce.

16. Heidegger, *Nietzsche*, vol. 3, 8. One could make the same argument about some variants of postmodernism.

17. Heidegger hardly does justice here to the subtlety of historicist thinking. For fuller explorations of the problem, see Charles Bambach, *Heidegger, Dilthey, and the Crisis of Historicism* (Ithaca: Cornell University Press, 1995); Jeffrey Andrew Barash, *Martin Heidegger and the Problem of Historical Meaning*, 2nd ed. (New York: Fordham University Press, 2003).

the domination of representational judgment has led to a fateful split between thinking and the being of beings, we might try to heal the split by seeking an original *sameness*. As the German idealists would put it, perhaps we could resolve the primal division (*Ur-teil*) by transcending representational judgments (*Urteile*) and finding a higher unity of subject and object. However, if Heidegger's critique of the tradition is as radical as he intends it to be, then it must also apply to this notion. His remarks on truth as identity are less extensive than his account of correspondence; however, he does give us the ingredients for a thorough criticism.

Let us briefly review the main appeals to an identity of the thinker and what is thought in Western philosophy. (We may leave aside the Parmenidean "sameness" of thinking and being, because in Heidegger's interpretation, as we have seen, this is not really an identity but a mutual dependence.) Aristotle's god is a pure act of self-beholding (*noesis noeseos*). The god is the most perfect of all substances because it is always a full performance of the most perfect activity (contemplation—an activity that requires no matter), and is contemplating that which is most perfect: itself.[18] The Cartesian *cogito* is a first-person version of this self-contemplation; it serves as the foundation of Descartes' metaphysics, just as Aristotle's god serves as the culmination of his. Kant strips the *cogito* of cognitive content and conceives of it as the transcendental unity of apperception—the ability of the subject to accompany all its cognitions with "I think" (*Critique of Pure Reason*, B131–32). But this apparently empty ability turns out to be a necessary condition for all thinking and underlies the legitimate employment of the categories (B143). Fichte conceives of self-consciousness as a *Tathandlung*, or primal, self-generating act. Hegel conceives of it as a far more inclusive and articulated process of externalization and re-internalization, or re-collection (*Erinnerung: Phenomenology of Spirit*, concluding sentence).

The Heideggerian critique of all these moments in metaphysics has to begin by pointing out that they are moments of more or less sophisticated self-presence—moments in which the act of beholding is presented to itself. Even and especially the Hegelian system, with its elaborate deferrals, alienations, and mediations, aims at *"the self-present present"* (200). But if such self-presence is taken as an absolute—the foundation or culmination of a system—then it violates the temporality of both being-there and be-ing. Being-there is more than present because it is radically temporal. Beings are present to being-there only by virtue of time, which exposes being-there to be-ing

---

18. *Metaphysics* Λ 9. The identity between thinker and what is thought is also found in the doctrine of *De Anima* (3.4, 3.7) that the intellect becomes the same in form as the things that it understands.

(the granting of the meaning of beings as such). Be-ing itself can never be present at all—that would reduce it to an entity. This entire complex resists characterization in terms of presence or self-presence. It is not that there is no self-awareness, but it depends on appropriation and cannot serve as its foundation.

Heidegger attributes the importance of self-awareness in modern philosophy to the interpretation of philosophical thought in terms of representational thought (457). If we take philosophy as a kind of representational consciousness, then we naturally assign special importance to the consciousness of consciousness, the moment in which we represent representation itself (202). The extreme case of this trend is Hegel's identification of "actuality (being) as the absolute with thinking as the unconditioned" (457). It is tempting to see Hegel and Heidegger as closer than they really are: both try to combat the separation of subject and object, include the particular as well as the universal in truth, and think historically. Yet there is no radical finitude in Hegel: all finitude is a means to the infinite. Heidegger, with Kierkegaard, insists on the irreducibility of the finite: contingency, decision, and sacrifice. If these are nothing but moments in an all-encompassing process of actualization, as Hegel has it, then there can be no genuine emergencies and no genuine ownness, no "uniqueness and estrangement of be-ing" (315).

Other than the Present Indicative

> The essence [of be-ing] cannot be exhibited like something present at hand; its essential happening must be awaited like a shock.
> —GA 65, 242

The representation of the known by the knower, the identity of knower and known, and even the pre-Socratic unity of being and be-holding have failed to enter the event of be-ing. If this tradition is fatally focused on presence, where is philosophy to go in the future? Could it be that it must become *futural thinking*, opening possibilities instead of describing givens? If so, could we still call this thought phenomenology? Or is phenomenology a philosophy of presence—and thus a philosophy of the past?

Philosophy has almost always been written in the present tense and indicative mood—but might there be a future-subjunctive philosophy? This is not simply a grammatical question.[19] Even when we philosophers use other

---

19. Nietzsche, of course, presents himself as a "philosopher of the future," and Derrida and his imitators have often experimented with moods and tenses. But Heidegger sees Nietzsche as the last metaphysician—thus as remaining within the present-indicative tonality. And one can

linguistic forms, or turn our attention to possibility, we tend to examine what possibility "is," as if it were always present now. Our goal is still to describe the being of beings, and this being is still tacitly understood as centered on presence—whether we are describing "the actuality of the actual" or "the possibility of the possible" (75). Our limitation may lie in the very project of *describing:* this way of thought may inevitably cast its topic as a present object. Even time, history, potential, and absence can be framed as quasi-present when we take them as objects of description; they are approached in a present-indicative tonality.

Grammatically speaking, most of the *Contributions* adhere to the present-indicative tonality of normal philosophical discourse. Heidegger writes, "be-ing essentially happens as appropriation"—which appears to be a statement of current fact. But he goes on to warn us that this is really "not a proposition" at all (260). As I argued in chapter 1, despite most of his surface grammar, Heidegger tends to think of appropriation as a unique future event. His goal is not to describe what is, but to prepare for the granting of a sense of what is, has been, and may be. He attempts to exceed presence and actuality for the sake of a broader and deeper encounter with time and possibility. We can then read the *Contributions* in something other than a present-indicative mood and tense, as evoking and anticipating an urgent happening; the primary tonality of the text is future-subjunctive. This tonality is sometimes reflected in its grammar: for example, the conception of be-ing as emergency is phrased as a "what if?" question (46; for more such questions see 113–14, 170, 246, 405). These phrases are not just "rhetorical questions,"[20] but acts of leaping into a possibility.

Can we call the *Contributions* phenomenological? If phenomenology is "ocularcentrist"[21]—focused on what can be "seen," in a broad sense, because it can present itself—then it remains within the present-indicative tonality, and the *Contributions* are not phenomenology. In fact, Heidegger never uses the term *phenomenology* to label his thought in this text. But this does not settle the question, since he is almost always reluctant to reject phenomenology outright.[22] His negative remark on "pre-hermeneutic 'phenomenology'"

---

argue that even Derrida remains focused on universal patterns without entering into a unique and urgent moment (see below, p. 123).

20. Schürmann, *Broken Hegemonies*, 606.

21. Ansell-Pearson, "The An-Economy of Time's Giving," 274.

22. An exception may be this note from 1937: "*Appearing*—only as starting point in the leap into being-there. (*Not* phenomenology, it is too directly [focused] on 'hyletic' data for a consciousness.) . . . *Self-showing*—presencing from *which concealment?*" (GA 87, 101). The suggestion is that phenomenology is too centered on what is given and shown, and too indebted to the tradition. However, one could argue that this criticism applies only to Husserlian phenomenology, not to phenomenology as a "possibility" (SZ 38).

(188) leaves us wondering whether he would adopt the label "phenomenology" for his own thought.[23]

Many interpreters of the *Contributions* call the text phenomenological. Few give grounds for this view, but Friedrich-Wilhelm von Herrmann does provide an argument that the *Contributions* are "hermeneutic phenomenology." The hermeneutic dimension of the text is hard to dispute. Although the *Contributions* do not present a developing, deepening interpretation in the manner of *Being and Time*, they say that being-there "is to be won only hermeneutically, i.e., according to *Being and Time*, in the thrown projection" (321). Being-there is involved in a hermeneutic circle: its interpretive projections depend on meanings into which it is "thrown," and in turn create new such meanings.[24] Von Herrmann argues that as thrown throwers, we can project the truth of be-ing only when the "appropriating throw" of be-ing grants it to us as projectable; the truth of be-ing is *given* to us, and thus it is a phenomenon.[25] The weakness in this argument is that the granting and giving in appropriation is nothing like the presentation of a phenomenon to an observer; it is an inceptive seizure that precedes all observation. Furthermore, it is not clear that this event has already happened, so there is a speculative dimension in the *Contributions* that von Herrmann disregards. Von Herrmann also claims that "it becomes necessary for Heidegger to think the historicality of being itself when he undergoes the phenomenological experience that *the WAY [in which] beings emerge gets historically transformed*."[26] If this means that the being of beings changes over history, it is correct. But the deeper historicity is the historicity of *be-ing*—the event in which the being of beings is given. This event is "historical," in Heidegger's sense, not because it changes but because it would seize us in a unique, urgent moment— and here we have to speak future-subjunctively. It is not clear that a possible moment of emergency can be given in a "phenomenological experience." Finally, von Herrmann cites Heidegger's claim in 1963 that the label "phenomenology" "can disappear as title, in favour of the *Sache* of thinking, whose disclosure remains a mystery."[27] Like Husserl, Heidegger is devoted to the

---

23. Compare Heidegger's recommendation that his thought-path be described as one "through" (not "from") phenomenology to thought. "Phenomenology" here has the very broad sense of "allowing the most proper concern of thought to show itself": Heidegger, "Preface," in Richardson, *Heidegger*, xvi.

24. Friedrich-Wilhelm von Herrmann, "Way and Method: Hermeneutic Phenomenology in Thinking the History of Being," trans. Parvis Emad, in *Martin Heidegger: Critical Assessments*, ed. Christopher Macann, vol. 1 (London: Routledge, 1992), 328, 319–20, 327–28.

25. Von Herrmann, *Wege ins Ereignis*, 62.

26. Von Herrmann, "Way and Method," 321.

27. Ibid., 311. See Heidegger, "My Way to Phenomenology," in *On Time and Being*, 82.

end to the "things themselves," the matter that calls for thinking.[28] But is this matter a *phenomenon*, something that *shows* itself to the phenomenologist? If "the matter of thinking" is the being of beings, then it is manifest (or can be brought to manifestation), and it is a phenomenon to be investigated by phenomenology. But when Heidegger says that this manifestness is itself a mystery, he points to the question of *be-ing*—the giving of the being of beings. If this event of giving "remains"—and perhaps must remain—a mystery, then it does not seem to be a phenomenon at all.[29]

Reiner Schürmann also repeatedly claims that the *Contributions* are phenomenological.[30] Heidegger's "method and . . . thinking remain those of the phenomenologist who 'sees and grasps only that which *is*.'" But this is a mistranslation that quotes out of context: Heidegger writes of a "reaching out" (*Ausgriff*) that seizes one who "sees and grasps that which *is* only in order to help [being-there?—object not stated] out of these beings . . . into be-ing" (242–43). Heidegger's thinking, then, reaches beyond given beings. It strives for appropriation as "*the* event" that is, as Schürmann puts it, the "always eclipsed manifestation" of phenomena. But if this event is *always* eclipsed, it cannot itself become a phenomenon. Schürmann himself also claims that "*there is a No that weakens all manifestation.*" Given phenomena are subject to "a removal outside their simple being-given"; their givenness is structured by factors such as nothingness and the future, which are not themselves given.[31] It would seem that phenomenality—and hence phenomenology—point to a different theme and a different kind of thinking, outside the present-indicative tonality.

However, maybe phenomenology can do more than describe what shows itself. Can phenomenology think of the intrinsically concealed—that which can never, in principle, become present? If this task lies beyond phenomenology, we will have to say that phenomenology remains within the present-indicative tonality and that the *Contributions* are not phenomenological—for Heidegger insists that be-ing is necessarily self-concealing. This is the root of the *Contributions*' esotericism and their "telling silence" (which we will consider soon).

Can hiding be shown? Can concealment be revealed? Can withholding be given? In some sense, yes: phenomenology is keenly aware that consciousness is largely a web of experiences of absence—allusions, intimations, expectations, recollections, and so on. Husserl addresses these experiences in

28. Von Herrmann, "Way and Method," 320.
29. Compare the claim in *Besinnung* that the essence of truth can never be investigated on the basis of self-showing: GA 66, 314.
30. Schürmann, *Broken Hegemonies*, 516, 538, 544, 556.
31. Ibid., 675n27, 566, 618, 600, 608.

terms of "empty" or "unsaturated" intentions. In his prototypical example, my consciousness of an object in space includes a consciousness of its far side; even though this side is not given to me in intuition, I expect that I *could* fulfill the intention.[32] The plausibility of Husserl's analysis, however, depends on my *ability* to gain intuitive fulfillment. Perfect fulfillment may remain an unreachable ideal, but at least it is an ideal that makes sense and toward which we can make meaningful progress. If the very idea of such fulfillment were senseless, then Husserl's principles would seem to dictate that I should put my expectations out of commission, since they could have no phenomenal support. There seems to be no room in Husserl's phenomenology, then, for a notion of something that can *never* show itself.

Heidegger's early thought may not accommodate this notion either. According to *Being and Time*, the being of beings is initially concealed, but it "demands that it become a phenomenon" (SZ 35). Phenomenological ontology, then, is a matter of "thematizing" or focusing on our background sense of the being of beings. This thematizing requires an indefinitely long process of reinterpretation ("hermeneutic" phenomenology), but *Being and Time* never claims that some dimension of being must remain permanently obscure. Heidegger comments that being "is found only in encounter,"[33] and says there can never be something further that is hidden behind being (SZ 35–36). Being is essentially phenomenal. This seems to follow, in fact, from the difference between being and beings. Whereas beings can be independent of us, being cannot (SZ 183, 212); so only beings, not being, can be hopelessly hidden.

But *Being and Time* is not without hints of a deeper obscurity: I can understand being only by brushing against the "nothing" of my death, which is essentially a possibility and can never become an actual, given phenomenon for me (SZ 266, 308).[34] In the years following *Being and Time*, Heidegger comes to think of the interplay of being and the nothing as crucial to the event of be-ing; to say that be-ing involves the nothing is to stress be-ing's self-concealment, as we will see in chapter 3. But these are also the years when Heidegger stops calling himself a phenomenologist. Once again, we have to ask whether phenomenology can reveal concealment.

In some late remarks, Heidegger speaks of a "phenomenology of the inapparent."[35] This enigmatic thought is clearly relevant to the *Contributions*,

---

32. E.g., Edmund Husserl, *Cartesian Meditations: An Introduction to Phenomenology*, trans. Dorion Cairns (Dordrecht: Martinus Nijhoff, 1960), 61–62.

33. *History of the Concept of Time*, 217.

34. On nothingness in *Being and Time* cf. Vallega-Neu, *Heidegger's "Contributions,"* 14, 17–18.

35. "Seminar in Zähringen 1973," in *Four Seminars*, 80; cf. 79, 89. Also cf. Heidegger's saying that thought must be brought "into the clearing of the appearing of the unapparent": letter to Roger Munier, February 22, 1974, in *Heidegger: Cahiers de l'Herne* (Paris: L'Herne, 1983), 115, cited by Marion, *In Excess*, 110.

which already suggest that appropriation is "most inapparent" (472).[36] Heidegger's remarks have generated extensive but inconclusive discussion. If "inapparent" (*unscheinbar*) merely means inconspicuous or initially hidden, then there is no paradox—all phenomenology is a phenomenology of the inapparent.[37] But if the inapparent is what *cannot* appear, then a phenomenology of the inapparent sounds like an oxymoron; Heidegger may be implying that we need a way of thinking that is not phenomenological at all.[38]

We are still faced with the contentious question of whether phenomenology can escape the present-indicative tonality. The answer depends in part on how broadly one defines "phenomenology." But this semantic issue is linked to substantive ones: what constitutes genuine thought, and is traditional phenomenology adequate for it?

Consider two recent formulations of phenomenology. First, Jean-Luc Marion draws on Descartes and Husserl in emphasizing the phenomenological reduction, which yields an "indubitable . . . given without remainder, without shadow, without aura." His "givenness" includes more than "the persistent presence of substantiality," and is even meant to include more than what shows itself phenomenally. Dimensions of "nothingness" or "absence," such as my own birth and death, which are not present phenomena, are still supposed to be "given" in Marion's sense. But Marion falters in his phenomenology of one's own death: "it is very likely a question of a pure event, but too pure to show *itself* and therefore also to give *itself* as a perfect event."[39] Here it seems impossible to avoid a doubt, a remainder, a shadow. My relation to my own death is *not* a relation to a given, but a relation to what may happen and yet can never be given to me; this is the future-

36. Cf. "The Way to Language," in *On the Way to Language*, 128. Beistegui characterizes the *Contributions* as a "phenomenology of the inapparent": *Truth and Genesis*, 115–16, 127. Françoise Dastur interprets the phrase in a way that fits well with my own interpretation of *Ereignis*: what is inapparent is "the nonappearance that resides *in* all appearing, the *event* itself of apparition and the *giving* of being": "La pensée à venir: une phénoménologie de l'inapparent?" in *L'avenir de la philosophie est-il grec?* ed. Catherine Collobert (Saint-Laurent, Quebec: Fides, 2002), 146.

37. Gérard Guest, "Aux confins de l'inapparent: l'extrême phénoménologie de Heidegger," *Existentia* 12 (2002): 123.

38. Jean-Luc Marion thus speaks of "this paradox—a phenomenology of the unapparent *as such*, and not simply of the not-yet-appearing": *Reduction and Givenness: Investigations of Husserl, Heidegger, and Phenomenology*, trans. Thomas A. Carlson (Evanston: Northwestern University Press, 1998), 60. According to Marion, in *Being and Time* being is already thought as intrinsically unapparent, because it cannot become present like an entity; the paradox of a phenomenology of the unapparent is "fully required" by the ontological difference (ibid.). This interpretation obscures the fact that in *Being and Time* Heidegger claims that the being of beings is simply not-yet-appearing (being can be thematized as a phenomenon, even though it can never appear as ontically present) (SZ 35); in contrast, the *Contributions* focus on be-ing (the giving of the being of beings) and claim that it is, at least in some ways, intrinsically unapparent.

39. Marion, *In Excess*, 18, 24, 30, 23, 39–44, 40. Schürmann more consistently says that nothingness and the future are not given, but they structure the given: *Broken Hegemonies*, 608.

subjunctive relation par excellence. When it comes to thinking of what cannot be present, Marion's thought loses the indubitability that he views as essential to phenomenology.

Adopting a broader, less Cartesian concept of phenomenology, Françoise Dastur argues that phenomenology is essentially concerned with the inapparent, in two ways. First, it seeks the origin of appearing—an origin that can never itself directly appear, but must be "reconstitute[d] 'after the event.'" Second, intentionality necessarily involves an expectation of more than is directly given, so phenomenology necessarily remains open to surprise. Dastur adds that by breaking the bounds of expectation, a traumatic event may reconfigure our possibilities in a way that can be understood only retrospectively: "We never experience the great events of our life as contemporaneous."[40] Dastur thus elegantly shows that both past and future harbor "phenomena" to which the phenomenologist has only indirect access, which must be reconstituted in their absence. By joining the two sides of Dastur's argument—the origin of appearing and traumatic surprise—we gain a concept of emergence as emergency: *Ereignis* itself. The event of appropriation cannot become present, for the two reasons Dastur explains: it is the source of givenness rather than something given, and it transforms meaning so radically that it cannot be comprehended as it is happening.

Is the thinking of appropriation "phenomenology," then? In Dastur's generous sense, yes—but this sense stretches phenomenology beyond the description of the given. Such an extension is probably implied by the phenomenological project itself, as Dastur argues.[41] We can see this development, then, as the fulfillment of phenomenology. However, one could also see it as the self-dissolution of phenomenology, its supersession by a more primordial way of thinking that "demands a transformation of questioning from the ground up" (193).

This new thinking is marked by its attention to the hidden and possible *as such*, by its distrust of all efforts to represent the inceptive event, and by its ambition to *participate* in the event, not simply to observe it. To assert that be-ing exceeds presence is not yet to exceed presence in one's thinking—because as long as thinking remains *asserting*, it is oriented to the present. This means that it is not enough to train our theoretical attention on happening or on the future; our entire way of existing must break loose from the present-indicative tonality. The creative reciprocity between be-ing and being-there is so intimate that it cannot be represented by theorizing, which tries to stand back, contemplate, and describe.[42]

40. Dastur, "Phenomenology of the Event," 181, 184–85, 186.
41. Ibid., 181.
42. A case in point is Marion's description of the relation between the given and its recipient. The recipient "is an obstacle to [the given], stops it in blocking it and fixes it in centering it. . . .

If our displacement beyond the indicative mood is to be more than grammatical, we also need a displacement in emotional moods, an "affective
shift"—for mood is not just the subjective veneer of experience, but a way of
being thrown into the world, revealing a constellation of possibilities.[43] All
seeing, all present-indicative contemplation, presupposes a mood (SZ §29).
The first inception begins with the mood of wonder, *thaumazein*.[44] This mar-
veling at the fact that beings *are* at all, that they are present and not absent,
generates metaphysics and the special sciences—theoretical investigations
of the present features of beings. These are legitimate pursuits within their
limits, but they do not address the question of *be-ing*, because they take presence for granted as the being of beings without inquiring into its origin. In
order to move beyond the present-indicative tonality we need new ways to
be *moved*, moods that are attuned to something other than the present.
There are many such moods: longing, dread, nostalgia, excitement. Futural
thought, thought of the possible as such, can be guided by a "principle of
hope," for example. But then the thinker has to think *hopefully*, not simply
theorize *about* hope.[45] From the theoretical point of view, everything becomes present or quasi-present; a theoretical description of hope would still
be attuned by *thaumazein*, and would treat hope and its "objects" as quasi-
present phenomena.

In contrast, Heidegger is experimenting with a nontheoretical thought
that is attuned by new moods; these moods are to be brought about, not simply described (15, 395). The moods of the *Contributions* are all attuned by the
tense situation of the transition from the first to the other inception. "Restraint" (*Verhaltenheit*) involves a kind of caution that holds back from imposing a representation on the nonrepresentable. As we will see, restraint
leads to "telling silence" as a mode of saying. Restraint is not diffidence, how-

---

[the recipient's] screen or its prism remains perfectly unseen as long as the impact, crushed
against them, of a given does not illuminate them all at once. . . . the impact gives rise for the
first time to the screen against which it is crushed, as it sets up the prism across which it breaks
up": *In Excess*, 50. These metaphors vividly express the relation between noesis and noema, but
they remain optical metaphors indebted to early modern philosophy. Marion's phenomenologist is still an observer, even if the observation is dynamic. But for Heidegger what is at stake is
not *seeing* at all, but leaping into the possible happening of one's own.

43. Charles E. Scott, "*Zuspiel* and *Entscheidung*: A Reading of Sections 81–82 in *Die Beiträge
zur Philosophie*," *Philosophy Today* 41 (1997), Supplement: 164. On mood, cf. *The Fundamental
Concepts of Metaphysics*, 59–68; GA 39, 81–83; Hans-Helmuth Gander, "Grund- und Leitstimmungen in Heideggers *Beiträge zur Philosophie*," *Heidegger Studies* 10 (1994): 15–31; Klaus Held,
"Fundamental Moods and Heidegger's Critique of Contemporary Culture," in Sallis, *Reading
Heidegger*; Maggini, "Le 'style de l'homme à venir'"; Trawny, *Martin Heideggers Phänomenologie
der Welt*.

44. *Basic Questions of Philosophy*, 135–51.

45. "Thinking means venturing beyond": Ernst Bloch, *The Principle of Hope*, trans. Neville
Plaice, Stephen Plaice, and Paul Night, vol. 1 (Cambridge: MIT Press, 1986), 4–5. The problem of possibility, of futural thinking, is central to the work of Bloch.

ever, but a self-collected rootedness that makes room for "great stillness" (34). "Restraint—as style—[is] the self-certainty of the founding that sets standards and of the endurance of the severity of being-there" (33). "Alarm" or "terror" (*Erschrecken*) is a shock at the withdrawal of be-ing. In contrast to the first inception, which wondered at beings, the other inception must be alarmed at be-ing's self-withholding. Alarm alerts us to the fact that beings *are*, yet be-ing lies in oblivion (15).[46] Restraint and alarm come together to constitute "intimation" (*Ahnung*, 14; *Er-ahnen*, 20). This is a premonition, an inkling of be-ing. "Awe" (*Scheu*) fits well with the other moods: it is a respect for the mystery of be-ing, an unwillingness to violate it. This awe lets be-ing hold sway in its own way, and listens for the "hint" of the final god (16).[47] This rather somber palette of moods is occasionally interrupted by "enthusiasm" (*Begeisterung*, 22) or "delight" (*Lust*) in the play between inceptions (169) or in creating (249). On the whole, however, the tone of the *Contributions* is one of agitated longing. Heidegger's characterization of the fundamental moods does not quite capture the violently prophetic flavor of much of the text.

All the fundamental moods that Heidegger emphasizes are appropriate relations to be-ing as a giving that does not give itself (22–23). They are the right moods for his project, because they are future-subjunctive moods; they respond to the mystery of be-ing as a possible event.

But is there really such a thing as "a mode of thinking which is intrinsically futural"?[48] Heidegger often speaks of futural or future thinking (*das künftige Denken*, e.g., 3). The first part of the text is called "Preview" and another part is devoted to "The Future Ones." Several passages are written in the future tense (70, 155, 227, 399–400). Heidegger is preparing for a future transformation of human beings (xvii, 3, 9, 248, 294, 300). But he also warns us that intimation is not simply about a future occurrence in the vulgar sense, but about "temporality as a whole: the time-play-space of the there" (22). And it would seem that futural thinking cannot just be speculation about what will happen—this would be groundless, *wishful* thinking. Futural thinking must open the future by drawing on the past.

Is appropriation, then, primarily a heritage (*Herkunft*) rather than a future (*Zukunft*), such that our projection of it only takes up what has *already* ap-

---

46. As Gander points out, alarm in the *Contributions* is a development of anxiety in *Being and Time*: "Grund- und Leitstimmungen," 21. A related theme, "pain," plays a prominent part in "Das Ereignis," where Heidegger writes that the experience of the inception is the pain of the parting.

47. This mood is a precursor to *Gelassenheit*, the "releasement" or "letting-be" that gains prominence in Heidegger's thought a few years after the *Contributions*.

48. Ansell-Pearson, "The An-Economy of Time's Giving," 269.

propriated us?[49] This would be a hasty conclusion. As we have seen, Heidegger claims that we have never yet been historical (492). So even if genuine history is an interplay between future and past, it may be that this interplay has not yet taken place. The whole relation between appropriation and projection, "time-play-space" itself, may be a *possibility* into which Heidegger is leaping.

We have not yet settled this question, but at least we should not be too quick to look for the prior, the "always already." This expression, ubiquitous in *Being and Time*, is conspicuous by its near-absence in the *Contributions*. The only three positive uses of it occur in passages on truth which can be read as the exceptions that prove the rule. The usual concepts of truth "always already [*schon immer*] presuppose" the truth of be-ing; however, be-ing cannot be reached by articulating presuppositions and assumptions, but only by a leap (93). With the essential happening of be-ing, the truth of beings is "always already [*je schon*] decided"; so "the decision concerning truth takes place in the leap into the essential happening of be-ing" (235). "Truth essentially happens only and always already [*immer schon*] as being-there and thus as the striving of strife" (390). These passages insist on struggle, decision, and leaping—none of which would be necessary if be-ing were a constant condition. The "always already" in these sentences does indicate a requirement, a necessity—but the necessity comes not from permanence, but from emergency, which is "the genuine futural itself" (113). Heidegger is claiming that truth will be decided *if* be-ing and being-there take place. If this event were "always already decided" in the strict sense, then there would be no event or decision whatsoever (102).

Clearly the question of how Heidegger thinks in this text is linked to the question of how be-ing itself takes place historically. What is the relation between future, past, and present in the event of be-ing? How does (or would) the history of be-ing happen? And how can we think of this history *historically*?

Bethinking as Be-ing-Historical Thinking

Can we think and speak in a way that does justice to history, to the dependence of presence on time? Can thinking become neither the expression of universals nor the representation of particulars but the event of thinking the event? As Heidegger puts it, we are faced with a decision—not a mere choice between givens, but a fateful scission—between history and the lack of his-

49. Sinn, *Ereignis und Nirwana*, 52, 73.

tory (96, 100). In his more confident moments, he trusts that the decision for history has come to pass: his "thinking became ever more historical" because be-ing "announced its historical essence" (451). He is no longer representing universals, but entering the momentous site of being-there in an inceptively historical way (374).

As we saw in chapter 1, Heidegger's early work already sought a way of thinking that did justice to history. His early notion of "formal indication" bore fruit in the hermeneutic phenomenology of *Being and Time.* Phenomenologists must acknowledge their own historical situatedness; the point is not to discard our prejudices, but to use them as an entry to the hermeneutic circle (SZ 195, 363). Heidegger puts it effectively in his lectures on Plato's *Sophist:* "The past comes alive only if we understand that we ourselves are that past. . . . we will be what we receive and appropriate [*aneignen und verwalten*] from what we were, and here the most important factor will be *how* we do so. . . . the proper meaning of actual research [is] a confrontation with history, a history which becomes existent only when the research is historical, i.e., when it understands that it itself is history."[50] The "confrontation with history" includes the *Destruktion* or dismantling of the metaphysical tradition (SZ §6). This does not mean getting rid of the tradition, but uncovering its deep currents and confronting the questions embedded in it—and in ourselves as its inheritors. The key to philosophical illumination is to remain within the movement of historically aware interpretation and to avoid clutching at the truth in the form of ahistorical propositions (SZ 19, 36).

This historical hermeneutics does not leave Heidegger committed to a crude relativism, which would hold that all claims are valid only within a historical era and cross-cultural discussion is impossible. Nothing in Heidegger's position denies that there are lasting conditions that transcend epochs and cultures, or even that there are eternal patterns (say, mathematical relations). His point is that truth as unconcealment is historical; even universal conditions must be revealed through a hermeneutic process that draws on the interpreter's particular heritage. This does not prevent a member of one culture from being initiated into another culture's interpretations.

If the hermeneutic phenomenology of *Being and Time* falls short, it is not because it falls prey to relativism but because it does not penetrate far enough into the historicity of being-there and be-ing. It does not fully live up to its claim that being-there is profoundly historical, and it runs the risk of objectifying be-ing. What Heidegger seeks now is a way of thinking that is truly

---

50. Heidegger, *Plato's "Sophist,"* trans. Richard Rojcewicz and André Schuwer (Bloomington: Indiana University Press, 1997), 158. For more on these themes, see Polt, "Heidegger's Topical Hermeneutics."

"be-ing-historical," that not only speaks of but participates in the event of appropriation.

One of the *Contributions'* most striking words for this new thinking is *Er-denken*, which we can render as "bethinking." *Erdenken* ordinarily means to think something up, to invent it (*erfinden*). Heidegger seems to be daring us to raise some typical objections to his thought: it is fantastic, arbitrary, nonobjective. The conception of truth as correct representation looks on inventiveness with suspicion: creativity must be subordinated to the way things are. The very word *Er-denken*, then, is part of Heidegger's assault on representational thought. Bethinking tries to step beyond being as presencing, and thus beyond the present-indicative tonality of traditional thought.

I propose that we can approach bethinking as *the event of thinking the event.* Bethinking is not just *about* be-ing, but *is* be-ing—if this claim is properly understood. Bethinking is a happening that belongs inextricably to the happening of appropriation itself, because bethinking is a crucial instance of the emergence of meaning that the word *appropriation* indicates. In bethinking, appropriation is displayed and instantiated.

Even though the notion of an identity of knower and known seems to be fatally infected by traditional metaphysics, in some crucial passages Heidegger assimilates his thinking to the topic of this thinking. The first section of the *Contributions* says, "the saying here is not opposed to what is to be said, but rather is this itself as the essential happening of be-ing" (4).[51] The land that the way of bethinking explores comes to be only through the way itself—and this land is where appropriation takes place (86–87). Bethinking is not cartography—the description of a given phenomenon—but an adventure, and this adventure is precisely what bethinking is "about." The event of bethinking *is* the event that it bethinks.

But what does this mean? The "is" here cannot express a conventional predication or identification, or even a Hegelian "speculative proposition."[52]

---

51. Cf. *Introduction to Metaphysics*, 90: "philosophy has no object at all. Philosophy is a happening that must at all times work out [*erwirken*] being for itself anew." Similar statements appear in *Besinnung*: "[The] word [of philosophy] never merely means or designates what is to be said, but rather is be-ing itself in the saying" (GA 66, 51). "Philosophy . . . *is* the imageless saying 'of' be-ing itself, a saying that does not express be-ing; instead, be-ing essentially happens as this saying" (GA 66, 64).

52. In a speculative proposition, such as "substance is subject" or "God is love" (when grasped in a Hegelian way), two concepts achieve a mutual determination. The "is" here functions, so to speak, as a mutually transitive verb that allows each of the terms it joins to realize itself through the other (*Phenomenology of Spirit*, Preface, ¶¶60–62.) Heidegger would object that Hegel's speculative propositions are ruled by his *logic*, and are thus part of the tradition of logical-representational thinking (cf. GA 65, 461). For Heidegger's explanation of the speculative proposition, see e.g., "Seminar in Le Thor 1968," in *Four Seminars*, 34; on the dialectical "is," see *Schelling's Treatise on the Essence of Human Freedom*, 81–82. On the Heideggerian "is" that joins thinking and be-ing, cf. Wansing, "Im Denken erfahren," 87–92.

It indicates a distinctively Heideggerian theme: the reciprocal "turn" in which be-ing and being-there come into their own. In the turn, being-there and be-ing attain the proper rapport that lets them flourish (262).

Our first clue to this turn is Heidegger's reading of the pre-Socratics. As we saw, the thinking of the first inception is a be-holding: it holds the gathering presence of beings. The being of beings as presencing needs be-holding, so that beings may be manifest; conversely, be-holding needs being as presencing, because be-holding responds to manifestation, rather than supervising or dictating to it. Like be-holding and presencing in the first inception, bethinking and appropriation will prove to be inseparable in the other inception.[53]

The first aspect of the turn is bethinking's belonging to be-ing. Bethinking is attuned to and by be-ing itself (86). In bethinking, be-ing appropriates thinking (464; cf. GA 66, 357–58). This distinguishes bethinking from the representational tradition (458): instead of trying to form correct assertions, bethinking lets itself be drawn into the happening of be-ing. In this sense, bethinking casts aside every "logical" interpretation of thinking (460).[54] To the objection that bethinking destroys the autonomy of thought by subordinating it to be-ing, Heidegger replies that thinking attains an "unconditional origin," or is self-determined, only if it is determined by "that which is to be thought by it" (462). Thought must not be considered in abstraction from its topic: thought fulfills *itself* when it is true to its theme. (We can see this as an implication of intentionality.)

Another reason not to picture bethinking as a slavish submission to something that holds us in its grip is the second aspect of the turn: be-ing's dependence on bethinking. Being-there is required in order for be-ing to take place—for being-there is the grounding of the truth of be-ing as appropriation (318, 455). Being-there grounds be-ing through a *leap*, a free transition to the other inception (460). At the same time, this leap grounds being-there itself, allowing it to own itself (303). Bethinking participates in this founding of being-there and be-ing: be-ing must be opened in an inceptive leap so that be-ing can determine the character of bethinking (458).[55] Given the fusion of daring and compliance in the leap, bethinking, as a form of leaping, can be neither a slave to be-ing nor be-ing's master. Instead, be-ing and be-

---

53. Heidegger even uses the word "ap-prehension" (*Ver-nehmen:* GA 65, 458) to characterize bethinking, just as he had used it as a name for Greek be-holding in *Introduction to Metaphysics*.

54. As Greisch puts it, thought belongs to appropriation, and "to talk about belonging, to treat it like an object, is already to betray it": "Les 'Contributions,'" 607.

55. On thinking as leaping, see George Kovacs, "The Leap (*der Sprung*) for Being in Heidegger's *Beiträge zur Philosophie (Vom Ereignis)*," *Man and World* 25, no. 1 (January 1992): 39–59.

thinking are interdependent; they belong together because they both come into their own together. In this sense, bethinking "is" appropriation.

The joint happening of be-ing and bethinking involves creativity—not as the willful imposition of a new form but as responsive engagement with the emergence of meaning (24). Be-ing is the happening in which meaning emerges, in which the being of beings becomes a live issue for us. But this event cannot happen unless we dare to bethink it—to leap into it as a possibility. It is not that we *make* be-ing, but that we are needed as participants in the event of be-ing, the event that in turn affects how we, as thinkers, can think.[56] The process of drawing a landscape offers some parallels to the creativity of bethinking. A landscape drawing, if it is a genuine work of art, not only represents a place—an entity—but also alerts us to its meaning (its be-ing). The artist elicits this meaning in the course of drawing. The meaning was not simply "there" before the drawing was drawn, just waiting for someone to express it on paper; it was latent, diffuse, taken for granted. The meaning cannot come alive, then, cannot fully *happen*, until the drawing draws it out. We could even say that the artist *in-vents* the meaning—as long as we use this word in its root sense of "coming upon" an opportunity in an innovative and illuminating way.[57] In-vention is not planning or willing; it is a venturesome openness to an experience in which the artist himself may be transformed. It is neither the discovery of a previously formed object nor the creation ex nihilo of a form, but the attentive cultivation of meaning. It is neither a mere acceptance of the given nor an imposition that negates the given, but a creative reception of the given—an event of appropriation. In this way, in-vention undercuts the opposition between creativity and truth. It allows meaning to flourish—and allows the finder of meaning to flourish as well. Similarly, be-thinking (*Er-denken*) is the in-ventive finding (*Er-finden*) of the event of be-ing. Heidegger thinks of *Er-denken* in the middle voice: bethinking is a kind of thought that generates opportunities for itself to be affected by an event greater than itself.

Bethinking *is* appropriation. This "is" means that bethinking is one of the happenings that elicit the upsurge of meaning that sustains in-vention. It is a signal way in which the truth of be-ing is fostered. Instead of functioning as a moment of self-presence, bethinking is a moment of thrown throwing

---

56. "The language of *Contributions* . . . enables the e-vent of being to appear as it appears in thinking and—in turn—it enables language and thinking to appear as events of be-ing": Vallega-Neu, *Heidegger's "Contributions,"* 3. Ruin also states the point well: "only in and through this mode of thinking will the truth of being appear as the very event of that truth": *Enigmatic Origins,* 260.

57. Compare Heidegger's suggestion that imagination can be understood as appropriation itself—the happening of the clearing (GA 65, 312).

in which we appropriate the event of be-ing that appropriates us.[58] Bethinking both provokes and depends on the emergence of the being of beings.

In calling for thinking of and as a unique event, Heidegger is not forbidding us to think in broad terms, to look for deep connections, or to identify lasting grounds. What matters is staying attentive to *how* we are finding and expressing these patterns. If we find them as simply given, as present, then we have not taken any essential step beyond the traditional tonality. But if we in-vent the patterns, we can enter bethinking. Again, "in-vention" does not mean creating forms willfully, but cultivating and articulating meanings as they come forth. Meanings come forth in unique moments—"*shocks* of time" (17)—when bethinking and be-ing let each other happen. "Bethinking sets [us] forth into that history whose 'events' are nothing other than the shocks of appropriation itself" (463). Moments of bethinking are rare, and they cannot be reproduced. A statement or word that is bethought should not be taken out of context and parroted; its sense lies in a move made at a particular moment, not in a conjunction of ahistorical concepts. The only way to build on a former achievement of bethinking is to retrieve it, letting it resonate in one's own place and moment, so that it is both distant and familiar (8).

This may all seem far too nebulous and arbitrary. What are the standards for judging an attempt at bethinking? Heidegger would reply that there are none. Whereas representational thought takes assertion and logic as its guidelines, in bethinking no guideline at all comes into play (458). If bethinking is truly originary, then it cannot be subjected to some criterion external to the topic that is in-vented in the event of bethinking. Bethinking is determined *only* by what is to be thought (462). Be-ing attunes bethinking to itself, as being emerges in the event of bethinking; there is no external method or test that can pass judgment on this event. This may sound supremely irresponsible; Heidegger's thought cannot be verified or falsified by public standards, so it seems arbitrary and illogical. However, he retorts that logic is the *least* rigorous approach to be-ing: logical thinking imposes a regime of assertibility on be-ing because it carelessly assumes that assertion provides our primary access to be-ing (461).[59] When we confront fundamental questions, there is no avoiding a leap, a Promethean or "titanic" venture with no logical safety net (462). Only through leaping can we discover what is truly compelling; the necessity is discovered in the execution of the thought (56). Bethinking does have a ground, then, but it emerges *with* the venture of thinking—and it is

58. In this sense, one can say that bethinking is thinking "all the way into and from out of be-ing": Kenneth Maly, "Soundings of *Beiträge zur Philosophie (Vom Ereignis)*," *Research in Phenomenology* 21 (1991): 177.

59. A parenthetical remark suggests that Heidegger might concede that logic can play a legitimate role in "expressing" the *results* of bethinking: GA 65, 461.

not a Cartesian ground, a certainty, but a field of tension that always invites further questioning. Bethinking "rests" in its theme precisely because it never stops questioning (57). Instead of laying out an answer, it is devoted to the urgency of the question. This does not mean that bethinking is just a preliminary to adequate representation; instead, it is adequate to the elusiveness of be-ing itself, which can never be said definitively (460).

Bethinking should no more be judged by a set standard than a poem should be judged solely according to rules of versification. However, this does not mean that bethinking is immune from all judgment. A poem can certainly fail, even it conforms to formal rules: it can fail to *find* its voice or theme. A successful poem is apt or appropriate. Similarly, bethinking has to find its own appropriateness. The "project" of bethinking is not subject to arbitrary whims, because it must learn to adapt itself to the new dimension that it itself opens up (56, 86). Accomplished thinkers have a tact and sureness in their performance, like the sureness of a dancer or musician—a stylistic "self-certainty" (69). In bethinking, as in art, there is a rigor that exceeds the rigor of representational propositions (65). (A quantitative topography of the Grand Canyon is *precise*, but it would be wrong to see it as more *rigorous* than a poetic evocation of the canyon. The poem responds to the place as a whole, as it presents itself; the measurements simply ignore this experience. In this sense, the quantitative account of the canyon is loose and careless.)

We might grant these points, but still wonder whether Heidegger actually achieves bethinking. He often calls his thought preparatory (465) or transitional, on the way to "simple doing" (463); much of the book seems to be *about* bethinking, rather than the "doing" of it. But if bethinking cannot be judged by other modes of thought, this would be a waste of time; a *representation* of bethinking would automatically *mis*represent it. Only one who has reached the unity of thought and be-ing has the right to complain about their separation—and Heidegger himself is unsure that he has reached such unity. When he says that bethinking is appropriation, is this a present-indicative statement, or is it future-subjunctive in the worst sense—an exercise in wishful thinking? Bethinking begins to seem like an idle construct. Even worse: if bethinking "is" appropriation, then appropriation is an idle construct too.

This is a serious objection, but it would be ungenerous to accept it completely at this point. Heidegger does find the words to name his theme in a powerful way (such as the word *Er-denken* itself)—and bethinking may, above all, be the art of finding words, the art of "naming" be-ing (460, 463). Bethinking is poetic: it practices the art of finding names.[60] In poetry, an in-

---

60. On the language of the *Contributions* as "poietic," cf. Vallega-Neu, *Heidegger's "Contributions*," 3, 35, and Daniela Vallega-Neu, "Poietic Saying," in Scott et al., *Companion*.

herited word is adapted to the unique exigencies of a moment. The word then *names* what is at stake at this moment, instead of categorizing it. The name helps what it names to come forth in its singularity. The name and the named become engaged: the named is elicited by the connotations of the name, but at the same time the connotations are transformed to fit the named. The name and the named come to own each other. This is a process of mutual adjustment and simultaneous emergence—a matchmaking and a marriage, not a representational correspondence. Poetic naming is the happening of appropriation in language. Heidegger does engage in bethinking, then, whenever he arranges an appropriate engagement between name and named.

Are the *Contributions to Philosophy*, then, a contribution to poetry? Is appropriation Heidegger's muse? Are thought and poetry the same? In the 1930s Heidegger is engaged in an intensive meditation on poets, particularly Hölderlin. He explores the affinities between philosophy and poetry, considering, for example, the "poetic thinking" of Parmenides and Heraclitus and the "thinking poetry" of Sophocles. Although he always maintains that there is a distinction between the two, he is more concerned with showing what they have in common. "The poet always speaks as if beings were expressed and addressed for the first time. In the poetry of the poet and in the thinking of the thinker, there is always so much world-space to spare that each and every thing—a tree, a mountain, a house, the call of a bird—completely loses its indifference and familiarity." Unlike science, which presupposes the opening of a "world-space," poetry and philosophy participate in the event of appropriation—the emergence that "first rips space open."[61]

But what is the difference between them? Does poetry name beings, while philosophy names be-ing? In "Das Ereignis" Heidegger proposes that, by finding names for the holy, the poet finds ways to be at home amidst beings; in contrast, the thinker does without the holy and seeks to inhabit the permanently uncanny, un-homely abyss of be-ing. But do we have the words to name be-ing? Heidegger's goal in the *Contributions* is to bethink be-ing without basing it on beings (75–76); he wants to in-vent the event of giving without relying on the given. However, all language remains the language of familiar beings (78, 83). Our repertoire of names is so bound to beings that we find ourselves at a loss for words when we try to bethink and bespeak pure be-ing. If bethinking succeeds, it will reach a peak of historicity for which we still lack the language (463). Here Heidegger slips back into the danger of turning bethinking and appropriation into speculative constructs—a problem we will return to in chapter 4. He can only hope that we (and he) will shift into hearing the language of beings

---

61. *Introduction to Metaphysics*, 154, 28, 195. "Poetry makes beings more beingful [*seiender*]": *The Essence of Truth*, 47. Cf. *Nietzsche*, vol. 2, 208.

as the language of be-ing (83). We could argue that poets hope for a similar shift. The goal of poetry is to rejuvenate and transform our ways of perceiving what is—in other words, to participate in and even "found" the emergence of meaning, the event of be-ing (11). How does this differ from bethinking?

Does poetry experience the world as if for the first time, while philosophy experiences it as if for the last? For the poet, things are wondrous—even an old man or a familiar ruin are encountered with an arresting strangeness, so that we see them as they have never been seen before. Poetry opens new prospects. But philosophy typically takes a retrospective position, summing up the sense of all that has unfolded—not unlike the way one's life flashes before one's eyes when one seems to have reached one's final moments. Philosophy may begin with wonder, but it tries to replace wonder with understanding (Aristotle, *Met.* A 2). The owl of Minerva spreads its wings only at dusk (Hegel, *Philosophy of Right*, Preface). But these thoughts will not apply perfectly to Heidegger. He is quite capable of structured and synoptic thought, and we will see at the end of this chapter that the *Contributions*, tentative and fragmentary as they are, do form a kind of whole. But he does not want bethinking to be retrospective—in fact, we have seen that it itself is a possibility at least as much as an activity. Bethinking must be *inceptive* thinking, opening the other inception.

Inceptive Thinking

In philosophy we soon discover that when we begin to think, we are far from the beginning. We begin as latecomers, the inheritors of derivative concepts and opinions (GA 39, 3–4). What is first for us, as Aristotle likes to put it, is not what is first by *physis*. How can we reach what is truly first? What does come first? For a sign that these questions are important to Heidegger, we need look no farther than the titles of two texts closely linked to the *Contributions: Über den Anfang* (GA 70, *On the Inception*, 1941) and *Die Stege des Anfangs* (GA 72, *The Bridges of the Inception*, 1944).[62] What is an *Anfang*? Could it be no less central to Heidegger's thought than *Ereignis*? In fact, the two words name the same theme. "What is the *inception* . . . ? It is the essential happening of *being* itself. . . . The *inception* is *be-ing itself* as appropriation" (58).[63] The question of inception, then, leads directly to the central enigmas of the *Contributions*, as does the question of inceptive thinking (§§20–31).

---

62. Heidegger told Friedrich-Wilhelm von Herrmann that these are among the texts "especially close" to the *Contributions: GA 66, 434.

63. "Here, ground is . . . a gathering that grants the Open where all beings are. '*Ground*' means *being itself and this is the inception*": *Basic Concepts,* 74.

An inception is not an ordinary beginning (*Beginn*). A *Beginn* is simply the start of some process; there is nothing necessarily profound or fundamental about such a moment. But Heidegger usually reserves the term *Anfang* for great, founding events.[64] What qualifies an inception to play this role? What happens in an inception?

To begin with etymology: an *Anfang* suggests a moment of seizing (*fangen*). Similarly, the Latin *incipere* is based on *in-capere:* to take in hand, to undertake, to seize.[65] Who or what is doing the seizing, and what is being seized? Presumably we, as being-there, are seizing the day—resolutely deciding to start upon some path. In doing so, we seize be-ing: we explicitly receive the gift of the significance of what is. At the same time, be-ing is seizing us: we are not creating meaning from scratch, but are responding to an event of meaningfulness that is happening *to* us. *Introduction to Metaphysics* puts it dramatically: "the almighty sway of being violates being-there (in the literal sense)."[66] We must be ripped away from our habitual existence, and ripped open so that we can receive being. Since normality is ruptured at such moments, we can call them moments of de-rangement, *Verrückung* (14).[67] For the everyday position, all deep experiences are deranged, because they reposition and rearrange us. We might call these moments *seizures.* But we should not overemphasize this aspect of inception, for Heidegger does not want us simply to be overwhelmed by some external power. In an inception, we respond to the superior power of be-ing with our own powers.

If in an inception we seize and are seized, possess and are possessed, then an inception is precisely an event of appropriation. Appropriation is the event in which the being of beings is given. Every gift affects the future, in that it begins a new relationship or perpetuates an old one. But the gift of being opens a whole realm of possibilities, an arena in which we can act and encounter entities.[68] Appropriation is inceptive because it initiates an epoch, an enduring way of experiencing and conceiving of beings. In this epoch, be-ing itself then withdraws, fading into the background to allow beings to come to the fore.[69] An inception, then, is a moment of seizure when be-ing and being-there both come into their own, when the difference be-

---

64. GA 69, 156; GA 70, 9–10; GA 39, 3–4; GA 51, 108; "The Origin of the Work of Art," in *Off the Beaten Track*, 48–49. GA 70 as a whole is an exploration of the dynamic of inception, an attempt to use the word *Anfang* as a name for be-ing itself. On inception and inceptive thinking cf. Fried, *Heidegger's Polemos*, 116–35.

65. *Oxford Latin Dictionary* (Oxford: Clarendon Press, 1968), s. vv. *incipio, capio.*

66. *Introduction to Metaphysics*, 190.

67. On *Verrückung* in the *Contributions* cf. Oudemans, "Echoes from the Abyss?" 72, 76.

68. In this sense, the inception "is not the past, but rather, because it has decided in advance everything to come, it is constantly of the future": *Basic Concepts*, 13.

69. The concept of the epoch is developed more after the *Contributions*. See e.g., "The Anaximander Fragment," in *Early Greek Thinking*, 26–27.

tween something and nothing takes place, when a space opens up in which beings can appear.

Such events are rare. In fact, it seems that for Heidegger, there may have been only one inception in Western history so far—the Greek "first inception"—and it did not fully happen, because the Greeks could not recognize and "ground" it.[70] The first inception demands "the other inception," the inception that may ground Western being-there more deeply by wrestling with the hidden possibilities of the first. Although the first inception can never be duplicated, it can and must be *retrieved* (55, 73, 169, 171, 185; GA 69, 22–23). This retrieval would not tame and explain the inception, but would itself constitute a new inception (55). An inception, then, is unique, a one-time event. It does not reproduce anything, nor can it be reproduced. But it does not stand alone, a solitary monument in the past that bears no relation to us; instead, it reaches forward and seizes us, calling on us to seize it in return. This retrieval is not reproduction, but a fresh encounter with the possibilities of the first inception. This is how the first inception remains effective.[71]

When Heidegger says that an inception is unique, he does not simply mean that it differs externally from other occurrences, so that it is "new" (55). Instead, an inception has a special kind of temporality that takes it out of the realm of reproducibility. As an event of appropriation, it involves temporal ownness: the inception lays claim to a human group and an era, and they in turn lay claim to it. This mutual belonging makes the inception not just different, but nonreproducible. Yet although the inception itself cannot be reproduced, it *generates* reproducibility.

A few examples will bring home these points. Normally we live in the realm of the reproducible. I ride the bus to work, just as anyone would ride it; I am one more reproducer of a widely shared pattern of practices. At work, I reproduce some other pattern, and my own activity could, in principle, be reproduced by some qualified replacement for me. In this system, production means reproduction—bringing forth case after case that instantiates the form. Reproducibility is also central to everyday thought and language. We usually traffic in well-worn words and ideas, use them as anyone would use them, apply them in the same way we have applied them before. When we form concepts, we do so by abstracting a feature that displays itself as com-

70. *Basic Questions of Philosophy*, 180.
71. Cf. Neu, *Die Notwendigkeit der Gründung*, 124, 153–54; Beistegui, *The New Heidegger*, 86. As Joseph P. Fell points out, the first and the other inception are "contemporaneous" in that the future draws on the past: "Heidegger's Notion of Two Beginnings," *Review of Metaphysics* 25, no. 2 (December 1971): 220–21. As Vallega puts it, "The first and the other beginning do not define points in history, as if we were to accomplish a move from point A to point B. It is in the encounter of first and other beginning, in their playing off each other, that they enact the opening of beyng [*Seyn*]. [Thus] there is not an unchanging origin or beginning to which thinking might return": "'Beyng-Historical Thinking,'" 55.

mon to a group of beings, that is reproduced in each of them. This concept can then be applied to other cases, which are represented as reproductions of the universal (§27, §265). Once a concept is established, it apparently makes no difference who uses it or when; its meaning floats free of the situation, so that it can be reproduced under any conditions.

The natural sciences embrace reproducibility as an essential part of the correct method of knowing. If the relevant conditions of an experiment are reproduced, the same product must result—and this is the sign of a law. Scientific language is also disciplined according to the rule of reproducibility: ambiguity has to be avoided, so that terms can be applied unerringly, efficiently, and in a way that is indifferent to their particular user. This is why many scientific texts can now be translated by computers.

Reproducibility is at work not only when we are producing item after identical item, as on an assembly line. The news, for example, is constantly new—an ever-flowing stream of fresh information. But this information is almost always categorized in the same way; our standards for what counts as important, the concepts and language that are at work in our accounts of events, remain unchanged from day to day. In news reporting, as well as in normal scientific research, we encounter new things, but our mode of encountering them is the same as it ever was.[72]

The farther we get from the realm of production, from everyday language, and from the modern scientific method, and the more we engage in poetic activity, the less can be reproduced. Poetic moments are singular, nonreproducible. But this should not be confused with "creativity" or "originality" in the sense of mere novelty. Borges makes this point effectively in his story "Pierre Menard, Author of *Don Quixote*." Twentieth-century Frenchman Pierre Menard set out to write *Don Quixote*—not a modern adaptation, but *the Quixote*. He used exactly the same words Cervantes had used. But his book had a completely different meaning—and in fact, Borges slyly concludes, the Menard *Quixote* is far more profound than the original.[73] Likewise, a great performance of Mozart today cannot mean the same as it would have meant two centuries ago. Each genuine appropriation is a unique event, even if it follows an established pattern, such as a musical score. This is why the other inception cannot be a nostalgic, classicist reproduction of the first (504); that would be as quixotic as an attempt to write *Don Quixote* again and have it mean what it meant when Cervantes wrote it.

Another approach to uniqueness is offered by the Japanese tea ceremony.

72. At news.google.com, journalistic information is sorted into categories and ranked according to importance—by computers alone.

73. Jorge Luis Borges, "Pierre Menard, Author of *Don Quixote*," in *Fictions*, trans. Anthony Kerrigan (New York: Calder Publications, 1991).

The art of tea requires years of practice and intense concentration. Each step in this process has been ritualized and turned into an exquisite and delicate experience. One might suppose that a ceremony, a ritual, is the quintessence of reproducibility and routine—but in fact it is the opposite. There are rules for the tea ceremony, of course, but this does not mean that the point of the ceremony is to follow the rules; if so, it could be performed by robots. The rules are *occasions* for carrying out each action in an inceptive, unique way. What matters ultimately is not reproducing the forms, but imbuing those forms with spontaneity and singularity. The tea ceremony (or simply "tea," as it is known to its adepts) is diametrically opposed to the assembly line. The goal of tea is not simply tea; the process is not subordinated to the product. Each motion in the ceremony is a unique end in itself. The art of tea cultivates singularity. In part, it does so by introducing innovations: a ceremony should include a new painting or piece of pottery, or a new poem composed to evoke the current season. In part, tea cultivates singularity by preserving certain precious objects: the tool used to scoop out the powdered green tea from its container may be a small piece of bent bamboo that is centuries old, has been handed down from master to disciple for generations, and even has a proper name. Singularity can be promoted, then, either by doing something new or by preserving something old—just as the realm of reproduction involves not only the lockstep imitation of established forms, but the more subtle technicism of frenzied rearrangement and permutation that we find in the entertainment industry.

What distinguishes an event as unique, then? It is a special mode of temporality that is lacking in everydayness, and that even defines everydayness by its absence. In the art of tea one tries to do things for the first and last time.[74] The tea, for instance, is to be smoothed and scooped as if it had never been touched before and as if it would never be touched again. In fact, we should remove the "as if": when lived profoundly enough, each moment really *is* unique, nonreproducible, and singular. However, the routine reproducibility of everydayness covers up the possibility of this type of experience. Heidegger tries to regain temporal uniqueness when he says that the poet speaks as if beings were addressed for the first time, or when he writes of authentic being-toward-death, in which we recognize that each moment may be our last.

Now we can say more about why be-ing itself takes place as an inception. In everydayness, nothing seems to be done for the first or last time. Every act, perception, and thought is "more of the same." Everything happens as if it had happened before and could happen again. New beings are constantly

---

74. I owe this phrase to tea master Akira Ron Takemoto.

given to us—but the *way* in which they are given remains unquestioned. This way in which entities are given—the difference entities make to us as entities—is their being. In order for the being of beings to be brought into question, we have to participate in an event that is not just more of the same, but takes place for the first and last time, because it establishes the very mode in which entities are given to us. This event of be-ing sets the standards for how we identify beings; be-ing itself, then, cannot be measured by these standards. Be-ing must seize us, and we must seize it, in a moment that cannot be subordinated to some prior scheme. In this sense, inceptions are "the *shocks* of time" (17). They are not parts of an overarching history but unique sources of historicity, wellsprings of time.

This brings us back to the thought that although an inception cannot be reproduced, it *generates* reproducibility. What is the source of the patterns and models we use to approach beings? For the everyday perspective—our immersion in given beings—this question does not even arise. Beings simply seem to present themselves immediately according to these patterns. But for Heidegger, the patterns of the reproducible realm, the seemingly timeless forms we follow, erupt from a singular moment of appropriation, an inception. This is why singularity outranks eternity (17).

The uniqueness of be-ing lies concealed, then, in the background of the reproducibility that it generates. The arc of history is necessarily one of decline—the inception must always outstrip and outrank the epoch that follows from it. Throughout this epoch, however, the obscure origin remains potent and provocative: "the inception is what is *concealed*, the origin that has not yet been misused and managed, which by always withdrawing reaches out the farthest" (57).[75] Be-ing is the forgotten explosion to which the luminous cosmos we behold is beholden.

But in privileging the unique moment of origin over its imitators and successors, is Heidegger reverting to a classic metaphysical scheme? Is his notion of an inception—and of *Ereignis* itself—any more than a variant of the Platonism that opposes the perfect, single form to the imperfect, plural copies? The Derridean notion of iterability gives us a way of sharpening these questions.[76] This notion is part of Derrida's project of undoing the hegemony of presence—a project that often uses Heidegger's thought against the supposed remnants of metaphysics within this thought itself. Heidegger tries to show that presence is made possible by time and appropriation, which cannot be understood in terms of presence. Similarly, Derrida tries to show that

75. Cf. *Introduction to Metaphysics*, 165: "The inception is what is most uncanny and mightiest. What follows is not a development, but flattening down as mere widening out."

76. Cf. Rodolphe Gasché, *The Tain of the Mirror: Derrida and the Philosophy of Reflection* (Cambridge: Harvard University Press, 1986), 212–17.

presence (whether it be conceived as pure being, absolute truth, perfect self-consciousness, unambiguous reference, the center, the foundation, or the original) cannot come into effect *as* presence without relying on its other, on some type of absence or imperfect presence (the margins, the traces, the off-shoots, the imitations). To say that all origins are characterized by iterability is to say that they are intrinsically subject to absence, reproduction, and alteration. Otherwise, the original could not serve as the origin *of* its derivatives. The original has to be able to give way, to become absent, in order for its derivatives (its imitations or reproductions) to be able to come forth. Furthermore, the derivatives are alterations of the original, because they are other than it. The original thus proves to have within it a necessary reference to its derivatives—a fact that calls into question the very concepts of original and derivative. There is no original presence, because presence must be infected by re-presentation. Since all signification relies on the ability of signs to be *reproduced*, iterability is at work in the happening of meaning itself, which cannot be understood as a unique event.[77]

In some respects Derrida's line of thought echoes the account of thrownness and projection in *Being and Time. Dasein* is "always already" in a world; we are "thrown" into a situation that is not of our own making. There is no way, then, to begin with a completely pure origin (e.g., SZ 150). Furthermore, Heidegger defines death as the possibility of the impossibility of being-there (SZ 250) and claims that without this possibility, projection itself would not be possible; it is essential to our life that we are mortal, that any of our choices could be our last. Similarly, Derrida makes a more general argument that every presence is made possible by the possibility of its own absence.[78]

Yet Derrida's argument for iterability is in some respects more traditional than Heidegger's thought, at least in the *Contributions*. First, Derrida in fact puts forth an argument, a line of reasoning. Heidegger, in contrast, tries to open himself to the event of the giving of the being of beings. There is no

---

77. "Representation does not suddenly encroach upon presence; it inhabits it as the very condition of its experience": Jacques Derrida, *Of Grammatology*, trans. Gayatri C. Spivak (Baltimore: Johns Hopkins University Press, 1976), 312. "The present in general is not primal but, rather, reconstituted . . . there is no purity of the living present": Derrida, "Freud and the Scene of Writing," in *Writing and Difference*, trans. Alan Bass (Chicago: University of Chicago Press, 1978), 212. "A sign is never an event, if by event we mean an irreplaceable and irreversible empirical particular. A sign which would take place but 'once' would not be a sign": Derrida, *Speech and Phenomena, and Other Essays on Husserl's Theory of Signs*, trans. David B. Allison (Evanston: Northwestern University Press, 1973), 50.

78. Much like Derrida, Schürmann extends the notion of mortality into the view that all founding principles are fated to collapse. Unfortunately, he provides little argument to support this extension, claiming only that we all already know he is right: *Broken Hegemonies*, 596, 601, 602.

argument here (which is not to say that there is no thought). Rather than arguing his way to a universal pattern, Heidegger dwells with the contingent and unique happening of be-ing (464). Second, whereas Heidegger tries to escape transcendental thinking, Derrida's argument is transcendental, in a broad sense; it tries to uncover a necessary condition of the possibility of presence. To be sure, this is a very special kind of transcendental argument, because instead of ranking the condition over the conditioned, it shows that any such ranking undercuts itself. In this way it resembles ancient skeptical arguments, which, having done the job of casting doubt on dogmatic arguments, proceed to abolish themselves. However, as Rodolphe Gasché observes, even though Derrida is nondogmatic and nonsystematic, he persistently draws our attention to a certain "system" or certain "infrastructures" that are always already at play in any attempt to establish a dogma. Derrida tries to demonstrate, so to speak, that systems collapse systematically.[79]

With their emphasis on inception, do the *Contributions* betray Heidegger's earlier insights into presence as always already indebted and exposed to absence? In Derrida's terms, do the *Contributions* try to efface the iterability of the origin? Or does Heidegger's *Anfang* acknowledge its dependence on its successors?

First we must admit that Heidegger privileges the inception very heavily: "whatever is great can only begin great. In fact, its inception is always what is greatest."[80] Usually the *Contributions* speak as though there has been only one inception, the "first inception"; Heidegger is preparing for the "other inception." If an inception is so rare, does it not become an impossibly distant origin, a mythical golden moment? From a Derridean point of view, one could argue that Heidegger succumbs to yet another variant—another iteration—of the metaphysical trap, according to which we latecomers can only engage in futile attempts to represent the original moment of presence. One could also criticize Heidegger, from another point of view, for failing to recognize the inceptiveness that enters every human life and that is important to all significant experiences. I will develop this criticism in chapter 4.

However, there may be some ways in which Heidegger's notion of an inception eludes Derrida's argument. First, inceptions are not moments of presence—in fact, they can never be *given* at all. Instead, they are "shocks" of time itself (17). In inceptions, time happens. Whether we can think of the happening of time itself and not only of happenings within time is a problem we will postpone, but at least it is not the sort of problem that comes from privileging the present at the expense of time.

---

79. Gasché, *The Tain of the Mirror,* 250.
80. *Introduction to Metaphysics,* 16–17.

Second, if my interpretation of *Ereignis* is right, then an inception is a moment not as an evanescent "now" but as an emergency. It is *instant*, in the old adjectival sense of this word as a synonym for "urgent." It is a momentous moment of urgent import. From such urgency as instancy, the more superficial "instants" and "moments" emerge—the mere "news." Traditional metaphysics fails to address the emergency of being. Perhaps Derrida's rhetoric, too, despite its revolutionary tones, tends to divert us from crucial, urgent moments by diffusing import, by deconstructing all centers.[81] This thought is far from a refutation of Derrida—but it is legitimate to ask whether, in undercutting all attempts to place a primal presence at the head of all beings, he has overlooked a different sort of beginning: the inceptive emergency in which the import of beings comes to a head. To affirm inceptive uniqueness is not to insist on pure presence and deny time, for time, as Heidegger understands it, is not simply a series of absences and deferrals any more than it is a series of presents. It is a field of urgency that comes to a head at rare moments of emergence and emergency.

Finally, Heidegger's "inception" may escape Derrida's critique because of the special character of the relation between inception and successors in the *Contributions* (55). Granted that the inception can never be overtaken by its successors, it does *call for* them and thus stands in an essential relation to them, unlike traditional metaphysical origins, which are supposedly independent of their successors.[82] By opening a domain of meaning, the inception calls for reproductions within this domain. It also calls for a deeper response, an other inception, which never pretends to re-present a bygone present.

The other inception requires *inceptive thinking*. This cannot be a method opposed to the method of representational thought. The very notion of a technique of thinking belongs to the realm of reproducibility, which includes ordinary conceptual thought. Applying a technique of thought amounts to putting beings on an intellectual assembly line, so that we reproduce the same procedure with every entity that comes along. Furthermore, inceptive thinking cannot simply be a report about an inception, a representation of it—no such thing is possible. Instead, inceptive thinking must participate in the "enactment" of an inception (64). Inceptive thinking proves to be bethinking—the event of thinking the event.

---

81. Neu reaches a similar conclusion: "Heidegger, in contrast to Derrida, thinks *in decision*": *Die Notwendigkeit der Gründung*, 376. Derrida does not experience "an urgency that necessitates a leap into the abyss": ibid., 377.

82. An exception is Hegel, for whom the beginning is empty and abstract without the entirety of its successors. Hegel's difference from Heidegger and Derrida lies in the very idea of an "entirety," a complete truth.

We can also expect that we will be unable to represent inceptive thinking by means of representational thinking; an account of inceptive thinking must itself be inceptive. Of course, this raises the possibility that inceptive thinking may simply be unable to communicate with ordinary thought—a possibility that is all too apparent in the *Contributions*. Inceptive thinking threatens to become completely hermetic. However, metaphors and analogies can provide some access to it, because such moves are not impositions of a form, but juxtapositions that provide fertile spaces for the emergence of meaning.

We can compare inceptive thinking, then, to events such as the tea ceremony. In the art of tea, each motion is to be done for the first and last time, and each step in the process is not just a means to an end, but itself fulfills the end. The point of doing what one does is simply to do it—in a way that appropriately brings to life the singularity of the moment. What would it mean, then, to *think* in a way that fulfills the end of thinking at each step? What would it mean to think each thought for the first and last time?

This cannot mean that one is constantly shifting one's words, one's claims, or one's topic of thought. This superficial variation would provide novelty, but it could never guarantee true uniqueness. Instead, Heidegger thinks persistently about the same topic, and tends to use the same words, but tries to let the sense of the words respond on each occasion to the current experience of the matter at hand. The word *Ereignis*, for instance, always attempts to respond to the same topic, the happening of be-ing, but what it means must grow out of the context in each instance. It would be misguided to try to define appropriation representationally, so that one could always substitute the definition for the word *salva veritate*. Rather than reproducing a defined concept, Heidegger is performing the word, as one might perform a musical score. All the performances are linked, but they are also all unique. Each sentence, each word tries to leap into be-ing. *Ereignis*, like Heidegger's other key words, does not express a concept in the usual sense, so strictly speaking, it cannot be defined. Of course, this does not imply that we cannot discuss it in our own words—in fact, we must do so if we are ever to have our own experience of the matter at stake.

In inceptive thinking, the thinker must be prepared to change with the thought, to be de-ranged into being-there (14). To enter being-there is to seize and be seized by be-ing, to stand steadfastly in the site where be-ing takes place. In other words, here we do not subordinate the object of our thought to a reproducible process of representation. Instead, at each moment in our thinking, we respond to the topic of our thought by letting it appropriate us as we appropriate it. *Anfang* is *Einfang*: we ourselves are drawn or seized into the realm that our thought opens (56). This is why inceptive thinking necessarily affects who we are; it is essentially linked to the self. This does not mean that we should ruminate on our own subjectivity; instead, the self emerges from be-ing (67). Inceptive thinking in-vents the self.

Inceptive thinking is no license to dogmatize; it does not establish "first principles" and deduce further propositions in the rationalist style. What comes first is not a proposition at all, but the happening of unconcealment. Inceptive thinking dwells with this event, struggles with it, and recognizes that it calls for continual questioning (57). Such a way of thinking has to be tentative and incomplete—a way for perpetual beginners. When it comes to be-ing, we must begin again and again (17).

Heidegger tells us that inceptive thinking is not conceptual (36). Can we think at all without concepts? The only alternative might seem to be an intuitive, nonverbal feeling. But he is not calling for sheer feeling, or for "an indefinite, flickering representation" (64). The target of his attack is not expression and articulation in general, but the kind of conceptuality that dominates theoretical thought. For theory, a concept (*Begriff*) is a general representation through which we grasp or comprehend (*greifen, begreifen*) many particulars by bringing them under a common aspect. For Heidegger, this procedure is fatally Platonic, even if Plato's and Aristotle's own use of this thinking was still creative (64).[83] The problem, as we have seen, is that the act of grasping the common aspect is derivative (63): it begins with beings, which are taken for granted as present at hand. This type of thinking merely re-presents the universal aspects of what is present. What it misses is the event that inaugurates the distinction between something and nothing.

Heidegger points to the difference between theory and inceptive thinking by distinguishing between *Begriff* and *Inbegriff*. In English, we can make a different but still appropriate play on words by saying that inceptive thinking requires incepts, not concepts. Before we turn to Heidegger's brief statements on *Inbegriff* in §27, consider two everyday meanings of the word. First, *Inbegriff* means what is comprised in something—the sum of its contents (the *Inbegriff* of a suitcase is all the items in it). The word connotes completeness. In contrast, an ordinary concept leaves out all but one aspect of a being, disregarding its particularity and its situation within a world. "Inceiving," then, might attempt to do justice to the fullness and richness of the unique. There are also phrases such as, "he is the *Inbegriff* of generosity." In English, we might say epitome, essence, quintessence, or soul. For traditional metaphysics and logic, such phrases are rhetorical—they are deliberate category mistakes. What we mean is that the individual clearly illustrates the essence, but we exaggerate by saying that he *is* the essence. But maybe we can take

---

83. Hegel's *Begriff* is a special case. As we have seen, Hegel is far from simply thinking in abstract universals; yet he fails to embrace the historicity of the happening of be-ing.

these phrases more seriously. The judgment that an individual is generous allows him into the familiar (what we have previously called "generous"). But instead of reducing him to the familiar, we can familiarize ourselves with *him* by paying attention to his own way of being. In doing so, we will of course use concepts, but the concepts will be transformed and enriched. The Platonic order has then been undone: instead of getting to know "generosity itself" through this man, we keep our concept of generosity subservient to our experience of the man. To inceive, then, might mean to subordinate our universal representations to our experiences of what is. Instead of comprehending by generalizing concepts, we let our inceptive concepts respond to the fullness of what is comprised in a being.

So far, we have extrapolated from the usual German meanings of *Inbegriff*, and we have spoken of beings rather than be-ing. How does inceiving think of be-ing? Section 27 gives us some hints, but it also forces us to venture interpretations of some other fundamental concepts, or rather incepts: "juncture," the "turn," and "insistence."

After presenting his critique of ordinary conceptual thinking, Heidegger writes: "Inceptive thinking is the originary enactment [*Vollzug*] of the echo, the pass, the leap, and the grounding in their unity. Here enactment means that these . . . are in each instance taken over and withstood only by human beings, that they themselves are always essentially an other and belong to the happening of being-there" (64). Here Heidegger refers to the four main movements or "junctures" (*Fugen*) that structure his text. As we will see at the end of this chapter, these junctures are elements in the transition from the first to the other inception; they give the text a unity that centers on a moment of crisis. Inceptive thinking must not only be about this crisis and this transition, but must carry it out. I take the obscure phrase "they themselves are always essentially an other" to mean that the junctures are different every time, "in each instance" (*je*). Their character depends on how we participate in them. Inceptive thinking is one form of this participation.

Such thinking is devoted to "be-ing in the joining of those junctures" (64); be-ing is at stake in the transition to the other inception. But this transition needs to be taken over by human beings. What is happening involves *both* humans and be-ing. This is "the happening of being-there"—the event in which the being of beings is given to humanity, so that both humanity and being come into their own. Incepts thus always include a "co-grasping" of the turn in appropriation, the reciprocity between be-ing and being-there (64). Inceiving, then, is the event of thinking the event in which both be-ing and being-there take place *together*. This togetherness may be indicated by the word *Zusammengriff*. Is such "co-grasping" something that we do, or something that the turn does? Heidegger leaves it ambiguous. What is happening here cannot be divided into an active subject and a passive object; it is the bursting forth of an event in which being-there and be-ing first occur.

Section 27 also links inceiving to "insistence" or "instancy" (*Inständigkeit*, 65). Insistence in the *Contributions* resembles authenticity in *Being and Time:* it is a stance that enables proper ownness. Genuine selfhood—belonging to one's self—requires belonging to be-ing. Heidegger calls this stance a paradoxical "out-standing insistence" (*ausstehende Inständigkeit*). We understand be-ing only by with-standing its abandonment and standing ready for its call (64). This means dwelling in the place and time where appropriation may happen.[84] This "masterful knowing" (44, 62, 64, 281–82) is both the "innermost" (64) and the "outermost" happening (57); it gathers us into intimate belonging to our particular moment and site, yet it also takes us to the strangest limits of our ability to embrace what is and what is not.

The ordinary meanings of *Inbegriff* suggest that "inceiving" might mean subordinating our concepts to the fullness and particularity of beings. Maybe something similar is possible on the level of *be-ing*. To grasp the event of be-ing is not to apply preformed concepts to it, but to "insist," to take a stand within the happening itself. The particularity here is the uniqueness of a historical instant. This stance could also develop our appreciation of the uniqueness of *beings*. Under the sway of the *idea*, the particular is seen as merely accidental. But if we grasped (or inceived) the uniqueness of be-ing, we could grasp essence as the "essential happening of the rank and uniqueness of beings in each instance" (66). We could then experience beings as "happening only once" (91). Entities would no longer just be the many that are subordinate to the one. They would no longer be instances of the universal, but would shelter an instant, an event of be-ing. (The notion that be-ing can be "sheltered" in beings is a crucial thought that we will examine in chapter 3.)

By thinking of and in this instant, Heidegger wants to think of both be-ing and beings in a thoroughly historical way. His sayings are to be understood not as mere "formulas" (247) but "hermeneutically" (321), as moments of noticing the historicity of be-ing. His goal is not to construct an ontology, theology, or anthropology—if an "–ology" is a conceptual representation of the general, permanent aspects of a certain type of thing. But neither is he merely pointing out particulars in their manifold becoming—if particularity, multiplicity, and becoming are conceived merely as the counterparts of universality, unity, and permanence. Instead, he is thinking historically about how the sense of what is, as a whole, is transpiring at a historical moment—transpiring not for anyone in general, but for "us," where the very meaning

---

84. Inceiving requires "insistence in the fundamental decisions in each case": GA 69, 115. For an earlier formulation of this thought see *The Fundamental Concepts of Metaphysics*, 9.

of the "we" is called into question in this thinking (48). Attentive readers of the *Contributions* are thus forced to reflect on the historicity of their own ways of reading and thinking. Heidegger also continually draws attention to the resources and pitfalls of his language: he plays on words, explores the histories of ideas, and engages in arduous, churning reformulation. He acknowledges the roots of his concepts and uses them in a way that leaves open the possibility of further transformations. Concepts thus become not ahistorical generalizations, but historical events themselves.

"Inceiving" itself is not a theoretical concept, but an incept. Heidegger does not use the word *Inbegriff* to pick out a common feature of a pre-given set of beings; he uses it to draw on language in a way that provokes us into taking part in the unique happening that gives us the being of beings. Although this happening cannot be conceptualized in the traditional sense, it is not simply ineffable; we can find suggestive, poetic names for it, as long as we keep our words and thoughts flexible and responsive. However, there is no denying that a murky vagueness inhabits Heidegger's account of inceiving. A certain constraint becomes apparent in these passages, as in much of the *Contributions to Philosophy*. Not all is being said—and not all can be said. This necessary reticence is our next theme.

Telling Silence

> Supremely thoughtful utterance does not consist simply in growing taciturn when it is a matter of saying what is properly to be said; it consists in saying the matter in such a way that it is named in nonsaying. The utterance of thinking is a telling silence [*Erschweigen*]. Such utterance corresponds to the most profound essence of language, which has its origin in silence.
> —*Nietzsche*, vol. 2, 208

> What the essential thinkers never say is always simpler than what they say.
> —GA 66, 299

Heidegger is not a man of few words; in the *Contributions* he is positively loquacious. But he tells us that he is not telling us everything—in fact, at the heart of his language there is silence. This is not a refusal to say something that could be said, but an *inability* of which he is keenly aware. As I noted in my introduction, the *Contributions* are esoteric not because they are secretively keeping quiet something that could be said out loud, but because their theme—be-ing itself—is intrinsically mysterious. Heidegger is trying to respond to be-ing with appropriate language, but it is impossible to say be-ing directly—or indirectly (79). Nothing we can say will make be-ing show itself with perfect clarity.

The "logic" of this silence is "sigetic" (§§37–38), from the Greek *sigan*, to keep silent.[85] "Sigetic" is a rejoinder to the logical tradition, just as *sigan* is a counterpart to *legein*. "Sigetic" is an artificial term, and Heidegger warns us not to be satisfied with introducing it as a technical concept that will replace "logic" in some "system" of Heideggerian philosophy (79). Neither is sigetic an irrationalist rejection of logic; it does not invalidate the correctness of logic within its own domain, but this domain is limited and made possible by the domain of sigetic. Telling silence includes the logic of beingness, just as the grounding question incorporates and transforms the guiding question (79). In other words, the question of how be-ing essentially happens includes the search for the universal characteristics of beings, while changing the meaning of this search; in just the same way, sigetic incorporates logic. In order to understand this, we need to consider the relation between be-ing and beings, and Heidegger's interpretation of *logos*.

In chapter 3 we will look more closely at be-ing and beings, but we can already see that be-ing cannot be put into words as beings can. The givenness of beings depends on a givenness of their being; our everyday encounters with things are sustained by a prior familiarity with what is, as such and as a whole. This prior familiarity normally lies in oblivion; we take it for granted. Being, as it were, *gives way* to beings: it gives them a way to present themselves, but at the same time, it fades into the background. Experiences such as anxiety can wake us up from our immersion in entities and make us aware of their being, but awareness of the being of beings is not the same as the ability to put it into words. In fact, in moments of anxiety words may fail us, returning only when we return to beings. The dis-quieting experience of the difference between something and nothing calls for an infinity of words—but also shows that no words are adequate.

Metaphysicians have tried to put the being of beings into words, to articulate the structures of presence. But even if we grant for the sake of argument that they have succeeded, further challenges face anyone who tries, with Heidegger, to raise the question of *be-ing*—the question of how the being of beings is itself given. First, "every saying already speaks *from* the truth of be-ing and can never directly leap over itself to get to be-ing itself" (79). Be-ing always lies behind our backs: it enables the articulation of beings, so

85. Cf. Jean Greisch, "La parole d'origine, l'origine de la parole: Logique et sigétique dans les *Beiträge zur Philosophie* de Martin Heidegger," *Rue Descartes* 1–2 (1991): 210–12; Daniel Panis, "La Sigétique," *Heidegger Studies* 14 (1998): 111–27.

that whenever we address something, we presuppose an event of be-ing that we cannot articulate. Since we are already in the grip of be-ing, instead of trying to represent it we should respond to it with cautious and tentative respect. This implies a second point: all language is the language of beings (78). We have no words that belong exclusively to be-ing. We cannot simply make up such words, either, because there is no saying without the ability to hear; a language of pure be-ing would be unintelligible (78). Our everyday language is a formidable means of dealing with the endless nuances of beings. Our metaphysical language, too, is a language of beings, because it represents the being *of beings*. Metaphysics at its best is still focused on entities, not on the event of the granting of their sense. This event has given way to beings and their being. Here, words fail us (36). In this sense, language is rooted in silence. Be-ing cannot be illuminated by a floodlight; it generates sparks that point to the silent center.

Heidegger adds that we have no way of naming be-ing mediately, through dialectic (79). Dialectic, especially in the Hegelian sense, is the apotheosis of logic—which cannot apply to the bethinking of be-ing because it is a remote derivative of the primordial happening of truth. In the first inception, presencing is grasped as gathering gatheredness—*logos*. But then *logos* is taken as the human apprehension of this gatheredness and as the ability to articulate it in language. Even more superficially, *logos* becomes *assertion*. This is how *episteme logike*, logic, arises: it is an analysis of assertions and the rules that govern them.

We can now see why sigetic includes logic (79): the event of truth "includes," or makes possible, the display of beings and their features. The language of beings addresses only this display—so this language and its logic are enabled and enveloped by a basic mystery, a silence. Before the human articulation of gatheredness, perhaps even before the gathering (the event of presencing), there is a giving-withdrawal, a self-concealment of be-ing.

What is the appropriate response to this self-concealment? Wittgenstein would say: when we cannot speak about something, we must remain silent. But Heidegger does not propose utter silence, *Schweigen*, but *Erschweigen*, a *telling* silence. To keep quiet altogether would be to give up the search—but an intrinsically mysterious theme demands to be honored by a search. In this case, seeking and finding are the same (80). To question is to recognize and honor the problematic as such, whereas either keeping quiet or proposing a solution would deny the question-worthiness of be-ing.

How, then, can we speak in a language that maintains the seeking and respects the mystery? Heidegger proposes a discreet kind of saying that recognizes its own limits. This saying allows the "noblest" language of beings to be said and heard as the language of be-ing (78). Inceptive thinking "lets be-ing tower into beings, by saying the grasping word with telling silence" (58). But how does this work? How can words that ordinarily refer to beings evoke be-ing, while still allowing it the silence that is its own? There is a deep difficulty here that Heidegger does not intend to cover up: all attempts to speak of be-ing can be understood in terms of beings. The words disclose something familiar, and thus close off what is supposed to be revealed. So we must go along with entity-language for a while, and then turn our thinking around at just the right moment (83–84). This turn involves a change in our mood and mode of existing: reticence as a style of writing must spring from restraint as a style of being human (36). Restrained existence experiences be-ing as a gift that leaves us speechless (according to "Das Ereignis," what is closest to thanking is silence). To turn to be-ing in this way would require a deep change in us and our world; a "great stillness must come over the world for the sake of the earth" (34). The earth is the dimension that precedes and sustains articulate meaning—the obscure foundation of the patterns of the world. To let stillness come over the world would mean allowing ourselves to hear the echoing of our familiar words for beings within the uncanny space of be-ing.

Heidegger does not think of this as symbolizing be-ing by means of be-ings (79–80). The language of entities as a symbol for be-ing would easily fall into the traditional opposition between the sensuous and the ideal. But neither are we simply assigning an available label directly to be-ing, as if it were a botanical specimen. The "key," perhaps, is to enter into meaning without expecting a key; we must not expect truth to take place in the form of an answer or a total illumination. It can, however, take place, as long as we are drawn into being-there. Once again, Heidegger is suggesting that this happening of truth in thought *is* an event of appropriation. Our words can bespeak appropriation only if appropriation itself comes to pass when we speak.

The Juncture and the Quarry

Are the *Contributions* any more than a loosely grouped set of abortive, meandering attempts at inceptive bethinking? Is this text "no more than a set of notes for a book in preparation, but an extremely rich one"?[86] It certainly looks like a group of fragments that are only *on the way* to becoming a book. However, as soon as he had written the text by hand and ordered its sections, Heidegger had his brother produce a typescript, and referred to the text ever

---

86. William J. Richardson, "Martin Heidegger," in Babich, *From Phenomenology to Thought, Errancy, and Desire,* 625.

since then as "the *Beiträge*"—which suggests that in his view the book was finished, even if it was unpublished.[87] To put the problem in a nutshell: are the *Contributions* a whole?

What would it mean to be a whole—a work with integrity? At one point Heidegger writes that the *Contributions* are only an anticipation of a true "work," which would deserve the name *The Event of Appropriation;* "work" here means "the self-developing structure in the turn back into the towering ground" (77). The *Contributions* cannot yet "join the free juncture of the truth of be-ing from be-ing itself. If this should ever succeed, then that essence of be-ing in its trembling will itself determine the jointure of the thinker's work" (4). These statements are cryptic—but we can at least say that the wholeness of a work would be determined by its relation to be-ing. Heidegger is not sanguine about the *Contributions'* achieving such wholeness.[88]

The text is a broken text, then—broken off from be-ing. But this rupture is not a complete separation; the text is attuned to be-ing *as* what is concealed. To recognize oblivion is not to overcome it, but it is at least to establish some thoughtful relation to what lies hidden. This means that the *Contributions* do have some connection to be-ing as the "towering ground" that secretly affects their "juncture." The text, in Heidegger's words, is a quarry, a series of break-ins to the hard ground of be-ing; it has its own juncture, its emergent unity that answers to the emergency of be-ing.

The *Contributions* are not a whole that is wholly determined by be-ing; however, the text tries to initiate such a condition. As a transitional text, it has a transitional kind of integrity, and we can even call it a transitional "work." A work in an age of transition must be a *Gang:* "both a going and a way, a way that itself goes" (83).[89] A way that goes is a text that not only guides its reader to a goal but itself makes the journey. The *Contributions* are not just

---

87. Apparently Heidegger's only afterthought about the general structure of the text came in May 1939, when he noted that "Das Seyn," originally designated as part 2, was really a new effort to grasp the whole; on these grounds the editor has made it the last part, part 8 (Editor's Epilogue, GA 65, 514). This is arguably an overreaction to Heidegger's note: see Babich, "Heidegger Against the Editors," 329–30; Dennis J. Schmidt, "On the Memory of Last Things," *Research in Phenomenology* 23 (1993): 98–99. In "On 'Be-ing,'" Parvis Emad assumes that the editorial transposition is correct.

88. A note from 1937 or 1938 is evidence of Heidegger's ambivalence: "These 'contributions to philosophy' are meant to make the breadth of the question of being visible in a new approach; here the point is not to develop the details, because that would all too easily narrow the real field of vision and allow the basic impetus of the questioning to get lost. But even here, I have still not reached *the* form that I require for a publication as a 'work' . . . for here the new style of thinking must announce itself—restraint in the truth of be-ing; the saying of telling silence—the ripening for the essentiality of the simple": GA 66, 427.

89. This passage anticipates Heidegger's motto for the *Gesamtausgabe* as a whole: *Wege, nicht Werke.* The motto is explained in GA 1, 437–38.

an invitation to leap, but the performance of leaping. What we need to understand is the coherence of that performance.

Let us begin with the image of the quarry—an image that has much to do with beginning. Heidegger introduces the themes of "Be-ing" (part 8, originally part 2) with the words, "Here lie the boulders of a quarry in which bedrock is broken" (421). In the other inception, philosophy is "no edifice of thoughts anymore, but boulders apparently fallen at random in a quarry where bedrock is broken and the rock-breaking tools remain invisible. Are the blocks closed forms, or the unwieldy supports of an invisible bridge—who knows?" (436). As a quarry, the *Contributions* try to reach primordial bedrock, *Urgestein* (187, 421, 436). The bedrock is appropriation as the giving of being. But this giving is not simply handed to us; it is given as a task and a challenge, given only to and in *questioning*. This ground—as we will see in chapter 3—is an *Abgrund*, an abyss. So we cannot begin with a self-evident first principle that serves as a foundation for an edifice. We must begin at the beginning and *stay* there, continually digging into the bedrock. Each moment needs to be a new beginning, in which we reinterpret and rediscover what is primary. The thoughts have to be "mined" from the basic mood on each occasion (21). The text is repetitive because Heidegger is trying, again and again, to stay with the same (82), to start from the beginning in confronting the problems at stake.[90] This is repetition as renewed retrieval, not as reproduction. Heidegger's aim is to inceive—to perform and re-form his concepts and words on each occasion. He envies poets, who manage to capture the essential in a single, surveyable form (59–60). He tries to do the same himself, struggling to sum up everything in a nutshell—while fully realizing that this cannot be done, that no single sentence can convey the whole.

In a sense, of course, it is impossible to begin at the beginning. Every use of a word draws on its other uses, and every fundamental concept of a philosophy is linked to its other fundamental concepts; they all shift together, and need to be understood in terms of each other. (Hence the saying that the best way to begin to read a philosopher is to read him for the second time.) If we grasp this point, we can see how a text that consists of individual moments of attempting to reach "bedrock" could be more than a set of aphorisms. It could create a resonance among these moments—not a linear development or an "edifice of thoughts," but a mutual affinity. Such a resonance echoes through the *Contributions*, even if the blocks of the quarry seem to have fallen at random.

90. Heidegger characterizes *Besinnung*, which has a similar style to the *Contributions* although a more scattered overall organization, as follows: "*not a system, not a doctrine, not aphorisms, but a sequence of shorter and longer leaps of questioning into the readiness for the appropriating event of be-ing. The 'repetitions' [are] necessary, since each time the whole [is] to be said*": GA 66, 434.

"Are the blocks closed forms, or the unwieldy supports of an invisible bridge—who knows?" Heidegger would certainly like the moments of the *Contributions* to support a bridge to the other inception, even if they are misshapen. But he himself does not know whether the bridge can be built. (The answer may now depend more on us than on him.) If there is a bridge, it is "invisible," like the rock-breaking tools. While we can reveal many of these tools, some mystery has to remain, because the text is intrinsically esoteric—it is concerned with a self-concealing topic. We will not be able to turn the quarry into an edifice. Or, to vary the metaphor: the great philosophies are unclimbable mountains, but they provide the highest peaks in a land and point to its bedrock (187). The point is not to ascend the mountain—to master Heidegger's thoughts in a crystal-clear representation that he himself did not possess or desire. Our goal, instead, should be to experience the thoughts as pointing to the bedrock and pointing to the bridge—as an impetus to a fresh confrontation with be-ing.

Even if we grant that there can be a resonance among separate attempts to reach bedrock, the image of the quarry does not take us very far in understanding the *unity* of Heidegger's text—especially since he suggests that the blocks in the quarry seem "unwieldy," *ungefüge* (436). In order to grasp the book's unity we need another word, one with connotations from both carpentry and music: *Fuge*, which can be translated as "juncture." The notion of the *Fuge* is part of Heidegger's answer to the problem of how to think historically. Traditional modes of philosophical thought fall short of historicity. The most potent type of unity in the tradition, the system, is ahistorical: it derives logical implications from principles, without acknowledging the appropriating event that precedes reason, principles, and propositions.[91] This is true even of Hegel's system, which claims to be historical yet turns out to be the apotheosis of ahistorical logic. With the word *Fuge* and its relatives, Heidegger indicates a nonsystematic, historical order. This junctural order is determined by the structure of a historical moment, a moment of emergency in which we are faced with a "decision" on the level of be-ing itself. The distinctive "rigor" of inceptive thinking is to be found not in systematic reason, but in "the freedom of the joining [*Fügung*] of its junctures" (65).

The age of systems is gone (5).[92] The ideal of the system, claims Heidegger, is possible only within modernity, where truth is interpreted as certainty and is sought mathematically—that is, in terms of what the subject can de-

91. Cf. *Basic Questions of Philosophy*, 125–26.

92. However, philosophy necessarily seeks the juncture of be-ing and in this sense is always systematic: *Schelling's Treatise on the Essence of Human Freedom*, 29.

termine a priori about objects (65).[93] This approach to the world is an aspect of "machination," which understands entities as what is calculable, explicable, and useful—what can be accurately produced and reproduced (132). Although it may be impossible to prevent readers from taking the juncture of Heidegger's thought as a system (59–60), to do so would be to interpret it from the perspective of modern subjectivity and objectivity. Instead he is trying to think of the event of be-ing, which precedes both subjectivity as the capacity to represent and judge, and objectivity as the representedness of beings. In the other inception, propositions and principles are no longer decisive (130): thinking must follow appropriation, which can never be calculated (242).

When Kierkegaard rebelled against the Hegelian system, he did so in the name of decision: he tried to make room for the individual's decisive leap as a source of meaning that cannot be reduced to a merely logical transition. Heidegger sees this as a religious rather than philosophical objection to Hegel.[94] But he, too, opposes system to decision (88–90). However, Heideggerian decision is not a matter of human choice (87, 90, 103). Choices choose between options that are given in advance (100): I have two shirts and choose which to wear. But be-ing first enables beings as such to be given to us, so it cannot be a matter of choice. If be-ing essentially happens as decision (92, 95), this means that it takes place when a sense of the givenness of beings is carved away from alternative senses. Such moments, however, do not simply wash over us; we do have a role to play. We can open the de-cision if we can leap into the happening of be-ing, if we can dare be-ing instead of resting satisfied with beings (88, 91).

Junctural unity, then, would center on a moment of decision. Such a moment is "critical" in the sense of *krinein*—a moment that decides a course of events, a moment that can involve our choice but is not reducible to our choice. The word *juncture* is especially helpful here, since it means not only a joining or connection in general, but a crossroads or crux—a crucial moment. A juncture is a historical unity, the coherence of a moment of emergency and emergence.

The German *Fuge* does not ordinarily refer to a critical moment, but either to a carpenter's joint or to a musical fugue. Its musical sense is secondary

93. Euclid becomes a model for philosophy only in the modern age, because it is with modernity that *mathematical* order comes to be seen as the standard of all truth. At the same time, the mathematical comes to be interpreted as that which is imposed in advance by the representing subject, whereas for the ancients, including Euclid himself, mathematics was purely a matter of discovery: David R. Lachterman, *The Ethics of Geometry: A Genealogy of Modernity* (New York: Routledge, 1989).

94. *Schelling's Treatise on the Essence of Human Freedom*, 24. Heidegger's clearest statement of his relation to Kierkegaard and existential philosophy is in GA 49, 19–76.

in the *Contributions,* but not absent and not inappropriate. A musical work evokes a mood and depends on remembrance and expectation; its unity is temporal. The *Contributions* are fugal in that they immediately announce a set of themes that are then played out contrapuntally. The text repeats, varies, and interlaces these themes, guided by the leitmotif of appropriation but expressing a variety of moods.[95]

The main sense of *Fuge* in the text, however, is that of a joint. It is associated with the words *fügen* (join), *sich fügen* (comply), *verfügen* (enjoin, govern, have at its disposal), *Gefüge* (structure), and *Fügung* (joining, dispensation).[96] In general, this family of words suggests well-adjusted arrangement. Heidegger's main explanation of *Fuge* (81) involves a threefold sense: (1) the attempt to grasp the impossible, the "fully unfolded fullness" of be-ing; (2) the pursuit of one path over other, possibly more essential paths; (3) the dependence on the dispensation of the truth of be-ing. In short, the *Fuge* is the way the text is joined together by its be-fitting dedication to be-ing.

To confirm that junctural order also involves a *critical moment,* we have to consider several pieces of evidence. Heidegger opposes both juncture and decision to the system (81, 88–90). He also claims that historical readiness for be-ing replaces systematic deduction (242). Juncture must involve such historical readiness—as is confirmed by the saying that joining is devoted to the enigma of history (274). Similarly, "The juncture is the enjoining that complies to the call and thus grounds being-there" for the sake of a "still possible transformation of Western history" (82). *Fuge,* then, is clearly supposed to involve a decisive inception, a critical moment—for crisis and emergency let history begin or decline (45). The *Contributions* are situated at this juncture, this transition, where we glimpse the possibility of the other inception. This moment of crisis gives the text its unity and determines its "joinings" or "junctures" (*Fügungen*). As Heidegger puts it, the structure of the *Contributions* is "drawn from the still unmastered fundamental outline of the historicity of the transition itself" (6). The text proves to have a *dramatic* unity; it consists of several acts in a play whose plot concerns the foundation of the site for the transition to the other inception (82).[97] Let us see how this works.

---

95. On the quasi-musical character of the *Contributions* see Brogan, "Da-sein and the Leap of Being," 172–73; Richardson, "Dasein and the Ground of Negativity," 37; Ruin, "Contributions to Philosophy," 361; Iain Thomson, "The Philosophical Fugue: Understanding the Structure and Goal of Heidegger's *Beiträge,*" *Journal of the British Society for Phenomenology* 34, no. 1 (January 2003): 59–63; Wood, "Fugal Lines," 255, 266.

96. Cf. GA 65, 4, 18, 45, 81. Surprisingly, the *Contributions* make no use of the archaic word *Fug,* "proper fittingness," which plays an important part in *Introduction to Metaphysics* as a rendition of *dike: Introduction to Metaphysics,* 171.

97. Hans Ruin's phrase "kairological writing" applies well to the *Contributions: Enigmatic Origins,* 208; "The Moment of Truth: *Augenblick* and *Ereignis* in Heidegger," *Epoché* 6, no. 1 (1998):

Part 1, "Preview," is an overture—an approach to the task ahead. While it touches on all the elements of appropriation, the emphasis is on the challenge that faces philosophy as inceptive, reticent thinking, and on the "decisions" that confront us at this historical moment.

Part 2, *Der Anklang* ("The Resonance" or "The Echo"), characterizes our current situation as an emergency. Modernity is described in terms of machination, nihilism, and the scientific oblivion of be-ing. Our world is one of technological objectivism and its concomitant subjectivism. Quality has become quantity (135); reproducibility has supplanted singularity and belonging. This experience of emergency provides the motivation for the gestures that are to follow. The moods here are alarm and awe that arise from restraint (107).

Part 3, *Das Zuspiel* ("The Interplay" or "The Pass," as in a ball game), turns to the first inception and its ramifications in order to awaken the question of be-ing in a retrieval of and confrontation with the tradition. Heidegger says somewhat surprisingly that the guiding mood here is one of delight (169), the excitement of the recovery and discovery of the problems that underlie the tradition. However, he also tells us that the "necessity" of the pass comes from "the resonance of the emergency of the abandonment of being" (82); this juncture is a response to the urgency uncovered in the previous juncture.

Fresh from the confrontation with the first inception, Part 4, "The Leap," ventures to name the fundamental traits of be-ing in the other inception. Here we find key thoughts on be-ing, the nothing, and essential happening. In its mood, this part is daring, but not aggressive or reckless, because it is constantly attuned by awe toward the mystery of be-ing (227).

Part 5, "The Grounding," follows "The Leap": since be-ing cannot serve as a metaphysical ground but is instead an abyss, our foundation must grow from an *Ur-sprung* or primal leap. What is founded is being-there—the site or "there" where be-ing needs to take place. "The Grounding" explores what is required of being-there in the other inception. Also included in this part are the themes of truth and time-space; these are intimately connected to the theme of being-there, for truth (unconcealment) requires being-there as the time-space, the "site of the moment," where it happens.

Parts 6 and 7, "The Future Ones" and "The Final God," are brief intimations of what is to come—those few creative leaders who make the leap thanks to their insistence in being-there, and the god whose "hints" may greet them (82). Here Heidegger is at his most prophetic.

---

84. The *kairos* is a critical moment or turning point. For its importance in Heidegger's earlier work, see Kisiel, *The Genesis of Heidegger's "Being and Time,"* Index of Subject Matter, s.v. "kairology."

"Be-ing," originally designed as the second part of the text, casts its net wide and serves as a review. The emphasis, however, is on the fundamentals: the project of bethinking and the essence of be-ing.

This sequence of "junctures," or acts in the drama of the crisis, is certainly not a system. We should not overstate its unity, either; many of the connections are somewhat tenuous, and parts of the text still do resemble a quarry whose blocks have fallen at random. However, the junctural order shines through. Ultimately, all the junctures try to say "the same about the same," but from different domains of appropriation (82). The junctures are all moments within the overarching moment of crisis.

The structure of the *Contributions* is not "logical"—it does not prove a series of propositions. Instead, it is a deeply historical structure, in keeping with Heidegger's conviction that be-ing itself is historical. "What is said, is asked and thought in the 'interplay' of the first and the other inception, from the 'resonance' of be-ing in the emergency of the abandonment of being, for the 'leap' into be-ing, to the 'grounding' of its truth as a preparation for the 'future ones' 'of the final god'" (7).

What remains to be said is that these junctures are not merely formal modes of presentation, not just stylistic features of Heidegger's text; they also concern the substance of what he has to say. We saw that he explains *Fuge* in terms of a dedication to the "fullness" of be-ing itself (81), and that he wants to grasp "be-ing in the joining of those junctures" (64). Be-ing itself deploys itself in these moments when history happens as the event of appropriation.

3

Straits of Appropriation

O ur basic account of appropriation is in place, as is our investigation of Heidegger's way of thinking. Our main findings can be recalled as follows. The *Contributions* respond to the problem of how the being of beings is given to us. Heidegger consistently approaches this problem in terms of ways of belonging that precede theoretical abstraction. In the *Contributions*, his goal is to think in a way that participates in be-ing (the giving of the being of beings) as a unique, possible event of owning. To bethink be-ing is to take part in the founding of the there—the event that makes possible all our interpretations of ourselves and other beings.

These leading features of the *Contributions* open up a wide range of problems. Since every page of the text is a resourceful and suggestive attempt to confront these problems, a thorough commentary would have to pass painstakingly through each section. This chapter tries to do both less and more. It will not interpret all the relevant passages in detail (although I pause for a close reading of the crucial §242). Instead, it tries to focus on the central issues, to find some interpretive keys to them, and to take a few independent steps beyond Heidegger's statements.

As we saw at the end of chapter 2, the *Contributions* have a "junctural" structure centered on the transition from the first to the other inception. First, Heidegger tries to show the need for such a transition by describing the present as an age of the oblivion of be-ing; he then prepares the way for the transition by confronting the first inception. I will generally avoid commenting on the more polemical aspects of Heidegger's account of the tradition and modernity, on the assumption that what matters most in his polemics is the positive vision that motivates them. This vision is articulated in parts 4–7 of the *Contributions*, where he dares to leap into be-ing and find a new ground for being-there. These passages try to set the other inception into motion, and they raise the complex of problems that I will be considering now.

What happens in the other inception? The event of be-ing appropriates being-there; being-there grounds time-space; within this time-space, being-there shelters the truth of be-ing in beings; the gods or "the final god" then have an opportunity to make a difference to us. My interpretations, then, will begin with be-ing (its self-concealment, its relation to the nothing, its "fissure"); next I turn to being-there (the relation between be-ing and being-there, the relation between being-there and man, the problems of selfhood, leaping, and grounding); I then consider time-space and the relation between be-ing and beings (including "sheltering" and "simultaneity"); finally, I discuss the gods. This order of presentation is close to Heidegger's, although he devotes a separate division, 5(c), to truth; I have found it less redundant to incorporate this theme into my discussion of the others.

We must try to think of these issues not as eternal traits of some universal pattern, but as problematic points in a juncture, a critical event. Heidegger economically suggests the event-character of his central mood, restraint, by emphasizing the *Zug* ("trait," but also "train," "pull," or "current") in *Grundzug*, creating a term that could be translated as "fundamental *pull*" (17). In English we could say that the features of appropriation are not its properties, but its appropriating and expropriating emergencies; not predicates, but predicaments; not traits, but straits.

Be-ing: The Withdrawal, the Abyss, and the Fissure

We have said a number of things in general about be-ing, but we now need to leap into its straits. These include be-ing's self-concealment or withdrawal, its essential relation to the abyss of the nothing, and its "fissure" into several dimensions of the event of appropriation, such as urgency, mastery, and singularity.

The Withdrawal of Be-ing

What if be-ing itself is "self-withdrawing" and essentially happens as "refusal"? What if this refusal is the highest kind of donation (246)? With this thought, Heidegger approaches the concealment (*Verbergung*) of be-ing—a topic we have touched on before in terms of the intrinsic esotericism of the *Contributions* and their "sigetic" style. When the *Contributions* claim that be-ing is intrinsically self-concealing, they seem to have left behind both Husserl and *Being and Time*. This position no longer seems to be phenomenology at all. It may even seem to reduce be-ing to an elusive *entity*, an entity whose hiddenness can never be confirmed phenomenologically—some sort of arbitrarily posited *deus absconditus*.

To avoid this misinterpretation, we must first see that Heidegger is not claiming that be-ing is *utterly* hidden—it can, after all, "appropriate" us. We should not picture this as a condition in which be-ing, like a thing, gets partially uncovered—a sort of ontological peek-a-boo. Instead, be-ing shows itself to us *as* concealed—or, better, its very self-concealment is the supreme gift (246, 267; GA 66, 295). By withdrawing or giving way, be-ing gives *us* a way to be there and to find a proper relation to beings.[1]

An ontic analogy may help. A mother is sewing a simple dress for her daughter. The estranged father, meanwhile, has spent all he has on a beautiful store-bought dress. But he eventually decides not to give the dress to his daughter, but to tell her that he cannot give her anything. By withholding the dress, he gives a greater gift to both the mother and the daughter—not a material present, but the opportunity for the daughter to appreciate the mother's act of giving.[2] Similarly, by withholding itself from us, be-ing allows us to extend beyond that which is given—given entities and even the given sense of their being—and attend to the event of giving. The thankfulness of thinking—to borrow a theme that emerges shortly after the *Contributions*—is grateful not for the gift, but for the *giving*, which gives itself in its self-concealment.

The proper response to this withholding-as-giving is not to try to possess it or make it present. We can establish the right relation to be-ing—and step into being-there—only if we learn to renounce the desire for presence. This renunciation permits an annunciation of the "refusal" (*Verweigerung*). The "knowledge of refusal" (63) is not a getting or having, but allows the self-concealing to come forth as such. This is the "resonance of be-ing as refusal in being's abandonment of beings" (108). A resonance is the manifestation of an absence, a giving of withdrawal. To learn to hear the resonance is to step into telling silence.

But what justifies us in looking for a "giving" at all? Why not remain con-

---

1. In this way, freedom becomes possible. "In order that something may truly be given-over as a gift . . . [the giver] must inconspicuously withdraw in the giving, for the sake of the freedom of what is given": Holger Helting, "Heidegger und Meister Eckehart," in *"Herkunft aber bleibt stets Zukunft": Martin Heidegger und die Gottesfrage*, ed. Paola-Ludovica Coriando (Frankfurt am Main: Vittorio Klostermann, 1998), 87.

2. This story comes from an episode of the television drama *Homicide*. I thank Julia and Tom Davis for a conversation in which we explored this analogy.

tent with what is given? Here our ultimate "justification" is not a rational one, but an experience of emergency. We experience a crisis—or some of us do—when we recognize that our sense of the being of beings is limited and contingent. We ask how it comes to pass that this sense of being, and not some other, has been granted to us. This question leads us to search for an event of giving, an event that cannot itself be given.

Perhaps all philosophy begins with an experience of contingency, a felt need for a justification or explanation that would provide a ground for something. The danger is that this project will drown the contingency in necessity, leading us to forget the original experience. Heidegger's project is different. While respecting the impulse that drives us toward a primal source, he thinks of this source as an un-ground or abyss that is itself radically contingent. The effect is to heighten the urgency of the original experience rather than to cover it over.[3]

However, Heidegger often implies that be-ing *has* to withdraw. This suggests an insight into a necessity, which calls for an elucidation. But would an explanation of be-ing's obscurity violate this obscurity? Would it impose crassly on the mystery? Perhaps not. It could be that, while respecting the esotericism of Heidegger's text and his topic, we can reveal a few of the grounds for his claims.[4] Be-ing's self-concealment seems to have several modes, not all of which can be considered necessary or inescapable. Some seem to be contingent features of Western history; others are intrinsic features of everydayness, but we can emerge from this everydayness, at least for a while; finally, some are inescapable aspects of be-ing itself and can never be overcome, even if we can glimpse the reasons why we cannot overcome them. This classification of modes of concealment will work well enough to allow us to carry out our search for grounds. Still, we should remember that the "traits" of be-ing are really straits—and that all necessity, Heidegger insists, is grounded in emergency. (As we will soon see, he even tries to find an al-

---

3. In this respect Heidegger is akin to the late Schelling, who tries to think through the original givenness of beings and their sense without effacing their contingency. Schelling elegantly characterizes the object of his thought as the *Urzufall*, the primal contingency or accident: *On the History of Modern Philosophy*, trans. Andrew Bowie (Cambridge: Cambridge University Press, 1994), 116. For both thinkers, the question "Why is there something instead of nothing?" retains its urgency and pathos, because it is a meaningful question that can never adequately be answered. As Otto Pöggeler observes, *Ereignis* happens contingently: for example, "Every pure work of art . . . lets the history of Truth be seen as that which possibly might not have been, i.e. as event (*Ereignis*)": "'Historicity' in Heidegger's Late Work," trans. J. N. Mohanty, *Southwestern Journal of Philosophy* 4 (1973): 63 (translation modified). In this sense it can be said that *Ereignis* is a "miracle": Aldo Magris, "I concetti fondamentali dei 'Beiträge' di Heidegger," *Annuario Filosofico* 8 (1992): 248.

4. For another attempt to explore the theme of be-ing's self-concealment—and a refreshing admission of its difficulty—see Stambaugh, *The Finitude of Being*, esp. 111.

ternative to the traditional doctrine of the modalities—necessity, actuality, and possibility.) Although we may detect some relative necessities, our thought must still be guided by an urgency and affliction that cannot be explained away by a theoretical scheme. The urgency is itself contingent: it stems from the experience of thrownness (45). If we were not thrown into an emergency, be-ing and being-there would never happen at all; then there would be no question of seeking necessities within this happening.

Now we can review the various modes of be-ing's self-concealment, moving from the relatively contingent to the relatively necessary. The most contingent concealment seems to be the "oblivion of being" that infects Western thought from early on. This seems to be a happening that could have been otherwise, a happening that pertains to one unique course of history. The root of this oblivion is the abandonment of be-ing. Heidegger's accounts of this original fall do not always maintain a clear distinction between being and be-ing (page 114 speaks of both *Seinsverlassenheit* and *Seynsverlassenheit*). Presumably he means that because be-ing abandoned us (did not come into question for us), we were unable to experience the being of beings as a question. We made a distinction between beings and their being, and even described this being, but we did not ask sufficiently about its source. Humanity was unable to master the difficult art of turning back from being to beings while keeping being in question (453).

Perhaps this failure was not completely contingent: it was necessary in order to establish the initial distinction between beings and their being. In order to grasp the *idea*, or the beingness of beings, the Greeks had to remain oblivious to be-ing (453). If this is so, then without the abandonment of be-ing we would never have become philosophical and scientific at all. Here is one way in which abandonment proves to be a gift.

Is there also an *inherent* tendency for be-ing to abandon us? There does, at least, seem to be an inherent tendency to become absorbed in beings at the expense of their being. This tendency is part of what *Being and Time* called falling (SZ §§35–38). The being of beings makes it possible for us to encounter beings; for that very reason, it cannot be grasped as if it were itself an entity, and it tends to remain in the background.[5] In sections 177 and 201 of the *Contributions*, Heidegger thinks of this tendency as "being-away"; it is an "essential," "necessary" way in which humans relate to being-there (302). This may sound exactly like *Being and Time*, but note that humans and being-there are separate here. Instead of speaking of authenticity and inauthenticity as modes of being-there, where being-there is assumed to be equivalent to humanity, Heidegger now seems to identify humanity with in-

---

5. *Basic Questions of Philosophy*, 178.

authentic being-away, and being-there with authenticity (323). The "necessity" of falling or being-away is, so to speak, a contingent necessity: it is necessary only as long as we fall short of genuine ownness. In *Being and Time*, even if we attain authenticity, we are doomed to fall back into inauthenticity for the most part, because the tendency to fall is a basic existential characteristic of being-there. The *Contributions* seem to entertain the rather utopian prospect that inauthenticity might be left behind.

Even if we leave fallenness behind, however—in brief or protracted episodes of authenticity—we have no hope of making be-ing perfectly accessible. As we saw when we considered telling silence, Heidegger claims that "every saying already speaks *from* the truth of be-ing and can never directly leap over itself to get to be-ing itself" (79). This is a still more necessary concealment. As the background to all presentation and representation, be-ing eludes all attempts to picture it. We can never completely control or understand be-ing, for all possibilities of control and understanding grow out of be-ing as an event that exceeds them. Just as a snake swallowing its tail can never make itself disappear, our understanding can never get its sources totally into its view in such a way as to conquer them and make them superfluous.

This predicament pertains to what Heidegger calls "earth." The word points to the limitations of all orders of intelligibility. Truth happens only in the strife between world and earth; genuine unconcealment requires both intelligibility and unintelligibility. When we recognize the limits of our understanding, this understanding becomes more intense and more heedful—so we can renew the world by rescuing the earth (412). This renewing power is found in artworks, which have the paradoxical capacity to reveal the hidden *as hidden*.[6] The *Contributions* extend this insight beyond art, to all the great accomplishments of being-there—creations, acts, and sacrifices (349, 391). The strife between earth and world is thus essential to being-there (72, 322), to history (96, 275), to language (510), and to be-ing itself as appropriation (29, 34).

In what respect is the earth hidden or unintelligible? "Earth" has to do with our immersion in the multiplicity of given beings, beings that are not exhausted by our current interpretations of the being of beings. In this sense, earth is nature—not nature as it is studied by natural science, which has already interpreted its basic features, but nature as the mystery that sustains all interpretations (91, 277–78). Heidegger asks us to experience our depen-

---

6. "The Origin of the Work of Art," in *Off the Beaten Track*, 25. As Richardson puts it, there is a "subversive element" in truth, the concealment that haunts it: "Dasein and the Ground of Negativity," 48.

dence on this mystery as part of be-ing, part of how the being of beings is itself given. The import of beings as such comes to pass only for us, and we ourselves are beings who are "besieged" by the other beings that throng around us (481–82).[7] Our condition, then, is one of openness to beings as beings, but also one of indebtedness to the obscure earth (259).

As we saw in chapter 1, Heidegger views this insight—that thrownness and "earth" are essential to be-ing itself—as a decisive step beyond transcendentalism (231, 239, 259, 448). A transcendental approach would hold that the being of beings must be given in our understanding prior to all beings, because it is impossible to experience beings unless the being of beings is already in place. Heidegger now replies that even though our understanding of beings would be impossible without the being of beings, understanding always grows from and rests on an opacity that continues to resist our interpretations. The givenness of beings, then, is not reducible to the being of beings as we understand it. Heidegger is thus at pains to avoid thinking of "projection" transcendentally, in terms of forms of representation that enable us to encounter objects (447). The notion of the "understanding of being" in *Being and Time* was ambiguous between such a transcendental faculty and the thrown grounding of the there (455). Now we must be clear that projection, properly speaking, is not a condition of possibility for representation, but a thrown clearing (448).[8]

But how does such a clearing first emerge? As we have seen, Heidegger answers this question in terms of a radical and unique inception. This involves a further dimension of self-concealment: inceptions are inexplicable (188). Explaining, providing grounds, can succeed only *within* the order of unconcealment opened up by the inception. This means that the inception, be-ing itself, cannot be grounded—it is an "abyss" that can never be articulated conclusively (460). All articulating and defining presuppose an inceptive event that eludes definition.[9] It follows that the happening of be-ing cannot be guaranteed, mastered, or founded metaphysically on some absolute entity or certainty. Here, if we may use these terms, we find a kind of necessity that

7. We can see the beginnings of this standpoint in Heidegger's 1928 concept of "metontology": *The Metaphysical Foundations of Logic*, 156–58. Metontology means thinking about beings as a whole, in so far as our thrownness into beings is a precondition for the emergence of the sense of their being.

8. This is why Friedrich-Wilhelm von Herrmann proposes *"re*-writing" *Being and Time*'s analytic of being-there "in the perspective of *Ereignis*": Emad, "A Conversation," 149. The "core structure" of *Ereignis* involves "the appropriated projection from out of the appropriating-throw" (ibid., 156; cf. 163–64).

9. As Beistegui puts it, what is "individuated" is only "the visible side of the invisible essence of truth": *Truth and Genesis*, 127. The event by virtue of which individual, clear characteristics emerge is not itself accessible as a clear phenomenon.

springs from contingency: the giving of the being of beings is contingent, and for this very reason we are necessarily unable to give a ground for it or represent it conclusively.

We could also put it this way: the happening in which the being of beings is *given* cannot itself be given, because this event of be-ing sets the parameters for what givenness itself means. The giving of givenness cannot be given. If it were, that would imply a sense of givenness that outranked the event of the granting of this sense, which is impossible. When we hold and behold beings in their being, as a given gift, we are beholden to a giving that is itself self-withholding, that cannot give itself.

Many of these aspects of the withdrawal of be-ing are ingredients in Heidegger's meditation on truth as "the clearing for self-concealing" (348–49). Clearing and concealing are intertwined in the genuine happening of unconcealment, the happening in which "appropriation becomes truth" (349). If we forget about the concealment in *a-letheia*, truth loses its depth and its abyssal essence (332). Concealment preserves be-ing against the indifferent obviousness of inauthentic understanding, for which the availability of things is unproblematic. Furthermore, if we pay attention to mystery, we can treat individual beings appropriately—"according to the directive that belongs to each of them" (348). We will look more closely at this suggestion when we consider the relation between concealment and sheltering.

Be-ing and the Nothing

Another way to approach the withdrawal or self-concealment of be-ing is in terms of "the nothing" (*das Nichts*) or the "not." Negativity dwells in the heart of be-ing (246, 267). This "not-granting" (8) is not simply a lack or absence, but also a *giving* (246; cf. 267 and GA 66, 295). Heidegger struggles to express this combination of donation and withdrawal: "The ripeness is pregnant with the originary 'not'" (268, cf. 410).[10]

But the nothing is not only the self-concealment of be-ing; it takes various forms in accordance with different moments of the essential happening of be-ing (410). In fact, *das Nichts* is one of the most flexible and ambiguous words in Heidegger's repertoire.[11] Let us consider some of its major appearances in the *Contributions*.

First, the nothing is not reducible to negation as a logical function (410).

---

10. The notion of a pregnant emptiness is developed in GA 65, 379–82.

11. For accounts of the *Contributions'* sayings on being and the nothing in the context of Heidegger's development and the philosophical tradition, see Alessandra Cover, "Essere e negatività nei 'Beiträge zur Philosophie' di M. Heidegger: Linee per uno sviluppo del problema dalle prime lezioni friburghesi alla *Abhandlung 'Hegel. 1. Die Negativität'* (1938/39, 1941)," *Verifiche* 22, nos. 3–4 (July–December 1993): 319–63; Polt, "The Question of Nothing."

As Heidegger had argued in "What is Metaphysics?" propositional negation and affirmation are merely surface phenomena. They depend on a prior givenness of beings in their being (247).[12] However, there may be a deeper sense of affirmation and negation: those who dismiss talk of the nothing as nihilistic are incapable of "essential, 'creative' yes-saying" (246). Here the echo of Nietzsche is unmistakable—but is it misleading? The answer depends on how one reads Nietzsche—and Heidegger's own readings of Nietzsche range from appreciation to denunciation.[13] Nietzschean yes-saying can be read as a glorification of the will to power and an insistence on *beings* as eternally recurring; in this case, there is hardly any sign in Nietzsche of a Heideggerian openness to *be-ing*. However, Nietzschean yes-saying may also be an embrace of the here and now and a rejection of the ahistorical realm of metaphysical absolutes. In this case, Nietzsche is not far from Heidegger's "insistence" and his rejection of the *eidos* in favor of appropriation. Be this as it may, the distinctively Heideggerian aspect of his "yes-saying" is gratitude for the giving of the being of beings—a gratitude that acknowledges the self-withdrawal of this giving.[14]

In addition to this withdrawal, "the nothing" points to the *difference* of be-ing from all beings. Be-ing, as we can say in English, is *no thing*. Heidegger claims at one point that this sense of the nothing is relatively trivial (*nichtig*); rather than appreciating the happening of be-ing itself, it limits itself to the assertion that be-ing is not an entity (246). But another passage finds more depth in the "no-thingness" of be-ing: be-ing is unfamiliar (*ungewöhnlich*, 480–81).[15] In part, this is because in our age, beings and being-there have been "expropriated" (*enteignet*) from be-ing (120, 231). But it is not just that we are not used or habituated (*gewohnt*) to be-ing. Be-ing is *intrinsically* unfamiliar: it has to exceed our habitation (*Wohnung*). Be-ing essentially happens as estrangement, *Befremdung* (27, 230, 241, 249, 283, 347, 406). This line of thought brings the concept of anxiety into the *Contributions*. Anxiety *ent-setzt*: it terrifies and alienates, but by the same token, it sets us free from our fixation in beings. Anxiety is crucial to the event of be-ing as appropriation: "Be-ing *ent-setzt* in that it appropriates being-there" (483; cf. 470, 482). Only by remaining open to the unfamiliarity of be-ing can we find some

12. Perhaps for similar reasons, Heidegger makes "otherness" subordinate to the nothing that holds sway within be-ing itself (GA 65, 267). This is an implicit rebuke to the attempt in Plato's *Sophist* (258b) to derive nonbeing from otherness.

13. See the lectures and essays collected in Heidegger's *Nietzsche*. The most condemnatory piece is probably "Nietzsche's Metaphysics," in *Nietzsche*, vol. 3, 187–251.

14. Heidegger's "yes" is not an "agreement [*Zu-'stimmung'*] to something present at hand, but attunement to the voice of stillness [*Gestimmtheit auf die Stimme der Stille*]" (GA 66, 312).

15. Heidegger's two assessments of be-ing as "no thing" reflect his ambivalence toward the "ontological difference." See below, p. 193.

liberation from the beings that "besiege" us (481–82) and discover that we are ourselves "strangers" (487).

It seems paradoxical to claim that appropriation, the very happening of *ownness*, involves alienation and expropriation, or dis-owning (*Ent-eignung*: GA 66, 312; GA 70, 121–23). But we can never be at home with appropriation, precisely because appropriation first *establishes* our home. Appropriation itself can never *be* what is fully one's own, precisely because it *provides* ownness. In order to be completely habituated to what is one's own, one must take it for granted; to experience the *giving* of it is to loosen its bonds. This is not an escape from beings, but an opportunity to dwell among them in a way that appreciates appropriation as a contingent event, and thus freely and authentically to inhabit what is one's own.[16]

Death, too, is a point of access to appropriation. Death is not the mere absence of a present entity, but "the away" as the other of the there (324). Here as elsewhere, Heidegger proposes a symbiosis (and synthanasia) between there and away, be-ing and nothing, ground and abyss (325); unconcealment and belonging verge, and must verge, on darkness and estrangement. Death is the possibility of the impossibility of existence (SZ 250, 262). But if being-there is the thrown projector of be-ing, and to project is to open *possibilities*, then death also affects be-ing itself. Our ability to receive and cultivate the being of beings is never guaranteed, so being must be given contingently.[17] Be-ing excludes a final ground; it takes place "abyssally."

A powerful passage in *Besinnung* expands on the notion of "abyss" as the nothing within be-ing.

> *The nothing is the first and highest gift of be-ing,* the gift that be-ing as appropriation donates with and as itself to the clearing of the originary leap as abyssal ground [*Ab-grund*]. Abyssal ground is not meant metaphysically, [as] the mere *absence* of ground, but [as] the essential happening of the urgency of grounding, an urgency that is never a defect, and not an excess either, but rather the *that* [*das Daß*] of be-ing, which is superior to both defect and excess—the *that* of be-ing as the "that" of the "is." [GA 66, 295]

16. See the discussion of "belonging-yet-not-belonging" in chapter 1 above (p. 40). As Susan Schoenbohm puts it, be-ing "eventuates (as) a kind of double-movement, a drawing of thinking *both* into *and* back out of familiarity": "Reading Heidegger's *Contributions to Philosophy*," 25. Schürmann stresses expropriation throughout *Broken Hegemonies* (e.g., 587). The flaw in Blackburn's caricature of Heidegger as subscribing to the schema of a "golden age" of unity and a "fall" that instituted "estrangement" ("Enquivering," 44) is that for Heidegger, as much as for Hegel (if not more), estrangement is necessary and fruitful.

17. On death in the *Contributions* in relation to the philosophical tradition cf. Müller, *Der Tod als Wandlungsmitte*, §§11–18, §20. In *Broken Hegemonies*, Schürmann insists on the importance of mortality, which he identifies with the expropriation or "singularization to come" that undercuts all hegemonies (e.g., 25, 538, 582).

This passage confirms our interpretation of Heidegger's "be-ing": the question of be-ing is the question of the "that" (the giving) of the "is" (the being of beings). Be-ing *calls* for grounding in a way that is urgent, rather than logically necessary. If the grounding were logically necessary, then be-ing would have some sort of a priori guarantee. Instead, it happens contingently, in a decisive emergency, an originary leap. Be-ing essentially "trembles," and this trembling is the nothing (266); that is, be-ing evades every attempt to base it on an entity or a certainty. To leap into be-ing, then, is to open an abyssal ground, an area where entities can be recognized as indicating an event that is not an entity at all and can never be mastered.

As we have seen, the inceptive leap tends to fade into the background, to conceal itself behind beings. It can come to make (almost) no difference to us that there is something instead of nothing. We may become indifferent to the very question of being. Here we have one last meaning of "the nothing": indifference as "the *being of unbeings*, the *higher nothing*" (101). The nothing, in this sense, is the "essential decay" (*Ver-wesung*, 115) of import that tends to set in after the inception. This decline, too, belongs to the happening of be-ing.

The Fissure of Be-ing

By connecting be-ing to the nothing (in various senses) and thinking of be-ing as self-withdrawing, Heidegger attempts to think of a dynamic deeper than any metaphysical analysis of the being of beings. Nevertheless, in some of the most open-ended sections of the *Contributions* he experiments with rough parallels to elements of traditional metaphysics. He responds to the idea of the great chain of being with a meditation on be-ing's *Stufen* (stages, levels, or strata) (§§152–55), and to the doctrine of modalities with his thoughts on be-ing's *Zerklüftung* (fissure or rift) (§127, §§156–59).

Heidegger claims that the traditional concepts of possibility, actuality, and necessity are outgrowths of the fundamental experience of the being of beings in the first inception: being as *physis* (281) and *ousia* (244). Supporting this claim would take nothing less than a metaphysical history of the modalities—a history that would encompass not only philosophical concepts but the manifold ways in which the West deploys power, determines truth, and conforms to laws. We can hardly do this, but we can set down a few guidelines for such an interpretation. In the first inception, beings emerge with the sense of abiding presence. Anything short of presence is interpreted as on the way to or from presence, as indicating presence, or as imitating it. We thus have different "modalities" of being as presence. On this basis, we can also develop more superficial, logical theories of modality (a possible truth can be expressed in a noncontradictory proposition, a necessary truth cannot be denied without contradiction).

The modal multiplicity of presence is apparent in Aristotle's theory of actuality and potentiality.[18] Aristotle affirms the being of potentiality (*Met.*Θ 3, Δ 7) but also assigns it a certain nonbeing (*Met.* N 2 1089a25). It is subordinate in several ways to actuality, which is the fulfillment (*entelecheia*) or being-at-work (*energeia*) of potential (*Met.* Θ 8). Potential intrinsically points to its fulfillment, to the actualization of a form. To move is to activate this potential, to get on the way to fulfillment, so motion is the actuality of the potential as potential (*Physics* 3.1). These principles are reflected in Aristotle's ethics of self-actualization, his aristocratic politics, his nonevolutionary biology, his teleological physics, and his intellectualist theology.

In modernity the metaphysical history of modality takes a turn, in that potentiality is liberated from actuality in a certain sense. "Energy" no longer means the actualization of a form, but the potential to do work; work is conceived in terms of motion as change of place, rather than as the fulfilling of an essence. Energy is set free as power in an ateleological universe. It may be no exaggeration to say that this is the root of all distinctively modern phenomena: an ethics of freedom, liberal politics, evolutionary biology, a physics without final cause, and the death of God conceived as the most perfect (actual) being.[19]

Heidegger himself is "modern" in the sense that he rejects the Aristotelian priority of actuality over possibility, at least as regards human beings: assigning an objective goal to life is "*the* misunderstanding of human existence."[20] Our possibility is not inferior to actuality or necessity, but is "the most primordial and ultimate positive way in which being-there is characterized ontologically" (SZ 143–44). (This is the sense in which Heidegger's earlier thought can fairly be called "existentialist.") To exist as being-there is not to *actualize* a possibility but to maintain it as possible, to live in accordance with it as enabling one to be (SZ 143).

Of course, Heidegger is hardly a wholeheartedly modern thinker. Modernity, in his view, fails to escape the metaphysics of presence; power and motion are ways of being present, no less than Aristotelian *energeia*. Furthermore, by eliminating ends and forms from its worldview, modernity tends to reduce all phenomena to measurable and calculable objects. It also "liberates" humanity by conceiving of it as an utterly self-determining subject, overlooking thrownness and historicity.

18. For Heidegger, the concept of *energeia* or actuality is the key to Aristotle's thought: "On the Essence and Concept of *Physis* in Aristotle's *Physics* B, 1" (1939), trans. Thomas Sheehan, in *Pathmarks*, 216. Cf. Heidegger, *Aristotle's Metaphysics Θ 1–3: On the Essence and Actuality of Force*, trans. Walter Brogan and Peter Warnek (Bloomington: Indiana University Press, 1995), 153–55.

19. Richard Polt, "Potentiality, Energy, and Sway: From Aristotelian to Modern to Postmodern Physics?" *Existentia* 11 (2001): 27–41.

20. *The Metaphysical Foundations of Logic*, 185.

What is needed, then, is a step beyond both the ancients and the moderns, which must begin as a confrontation with the first inception. We must ask how the being of beings came to have the sense of presence, and how being is given in the first place. *Being and Time* was on the way to these questions, but it managed only to describe being-there, without reaching the happening of be-ing. For example, when it claimed that being-there's possibility is higher than actuality, it had to resort to traditional ontological concepts without explaining the origin of our understanding of being in general.

With the "fissure," the *Contributions* go farther than *Being and Time:* they indicate a plurality within the happening of be-ing itself, which is irreducible to presence (75). The traditional doctrine of modalities will be insufficient here, because it speaks only of necessity, actuality, and possibility as aspects of presence as the being of beings. We need a way of finding plurality within the *giving* of the being of beings. The doctrine of modalities can provide some inspiration for this project, but we must resist the temptation to draw up an ahistorical table of modalities in the traditional manner (237, 280). Ideally, we should also be able to understand how the traditional modalities are subordinate to the fissure of be-ing—without turning be-ing into a first cause in a metaphysical sense.

The need to perform these balancing acts accounts for the provisional tone of the discussions of the fissure in the *Contributions* and for their ambiguous attitude to the tradition. Heidegger asks that we creatively forget the familiar modes of beingness as we seek the structure of the fissure (278), but he himself cannot resist trying to employ the traditional words to name be-ing (cf. GA 66, 290). "Refusal (the essential happening of be-ing) is the highest actuality of the highest possible as possible, and thus the first necessity" (244); he speaks of "the uniqueness, freedom, contingency, necessity, possibility, and actuality of be-ing's essential happening" (237). He wants us to hear these old words not as traits, but as straits. They are flashpoints, rifts that emerge as the volcanic event of be-ing deploys itself.

What can we learn from the quasi-Aristotelian phrase "actuality of the highest possible as possible" (244, 294)? The phrase suggests that the withdrawal of be-ing is something like *kinesis*—"motion" as what reveals the potentiality of the potential, setting this potentiality to work. Be-ing, Heidegger suggests, preserves possibility without subordinating it to actuality (presence). Be-ing cannot be understood in terms of a *telos* that is to be made actual; it happens only when it retains its problematic, questionable character and is not subservient to a further goal. The self-withdrawal of be-ing is essential to maintaining this problematic character—so the fissure involves "refusal" (244) and "abyss" (278).

The metaphysical concepts of potentiality and actuality have their limitations, of course, especially when it comes to understanding the *historicity* of be-ing. These concepts, along with the traditional concept of movement, depend on an understanding of the being of beings as *ousia*—constant presence (280). For Heidegger, the historicity of be-ing is not primarily a matter of "movement"; instead, it essentially involves a leap and a decision.[21] The leap springs open the abyss of the fissure and thus the necessity of grounding being-there (9). What is at issue in the fissure is the dynamics of this decisive, grounding leap, including the emergency that motivates it (237).

The theme of *Not*—urgency, emergency, exigency, pressing need—is central to Heidegger's thinking in the 1930s. Two slogans run throughout the texts of this period: all necessity emerges from emergency (45, 97), and we are living in the age of the emergency of the lack of urgency (11, 107, 113, 119, 125, 234–37).[22] These slogans say that we have lost touch with the tensions that animate history and expose us to the emergency of be-ing. Heidegger takes an apocalyptic stance, in the dual sense of apocalypse as revelation and revolution.[23] The fresh, authentic disclosure of beings in their being requires an inceptive, critical moment—a moment in which our comfortable dwelling is called into question. Revelation demands revolution. Emergence needs emergency.

Heidegger hopes to break through the bland complacency of the day by revealing this very complacency as a crisis. This restoration of urgency calls for individuals who are subjected to urgency and can awaken others to the experience (26, 99).[24] If urgency is restored, we can emerge from the somnolence of metaphysics (429) and the deracination of contemporary culture (119). We can then experience the need to raise the question of be-ing and shelter the truth of be-ing in beings (96). Heidegger is not optimistic about the prospects for reawakening urgency through philosophical activity. Eliciting urgency is not a matter of announcing new doctrines, but of "deranging" humanity into an emergency. What we need is not contri-

21. On being-there as "movement," see Thomas Sheehan, "Dasein," in Dreyfus and Wrathall, *A Companion to Heidegger*, 205: because being-there is drawn into its absence, it "has always-already come into its own, but its own-ness is its human finitude." The limitation of Sheehan's interpretation as an approach to the *Contributions* is that, by casting being-there as an "always-already," it renders absurd the notion of a leap into being-there.

22. Cf. *Basic Questions of Philosophy*, 158, 175–77. The origin of the idea is Heidegger's analysis of his time as one of profound boredom: *The Fundamental Concepts of Metaphysics*, 160–67.

23. We could also say that Heidegger proposes "a 'catastrophic' conception of history," in which history is dissolved and renewed at moments of turning down and going-under (*katastrophe, Untergang*): Vincenzo Vitiello, "Seyn als Wesung: Heidegger e il nichilismo," *Aut Aut* 248–49 (March–June 1992): 78. On inception as *Untergang* cf. GA 70, 83–87; on this dynamic as "tragic" see GA 66, 223.

24. Those who rescue us from emergency—certainly. But rescuers *into* emergency—where are they? "Überlegungen" X, §12.

butions to philosophy, but appropriation—which requires expropriation (113, 119).

One of the *Contributions'* richest discussions of emergency is §17, from which I have taken the epigraph to this book. Essential urgency, writes Heidegger, consists in our thrownness into beings, which determines us as the throwers of be-ing (45). At critical moments of inception or transition, this urgency engenders a unique mood that attunes and determines human beings, urging them to surpass themselves in creative leaps that establish a ground for beings (46). The section ends with a series of questions. What if the pressing urgency of thrownness and projection were the very way in which be-ing itself happens? What if be-ing happened as emergency? What if, with a deeper and more urgent grounding of unconcealment, be-ing would take place more intensely, and come to pass as the appropriating event? What if the intensification of urgency were based on the innermost happening of be-ing in its intimate and mysterious connection to beings?[25] The *Contributions* as a whole are an exploration of this multiple "what if?"— an attempt to carry out a leap and a grounding of be-ing as inceptive emergency.

Another prominent feature of the fissure of be-ing is mastery (*Herrschaft*). The question of mastery concerns freedom and power. In their attitude to power, the *Contributions* stand between the *Introduction to Metaphysics* (1935), with its celebration of human "violence" and the overwhelming violence of being, and the condemnation of power found in *Besinnung* (1938–39) and later texts.[26] This striking reversal is presumably connected to Heidegger's disillusionment with the Nazi state, but it also has philosophical grounds: he comes to suspect that all notions of power are beholden to metaphysics. The

25. Elsewhere Heidegger says that emergency is the essential happening of be-ing because be-ing is what is most endangered—it is threatened by the semblance of being that each entity puts forth: "Überlegungen" IX, §78.

26. For a lucid account of this development see Fred Dallmayr, "Heidegger on *Macht* and *Machenschaft*," *Continental Philosophy Review* 34 (2001): 247–67. For a discussion of power in the *Contributions, Besinnung,* and the Nietzsche lectures see also Emad, "Mastery of Being and Coercive Force of Machination"; but Emad assumes that these texts all express the same position. *Introduction to Metaphysics* seems to be the height of Heidegger's embrace of the language of power (although the *Walten* or "sway" of being should not be confused with the overpowering of one entity by another). By the late 1930s, he is eager to distance himself from all concepts of power and violence: GA 66, 83, 187–88; GA 69, 62–84 (although the term "mastery" persists at GA 66, 16). The decisive philosophical factor in this change is probably his increasingly unsympathetic interpretation of Nietzsche (and of Jünger's "one-sided" Nietzscheanism: GA 90, 213); Heidegger concludes that the will to power is simply the last manifestation of traditional metaphysics. In a handwritten addendum to §96 of the *Contributions,* Heidegger criticizes his own phrase "the disempowerment of *physis*" because it suggests that *physis* is power in the sense of the will to power, whereas the will to power comes to power only through the "disempowerment" of *physis*.

Contributions, however, try to leave room for a kind of supremacy and might that is not merely manipulation.

Section 159 distinguishes mastery from both power (in a narrow sense) and violence. Mastery is "the origin that leaps forward" (281); it is "unconditionality in the realm of freedom" (282). It serves as an ongoing bequeathing (*Vermächtnis*, 281)—an origin that continues to provide a heritage. Mastery is needed whenever beings are to be transformed on the basis of be-ing. In short, the term *mastery* expresses the freedom and radicality of the inceptive leap that grounds a fresh donation of the being of beings. In contrast, power (*Macht*) stores up possibilities for violence in the face of an opposing power (282). Finally, violence (*Gewalt*) alters beings not on the basis of be-ing, but solely by means of other beings. An example of violence might be breaking a horse. Power is, for instance, the ability to break horses, combined with the other abilities that make an effective farmer. An example of mastery is, perhaps, Hesiod's *Works and Days*—a work that limns the possibilities and meanings of farming.

Mastery can also take the form of "masterful knowing" (43–44, 59, 62, 64, 281–82). Philosophy, as a questioning leap into be-ing, "masters all sheltering of the truth in beings and as beings" (44). As we have seen, thinking as bethinking is not merely *about* an inception, but *is* an inception; this originary force is the mastery in masterful knowing. This is why masterful knowing is typical of "the future ones" (386)—those who can found a new site.

Mastery retains the secret potency of an inception without needing power or violence (282). However, the final sentence of §159 suggests a possible harmony among the three: "Every act is an act of violence, to the extent that here violence is mastered in accordance with power" (282). Heidegger implies that an inceptive leap can take charge of power, manifesting itself in great deeds. In this case, an opening of new possibilities might not remain only on the level of poetry or thought, but could also take a political form. Section 25 explores this possible synergy between politics and thinking. Here Heidegger calls for two kinds of "mastery": a political mastery over the uprooted masses, and (as we might put it) a spiritual mastery that will establish new roots. As is typical in the texts of the mid-thirties, he claims authoritarian measures are necessary but insufficient. One must fight politically against liberal and egalitarian tendencies, but only spiritual leadership will establish a deeper "steadfastness" (62).

This brings us to another dimension of the fissure of be-ing: the split into the most extreme singularity and the most superficial reduction to commonality (62). This tension links Heidegger's political elitism to his philosophical attack on universals (343). Appropriation is the unique, nonreproducible event for the few and the rare—but it generates a realm of reproducibility in which a sense of the being of beings is common to everything and is taken for granted by all the inhabitants of the realm. Both uniqueness and universality are proper to be-ing.[27]

The political dimension here makes it easy to read the faults of the fissure in anthropological terms. Humans are faced not just with necessity, but with urgency. They have not just possibility, but mastery and freedom. They have both unique and ordinary experiences—and so on. But Heidegger would insist that the fissure concerns *be-ing*. Be-ing, of course, is an event that involves us—if we are capable of being-there. But the event does not happen "inside" us; it opens the world *for* us as including certain ways of being. This means that the fissure is not only different from traditional modalities, but prior to them. The necessity, actuality, and possibility of present-at-hand entities are merely aspects of their being—and this being becomes an issue for us only if we engage in a masterful, singular leap in response to urgency.

The *Contributions'* treatment of death, as we saw, is a clear example of Heidegger's attempt to give "existential," seemingly anthropological phenomena a role in the happening of be-ing itself. Death is the ultimate testimony to the negativity of be-ing (230, 284). The singularity and strangeness of mortal existence expose the singularity and strangeness of be-ing, revealing "the collision of necessity and possibility" in the granting of meaning itself. "Only in such areas" can one suspect what is really at stake in the "pallid and empty *mishmash* of the 'modalities'" (283). When we relate to entities as what *is, can be, or must be*, we can do so only because our ability to be has to be bounded by the possibility of the impossibility of existing—and these are not just facts about *homo sapiens*, but dimensions that open only for those who take a leap into being-there.[28]

This leap is also a leap into the "godding" of the gods, a happening that requires "the most abyssal fissure" (244). In appropriation, man and god are assigned to each other. This event separates out into rifts: "What comes into its own here is refusal and staying away, onset and accident, restraint and transfiguration, freedom and coercion" (280). We will reserve our interpretation of the gods until the end of this chapter. As a first clue, however, we can say that Heidegger's "godding," unlike Aristotle's divine *noesis*, cannot be sheer actuality. It surpasses the traditional modalities because it takes part in the happening of be-ing—a happening that exceeds presence and bursts forth in the fissure.

27. Cf. *Basic Concepts*, 43–44.
28. David Crownfield nicely sums up some of these dimensions of being-there: "the utter gratuity in which being-there occurs for the time being rather than nothing at all; the inescapable exigency, for each of us, of accepting the incomprehensible task of being-there; the constant hemorrhage of unachieved possibilities": "The Last God," 214.

Being-there: The Happening of Ownness

The word *Dasein* is the most prominent piece of terminology that the *Contributions* preserve from *Being and Time*. Heidegger now hyphenates it in order to stress its root meaning. "Being-there" suggests a distinctive way of *inhabiting a place*, of standing in or "withstanding" the there (320). It is also a way of *being the there* (being-there "is" its own clearing or openness, in a "transitive" sense: 296). Finally, being-there is *the there for being* (the site where being can be given, the place that be-ing takes when it takes place).

Whereas in *Being and Time* being-there seemed identical to the entity man,[29] now being-there is not a given entity at all (GA 70, 29), but a *possibility* for man—the possibility of participating creatively in the emergence of the difference between something and nothing. Be-ing cannot happen without being-there, and being-there is not itself unless it responds to be-ing. Heidegger calls this mutual dependence "the turn" (407). Our ordinary self-interpretation fails to recognize the turn: we take ourselves as one kind of entity without asking how the being of entities is given to us—that is, searching for be-ing—and without interpreting ourselves as the ones whose most proper task is precisely to carry out this search (17). A central purpose of the *Contributions* is to alert us to this task, to incite us to make it our own. Although Heidegger distrusts the language of "goals" (138, 477), he himself ambitiously intends "to give historical man a goal once again: *to become the grounder and preserver [Wahrer] of the truth [Wahrheit] of be-ing, to be* the there as the ground that is required by the essence of be-ing itself: *care*" (16). Heidegger's thought is meant to "prepare that humanity" that will "empower be-ing" (430).

How does the reciprocity between be-ing and being-there, the "turn," come to pass? Would it be fair to call the notion of the turn a type of anthropocentrism? What is the relation between being-there and human beings? How would urgency urge human beings into a "decision" and a "leap" into being-there? Does this decision have anything in common with ordinary choices? How does the leap open up an abyssal ground? What does it mean to attain selfhood through such leaping? What is the relation between the few "future ones" who participate in the leap and the many who may follow? Can an entire nation achieve selfhood and attain the status of being-there? As we explore these questions, we will necessarily revisit some topics that have come up in our discussion of be-ing—necessarily, because

---

29. Against the preponderance of interpretations, Claudius Strube claims that *Being and Time* already implied a project of *transforming* man into being-there: *Das Mysterium der Moderne: Heideggers Stellung zur gewandelten Seins- und Gottesfrage* (Munich: Wilhelm Fink, 1994), 97–99.

the turn makes be-ing and being-there essential collaborators in the event of appropriation.

Be-ing and Being-there: The Turn

"The fundamental thought of my thinking is precisely that being, or the manifestation of being, *needs* human beings and that, vice versa, human beings are human beings only if they are standing in the manifestation of being."[30] This is how Heidegger puts things in a rare attempt to speak as straightforwardly as possible to a large audience, his televised interview with Richard Wisser in 1969. But just how straightforward is this statement? Much depends on the meaning of "manifestation" (*Offenbarkeit*). Does Heidegger mean that there is also a nonmanifest aspect of the being of beings, and that this aspect does *not* need human beings? This would surely be wrong. The entities given to us may well be independent of us, but the sense of their givenness requires some sense-grasping entity. Maybe, then, in speaking of "the manifestation of being," Heidegger was simply trying to avoid a misinterpretation of "being" as referring to entities. "Manifestation of being" would be a redundant expression.

This interpretation works well from the point of view of *Being and Time*, where Heidegger investigates the reciprocity between being-there (the entity who essentially understands being) and being (the sense of beings, which is essentially given only to being-there). But does this interpretation still work for the *Contributions*, where the issue at stake is *be-ing*? Heidegger's 1969 statement might also describe the *Contributions* if we are willing to stretch the sense of *Offenbarkeit*. Can we think of "manifestation" not as a static structure that is always already in place as long as human beings exist, but as an event of revelation?[31] Heidegger would then be saying that the being of beings can be manifested (given) in an event only if human beings rise to the occasion and become truly "human" (enter being-there); conversely, being-there requires us to "stand in the manifestation of being," where "standing" is not static, but means *taking* a stand steadfastly—adopting the stance that the *Contributions* call "insistence." Being cannot be given to us unless we take it. This interpretation also allows us to restore an intrinsic mystery: as we have seen, the being of beings can in principle be revealed, but the event of be-ing can in principle never be given, because it opens the sense of given-

30. "Martin Heidegger in Conversation," trans. Lisa Harries, in *Martin Heidegger and National Socialism: Questions and Answers*, ed. Günter Neske and Emil Kettering (New York: Paragon House, 1990), 82 (translation modified).

31. Cf. Stephanie Bohlen, "Von der Offenheit des Seins zur Offenbarung des Seyns: Heideggers Weg zum anderen Anfang des Denkens," *Archivio di Filosofia* 62 (1994): 539–52, esp. 541, 547, 550–52.

ness in the first place. This "withdrawal" or self-concealment of be-ing does not make be-ing independent of being-there. To the contrary, be-ing requires being-there just as much as being-there requires it—which is precisely why we can never control or survey be-ing, as we can control and survey objects from which we can separate ourselves and to which we have no essential relation (251, 254).[32]

The *Contributions* refer to the mutual need of be-ing and being-there as *die Kehre*, "the turn" (407). This should not be confused with the same expression as commonly used by scholars to mean the change from the earlier to the later Heidegger, although the two issues are not unrelated. *Being and Time* described being-there as the entity who understands the being of beings, but faltered in the attempt to describe how being-there's temporality serves as the "horizon" for being. In such a description, everything would have been "reversed," but "thinking failed in the adequate saying of this turning."[33] The limitations of *Being and Time*, as we saw in chapter 1, lie in the danger of taking being-there as a quasi-subject whose limits transcendentally determine being. The *Contributions* try to overcome transcendentalism by thinking of being-there as a thrown thrower whose very thrownness is part of its belonging to the event of be-ing. In this way, as Heidegger puts it in the "Letter on 'Humanism,'" his later thought "arrives at the locality of that dimension out of which *Being and Time* is experienced, [i.e.] the oblivion of being." Heidegger's marginal note clarifies that "oblivion" here is linked to the "withdrawal" or "expropriation" that is part of appropriation.[34] In short, the self-concealing event of be-ing is involved in a reciprocal "turn" with being-there; the thinking of this turn fulfills the "turn" in Heidegger's development, which is best understood not as a turn away from *Being and Time* but as a deeper insight into issues in the background of that text.[35]

What exactly happens in the turn? Be-ing "requires" (*braucht*) being-there or man (251, 262, 264, 317, 342). *Brauchen* means both to use and to need,

32. It can be misleading to say that there is "something about being itself, about its very event, its happening or unfolding, that strangely fails to touch us, that withdraws from us, that remains indifferent to us": William McNeill, "The Time of *Contributions to Philosophy*," in Scott et al., *Companion*, 134. Heidegger would reply that withdrawal is precisely a kind of "touch"—a distinctive relation, not the absence of all relations. (Mourners, for example, are intimately related to the departed dead.) Be-ing cannot happen in a way that is indifferent to "us," if "us" means being-there.

33. "Letter on 'Humanism,'" in *Pathmarks*, 250.

34. Ibid.

35. On the senses of *Kehre* cf. Fried, *Heidegger's Polemos*, 66–79; von Herrmann, *Wege ins Ereignis*, chap. 1, sec. 4; Louis J. Schiano Jr., "The *Kehre* and Heidegger's *Beiträge zur Philosophie (Vom Ereignis)*" (Ph.D. diss., Marquette University, 2001); Sheehan, "A Paradigm Shift," 195–96; Sheehan, "*Kehre* and *Ereignis*." In "Das Ereignis," the term *Kehre* is used in yet another way, to mean the essential happening of the truth of be-ing as the be-ing of truth.

so it appropriately suggests that neither being-there nor be-ing dominates the other. Be-ing as appropriation bears and "towers through" being-there, while being-there founds and projects the being of beings (261), grounding the truth of be-ing (262, 455). This event is an event of appropriation because it determines man as the "property" (*Eigentum*) of be-ing (263); man comes to "belong" to be-ing (251).[36] More specifically, man as being-there must establish the deepest clearing so that be-ing may find its proper concealment (342). This clearing will be the momentous site for the flight and arrival of the gods (264). If this site is founded and preserved, then be-ing can happen in its rarity and uniqueness (262). The richest account of this event is found in §255: "Only the assault of be-ing as the appropriating of the there brings *being*-there to itself and thus to the fulfillment (sheltering) of the insistently grounded truth within beings. . . . And *in turn:* only the grounding of *being*-there, the readying of the readiness for the captivating transport into the truth of be-ing, supplies what complies and belongs for the hint of the assailing appropriation" (407). This passage invokes several themes that we will discuss later, including selfhood, sheltering, and time-space. For now, we can simply say that in order to take the "hint" and enable both be-ing and being-there to emerge, we must open up a site within which beings can be appreciated as indicating the happening of be-ing.

The challenge here is to avoid personifying or hypostatizing be-ing—turning it into some hyper-entity or divinity that is calling us, manipulating us, or commanding us. Heidegger uses ontic language to speak of be-ing, as he says is inevitable (78). How can we hear this language as meaning something other than beings? He does not want us to think of be-ing as a cause, an explanatory *thing*. He does, however, want us to think of it as a source, an inception. Can we distinguish an inception from a cause? Can we think of a ground that is not an explanation or justification, but only a deeper mystery?

Maybe the notion of the turn can help us carry out these delicate maneuvers. We ourselves cannot "be there" unless we are appropriated by be-ing. Be-ing, then, has to be intimately involved with us. A cause, no matter how tight the causal link between it and us may be, can never be as intimately a part of us as our ability to grasp and interpret causes in the first place. Be-ing occurs on this level—the level of the originary event of opening rather than the level of things revealed within the open region. Because be-ing is not a cause but a primal opening, it is essentially mysterious. Of course, we can tell a likely story about the causal origin of our brains, or even of the universe as

---

36. "When man leaps into the history of being, he is no longer simply man; he too happens . . . as appropriation": Costantino Esposito, "Die Geschichte des letzten Gottes in Heideggers 'Beiträge zur Philosophie,'" *Heidegger Studies* 11 (1995): 48.

we know it. But the framework of this story—the sense of givenness that is at work in it—will remain a presupposition of the explanation instead of being explained by it. We get in touch with this sense of givenness, we do justice to it, only when we wonder: why is there something instead of nothing, and why is there sense instead of non-sense? These are "whys" that do not search for causes, but simply appreciate the event of giving.

The other side of the turn is be-ing's dependence on being-there. The giving of being cannot take *place* without us, because we are needed in the founding of such a place.[37] Only when the event of giving becomes an issue *for us* does the event truly happen. This aspect of the turn also helps us to avoid thinking of be-ing as some quasi-divine supreme entity. As Thomas Sheehan puts it, "the 'Big Being' story," in which "Being" reaches out from the "Beyond" and reveals itself to us, is completely undercut by the notion of the turn.[38]

This brings us to a recurring objection to Heidegger's thought. Is he guilty of a certain unjustifiable idealism, anthropocentrism, or subjectivism? Has he linked be-ing and being-there too closely? *Being and Time* expresses sympathy for idealism, understood as the view that being can never be explained by beings, but is the "transcendental" for all beings (SZ 208). The flaw in idealism is that it fails to explain how the understanding of being forms part of being-there's ontological constitution (SZ 207). For Heidegger in *Being and Time*, then, because the being of beings is transcendental it is not independent of being-there, as beings are. Being is given only for being-there. Any attempt to find an "objective" being by generalizing about the qualities of beings is hopelessly naive, because an appeal to beings presupposes a sense of being that first opens up the "there." The truly vicious subjectivism is not Heidegger's position, but the position that poses as objectivism; such a position, by failing to question its own sense of being as objectivity, ends up imposing this sense on beings uncritically and rigidly.

In the *Contributions*, however, Heidegger is trying to overcome transcendental thinking itself, in part through the notion of the turn. Where does this leave his old defense against the charge of subjectivism? He claims he has now left subjectivism behind for good (259). Being-there is required by be-ing, and being-there's thrownness is part of its belonging to be-ing. This means that the being of beings can no longer be conceived as the achievement of a subject, a mind, or even being-there as described in *Being and Time*. It would be wrong to say that Heidegger has made be-ing a product of

---

37. Heidegger puts it more bluntly (but perhaps less clearly) in "Das Ereignis," where he writes that all be-ing is being-there.

38. Sheehan, "*Kehre* and *Ereignis*," 10.

being-there, because although be-ing does need being-there, it also fundamentally transforms being-there and "forces it toward its self" (251). If being-there can be itself only through be-ing, be-ing is not subordinate to being-there. The way to transcend the transcendental—to get beyond thinking of being as a condition of the possibility of experience that we impose upon beings—is not to lapse into empiricism but to leap into the event of appropriation, as what enables us to attain being-there for the first time (250–51).[39]

Being-there and Humanity

We need to look more closely at the relation between being-there and human beings. *Being and Time* had said of being-there, "we *are* it, each of us, we ourselves" (SZ 15). But now the meaning of the "we" has become problematic (§19). Does "we" refer to human beings in general? But according to Heidegger, there is no human nature, no "'Man' in himself," but only historical man (441).[40] Or if there *is* some ahistorical human nature, then being-there cannot be identified with it. Heidegger must instead refer to "the being-there *in* man" (455),[41] or hazard that "somehow it is man and yet not man after all, and always in an extension and a derangement, who is in play

39. The charge of anthropocentrism has recently been revived by Miguel de Beistegui: *Truth and Genesis*, 116, 146, 282; and "Discussion: Response to Peter Warnek," *Research in Phenomenology* 33 (2003): 279–80. Beistegui's argument depends on a distinction between being as it is for us and being in itself. It is telling that precisely when Beistegui puts forth a notion of being "in itself," he starts capitalizing "Being" ("Response," 280; *Truth and Genesis* seems to use "being," "Being," and "beyng" indiscriminately, e.g., 138). This Big Being, as Sheehan dubs it, is not Heidegger's *Seyn*. It can only be some feature of *das Seiende*, such as the origination of beings (the "operation whereby the things themselves come to be": *Truth and Genesis*, 111); when Beistegui identifies "Being" with "nature" or "the real" (ibid., 24, 25), he is using "Being" to mean *that which is*, in a broad sense that includes the process of becoming (ibid., 219). It is legitimate to work on an ontology of difference and becoming, but the question of *Seyn* is about something else: the giving of our sense of givenness, which makes all ontologies possible. Heidegger would insist that this is not simply one "side of Being" (ibid., 26, cf. 337) which is no more fundamental than the other "side" (ibid., 338); the question of be-ing is always implied in any question about how beings come to be, because the latter question can be asked only when a sense of givenness has already been given to us. This is the core of truth in transcendentalism. Beistegui wishes to "articulate [the] pre-ontical zone . . . in a way that would not include the human as the being *for whom* it unfolds" (ibid., 146); but as long as the one articulating the "zone" is human, the articulation must presuppose that the zone has already unfolded *for* the human. (We can have "an experience without consciousness or subject" [ibid., 244] only if we take "consciousness" and "subject" in very narrow senses, and even then we cannot have an experience without being human.) All the same, Beistegui's reflections hold promise as a move in the direction of reintegrating be-ing and beings.

40. "Das Ereignis" even takes the *Contributions* to task for failing to think the human essence historically enough.

41. This expression appears already in 1929; see *Kant and the Problem of Metaphysics*, 164.

in the grounding of the truth of be-ing. And it is just this, which is questionable and worth questioning, that I call being-there" (313).

In the current oblivion of be-ing, we take it for granted that we are human, and that the meaning of humanity is settled: we take ourselves as present-at-hand cases of the human species (61), losing the possibility of creatively retrieving our shared past in an authentically historical moment. Being-there would involve interpreting ourselves not as instances of human nature, but as a historical instant at which the future and the past can open our world. Being-there is this possibility (301), rather than an invariantly present feature to be found in us. The concept of being-there is an "anticipation" (*Vorgriff*, 317)—a prime example of future-subjunctive thinking.

One could argue, however, that there must be some evidence of the possibility of being-there in order for us to say that it is possible at all—much less to insist that it is a crucial possibility for humanity. Is being-there some human achievement, past or present—humanity at its best, so to speak? Heidegger sometimes thinks this way, as when he says that being-there can initially be indicated by "extreme ways of being of man" (68). Man should perhaps regain these achievements and "win back again his own, thoroughly used-up and scattered essence" (440, cf. 301).

Of course, this is not an ahistorical concept of essence, but refers precisely to "historical man" (441). Genuine truth happens "ever since man is historical, and if he is historical" (355)—but elsewhere Heidegger pronounces that "man has never yet *been* historical" (492, cf. 454). He insists that being-there is not a characteristic of man (GA 66, 322). We cannot even use our current state as a *sign* of being-there—inferring that we must once have been-there, or must be essentially capable of being-there—for Heidegger also denies that being-there is a condition of possibility for man (GA 66, 321). So is being-there human in any way? If not, then where does the possibility of being-there come from? Why is it *our* possibility?[42] Being-there is "of" man in the sense that it is proper to (*eignet*) him. "But how?" (301).

Perhaps being-there is proper to the human essence in the sense that it is an essential *change* that is "determined uniquely and in advance" (GA 66, 322). Although we cannot predict whether we will become being-there, we can think of this transformation in advance and know its basic features (248). But such statements only deepen the mystery. If a transformation is allotted to us in advance, is it really a transformation, or is it only (in traditional terms) the actualization of our essential potential? Clearly the question of being-there calls our essence into question. Perhaps in order to think man's essence we must precisely think *away* from man. But toward what? This question,

---

42. Similar problems arise in *Basic Questions of Philosophy*, 179–81 and GA 49, 61–63.

suggests Heidegger, is itself part of the human essence (GA 66, 156). We are ourselves only when we seek beyond ourselves, holding ourselves open to questionability.

Is being-there equivalent to being *authentically* human? The notion that genuine disclosure occurs when we question what we normally take for granted bears a strong resemblance to *Being and Time*'s authenticity (*Eigentlichkeit*), which could also be interpreted as "ownness" or "propriety." Being-there, which in *Being and Time* can exist either authentically or inauthentically, now seems to be identified with authenticity (as is "care": 16, 35). Heidegger even suggests that authenticity is the very event of appropriation (GA 66, 145; cf. GA 67, 51).

The parallels to *Being and Time* suggest an answer to the question of why we should pursue the possibility of being-there. According to Heidegger, even in *Being and Time* he never held that being-there could be discovered by "staring" at humanity as if it were a present-at-hand entity (GA 66, 327). Consider the methodologically crucial §63: Heidegger's interpretation of existence is based on an "existentiell" projection of the possibility of authenticity—one possibility among others that he has chosen to pursue (SZ 312–13). The point of this procedure is not to subject ontology to an arbitrary point of view, or to discard all other possibilities of interpretation; understanding simply must begin with some particular take on the phenomena (SZ 151). We can then freely decide how revealing this approach is (SZ 315).

This does not quite get around the problem, however. How are we to decide whether the projection of being-there is revealing, if it is not only a take on phenomena but a leap into a new condition that has never yet happened? And why should we risk this particular leap—why does it have a special claim on us? These issues may become clearer if we can see why being-there could not possibly be a given characteristic of given human beings. I have argued that be-ing cannot in principle be given, because it is the event of the giving of the very sense of givenness. For the same reason, being-there cannot be given. To enter being-there is to ground the there, the site that is needed so that be-ing may take place; only within such a place can anything emerge as given. It follows that the site itself and the event of its grounding must exceed all given phenomena. Because being-there cannot simply be discovered as given, it must be projected (GA 66, 143–44, 325). To think of being-there, to know being-there, requires us to leap into it as a possibility.[43] In this sense,

---

43. "Being-there—more originary and earlier than human being as usually conceived—is the site of the play of being and the origin of its essential happening. Man, as the entry into this play, is that entity who has at each moment decided for or against being-there, knowingly or not, and who builds his history on the basis of this decision": Heidegger, "Die Frage nach dem Sein" (1937), *Heidegger Studies* 17 (2001): 15.

being-there is a *philo-sophical* concept, a concept motivated not merely by observation but by "love of wisdom," by a passionate venture into be-ing (GA 66, 63–64, 144). But we should also remember that Heidegger does not want the "projection" of being-there to be a willful creation. We do not make being-there; we take over it and "find" it by honoring what is worthiest of question (GA 66, 144). Here we might recall bethinking as in-ventive thinking. To in-vent being-there is not to dream it up, but to come upon it as a possibility to be retrieved.

This in-ventive leap into being-there is closely linked to the question of grounding that lies at the heart of the *Contributions*. Being-there "is not something that could simply be found in present-at-hand man, but rather the ground of the *truth* of be-ing, a ground necessitated by the grounding experience of be-ing as appropriation, through which ground (and its grounding) man is changed from the ground up" (294). Being-there will form the ground of a new humanity (262, 300, 329, 331). Yet man is also supposed to ground being-there (262, 318). There is, so to speak, a "turn" between being-there and man, a reciprocal grounding. Human beings must creatively transcend what they have been up to now in order to pursue the highest human, or even superhuman possibility—the possibility of being the there for be-ing—and then this possibility will provide a new basis, a new there, within which we can learn how to be human in a new way. If this should happen, then appropriation will happen—for appropriation is nothing but "*the appropriating event of the grounding of the there*" (247), which is also the "ap-propriation of man into being-there" (GA 66, 163).

Again, what would motivate such an event? Would it be necessary? Yes—in the sense of necessity that flows from emergency (26, 242). Emergency is part of the fissure of be-ing, one fault line along which the event of be-ing emerges. What is essential in it is the experience of thrownness (102, 231, 239). We must recognize that we have been thrust into a situation in which we are faced with the urgency of leaping into being-there, and that this thrownness is itself part of the happening of be-ing. Our projection of be-ing, then, our leap into being-there, becomes more than a whim; it participates creatively in an event of appropriation.

In chapter 4 we will return to the question of why we should leap into being-there, in the context of the larger problem of a philosophy of possibility.

The Leap and Decision

Although the leap into being-there is supposedly not an arbitrary choice, it does involve "decision" in a unique sense.[44] Being-there is a "crisis" (295), a

---

44. On decision cf. Müller, *Der Tod als Wandlungsmitte*, §§3–10, and De Carolis, "La possibilità della decisione."

moment that *decides* whether we will be de-ranged into the other inception. Such a decision is not a matter of human preference, which picks one given thing over another; the de-cision awaits the bursting forth of the event of appropriation (87, 100, 103). But this is not to say that we have no role to play. In order to understand decision, we must keep in mind the turn (95): be-ing cannot happen unless human beings leap into the possibility of being-there. We must "open de-cision for ourselves by leaping" (88). This implies a certain responsibility on our part—understood not as autonomy but as responsiveness to an urgent demand.[45]

The leap, then, is not a subjective choice but a venture that calls into question who the venturers are by exposing them to an event that is greater than they. The hyphenated *Ent-scheidung* ("de-cision") indicates a division (*Scheidung*) that opens a domain of unconcealment, separating it out from other such possible domains. The de-cision thus establishes both the way in which beings are given and our way of being-there—our way of being those to whom beings as such are given. Choices, in contrast, are carried out by someone who is already an established self, and they concern options that are laid out in advance (100). De-cision, then, is prior to choice. It happens not within the will of a subject but as the essential happening of be-ing itself (92, 95, 103). The leap that opens up de-cision for us is neither an arbitrary choice nor a necessity that is forced upon us, but a free venture in response to emergency. Instead of surveying a set of given options and choosing one, we are motivated by a plight that impels us to risk our own identity in a leap into the happening of be-ing, into a de-cision that will transform us and reveal beings in a new way.

What is at stake in this decision, at this juncture? The decision is between history and its loss (96, 100), or between being and nonbeing (where "being" means "the essential happening of being," i.e., be-ing) (101). Will history happen? Will be-ing happen? The two questions are the same, for "history" means the taking-place of be-ing itself.[46]

But if decision is part of the essence of be-ing, can there ever be a decision between be-ing and its lack? The very happening of a decision would already involve be-ing. The real decision, then, decides between decision itself and indecision, between the urgency of the either/or and the indifference of the neither/nor (101–2). To put it otherwise: in order for there to be sense, this

---

45. "As we find ourselves in major decisions, we find ourselves already to be responsible in the sense that we are called to take a stance in them": Daniela Vallega-Neu, "Discussion: Human Responsibility (A Reply to Peter Warnek)," *Research in Phenomenology* 33, no. 1 (September 2003): 281.

46. As De Carolis puts it, "*only* on the basis of a historical experience can being truly unfold, and vice versa, *only* a happening that calls being into question can count as an authentic historical experience": "La possibilità della decisione," 176.

sense must distinguish itself from other senses—or, at the most fundamental level, from non-sense as the blurring of all distinctions. The happening of sense—the event of be-ing—thus requires decision, and the ultimate decision is the decision against indecision.

This paradoxical reduplication of decision recalls *Being and Time*'s Kierkegaardian characterization of resoluteness as the choice to choose (SZ 268, 270). But it also points forward to Heidegger's later attack on "the will to will" as the triumph of modern subjectivity.[47] What happens in this development? Did Heidegger endorse a subjectivism in *Being and Time* that he rejected later? That is certainly not how he reads *Being and Time* in the *Contributions* (87–88), nor would it be a fair reading in terms of *Being and Time* itself, for there he emphasizes that resoluteness (*Entschlossenheit*) is not blind stubbornness, but a disclosedness (*Erschlossenheit*) of the world that enables us to encounter beings clear-sightedly (SZ 297). Still, the emphasis in *Being and Time* is on individual selfhood, whereas the *Contributions* emphasize be-ing. There has been a shift, although Heidegger has not yet shifted so far from subjectivity that our relation to be-ing is primarily one of waiting in a *Gelassenheit* beyond all will.[48] The *Contributions* are still willing to speak of willing: we need a "will to appropriation" (58) and "a will to ground and build" (98); "the *moment* as the lightning flash of be-ing" requires questioning as "the will to know and experience" (409). The peculiar position of the *Contributions*, then—and perhaps their advantage—is that they leave room for both human will and the de-cision of be-ing, and in fact see these two as linked. Thus, the ultimate de-cision—be-ing or not—necessitates a series of human decisions, including the decision to dare decision altogether (91).

The *Contributions* themselves aspire to such daring; their central two parts concern leaping as the founding of the site for be-ing. But what is a leap? One of Heidegger's most striking discussions of this question is the opening of *Introduction to Metaphysics*. The question "Why are there beings at all instead of nothing?" is the most "originary" (*ursprünglich*) of questions.[49] Heidegger explains this word through a complex train of thought. The why-question is radically broad, questioning all beings; human beings, then, are not its focus. Yet by virtue of our ability to ask such questions, we do have a special position after all—we are the beings who are aware of beings as such and as a whole. We are the point at which the totality of what is wakes up to itself. But then, why is our seemingly all-embracing consciousness limited to our

47. E.g., "On the Question of Being," in *Pathmarks*, 312.

48. *Gelassenheit* originates its own peculiar reduplication—a will not to will, that is, "a renouncing of willing": "Conversation on a Country Path About Thinking," in *Discourse on Thinking*, trans. John M. Anderson and E. Hans Freund (New York: Harper and Row, 1966), 59.

49. *Introduction to Metaphysics*, 2.

finite circumstances? As Pascal puts it: "When I consider the brief span of my life absorbed into the eternity which comes before and after . . . the small space I occupy and which I see swallowed up in the infinite immensity of spaces . . . I take fright and am amazed to see myself here rather than there: there is no reason for me to be here rather than there, now rather than then. By whose command and act were this time and place allotted to me?"[50] Now our questioning leaves mere wonder behind and feels vertigo: what gives us the right to question everything from our finite position? Is this questioning legitimate? What is its ground? "What is asked in this question rebounds upon the questioning itself, for the questioning challenges beings as a whole but does not after all wrest itself free from them." This recoil of the question upon itself does not, however, happen automatically; it requires "force of spirit" and a leap. Such a leap is a "happening," not just any "arbitrary process." The leap "attains its own ground by leaping, performs it in leaping [*er-springt, springend erwirkt*]."[51] In this sense it is an *Ur-sprung*, an originary leap.

It may seem that the why-question here has little relevance to the *Contributions*, which are focused on the still deeper question: how does be-ing essentially happen?[52] But this question is already implicit in *Introduction to Metaphysics*. The why-question bears within it the question, "How does it stand with being?" And although this is in part simply an attempt to clarify the sense of the being of beings, it also involves the question of the "fundamental happening" in which this sense is granted to being-there.[53] Could it be that this event belongs together with the "happening" of radical questioning as the two sides of *Ereignis*?

If so, then Heidegger's remarks on the originary leap in *Introduction to Metaphysics* can also shed light on the leap at the heart of the *Contributions*. What precisely "happens" in an originary leap? What does it leap away from, and what does it leap toward? Why is a leap required at all? In what sense does this leap create a ground?

When one is *not* leaping one is stepping, standing, or lying down—relying on the presence of some ground. We take it for granted that the ground will support us. In the realm of thought, to have grounds and avoid leaps means to be able to give a reason for our every claim. To leap, then, means to dispense with the constant safety of a ground. One might leap across a crevice, springing from one spot of ground to another. One might leap into an apparent abyss, without any guarantee of finding safe ground again. Fi-

50. Blaise Pascal, *Pensées*, trans. A. J. Krailsheimer (New York: Penguin, 1966), 48 (no. 68).
51. *Introduction to Metaphysics*, 5, 6, 7.
52. For a criticism of *Introduction to Metaphysics* along these lines see GA 66, 267–77.
53. *Introduction to Metaphysics*, 35, 215–16.

nally, in thought there is an even more extreme leap: one might leap into an abyss and take the risk that when one looked back at the ground from which one had leapt, one would discover that it had never been a reliable ground at all. This is the kind of leap Heidegger has in mind—a leap "away from all the previous safety of [our] being-there, be it genuine or presumed."[54]

What are we leaping away from? In one sense, the ground is everything, every entity. We no longer take beings for granted, but ask what grants them as such. Traditional metaphysics halts our fall into the abyss by finding an entity that grants all beings: God as the *causa sui*, the being that grounds itself and all else. But Heidegger suggests a greater leap that cannot be halted by the same means: we leap away from the very *sense* of what it means to be that we have so long taken for granted. Without the ontology of presence and substance, the metaphysical concept of God becomes problematic (which is not to say that we necessarily fall into atheism). There is no entity, then, that can halt our fall into the ungrounded. The question of be-ing—Heidegger would insist—is essentially abyssal.

One might ask whether it is not reason itself that leads us to the question of be-ing; after all, reason searches for sources and origins, such as the source of our sense of being. And if a question is rational, it is not a leap. Heidegger could point out in reply that Leibniz, who pursued the principle of sufficient reason to the point of asking why there is something instead of nothing, did not go so far as to ask "how it stands with being." Maybe his failure to do so was not a failure of reason, but a failure to do something other than search for grounds, to leap away from his understanding of being as essentially involving grounding. The question of be-ing, when properly carried out, is not a search for a ground—a sufficient reason—but an act of appreciating and entering into the very event of giving.

The leap, then, leaps away from beings and away from the sense of being that we have taken for granted. Where does it bring us? Can we find any footing anymore? Is the "event" into which we enter anything more than an endless free fall? Recall that the originary leap does not leave us floating in a void, but brings us back to our enigmatic situation as the beings who are capable of questioning the being of beings. We are both particular, finite, situated entities and entities who stand in a clearing where entities as such can make sense to us. In a way, then, Heidegger embraces Pascal's vertigo. Pascal takes fright at the thought that he, who can contemplate all beings, is himself one particular being—limited to a time and place—and this fright impels him to search for God as a sufficient reason for his own situatedness. But Heidegger would answer that it is precisely thanks to our situatedness that we can

54. Ibid., 6.

relate to beings as a whole and search for grounds. The being of beings is given to us only through our habitation of a site and moment, through our receiving and appropriating the meaning that is passed on to us. The leap means inhabiting the there without lapsing into habit—appreciating the emergence of beings in their being without losing touch with emergency, with the distress that reminds us that we possess no safe ground. "Being-there itself essentially happens as *emergency*, authentically founds [*setzt*] emergency itself and thus first founds the 'where' of the 'there.'"[55]

In this way, then, leaping can be grounding—not as the establishment of an unquestionable basis but as the embrace of questionability and finitude themselves, as an appropriation of our thrownness that does not pretend to overcome it. Our ultimate decision decides against indecision, but not against undecidedness: we decide to accept uncertainty and risk.[56] A marginal note to §34 warns us that the term *leap* can create the false impression that this is a matter of a single act, one leap over a ditch. Presumably this would be a false impression because, as an acceptance of uncertainty, the leap can never be over and done with; it keeps calling on us to carry it out again. The few who can keep performing this originary leap will found a new site and a new selfhood. They will spring open (*erspringen*) being-there and be-ing in their leaping (88, 227, 458).[57]

The notion of an originary leap inevitably recalls Kierkegaard's leap of faith. Both Kierkegaard and Heidegger oppose the view that our every relation to beings can be grounded on true and certain propositions about them. For Kierkegaard, a genuine way of existing requires a sheer decision, a free commitment, which it would be ludicrous to base on any speculative claim

---

55. Heidegger, "Die Unumgänglichkeit des Da-seins ('Die Not') und Die Kunst in ihrer Notwendigkeit (Die bewirkende Besinnung)," *Heidegger Studies* 8 (1992): 7. These notes probably date from the period of the *Contributions*. On emergency as enabling the there, cf. *Basic Questions of Philosophy*, 132–33; for a perceptive interpretation see Frank Schalow, "Decision, Dilemma, and Disposition: The Incarnatedness of Ethical Action; Heidegger and Ethics," *Existentia* 12 (2002): 243–45. Regina is wrong to denounce the "precariousness" of beings in *Being and Time*'s account of anxiety and to claim that this account implies a willful, subjectivist nihilism that is overcome in the *Contributions*: "Phenomenology and the Salvation of Truth," 274–75, 277, 294. First, anxiety is not produced by the will of the subject, but comes over one. Second, in the *Contributions* beings remain questionable or "precarious," particularly when we are exposed to the questionability of be-ing. Since this exposure requires a "leap" on our part, the *Contributions* are, if anything, more "willful" here than *Being and Time* was. Regina obscures this element of human decision by claiming that "the leap is inspired not by the initiative of the subject, but by *Ereignis* itself" (292); an inspiration for a leap is not itself a leap.

56. As Daniela Vallega-Neu observes, "Every decision carries the possibility of failing as well as the necessity of losing something," so a certain "vulnerability" is part of the great decision in which Heidegger is trying to participate: "Thinking in Decision," *Research in Phenomenology* 33, no. 1 (September 2003): 262.

57. See Sallis, "Grounders of the Abyss."

about what is. He would endorse Heidegger's reversal of the German proverb *erst wägen, dann wagen* (weigh before you dare, look before you leap). "Who will leap over this weighing and dare the unweighable . . . ?" (238). Leap before you look, say both Heidegger and Kierkegaard—for it is the risk of a commitment that first opens our eyes and sets the standards by which we can judge the world. The ground for our judgments is a leap; as long as we remember that, we will have as firm a foundation as finite beings can ever have.

To be sure, Kierkegaard is speaking from the point of view of subjectivity, which Heidegger claims to have left behind. Heidegger would be wary of falling into a voluntaristic subjectivism, of resorting to freedom understood as being the self-sufficient cause of one's own acts. Yet freedom in a deeper sense, perhaps as "mastery," is surely in play here (consider Heidegger's call for a decision to decide).[58] And Kierkegaard himself may have a conception of freedom that is far more subtle than the traditional notion. Freedom consists in "freely appropriating that which is given, and consequently in being absolutely dependent through freedom."[59] Kierkegaard, too, understands freedom in terms of a certain appropriation.

The grounding that happens in the leap, then, both allows the truth of be-ing to happen in its abyssal way and builds on it as a ground (307). In this event, time-space opens, the future ones come forward, the truth of be-ing is sheltered in beings, and man attains being-there by becoming insistent (308). We can grasp these happenings more deeply by asking about selfhood.

Selfhood, Insistence, and Death

Assuming that selfhood involves freedom, we can draw on Kierkegaard's insight into freedom in order to grasp the character of the self. Selfhood involves the free appropriation of the given. But if something is already given to us, how can we take it? A gap must distance us from the given, so that this gap can be bridged in the act of appropriation by which we adopt the given. Selfhood, then, paradoxically combines distancing and adopting.

Furthermore, both distancing and adopting are paradoxical in themselves. The paradox of distancing is that in order to be oneself, one must question

58. The *Contributions* unfortunately do not provide an extensive meditation on freedom as such. But the notion of "freedom to the ground of be-ing as the grounding of the there" (GA 65, 414) can be connected to Heidegger's earlier reflections on the connection between freedom and truth. In brief, we are free only when we are set free into an open region in which we can encounter and deal with beings as such. See especially "On the Essence of Truth," in *Pathmarks*; *The Essence of Human Freedom*; *Schelling's Treatise on the Essence of Human Freedom*.

59. Søren Kierkegaard, *Journals*, July 18, 1840, in *A Kierkegaard Anthology*, ed. Robert Bretall (Princeton: Princeton University Press, 1946), 12. Kierkegaard goes on to comment that the attempt to give language to oneself ends either in silence or in gibberish.

one's own being. Someone who has never felt one's identity to be a problem is no one. Our identity is not simply a matter of having a given set of features; we must be able to grapple with the problem of whether and how the given defines us. We could say that our most proper feature, then, is precisely our ability to decide which features are proper to us.

But in order to find oneself, one cannot simply reject the given; one must ultimately appropriate it as one's own. The paradox of adopting, then, is that in order to become oneself, one must tie oneself to something that exceeds the freely deciding self, something other than the self. This truth may seem less paradoxical if we think of the self that is exceeded as small and undeveloped, and the larger self as inhabiting a greater space that allows the self to be fulfilled. Candidates for such a space include love, family, culture, class, nation, humanity, and religion.

The paradox common to both adopting and distancing is that one must abandon the self—or a semblance of the self—in order to attain true selfhood. The "self" that is abandoned in distancing is a set of given properties. The "self" that is abandoned in adopting is a subject with pretensions to absolute autonomy and independence. One must sacrifice both semblances of selfhood in order to become someone who is freely engaged in the world, who realizes himself through his commitment to more than himself.

For Heidegger, the distancing in selfhood happens in events of expropriation, moments when we brush up against the "nothing" that shadows all being, including our own. In such experiences we learn that "we cannot wholly belong to any thing, not even to ourselves."[60] This distancing is a prerequisite for the adopting in selfhood, which happens in the event of appropriation. In this event, we appropriate be-ing and are appropriated by it. We thus take part in the greatest of all happenings, the event that allows all lesser dimensions, such as family or nation, to emerge. When we join the event of appropriation, we come into our own. We exceed "the self as the merely selfsame" (320) and enter the realm of greater and truer selfhood.

When we were considering the relation between man and being-there, we asked what gives being-there the right to serve as our defining possibility—the possibility that is most our own—if it is not the essence of human beings as they currently are. We may now be closer to an answer. To enter being-there is to engage with the being of beings—including our own being. Being then becomes an issue for us, a problem that is our *own* precisely because it is problematic for us. Until this happens, we may have an identity as a set of given features, but we are not yet ourselves—for being a self requires distance from the given as well as an appropriation of it. For us, to have an

60. *Introduction to Metaphysics*, 31.

essence means to be in constant danger of losing it (489). Being-there, then, is not *what* we are; it is the condition we must enter in order to wrestle with *who* we are. We can *be* only by asking, "Who are we?" (51). As *Being and Time* points out, such a question has meaning only for an entity whose own being is at issue for it (SZ 42, 45). And such an entity must be appropriated, brought into its own, by encountering the being of beings as a question "for the first time" (492). To be appropriated does not mean to be defined as this or that, to be stamped with an essence in the traditional sense, but to enter a space within which being becomes a problem. Selfhood emerges in this strait; it is not a given trait of human beings (319).

Being a self, then, may be indissociable from participating in the event of appropriation. We would then expect all the elements of selfhood to derive from this event. For example, the "turn" between be-ing and being-there as thought in the *Contributions* can be understood as the ground of the thrownness and projection ascribed to being-there in *Being and Time;* leaping into the turn allows us to experience ourselves as "thrown throwers" (45). The difference in emphasis between the two texts is that whereas in *Being and Time* projection is primarily the pursuit of a possible way for an individual to be (SZ 143), in the *Contributions* it is an "incursion into the open" (239), an entry into the sense of the being of beings. And thrownness in the *Contributions* reveals not just facticity, but the appropriating throw of be-ing itself.[61] We can clarify the differences in emphasis by observing, first, that according to *Being and Time*, projection not only resolves who one is as an individual but also enables all beings to make sense (SZ 144–45). As for facticity, it is defined in *Being and Time* as the condition by virtue of which being-there "can understand itself as bound up in its 'destiny' with the being of those entities which it encounters within its own world" (SZ 56). Who we are and what we make of our surroundings cannot be separated from our belonging to those surroundings. In short, *Being and Time* already connected thrownness and projection—essential elements of selfhood—to the question of the origin of the sense of being. The difference between *Being and Time* and the *Contributions* is that the former proposes that thrownness and projection make our understanding of being possible, while in the latter what is primal is the very happening of be-ing and being-there, the event from which the structures of thrownness and projection emerge.

As we have seen, Heidegger now takes care to avoid the transcendental overtones of *Being and Time*, insisting that being-there is not a subject that determines the conditions of the possibility of experience (447, 448, 452, 455). Instead, it is claimed by its past and opened to its future, so that it re-

---

61. Emad, "'Heidegger I', 'Heidegger II', and *Beiträge*," 137, 139.

lates to be-ing creatively and responsively rather than imperiously. Being-there is not a foundation or launching pad for the difference things make to it; it itself is launched or thrown, and must acknowledge this thrownness in order to be itself (231). The leap is such an acknowledgment: it is "throwing one*self* openingly 'into' being-there. Being-there grounds itself in the leap . . . the self first becomes its own 'self' [*das Selbst wird erst "sich" zu eigen*] in the leap, and yet [this is] no absolute creating" (303). Despite some echoes of idealist talk of freedom as self-positing, Heidegger is claiming that freedom and selfhood come not from acts of will but from releasing oneself into an openness that is not of one's own making. This renunciation or external-ization (*Entäußerung*) is "the opposite of self-surrender" (28).

Selfhood happens only through "insistence in the happening of owndom [*Eigen-tum*]" (320). The ending -*tum* suggests that owndom, like a kingdom, is not an abstract quality but a domain—the region belonging to and gov-erned by owning (311, 320). Owning (*Eignung*) is both dedication (*Zueig-nung*) and assignment (*Übereignung*): owning happens when being-there is dedicated to itself in its assignment to appropriation (320). Identity can come alive as a question ("who are we?") only when one's own being, along with the being of all beings, becomes an urgent issue. Only urgency brings us to ourselves (45). The self, then, is not a possession but "insistence"—the stead-fast, persistent withstanding of this emergency. The word *inständig* usually means "insistent," like a pressing request; in English we can call such a re-quest *urgent*. To be *inständig* means to let oneself be drawn urgently into the urgency of be-ing. It also means to in-sist in the etymological sense: to *stand within* the site and moment that the urgency of be-ing tears open. Insistence is genuine being-there (298–99; GA 49, 54).

Without insistence, be-ing itself cannot happen. Selfhood is "the momen-tous site of the call and the belonging" (52). The call is the call of be-ing; if we hear it (*hören*), we can belong to it (*gehören*) (cf. 407). Selfhood thus happens in the moment of the turn, the belonging-together of be-ing and being-there, and insistence is what lets this belonging-together take place (233). This is why incepts—acts of thought that take part in the very event of appropriation—are rooted in insistence (65). "*Sheltering insistence*" now takes the place of traditional intellection (265).[62]

Curiously, in 1930 Heidegger had used the word *In-sistenz* to name the in-authentic alternative to *Ek-sistenz*. It is worth comparing *Inständigkeit* to *In-*

---

62. Insistence in the *Contributions* is much like authenticity in *Being and Time*. Authenticity is a way of existing that does not evade the fact that one's own being is at issue, and accepts the challenges and limitations that come with this condition. To be authentically is to be oneself (SZ 129, 322). Furthermore, authenticity is needed to form "appropriate existential concepts" (SZ 316). Similarly, in the *Contributions* insistence is the key to both selfhood and truth.

sistenz in order to see the authentic and inauthentic senses of "standing in." *In-sistenz* is an absorption in present beings that naively treats them "as if they were open of and in themselves," forgetting about the original event of opening.[63] When we in-sist in this sense, we lose sight of ek-sistence—the opening of the present by the future and the past. To rejoin ek-sistence is to drop one's attachment to beings as something simply given and to start questioning the source of their givenness. This nonattachment, however, is not the extinction of involvement but rather *Inständigkeit* as a passionate engagement in one's own historical juncture—an engagement that, as we will see, must return to beings in order to "shelter" the truth of be-ing within them. And while *Inständigkeit* abandons all static, thinglike conceptions of the self, it does so for the sake of a deeper selfhood. Perhaps thoughts such as these lie behind Heidegger's exclamation, "Not Buddhism! The very opposite" (171).[64]

Insistence is a requirement not only for being oneself but also for being exposed to death (230); mortality is a problem only for those who are insistently attuned to the differentiation of being and nonbeing. This means that death is a strait of being-there—not necessarily of man (324), and not at all of beasts. As in *Being and Time*, "death" does not mean the cessation of bodily functions, but the constant possibility of the impossibility of being (SZ 247, 250, 262). This possibility pervades being-there: to be where the event of be-ing takes place is also to be subject to death. Being-there thus includes "being-away" as a constant possibility, both as death (324) and as inauthenticity (301, 323–24). The there—the ar-rangement of sense, the range of possibilities for the emergence of beings—is essentially liable to de-rangement (324).

Being-there is finite—not simply because it will someday stop (324) but in the very structure of the possibilities that it projects, which are always shadowed by finality: every course we pursue may well be our last and may exclude every other. This finitude gives weight to our choices, making being-there temporally unique: authentic being-there can happen only for the first and last time. The fragility of being-there gives urgency to our being, granting us decisiveness and historicity (282). If we were immortal—constantly guaranteed the chance to develop different possibilities and revisit

---

63. "On the Essence of Truth," in *Pathmarks*, 150. Theodore Kisiel has suggested to me that in order to avoid confusion with *In-sistenz*, the best translation of *Inständigkeit* would be "instantiation" or "instanciation." These words nicely suggest the uniqueness of a moment of being-there. However, "insistence" lends itself more easily to English usage, and also appropriately implies urgency and decision.

64. Cf. Müller, *Der Tod als Wandlungsmitte*, 357–58. Nevertheless, Sinn points out some legitimate parallels between Heidegger's notion of the moment and the Buddhist notion of sudden enlightenment: *Ereignis und Nirwana*, 72, 75, 226; see also index of subjects, s. vv. "Augenblick," "Blitz," "Jähe."

our choices—the urgency and uniqueness of our being would fade away. This is what happens in everyday inauthenticity, which fails to look death in the eye and drifts along in a pseudoimmortality.

Because of the turn, death is not only a fact of human affairs but also a feature of appropriation itself, as we have seen. Appropriation happens only in projection (451–52), and projection is haunted by death. All possible senses of the being of beings must emerge from contingent ventures in the face of death. We are claimed by a sense of being that we in turn must claim; this claiming is necessarily finite—it is a singular path that excludes others and that may be our last. The uniqueness of mortal being-there is thus "testimony" to the uniqueness and strangeness of be-ing (230, 284).

Would be-ing happen more fully or more clearly if being-there were immortal? Heidegger would deny this. Death does not cripple openness but makes it possible (283).[65] Without the urgency and uniqueness that mortality imparts, the difference between what is and what is not could not become significant for us. All openness is finite; infinite openness, like unlimited white light and noise, would be tantamount to oblivion.[66]

The Few and the Many

True being-toward-death, writes Heidegger, is required for the coming creators, the founders of the other inception (285). Who are these "future ones"? They receive attention in the briefest juncture (part 6), but they are invoked well before then. They are the partners Heidegger imagines and hopes for; they are his intended audience, for the text is addressed to the few and rare who at unique moments dare to confront the uniqueness of be-ing (11). These few are futural; they are the ones "to come." What is the sense of this expression, and of the future tense that enters the text not only in part 6 (e.g., 399) but at other key moments (70, 155, 227)? Does Heidegger succeed in thinking futurally, or does he substitute prophecy for philosophy? Nietzsche, the "philosopher of the future" who is Heidegger's obvious inspiration, is also the greatest philosophical creator of a new prophet—his Zarathustra. Is Heidegger following Nietzsche into the dubious domain of mythmaking and forecasting?

65. Cf. Walter Brogan, "The Community of Those Who Are Going to Die," in *Heidegger and Practical Philosophy*, ed. François Raffoul and David Pettigrew (Albany: State University of New York Press, 2002), 244.

66. This is how I would interpret Joan Stambaugh's dictum, "through concealment being saves itself from boundless unconcealment": *The Finitude of Being*, 111. Stambaugh herself is unsure of what the saying means, but it accords with Heidegger's saying, "complete opening— *would be no opening any more* (*pure openness*—nothing)": "Das Wesen der Wahrheit: Zu 'Beiträge zur Philosophie,'" *Heidegger Studies* 18 (2002): 10.

The future ones are not simply a group that will come upon the scene tomorrow. Some are here today (400). (If only Heidegger had told us who they are!) One, at least, lived a century before Heidegger's words: Hölderlin (401).[67] Futurity, then, does not mean being chronologically later; in a sense, it means being earlier. The future ones are opposed to "the various arbitrary and unchecked later ones, who have nothing more ahead of them and nothing more behind them" (96). These "later ones" are epigones; they may race forward in an illusory "progress" that merely rearranges the current representations of beings, but they are incapable of deep transformation because they fail to participate in the nonrepresentable happening of be-ing. The future ones, in contrast, reach forward because they reach back: "Hölderlin is the most futural of all because his provenance is broadest, and in this breadth he *traverses* what is greatest and transforms it" (401). To exist futurally, then, is to engage with the sweep of our history and grasp its uniqueness, thus opening another unique history—the other inception. The future here is not a later point on our established timeline, but a new domain of sense and truth.

For this reason, although Heidegger's discourse *is* prophetic, it is not simply forecasting. Prophecy at its root is not prediction but "speaking out"; the biblical prophets speak out to the Israelites by bringing them back to their responsibilities, challenging them to heed the word of God. This bringing-back is not only a remembrance of commitments but also a revelation of the present and future in the light of these commitments. Through such communicating and struggling, "the power of destiny" as the happening of a people is set free (SZ 384). And when destiny is free, a new inception becomes possible.

We asked earlier whether the event of appropriation is not only a unique happening, but one that has never yet happened, an event reserved for the future. Maybe we can now answer: yes, if we rightly understand "future." Appropriation is futural not only because it has not yet fully occurred, but also because it engages (will engage) the whole domain of our history, and in this way opens (will open) a new domain. Appropriation is the event of the grounding of the there (247); such grounding requires grounders, and to be a grounder is to be futural.

The future ones include thinkers, poets, and men of action (those who would ground being-there by deed and sacrifice, 96). Different domains require different ways of grounding, but all will be united by their recognition of urgency (98), their alertness to the final god (395), and their "masterful" knowing (396). Heidegger quickly deflects the notions of a master race and

---

67. *Basic Questions of Philosophy* also names Schiller, Kierkegaard, van Gogh, and Nietzsche as "harbingers of a change of history" (182).

political control: masterful knowing cannot be applied to current business (396). As we saw, mastery is distinct from power and violence—although not incompatible with them (282). It is a free creativity that opens new possibilities by its "bequeathing" (281). To be futural is to be masterful—not by forcing beings to obey one's will but by participating in a new event of be-ing. "This knowing knows the hours of the happening that first forms history" (397).

Knowledge here is not the possession of facts but the *search* for be-ing (17). Seeking is essentially futural (398), not because it has not yet achieved its goal, but because it reaches beyond the given and present in order to explore the questionable realm of the *giving* of presence and givenness themselves. In this way, the future ones enter selfhood (398). By questioning, they attain the *distance* from the given that is needed to become oneself; and since seeking be-ing is also finding it (17), they *adopt* a larger happening and thus come into their own. Their own being comes alive as an urgent issue in the midst of the emergency of be-ing itself.

This emergency is echoed in the crises of Heidegger's time: the collapse of will, thought, and institutions, hiding behind the facade of the massive, the masses, and technical machination. We live in the age of *Untergang*, writes Heidegger (7, 397). But this "going under," as understood by the few future ones, is not a mere downfall but an opportunity to "undergo" the event of appropriation; they are ready to sacrifice themselves in order to gain true selfhood (397). Like Zarathustra in the opening of Nietzsche's book of prophecy, they are willing to go under so that they may be transformed and transform others.[68]

What about these others? What about the many who cannot yet take part in the event of appropriation but who may be secretly gathered into a people, a *Volk*? Ultimately, writes Heidegger, it is a *people* that must ground the truth of be-ing (97). Conversely, unless the people grounds this truth, it is not yet a true people—so its pioneers, the future ones, must often seem pitted against it (398). Yet the future ones, not the man on the street, are the genuine voice of the people (319). Only they can set the people "free for its law, which is to be won by struggle—its law as the ultimate necessity of its highest moment" (43).

These remarks encapsulate Heidegger's political attitude in these dark years; disillusioned with Nazi ideology, increasingly isolated and apparently irrelevant, he still dreams of a German rebirth. Heidegger apparently hopes

---

68. "When Zarathustra's tragedy begins, so does his downgoing. The downgoing itself has a history. It is the history proper; it is not merely an end": Heidegger, *Nietzsche*, vol. 2, 31. On sacrifice as the act that makes the other inception possible by combining "the greatest decision and the most docile submission" see Maurizio Ferraris, "Il sacrificio di Heidegger," *Aut Aut* 248–49 (March–June 1992): 133.

to create "the philosophy of [the German] people"—and make the Germans "the people of [his] philosophy" (43). But despite his craving for a revolutionary moment of urgency, the *Contributions'* reflections on the *Volk* are far from a political manifesto; they are uncertain, vague, and focused on the essential happening of the people rather than on any concrete policies. Heidegger has come to realize that there is a gap between politics and philosophy. Because philosophy "*opens* experience" rather than directing and constraining it, philosophy can never "ground history *immediately*" (37).

What does it mean to be a people? Although this question is "essential" (42), Heidegger addresses it only tentatively, and for the most part negatively. Above all, the people's highest goal must not be to maintain itself as one entity among others, but to watch over the truth of be-ing (99, 321). The people must never be an end in itself (98–99, 139, 319, 398). It can become itself only by attending to be-ing as an event greater than itself. Selfhood, for a people as for an individual, consists not in remaining selfsame but in experiencing one's own being—and thus being in general—as a question. We must ask "Who are we?" in order to be who we are (48–49). Because we fail to put ourselves in question, we take ourselves as instances of a set human essence, rather than as instants in which insistence may elicit the event of be-ing. Participation in history is then reduced to "incidence [*Vorkommen*] within a belonging-together that has come to be" (61); a people is nothing but a co-incidence.

How could a deeper belonging-together be "prepared" (61)? Only through a mysterious happening that would bind together the few and the many. The "originary gathering" of the people lies in wait within appropriation (97). As for how such a gathering might take place, Heidegger is nearly silent. He no longer has faith that political measures can bring it about—although he does not rule out the possibility (98). The rebirth of the people is more likely to happen through a religious awakening. The people must seek its own god; the future ones will lead this search (398).[69]

The *Contributions* absolve Heidegger of any charges that he was an uncritical supporter of Nazism until the bitter end. He insists that race and the body can never be absolutes. They enter history only as part of the earth; when the earth conflicts with the world, a people can come to belong to its god (399). It is grotesquely ahistorical to make "blood and race . . . the bearers of history" (493). Physical traits are not a foundation for the cohesion of a people. They are part of the given into which a people is thrown, but thrownness is not yet the cultivation of be-ing. The people's leaders must find

---

69. A particularly bitter marginal note to §30 calls the German people slavish and querulous, and asks how such a people can ever come to its own self.

ways to project possibilities on the basis of this throwness, possibilities relating to a god who can draw the people beyond collective navel-gazing and "set it back into beings" (398). The leitmotif of Heidegger's critique of Nazism, then, is that it turns the people into a fixed, self-centered subject, instead of recognizing its potential as being-there. A "'total' world view" typically overlooks its own "concealed ground (e.g., the essence of the people)" (40). The National Socialists reduce the *Volk* to "the communal, the racial, the lower, the national, the permanent" (117), forgetting that, as Hölderlin says, nothing is more difficult than the free use of the national (GA 39, 294). If a "*völkisch* principle" is ever to play a role in our destiny, it will have to be handled by those who have a "higher rank of spirit" (42; cf. 24, 319, 479).[70]

This is not to say that Heidegger feels any nostalgia for the Weimar Republic. Instead, he lumps all the political ideologies of his time together, claming they all posit man "as what is already known in its essence" (25). The "innermost essence of 'liberalism'" is self-certainty, presumably because the liberal insistence on individual rights presupposes a settled conviction about what it means to be an individual subject (53, cf. 319). When Nazism exalts the body over the mind and soul it merely becomes "biological liberalism" (53), since it still presupposes that it knows what it means to have a soul, a mind, and a body. By rejecting modernity wholesale in this way, Heidegger in effect withdraws from political practice altogether. The same attitude recurs in *Besinnung*[71] and is only strengthened by the Second World War.[72] In chapter 4, I will offer reasons to be skeptical of this attitude. But for now, we

70. The wide range of existing interpretations of the *Contributions*' statements on Nazism is conveniently indicated by the titles of Vietta's *Heideggers Kritik am Nationalsozialismus und an der Technik* and Rockmore's *On Heidegger's Nazism and Philosophy*. The fifth chapters of both books discuss the *Contributions*. Vietta's perspective is closer to the truth. Rockmore supports his claim that Heidegger continues to share the Nazis' "end in view" (186) only by defining this goal broadly as "the realization of the Germans as German" (189) or "the realization of the destiny of the German people" (191, cf. 201), even though Rockmore observes that Heidegger denies that the people is an end in itself (192, 196). By these standards, anyone with patriotic sentiments or concern for a community should be called a Nazi. Still, there is truth in Tertulian's remark that the *Contributions*' antiliberal, revolutionary themes "evoke, in a sublimated form, the spirit of the movement of 1933" ("The History of Being and Political Revolution," 222) and in Michael E. Zimmerman's observation that there are "disturbing echoes" of Nazism in Heidegger's "themes of degeneration, nihilism, transformation, the new beginning, the leap, the rescue, the sacrifice, ruthlessness and daring": "For a New Beginning?" *Times Literary Supplement*, March 16–22, 1990, 295. Cf. Thomä, *Die Zeit des Selbst*, 766–68.

71. Heidegger sees no essential difference between "the rational conformity to plan of 'total authority'" and "the 'common sense' [Heidegger uses the English words] of the democracies": GA 66, 234.

72. The most notorious case of Heidegger's monochromatic vision in the postwar period is his claim that extermination camps (i.e., Nazism), hydrogen bombs (America), blockades (the USSR), and mechanized agriculture (modernity itself) are all "essentially the same": "Das Gestell," in GA 79, 27.

turn to time-space—the venue for the proper selfhood of a people, the place and time where owning can happen (51).

Time-space: Evoking the Momentous Site

Heidegger develops the theme of "time-space" in some of the most puzzling and original sections of the *Contributions*. In what mood are these sections to be read? Are they present-indicative descriptions of temporality as a quasi-present, constant transcendental structure? Or are they subjunctive—perhaps even optative or imperative—evocations of a possible happening?

If so, then the *Contributions'* treatment of time-space would seem to be quite different from *Being and Time's* account of temporality. *Being and Time* traces ordinary time back to being-there's temporality as the existential structure that opens the "horizonal schemata" within which we encounter beings (SZ §69c). The present is only one such schema, so Heidegger certainly intends to exceed the restrictions of presence. However, his way of describing temporality in *Being and Time* still seems to move within the present in a larger sense. Temporality is presented here as a quasi-present phenomenon—its schemata can become present to the interpreting observer. Furthermore, it presents itself as permanently present, as more basic than any passing event. Temporality is a structure that is always already in effect. To be sure, it is relatively dynamic: it reaches "ecstatically" into future, past, and present; it "temporalizes" itself (*sich zeitigt*) and thus *happens* in some sense (SZ §65). Furthermore, *authentic* temporality is a possibility rather than a constant, and only by choosing this possibility can we authentically grasp temporality at all. However, on the whole the account of temporality in *Being and Time* appears to describe the fundamental features of *eventfulness*, instead of evoking an *event*; it seems to be on the hunt for essences rather than possibilities.[73]

The *Contributions* shift from the structure of being-there's understanding of being to the event of be-ing. "'Time' in *Being and Time* is the *indication* and *suggestion* of what happens in the uniqueness of ap-propriation as the truth

73. For example, "Anticipation makes being-there *authentically* futural, and in such a way that the anticipation itself is possible only in so far as being-there, *as being* [*als seiendes*], is always coming towards itself—that is to say, in so far as it is futural in its being in general" (SZ 325). The emphasis here is on being-there's *Sein überhaupt*, not on the moment of authenticity. Similarly, Hans-Helmuth Gander observes that "historicity" in *Being and Time* functions as an "'ahistorical' structure . . . contrary to Heidegger's own basic programmatic intention, historicity itself is no longer temporal and historical": "Sein—Zeit—Geschichte: Überlegungen im Anschluss an Heideggers *Beiträge zur Philosophie*," in *Histoire et avenir: Conceptions hégélienne et posthégélienne de l'histoire*, ed. Ingeborg Schüßler and Alexandre Schild (Lausanne: Payot, 2000), 185.

of the essential happening of be-ing" (74). *Being and Time* tries to show that being-there's temporality makes being intelligible; in contrast, the *Contributions* try to in-vent the self-concealing event of be-ing and bethink the emergence of being-there, with its own distinctive time and space, as part of this event.

However, some of the *Contributions'* statements on time-space can still easily be read as descriptions of invariant structures. *Die Zeit räumt ein, niemals berückend. Der Raum zeitigt ein, niemals entrückend* (386): whatever this may mean, it has the neat symmetry that one expects from a description of a framework—not a happening. But can we emphasize the verbs in these phrases, and interpret their present-indicative grammar in a way that points not to an eternal structure, but to a possible event? An initial hint is provided by one telling line that is more imperative than indicative—it ends with *muß*: "The abyssal ground is thus the intrinsically timing-spacing-oscillating momentous site of the 'between' as which being-there must be grounded" (387). Is this "must" some a priori, transcendental necessity? Or is it a situated, historical necessity that may someday become urgent?

In addition to these questions of mood and modality, we might focus on the meaning of the hyphen in *Zeit-Raum*. How are space and time related? The answer in Heidegger's thought as a whole is less than clear. *Being and Time* seems to give priority to time: a spatial "region" opens only on the basis of making-present, which is one dimension of temporality (SZ §70). Yet *Being and Time* also asserts, with little explanation, that because spatiality involves *ecstatic* temporality, "space is independent of time" (SZ 369). In 1962, Heidegger declares that "the attempt in *Being and Time*, section 70, to derive human spatiality from temporality is untenable." However, the same lecture claims that "true time itself . . . is the prespatial region which first gives any possible 'where.'"[74]

The *Contributions* are not completely consistent either; Heidegger sometimes wavers between assigning priority to time and making time and space equiprimordial. For instance, in one passage time is said to *schaffen* space, which can mean either that it provides space or that it creates space; however, Heidegger immediately adds that space must also be understood in terms of its own "spacing" (192). Elsewhere he speaks of "timing spacing—spacing timing" (261). Instead of subordinating one member of time-space to the other, he usually prefers to think of them as complementary dimensions of appropriation (377–78). Space and time belong together (189) because both are required in order for be-ing and being-there to happen.

Any attempt to synthesize these statements into a "reconstructed" Hei-

74. "Time and Being," in *On Time and Being*, 23, 16.

deggerian doctrine would be distinctly un-Heideggerian.[75] The more appropriate approach is to ask what is at stake in the problem of space and time. In the *Contributions*, the crux of the matter is the *owned* character of primordial space and time; our challenge is to think of how "time-space belongs to truth . . . as appropriation" (372). As we saw in chapter 1, *Being and Time* already tries to show that the neutral, mathematical space-time of modern natural science—a four-dimensional set of objects—derives from owned space and time. Primordial space and time consist of appropriate and inappropriate sites and moments—places and times where beings and events belong or fail to belong. The *Contributions* develop this insight and cast it in terms of the event of appropriation. This event is the grounding of the there (183, 247); it founds being-there, so that be-ing can happen.

If be-ing happens, it must have its own place and time. But this place and time are not just points on a map and numbers on a clock; they are the site and moment where and when home and inception hold sway—always shadowed by their others, estrangement and reproducibility. Appropriation takes time—not just because it lasts a while, but because it requires remembrance and awaiting as our belonging to a past and future (384). Appropriation also takes place—it stakes out the site that is our own, a "there" where beings can be given to us as beings. Only in a place can beings make a difference to us. Only at a time can we receive and interpret a legacy for the sake of a possibility, cultivating and eliciting historical import.

The there would open at a juncture, a moment of critical inception. We can call this juncture the *Augenblicks-Stätte*, the site of the moment—or the momentous site (for once, English has an advantage over German).[76] The there is the site of all "moment" as import—the place where the being of beings, their sense and importance, is implemented in our dwelling amidst

75. This is not to deny the value of several studies that explore the theme of space and time in Heidegger. For a clear overview of the problem of time and being, especially in Heidegger's early work, see Françoise Dastur, *Heidegger and the Question of Time*, trans. François Raffoul and David Pettigrew (Amherst, N.Y.: Humanity Books, 1999). For a critique of *Being and Time*'s account of temporality, see William Blattner, *Heidegger's Temporal Idealism* (Cambridge: Cambridge University Press, 1999).

76. On *Ereignis* as "momentous," see Theodore Kisiel's early but perceptive glosses: "The Language of the Event: The Event of Language," in *Heidegger and the Path of Thinking*, ed. John Sallis (Pittsburgh: Duquesne University Press, 1970), 102. McNeill elucidates the role of the *Augenblick* in the *Contributions* and relates this text to Heidegger's earlier explorations of the theme in "The Time of *Contributions to Philosophy*." On the moment in Heidegger see also William McNeill, *The Glance of the Eye: Heidegger and the Ends of Theory* (Albany: State University of New York Press, 1999); Ruin, "Contributions to Philosophy," 369; Ruin, "The Moment of Truth"; Heidrun Friese, "Augen-Blicke," in *The Moment: Time and Rupture in Modern Thought*, ed. Heidrun Friese (Liverpool: Liverpool University Press, 2001).

things. The momentous site is rooted in the proper, in belonging—understood as the coming-to-pass of one's own (*Eignung*, 51).

What happens in time-space? The words *Entrückung* and *Berückung* name ways of moving (*Rückung*) that cooperate to open the momentous site (70). (*Einrückung*, "moving into," also makes a brief appearance as a name for the present at 383.) I will use "transport" for *Entrückung* and "captivation" for *Berückung*—at the price of losing all trace of the common root. *Entrückung* (transport) means carrying away, removing—and in particular, rapture or ecstasy. *Entrückung*, then, names what *Being and Time* called the ecstases of temporality—our removal into the dimensions of future, past, and present.[77] *Berückung* (captivation) means a charm or spell, or in its more verbal sense, beguiling, luring, or enticing. The word suggests a seduction that draws one into an enclosed domain. If *Entrückung* is temporal, *Berückung* is spatial. While *Entrückung* draws out, *Berückung* draws in. Both words can have negative connotations (385): *Entrückung* is a dispersal or dissolution, and *Berückung* is an estrangement and bewitching. However, maybe these connotations are negative only as long as we picture ourselves as self-enclosed, static precincts. If we come to understand ourselves as being-there—a thrown and throwing openness—then it will be entirely appropriate to speak of a captivation and transport that carry us into time and space, enabling rather than destroying ownness. Heidegger would add that it is not enough to represent ourselves differently; what is needed is a de-rangement (*Ver-rückung*) of humanity into being-there (314, 372).

Time-space is—in a nearly untranslatable phrase—*die Entrückungs-Berückungsgefüge (Fügung) des Da* (371). The there fits together as the juncture of transport and captivation. The language of the "fissure," which Heidegger usually uses to name the multiplicity of be-ing, can also fit time-space: "time-space is the appropriated fissuring of the courses of appropriation" (372). Along its fissures, a series of tensions play themselves out. Heidegger lists them: belonging (to the past?) and the call (of the future?); the abandonment of being and the hint (of a new inception?); nearness and distance, emptiness and donation, impetus and hesitation (372). These words suggest that a contest takes place (or would take place) in time-space—the contest between our current lack of be-ing and the inceptive event of appropriation. Time-space is an "arena for strife" (260).

Heidegger traces this strife most closely in §242, which is one of the *Con-*

---

77. The term *Entrückung* is introduced in SZ 338–39. See also *The Basic Problems of Phenomenology*, esp. 267 and 302 (Hofstadter translates *Entrückung* as "carrying-away," "carrying-off," "remotion," and "removal").

tributions' most sustained and original trains of thought. This section demands a careful reading.[78] Each paragraph below presents a condensed paraphrase of one of Heidegger's main thoughts, followed by a more interpretive commentary enclosed in parentheses. I have taken some small liberties with the order of his statements, but I am faithful to the general movement of his thought. In broad terms, §242 moves from the themes of abyss and emptiness to a meditation on transport and captivation, and from there to an account of derivative space and time.

Ground as Abyss (379–80)

Time-space is the abyssal ground (*Ab-grund*) that belongs to truth. (Truth here means unconcealment. We have already seen how be-ing as appropriation would involve time-space; unconcealment must involve it too. But how do ground and abyss happen?)

The ground conceals itself while it sustains and towers through that which it grounds. (To seek a ground for the given is to seek something hidden—otherwise it would not need seeking, and would not be separate from the given. Yet the ground also pervades the given—otherwise it would not be the ground *of* the given. So the ground both lurks beneath the grounded and dwells within it. In this case, the grounded is the given beings and the given sense of their being; the ground is truth—the happening of unconcealment. Unconcealment is "in" beings themselves, for they are unconcealed. Yet unconcealing as such stays away; it remains in the back-ground.)

The abyssal ground is the staying-away of ground. (We would normally think of this as the absence of all grounds, but if the ground as such is self-secluding, then the ground itself essentially happens as abyss. As long as the ground *refuses* to come forth, it is abyssal.)

But there is a hesitation here: the ground does not simply stay away. It grounds, yet does not properly (*eigentlich*) ground (380). (What would it mean to ground *eigentlich*? Perhaps to provide an absolute, self-validating, fully self-disclosing ground. Such a ground is unavailable here, because be-ing happens contingently and secludes itself. If we are looking for certainty and security, unconcealment and be-ing will disappoint us. Alternatively, we could interpret "does not properly ground" as a contingent condition; maybe be-ing could *happen* in such a way as to provide a truly

78. For other readings of §242 see Beistegui, *The New Heidegger*, 80–93; Beistegui, *Truth and Genesis*, 154–65; Coriando, *Der letzte Gott als Anfang*, 87–106; Friedrich-Wilhelm von Herrmann, "Wahrheit—Zeit—Raum," in *Die Frage nach der Wahrheit*, ed. Ewald Richter (Frankfurt am Main: Vittorio Klostermann, 1997); Magris, "I concetti fondamentali," 263–68; Müller, *Der Tod als Wandlungsmitte*, 287–99; Neu, *Die Notwendigkeit der Gründung*, 204–14; Stambaugh, *The Finitude of Being*, 60–66, 116–22.

appropriating and potent ground, albeit not an absolute ground. It becomes clear later in §242 that this second reading is closer to what Heidegger intends.)

An ambiguous ground, an abyssal ground, lies between giving and nongiving, in the realm of the hint (*Wink*). Through this hint, we are beckoned (*erwunken*) into being-there. Being-there is *das Beständnis der lichtenden Verbergung*—withstanding the withholding, steadfastness within the clearing concealing. (The motto of this moment in §242 could be Heraclitus's fragment 93: "The lord whose oracle is at Delphi neither speaks nor conceals, but indicates."[79] If we learn to follow the indication, to take the hint, we can leap into being the there [385].)

Emptiness as Openness (380–82)

By withholding itself, the abyssal ground leaves behind a distinctive emptiness.[80] This emptiness is not a mere unoccupied void; it is an *openness* within which the given is given. (Compare Heraclitus's fragment 52: "Time [*aion*] is a child at play . . . the kingdom is a child's." Time-space is a *Spielraum*, a playspace or leeway [cf. 257 and SZ 368]. It grants *possibilities*. If the ground came forth as fully given and self-legitimating, there would be nothing childlike about it, nothing playful—and it would provide no possibilities, only necessities. There would be no gifts, only consequences. The world would be a deductive unity—as some philosophers and scientists hope that it is. The withdrawal of the ground, the *emptiness* of time-space, enables playspace to open.)

The empty openness has a definite character: it is attuned and fitted. ("Playful" though it might be, the openness is not an arbitrary whim or abstract freedom. It would arise as a concrete historical juncture, shaped and appropriated by a specific urgency. Unconcealment is never neutral, but has its own, unique texture. As Heidegger puts it in "Das Ereignis," every time in the history of be-ing is a *Frist*, an appointed time.)

Does the notion of emptiness presuppose an unfulfilled will, desire, or need? "Empty" seems to be a negative concept, defined only in relation to something that we were expecting and failed to find. (It seems that we cannot notice that something is absent unless either it was previously present—

---

79. For Heidegger's comments on the fragment see GA 16, 687 and GA 39, 127–28. On hinting, cf. GA 39, 32. For a careful elucidation of hinting that employs *Being and Time*'s phenomenology of signs, see Coriando, *Der letzte Gott als Anfang*, 62–70.

80. On "emptiness," cf. GA 65, 29, 338–39. The word invites comparisons with Buddhism, despite Heidegger's anti-Buddhist exclamation (GA 65, 171). The Mahamudra and Dzogchen schools understand emptiness as an "openness" or luminosity: *The Encyclopedia of Eastern Philosophy and Religion*, edited by Stephan Schuhmacher and Gert Woerner (Boston: Shambhala, 1994), s. v. "Shunyata."

which is not the case here—or we approach the experience with a *demand* for presence, which in this case would be illegitimate.)

Emptiness *is* linked to our being-there, but it is not a function of desire or need; what is decisive is the urgency that impels us to leap into appropriation, attuned by restraint. Since the word *emptiness* creates so many false impressions, perhaps we should give it up. (Unlike need and desire, urgency calls forth a new self. It is not a demand for presence, but a leap into being-there. A preexisting subject does not bring time-space into being by an act of will; rather, being-there comes about when it is swept up into timing and spacing. This account is not completely satisfactory, however. When Heidegger says, for example, that being-there is restraint "in the face of hesitating refusal" [382], the problem seems to arise anew. "Refusal" seems to presuppose a demand. What is the status of this demand? Maybe we can imagine a three-step sequence: a subjective demand for a ground; a relative "emptiness" or "refusal" in relation to this demand; finally, a "restraint" that respects the lack of a ground, no longer tries to master and represent it, and thus transcends the initial subjectivity in order to be drawn into a different way of being and thinking.)

Primordial Timing and Spacing (382–86)

In time-space, the divine becomes an undecidable problem for us. (The gods would now become urgently uncertain.)

This undecidability is prior to the "time" that flows by the present-at-hand and the "space" that surrounds it; time-space is the abyssal happening of unconcealment, not the beings that are unconcealed. (Now the theme of primordial "timing" and "spacing" is introduced.)

Time-space, as the happening of truth, lets appropriation spring forth in a leap; truth lets appropriation pervade the open. (If unconcealing happens, then appropriation can take place. The precise character of this relation remains elusive, as does the meaning of Heidegger's claim that truth is *not* "more originary" than appropriation: 383.)

The emptiness (if we may still use this word) *transports* us into futurity and having-been. The gathering of past and future constitutes the present. (Heidegger makes a transition from emptiness to transport. It is tempting to imagine emptiness as a sort of vacuum that draws us into past and future, but this would miss the sense of "emptiness" as a historical juncture with its own texture. This becomes clear in his next thought.)

The present is the moment of "moving into abandonment." This moment remembers belonging to being, awaits the call of be-ing, and withstands the abandonment of being. It is a moment of decision regarding the onset (*An-*

fall) of be-ing. (The distinction between being and be-ing is not obvious in these expressions. I propose that Heidegger means that in the first inception, we belonged to the being of beings; this belonging has abandoned us, and we await a new gift, the event of be-ing. Heidegger's concern, it would seem, is not to describe future, past, and present *in general*. He is intent on evoking a specific historical juncture as a state of abandonment, and he makes no claim that this state is necessary, or that it always characterizes the present. Such a claim would obliterate the character of decision to which he is pointing; it would eliminate the possibility of be-ing's "onset." The word *Anfall* suggests the unpredictable onslaught of an illness or an enemy: cf. 260.)

It might seem, however, that because time-space is an abyssal ground, a ground that *withholds* itself, there is nothing to be decided: there can be no granting. But this is a *hesitating* refusal; it bestows the possibility of bestowal and appropriation. (We return to the notion of a hint, which wavers between giving and withholding. Maybe only a hint can be the supreme gift—the gift of the possibility of giving.)

Because the refusal hesitates, it is not only temporal transport, but also spatial captivation. Captivation is a hold: it entices us into the site where the moment is held. In this site, abandonment is localized and withstood. (The decision regarding be-ing must literally take place; a place where be-ing is at stake must emerge. "Place" here is presumably something like "world"—an arrangement of givens and possibilities, an order where we find ourselves dwelling and where we have opportunities.[81] Even if it is the site of abandonment, it is not a meaningless wasteland, but a genuine place where we must stand and endure.)

At this point (384) Heidegger reviews his account so far; we should too. He is evoking the there, the momentous site where and when be-ing is at stake. The there is both temporal (transporting) and spatial (captivating). Time-space as a whole involves the hesitating withdrawal of the ground— the unavailability of a proper and potent foundation for the being of beings and their truth. This unavailability is experienced as something like a passionate longing; but this should be understood not as a desire or demand of an already-formed subject, but as a rapture that brings us into being-there. On one hand, this rapture *transports* us into pastness (recalling the belonging to being that characterizes the first inception) and futurity (awaiting the call

---

81. For two fine recent investigations of place, see Edward S. Casey, *Getting Back into Place: Toward a Renewed Understanding of the Place-World* (Bloomington: Indiana University Press, 1993), and J. E. Malpas, *Place and Experience: A Philosophical Topography* (Cambridge: Cambridge University Press, 1999). Although both studies draw on Heidegger, they attempt to refresh our understanding of an already given phenomenon (as the title of Casey's work indicates) rather than evoking a possible future site, as the *Contributions* do.

of be-ing, readying the other inception). On the other hand, the rapture *captivates* us into the present as the locale where the abandonment of being must be withstood and where be-ing may take place.

Time and space are distinct, but intertwined. Space is the captivating abyssal grounding of the hold; time is the transporting abyssal grounding of the gathering; captivation is the abyssal hold of the gathering; transport is the abyssal gathering into the hold. Time spaces in, never captivating; space times in, never transporting. (Heidegger has already used the word "gathering" [*Sammlung*] in connection with transport, and "hold" [*Umhalt*] in connection with captivation. Transport gathers past and future into present; captivation holds the abandonment of being within a site. What Heidegger seems to be saying in these formulas, then, is that the past and future need a place into which they can be gathered, and conversely, the place needs to serve as the site for the gathering of past and future. To say that time "spaces in" [*räumt ein*] and space "times in" [*zeitigt ein*] seems to mean that time and space enable each other to draw us into the site and moment where we can step into being-there. As we noted earlier, "transport" and "captivation" connote dissolution and estrangement; these connotations are belied, however, by the movements of gathering and holding, which suggest the opposite—a belonging, a coming-into-one's-own [385]. Appropriation may disown us as self-contained substances or subjects; but as this happened we would be appropriated—becoming the grounders of the there.)

Derivative Time and Space (386–87)

How does primordial time-space give rise to time and space? This question points to several distinct problems.

1. How did the concepts of space and time arise in the first inception, where *aletheia* remained unexplored?
2. How do they arise in the other inception, where time-space is explicitly grasped?
3. How is time-space to be empowered in the future through sheltering the truth of appropriation in beings?
4. How can the thought of time-space as the happening of unconcealment resolve traditional philosophical riddles concerning time and space?

(Heidegger continues to think *historically*. Problems 1 and 2 stand at the juncture between the first and the other inception, which give rise to separate ways of conceiving of space and time. Problem 3 looks forward to a decision regarding sheltering. Problem 4 might seem like an ahistorical, purely theoretical problem—but we are about to see that it is not.)

Being and Time took some steps toward addressing problem 2 by trying to grasp space and time in their pre-mathematical form. But what allows space and time to be mathematized? The answer is the happening in which the abyssal ground, barely grounded, is blocked by the "un-ground" (387). (It seems that problem 4 must also be addressed historically, in terms of this happening. But what *is* happening here? In an intriguing but undeveloped remark, the *Introduction to Metaphysics* distinguishes a "truly grounding" *Ur-grund* from an *Ab-grund*, which "refuses to provide a foundation," and contrasts both with an *Un-grund*, which "merely offers the perhaps necessary illusion of a foundation."[82] This suggests the following story. In the first inception, the event of unconcealing was glimpsed by the Greeks, who named it *aletheia*. But they could not properly ground this event by accepting and enduring its abyssal nature—its contingency and obscurity. Instead, they focused on the gift that emerged from this event: presence as the being of beings. As the ultimate *given*, presence easily offered the illusion of an unshakeable foundation; but it was actually subordinate to the *giving*, which was itself unavailable either as a present being or as the presence of beings. The understanding of the being of beings as presence allowed for an understanding of thinking as re-presenting, and representing becomes mathematical as soon as it engages in measuring. Space and time become quantitative when they are reduced to containers for present beings, which are the objects of measurement. In order to retrace the decline from *aletheia* and go even further "back"—to *Ereignis*—we can begin by noticing the owning [or appropriateness] that is at work in our everyday spatial and temporal experiences. This much was done in *Being and Time.* The next step is to experience the abandonment of the being of beings—the fact that it is no longer a living issue for us—and our belonging to be-ing—our assignation to the hidden, contingent event of the giving of the being of beings. Then time-space can go to work—or play—as a nonrepresentable, nonmeasurable, momentous site.)

The Fertility of Time-Space (387–88)

The hold of captivation offers an open expanse of possibilities. The gathering of transport offers the immeasurable remoteness of what is given as a task. (Heidegger has previously countered the notions of dissolution and loss that "captivation" and "transport" might suggest. He now addresses the opposite notion: that time-space might be confining and stifling. Despite its specificity and coherence, time-space is a fertile field, a nexus of distances and destinies.)

The abyssal ground is not groundless; it affirms ground in its hidden ex-

82. *Introduction to Metaphysics*, 3.

panse and remoteness. The "not" that holds sway in it is the "not" of the hint and of be-ing itself. (As stated at the beginning of §242, the abyssal ground is the staying-away of ground. But this is not equivalent to the denial of all grounds, or to nihilism. There is still the possibility of a genuine grounding. This would be a grounding that accepts the nothing within appropriation—that is, the contingency and strangeness of the happening of be-ing.)

From Time and Space to Time-Space (388)

Instead of beginning with time-space itself, we can also take the opposite way: starting with beings, we can examine their spatiality and temporality in a new way, in terms of the sheltering of truth. This interpretation will be guided silently by our knowledge of time-space as the abyssal ground, but it will awaken new experiences by beginning with the thing. (This final paragraph offers an important insight into the status of "The Origin of the Work of Art" and Heidegger's postwar essays on technology and "things." Various fields of beings can be approached in such a way that they point to the abyssal un-concealing of time-space. How is this possible? The key is sheltering, which is necessary in order for time-space to happen [386]. When be-ing is sheltered in beings, the momentous site will be grounded.)

I have read §242 not as an account of eternal essences, but as an evocation and anticipation of a motion—a unique and urgent happening. This is the aim of be-ing-historical thinking: to take part in the possible taking-place of be-ing. The text's tonality is future-subjunctive.[83]

But is a present-indicative interpretation also viable—an interpretation of §242 as a description of invariant structures? Probably so, for Heidegger retains the philosopher's penchant for finding grounds and patterns. One could even argue that this is a redeeming feature of his text—saving it from becoming rhapsodic prophecy and keeping it tied to thinking. Maybe we *ought* to analyze time-space and appropriation as universal structures, conditions that are quietly operative whenever and wherever human beings encounter other beings. Heidegger's thoughts on the degeneration of time-space into derivative time and space would not be a history or prophecy, then, but a phenomenology.[84]

Sections 98 and 150, for instance, appear to provide such a phenomenology. In §98 Heidegger claims that in the ordinary concept of time, "time is experienced in a disguised way as timing, as *transport*" (191). He sketches var-

83. Cf. Gander, "Sein—Zeit—Geschichte," 183.
84. According to Neu, Heidegger's investigation of time-space in the *Contributions* is still "phenomenological": *Die Notwendigkeit der Gründung*, 204. Coriando calls it a "phenomenology of the present": *Der letzte Gott als Anfang*, 95.

ious ways in which the subsidiary phenomena of constancy and presence emerge from primordial time-space:

Constancy and time: endurance (*Ausdauer*—akin to insistence?) is the basis of constancy as duration (*Dauer*). Endurance involves transports into past and future; it can happen only for being-there, whose remembrance and preparation allow the present to flare up in its uniqueness (257). It is as if being-there were stretched between past and future; the tension of this stretch allows beings to reveal themselves as lasting or constant—as merely continuing to be present.

Presence and time: endurance retreats from its transports, which fade into the background, creating the illusion that true beings are timelessly present. This is a familiar Heideggerian account: the present is opened by the future and past, yet seems to take precedence over them.

Constancy and space: constancy is the filling and fulfilling of space. Here "constancy" (*Beständigkeit*) seems to imply substantiality. A lasting substrate needs a location where it can stand firmly and endure. Space, however, is not "properly experienced" in the experience of substance. Like time, it fades away while constant substances come to the fore.

Presence and space: presence offers space for the beings that are set into it. Within this space, beings can be present as beings.

Section 150 follows a similar pattern, but focuses on the *idea* as preeminently constant and present. The *idea*, along with the distinction between essence and existence, is an impoverished remnant of the rich happening of time-space (271). Section 150's main addition to section 98 is its discussion of the "look" of that which is gathered into presence. This look constitutes "essence," and its ongoing duration constitutes "existence."

Heidegger's central thought in sections 98 and 150 is that being as presence is given by a richer happening that must be understood in terms of transport and captivation. When these fade into "indifference," then all that is left is an inert framework within which present beings can be represented (70; cf. 371, 373, 382). This leads to traditional concepts of space and time—which are not false, but rather have a certain truth if they are understood properly, in the context of be-ing as appropriation (378).

These passages can be read as descriptions of time-space as a quasi-present, constant structure—and maybe that is even the most fruitful reading. If we persist in interpreting time-space as a possibility, we will run up against the paradox of making a future event the basis of a traditional set of concepts. It seems that if transport can be "forgotten" (192), it must always already be in effect.

It may be possible to get around this reasoning by holding that time-space was anticipated to some degree in the first inception, but not yet "empowered" as it will be in the other inception (386). In any case, the present-indicative standpoint goes against the grain of Heidegger's thinking in the *Contributions*. As he says at the end of §98, it is a misunderstanding of space and time to take them as a particular kind of *Anwesendes*, a present something (192). He does not want "to lapse into the usual formal concepts of space and time" (261). His inquiry demands a new kind of questioning (193)—a leap out of the present-indicative tonality, into the possibility of a unique emergency.[85]

To confirm this interpretation, note that Heidegger tries to educe transport and captivation from hinting—which is "the inceptive essence of appropriation . . . in the other inception. This essence of be-ing [is] unique and happens only once . . . *physis* too is unique and happens only once" (385). If we take this statement seriously, then time-space is nothing like a universal structure or transcendental condition that always already hovers above every particular time and place. Time-space is *a* time and place—more precisely, *the* momentous site at which we may someday find ourselves. The time and place that originated the first inception were not time-space as Heidegger thinks it, but a separate emergency from which being as presence emerged. The task of thought, then, is not simply to describe time-space but to *ground* it (60, 237).

For a fuller understanding of time-space and the other inception, we need to turn to the relation between be-ing and beings—for in time-space, be-ing is supposed to be sheltered within beings (386).

---

85. A number of interpretations of §242 reflect the tension between a present-indicative reading and a future-subjunctive reading (which I see as truer to the radical impulses of the *Contributions*). For example, in Neu's reading, time-space does not concern matters that obtain "in general," but rather what occurs "in the *uniqueness* of being-there" (*Die Notwendigkeit der Gründung*, 203); in order to experience time-space as abyss, one must "be deranged into it by an emergency" (213). However, Neu also states that the abyssal ground of time-space "always already" indicates the ultimate ground, the truth of be-ing (206–7). This way of speaking makes be-ing sound like something permanently quasi-present, a structure that is "always already" in place and is more fundamental than any unique, contingent moment of emergency. Similarly, Costantino Esposito suggests the historical uniqueness of time-space yet also resorts to an a priori: "in the *Contributions*, history constitutes the very abyss of time, that in which being-there is always already transpropriated to being": *Heidegger: Storia e fenomenologia del possibile* (Bari: Levante, 1992), 185. Again, Beistegui characterizes "the taking place of place" as "a unique and singular event" (*Truth and Genesis*, 142) that is "the site of a singular historical configuration" (ibid., 145), yet claims it "does not cease to take place" and is "always operative" (ibid., 142; cf. 161 on the "always already"); time-space "does not mark one moment, one episode of history, but . . . [history's] very essence" (ibid., 173–74). Von Herrmann's reading is historical in that time-space involves the possibility of the "*onset* of the truth of be-ing" ("Wahrheit—Zeit—Raum," 253); but I would go farther and claim that time-space *is* this possibility.

Be-ing and Beings: Simultaneity and Sheltering

The philosophical tradition, charges Heidegger, has focused on beings and their beingness (*Seiendheit*) without raising the question of be-ing—how the being of beings becomes an issue for us. The tradition debates the nature of beingness without recognizing that it is neither a self-legitimating a priori structure nor simply an abstraction from particular beings, but a gift of the event of appropriation that opens the there. Before the *Contributions*, Heidegger conceived of the relation between being and beings as the "ontological difference"—but perhaps this concept was "a necessary impasse."[86] It can alert us to the question of being as other than all ontic questions; yet it also tempts us to conceive of being as a universal beingness (250, 465–69). The challenge, then, is to think through the relation between beings and *be-ing*, where be-ing is not a mere universal. Heidegger remarks that the differentiation (*Unterscheidung*) between beingness and beings originates in be-ing's essentially decisive character (*Entscheidungswesen*) (455).[87] Be-ing, this remark suggests, is a contingent event that unconceals beings in a particular way at a critical moment—and then withdraws. The event of appropriating opens the clearing, yet it cannot be recognized by representational thinking, which operates *within* this clearing and sees only the distinction between present beings and their beingness (466).

Even though be-ing cannot be understood in terms of beings, it does not occur "before" them; it essentially happens in and through beings, so Heidegger speaks of the *Gleichzeitigkeit*—synchronicity or simultaneity—of be-ing and beings (13, 223, 289). The expression intends to avoid all apriorism and transcendentalism; be-ing is not a condition of the possibility of beings, but happens together with the revelation of beings themselves.

We must also think of the relation between be-ing and beings in terms of the sheltering (*Bergung*) of the truth of be-ing, "by which beings as such first enter the there" (273). A being truly comes into being (*seiend wird*) when its own truth "as thing, tool, machination, work, deed, sacrifice" is sheltered in it (70, cf. 389). Sheltering enables beings to emerge as the beings that they

---

86. "Seminar in Le Thor 1969," in *Four Seminars*, 61. In a sense, the *Contributions* try to overcome the ontological difference, as Vallega-Neu observes: *Heidegger's "Contributions,"* 4, 28. But Heidegger intends to maintain, and even intensify, the distinction between beings and be-ing: cf. Gander, "Sein—Zeit—Geschichte," 181–82; Maly, "Turnings in Essential Swaying and the Leap," 154–55. The ontological difference was not different enough.

87. For a clear interpretation of differentiation in GA 66 and GA 69, see Beistegui, *Truth and Genesis*, chap. 5. Differentiation is also treated extensively in "Das Ereignis," where Heidegger conceives of difference (*Unterschied*) as a parting (*Abschied*) that is endemic to the event of appropriation as inception.

are, and enables be-ing as appropriation to take place. The conflict between earth and world is an essential part of this event; in order to appreciate how appropriation gives rise to a world, a configuration of what it means to be, we must remember that the world emerges from the earth, or the hidden ground of all meanings.

Heidegger hopes that appropriation will transform "all relations to 'beings'" (248). His quotation marks indicate that the very sense of what counts as an entity will change. Beings will no longer be taken for granted as present-at-hand things, but will be experienced as sheltering the inexhaustible truth of be-ing that is simultaneous with them.

The Simultaneity of Be-ing and Beings

The concept of simultaneity is not without precedent in Heidegger's earlier writings, but it is especially emphasized in the *Contributions*.[88] Unfortunately, the text cannot be said to give an *account* of simultaneity; the idea remains mostly at the level of slogans. It is easier to see what pitfalls Heidegger is trying to avoid than to understand how simultaneity would work. Still, we can extrapolate from some particularly striking slogans. "Be-ing is not something 'earlier'—subsisting for itself, in itself—but appropriation is the temporal-spatial simultaneity for be-ing and beings" (13). "The truth of be-ing and the essential happening of be-ing is neither the earlier nor the later. Being-there is the simultaneity of time-space with the true as beings" (223). These lines associate simultaneity with time-space, which I have interpreted as the distinctive character of a unique possible moment and place—the "momentous site" where be-ing would happen. This site or "there" can be grounded, and being-there can come forth, only if beings (the true) come forth "at the same time as" unconcealment (truth). This, in turn, can happen only if unconcealment retains traces of concealment, so that the "there" does justice to the mystery of be-ing. When self-concealing pervades all things within the clearing, "*world* arises, and together with it (due to the 'simultaneity' of be-ing and beings) the *earth* emerges" (349).

In order to interpret these statements we have to focus on the notion of thrownness, which the *Contributions* adopt from *Being and Time* and incorporate in their portrait of being-there as a grounded grounder, a thrown thrower (239). To be thrown is to be situated and indebted—not only in that

88. In 1927 Heidegger already writes that "beings and being are unveiled . . . with equal originality": *The Basic Problems of Phenomenology*, 320. Here he claims both that being is a priori (324–26) and that the understanding of being is always rooted in a "comportment toward beings" (327). "On the Essence of Ground" (1929) states, "*Transcendence means the projection of world in such a way that those beings that are surpassed also already pervade and attune that which projects*": *Pathmarks*, 128.

we owe our lives to the beings among which we find ourselves living, but also in that we have been given a sense of the *being* of these beings, a sense that we do not control or fully grasp. To be thrown, then, is to be appropriated by be-ing (239) as well as to find that one is oneself an entity amidst entities. All our attempts to interpret the beings that surround us must draw on the sense of being that has been given to us, without ever managing to construct a new, perfectly certain foundation for this sense. To put this in terms of the problem of the given, as we explored it in chapter 1: we must come to recognize that beings have been given to us together with a sense of their givenness, and that our attempts to describe the patterns of this givenness cannot exhaust the event of *giving* to which we are indebted. This event has thrown us "simultaneously" into beings and their being.

This thought opposes both empiricism and apriorism. An empiricist would hold that repeated experiences of beings give rise to our sense of their import—their being. But no experience is free of a given background of significance. For instance, a "pure noise" is a mere construct—we hear beings, not uninterpreted sounds.[89] All projection is thrown, so truth is not simply a matter of experiencing given beings and ascertaining data (245, 452). An experience is always informed by a sense of the difference it makes that there is something instead of nothing. Things always make sense to us—albeit in an obscure way—before we make sense of them.

An aprioristic account would turn this "always" into an a priori that determines experience in advance and is exempt from being transformed by any experience. In its transcendental version, apriorism holds that the limits of the experiencing subject constitute the being of all beings we can ever experience. *Being and Time* may seem to permit this reading, but as we saw in chapter 1, Heidegger is now at pains to rule it out (176, 223, 250–51, 253). The key, once again, is thrownness. Being-there is not just a thrower who projects the form of experience; this thrower is also thrown (239)—indebted to a given significance that is not fully understood. This obscurity calls for creative transformation. So even though each experience of beings occurs within a wider context of ways in which beings make a difference to us, there is room for experiences that can transfigure this context. (For instance, I cannot read *Ulysses* without some understanding of what it means to tell a story, but the experience of reading the book may well change this understanding.)

Heidegger claims that empiricism and apriorism are not enemies, but allies. Our concept of beingness is empirically abstracted from present beings; we then can interpret this abstraction as an underlying basis from which beings spring—an a priori ground. Hence "the '*a priori*' merely veils the de-

---

89. SZ 163–64; *Introduction to Metaphysics*, 36.

rivativeness" of the traditional concept of being (183; cf. 111–12, 216–17, 293, 425). Neither empiricism nor apriorism does justice to thrownness: neither grasps that we are already amidst beings and that they "simultaneously" make sense to us, in a way that we cannot fully understand. An insight into simultaneity will thus supposedly make the entire controversy between empiricism and apriorism obsolete.

Heidegger also claims that simultaneity is the key to avoiding an infinite regress, in which we would search for the be-ing of be-ing, and so on (288–89). Instead of a linear progression of deeper and deeper grounds, we are to think of an abyssal grounding in which beings and their being emerge together, needing no further ground.

None of this is meant as a merely conceptual solution to some philosophical conundrums; simultaneity is not a fixed relation that we can understand more or less clearly, but part of the unique possibility of the other inception. If simultaneity happens, "there is a moment of *history*" (349).

But how thoroughly is Heidegger committed to the possibility of simultaneity? Does he really implement it in his thought? He claims that even though be-ing is not the "cause and *ratio*" of beings, it is their "ground" (289). Even though be-ing is not a priori, it "essentially happens *before* all the beings that stand into it" (303); it has "precedence" (*Vorrang*, 428). Furthermore, Heidegger's stated goal in the *Contributions* is to leap into be-ing without starting from beings (75–76).

These statements are not as inconsistent as they may seem. Even if be-ing cannot happen without beings (whereas beings do not need be-ing: 30), be-ing may still rank higher than beings. While thinking of be-ing and beings as simultaneous, Heidegger hopes to reverse their traditional ranks. In the tradition, being serves beings; in the other inception, "beings are so that they may simultaneously bear the clearing into which they stand . . . all beings are sacrificed to be-ing, and this is where beings as such first get their truth" (229–30). In the "strife" of be-ing and beings (249), Heidegger wants be-ing to gain the upper hand. Nietzsche would call this a revaluation; Heidegger would rather say he is honoring be-ing itself as "mastery" (76). The new purpose of beings is to *shelter* be-ing—but this is not to say that be-ing lies "'above' beings and separate from them" (287). In order to take place, be-ing *needs* to be sheltered in beings. So even if we cannot grasp be-ing by starting with beings, we do have to return to them.[90]

---

90. As I read Heidegger, be-ing is neither reducible to beings nor separable from them; as Beistegui puts it, "It is always alongside beings that truth comes about [but truth is not] a function of beings": *Truth and Genesis*, 126. This interpretation lies between two extremes. According to Caputo, the later Heidegger focuses on an "Essential Being (*Wesen*)" that is "removed from beings": *Demythologizing Heidegger*, 118, 120. This interpretation simply neglects the

Sheltering and Truth

To "sacrifice" beings to be-ing (230) is not, of course, to annihilate them. Be-ings must continue to *be;* but they are to indicate the event of be-ing. They must refer to the emergence of the world in which they appear and belong. Appropriation can happen only if we experience the things around us as the haunts of be-ing.[91] As be-ing dwells in beings, the there opens. This is the primal event of truth, so truth essentially happens only "where it establishes itself in a being."[92] When sheltering takes place, the clearing is grounded in the beings that lie open within it (including things, tools, and artworks); this sheltering must also include self-concealment, and at its greatest peak it would gather all the ways of sheltering together into the being-there of a people (389–90). Unconcealment properly happens only if we encounter beings in their connections to the entire field of significance that is shared by a community, while remaining aware of the contingency and limits of this field. Since the field is historical, it is always finite and open to new possibilities. Sheltering lets the limits of meaning show up at the same time as it reveals a network of meaning in every experience of concrete beings. Beings are thus imbued with the richness of their place in a meaningful whole at the same

themes of simultaneity and sheltering. At the other extreme is Charles E. Scott's interpretation of the *Contributions*, according to which Heidegger wants to "re-think the meaning of the question of being so that be-ing's eventfulness suggests *only* the happening of beings": "Introduction," in Scott et al., *Companion*, 6 (my emphasis). Scott does distinguish be-ing as the "eventuation of beings" from all *particular* beings, because no single entity can properly define all the others (ibid., 9); but then "be-ing" seems to mean either the sum of all ontic events, or a pattern that characterizes all such events indifferently—neither of which is an event that founds the "there." Scott rightly stresses that Heidegger wishes to avoid positing a "defining ground" of beings (ibid., 6), but he goes too far in claiming that "for Heidegger's mature thought there is no dimension *in* which there are beings" (ibid., 5). (Consider the discussion of the "region" in "Conversation on a Country Path," in *Discourse on Thinking*, 65–87.) From Scott's perspective, Heidegger's tendency to assign "an Olympian role to 'the essential sway' of the truth of be-ing" is a retrograde feature of the *Contributions*, a remnant of metaphysics ("Introduction," 9). I prefer to try to understand why, despite Heidegger's opposition to traditional metaphysical and transcendental thought, he still wishes to assert a certain priority of be-ing over beings. As I will argue in chapter 4, the project is not altogether successful; but it is not simply a relapse into metaphysics, either. (Scott develops his own approach to the happening of beings in *The Lives of Things* [Bloomington: Indiana University Press, 2002]; see especially 57–67 on Heidegger. Scott claims here that *Ereignis* refers to "each being's arising into its own event" [65].) Lewis also makes be-ing sound too ontic when he glosses it as "the singularity of entities, the 'given fact' that they have but a single moment and site in which to be": "God and Politics in Later Heidegger," 392.

91. As Vincenzo Brutti puts it, the "betrayal" of be-ing can be overcome only if beings, man, and the gods can find a place again within the gift of be-ing: "Ritrovare ente e divino nell'essere: una lettura dei *Beiträge zur Philosophie* di Heidegger," in *Passione dell'originario: Fenomenologia ed ermeneutica dell'esperienza religiosa*, ed. Emilio Baccarini (Rome: Studium, 2000), 425, 440.

92. "The Origin of the Work of Art," in *Off the Beaten Track*, 42.

time as they resist total explanation in terms of this whole. Sheltering, then, preserves a mystery that we forget when we experience things merely as given objects. Recognizing the finitude of meaning incites us to allow meaning to evolve creatively and responsively.[93] In this way, sheltering indicates be-ing—the event of the emergence of meaning. These thoughts are elegantly conveyed by the phonic and semantic echoes in Heidegger's language: sheltering (*Bergung*) involves concealment (*Verbergung*) as well as unconcealment (*Unverborgenheit*); unconcealment is primal truth (*Wahrheit*), so in order for truth to happen it must be guarded and preserved (*bewahrt, verwahrt*) within beings.[94]

It may be possible, then, to approach be-ing not on its own terms (as Heidegger tries to do in the *Contributions*) but "by way of 'beings'" (389). Perhaps we can train ourselves to see beings as sheltering the truth of be-ing. This might require nothing less than "a derangement of [our] basic relation to be-ing itself" (389)—and to beings. Still, Heidegger envisions an interpretation of the "spatiality and temporality of the thing, the tool, the work [of art], machination, and all beings as the sheltering of truth. . . . The interpretation must awaken new experiences, beginning with the thing. . . . The way from [time-space and be-ing] and the way from beings must meet each other" (388). This programmatic statement gives us the connecting thread for many of Heidegger's essays, from "The Origin of the Work of Art" to postwar essays such as "The Question Concerning Technology," "The Thing," and "Building Dwelling Thinking." His plan is to focus on various realms of beings in a way that will point to be-ing as appropriation.[95] His statements in the *Contributions* also shed light on the concept of the "fourfold" (gods, mortals, earth, and sky) developed in "The Thing" and "Building Dwelling Thinking." These essays are not simply saying, in the present indicative, that beings participate in the fourfold; they are *provoking* us to imagine such a possibility, to be "de-ranged" into a new way of dwelling.

Artworks may be the clearest examples of sheltering. According to "The Origin of the Work of Art," the artwork lets beings show up as beings, as if for the first time, because it embodies the struggle between the self-conceal-

93. As Antonello D'Angelo puts it, finitude implies "groundlessness and conflict, and in this way keeps open the possibility of dynamism": "'Svolta' e 'attimalità' in Heidegger: Alcune considerazioni sui 'Beiträge zur Philosophie' e su 'Die Kehre,'" *La Cultura* 30, no. 2 (August 1992): 221.

94. Unfortunately, Emad and Maly often translate *Verbergung* as "sheltering" (e.g., *Contributions to Philosophy*, 244 = GA 65, 349) or "sheltering-concealing" (e.g., *Contributions to Philosophy*, 245 = GA 65, 350). The term *sheltering* should be reserved for *Bergung*. *Verbergung* stresses the withdrawal of be-ing, whereas *Bergung* stresses its latent potency in things and actions.

95. For a detailed interpretation of the various ways of sheltering see Neu, *Die Notwendigkeit der Gründung*, §§15–20.

ing earth and the illuminating world.[96] As *Introduction to Metaphysics* puts it, the artwork is being *within* a being (*das seiende Sein*); through it, "everything else that appears and that we can find around us first becomes confirmed and accessible, interpretable and understandable, *as a being,* or else as an unbeing."[97] Here, the sense of the givenness of beings is installed in a particular being; this being then sets standards for what can count as a being. The artwork reveals an order of belonging, a whole in which everything has its own time and place.[98] Yet it does not let us forget the finitude and contingency of this order.

Thinking about the preeminent rank of artworks within beings as a whole can lead us to the question of the stages (*Stufen*) of be-ing (§152). The traditional chain of beings, from the supreme being down to nonbeing, is part of the metaphysical way of representing beings in their beingness and organizing a system in terms of a particular concept of beingness (273–74). But even when such metaphysics has been surpassed, there is still the question of how to rank various entities: living things, inanimate nature, tools, deeds, and so on. This cannot be an ahistorical, systematic ranking, but must attune itself to *historical* necessity (274). We must approach beings as different areas in which the truth of be-ing is to be *sheltered*—for there are "stages and domains and degrees of sheltering" (410). The issue here is what roles various domains will play when we stage the transition to the other inception. For instance, "What should technology be?" (275). The question is not how to classify technological devices in a chart of beings, but how modern technicity can be experienced as sheltering the truth of be-ing, and how this experience may work together with others in order to initiate the other inception. Similarly, Heidegger considers the role of living things and nature, asking how we can relate to what is alive beyond the confines of modern biology (276)[99] and to nature as more than an object of science or recreation (277–78).

In all this, the point is not to discover how beings *already* shelter be-ing, but to elicit such sheltering as part of our leap into being-there. Has shel-

---

96. This is why art belongs to appropriation: Appendix (1956) to "The Origin of the Work of Art," in *Off the Beaten Track*, 55. On the relation of the "Origin" essay to the *Contributions* see von Herrmann, *Wege ins Ereignis*, chap. 2.

97. *Introduction to Metaphysics*, 170.

98. Cf. Heidegger, "Art and Space" (1969), trans. Charles Seibert, in *Rethinking Architecture: A Reader in Cultural Theory,* ed. Neil Leach (London: Routledge, 1997), 123.

99. For attempts to remedy Heidegger's comparative neglect of the body and life in the *Contributions* see David Farrell Krell, "Contributions to Life," in Risser, *Heidegger toward the Turn*; Neu, *Die Notwendigkeit der Gründung*, §19; Scott, "Seyn's Physicality"; Daniela Vallega-Neu, *The Bodily Dimension in Thinking* (Albany: State University of New York Press, 2005), chap. 5. Heidegger's brief remarks on "life" in the *Contributions* need to be considered against the background of his extensive confrontation with Nietzsche's concept of life (and indirectly with the Nazi use of Nietzsche): e.g., GA 46, 15–34, 165–68, 211–22, 233–48.

tering ever happened before, though? Some of Heidegger's genealogical accounts suggest that it has. For example, once sheltering is in place, then the secondary type of truth—true representation—becomes possible (344). Beings can now be correctly identified and described; the danger is that we will forget the source of the meanings in accordance with which we identify and describe them. Similarly, "The Origin of the Work of Art" presents a sort of sheltering as the precondition for essence as *eidos:* a Greek temple "gathers" a world and "first gives to things their look."[100] Perhaps sheltering happens in every inception, then.

What is clear, at least, is that sheltering happens only at times of greatness—and our times are not great. Beings have become "unbeings" (7–8, 30, 44, 119, 122, 317). This does not mean that everything has been destroyed, but that the *import* of everything is being destroyed. We are becoming indifferent to the difference between beings and nothing (101). Beings seem to stand on their own, without any meaning of being at all. "Beings can still 'be' in the abandonment of being; [then] *immediate* graspability and usefulness and serviceability of every sort (e.g., everything must serve the people) self-evidently constitute *what is in being [was seiend ist]* and what is not" (30). When we take it for granted that beings are, the difference they make dims down into indifference; they become, for us, nothing but things to be thoughtlessly exploited. This reduction of beings to unbeings is malignant (the German prefix *un-* carries the sense of badness as well as mere negation): it makes the world smaller and human beings emptier (495).

Humanity must now become the grounder and preserver of the truth of be-ing (16). We will have a double mission: to "stand within the truth of be-ing" and to shelter that truth "in that which, in accord with such preservation, sets itself as beings into the clearing of the there" (467). The task can also be called "gather[ing] the empowerment of be-ing" (430). Sheltering is essential to this task. (The notions of authenticity and care in *Being and Time* were only preliminary indications of sheltering: 16, 302.)

If we shelter be-ing in beings, taking our share of responsibility for truth, we will find new respect for the powers of what is. We will produce or preserve beings in accordance with their own "directive" (*Geheiß*), "so that [the clearing] does not become a void in which everything comes forth in an equally 'understandable' and controllable way" (348–49). Being-there will expose the "unrest of beings" as what we *"ground and create, and in creating, allow to confront us as an assault"* (314–15).

But how do beings command us? How do they assail us? Heidegger seems far more concerned with the directing power of *be-ing*. However, his state-

---

100. "The Origin of the Work of Art," in *Off the Beaten Track,* 21.

ments on earth and world give us some indications. The *world* is a sphere of meaning, an order of sense; it articulates the difference that everything makes to us. The world is a people's understanding of the being of beings. The *earth* is the unmastered and uninterpreted basis of experience, the non-sense that sustains yet resists our understanding. The most appropriate way of approaching beings is to appreciate both how they belong to a world and how, as earth, they are more than this belonging. Beings then make a difference to us both as fitting into a coherent whole and as resisting total explanation; they are involved in both disclosure and self-closure (482). According to the *Contributions*, all beings can be understood in terms of this tension (275, 389–91). An experience of be-ing as appropriation would bring this struggle to light and reveal everything—work, thing, deed, sacrifice—in a fresh way (391).

The strife of earth and world is crucial to sheltering (29, 275, 354, 410). If we experience things as sheltering be-ing, we will become aware of the emergence of the field of significance that allows them to be given. Experienced in this way, things refer to all the crucial dimensions of significance—the world. They are then revealed as much more than objects; they are points at which meaningfulness itself is gathered and displayed. Furthermore, we will allow things to exceed and challenge all our interpretations. Things are not exhausted by the world, because a world is precisely a way of approaching the unknown on which it is built; the world does not abolish obscurity, but is based on it and confronts it. The world grows out of the earth; in sheltering, we "grow back into" the earth while letting the world do its worlding (391).

When confronted with Heidegger's urgent but vague statements, we naturally want some *examples* of simultaneity, sheltering, and the conflict between earth and world. But no such examples are forthcoming in the *Contributions*, and the examples in Heidegger's essays are too often shrouded in myth or nostalgia. One of his more plausible examples of sheltering is a van Gogh painting of a pair of shoes. It presents us with particular, literally earthy, things; but these shoes evoke the entire world of the peasant, the meaningful routines and endeavors into which the shoes fit. The shoes get the meaning of their being from this world—the world tells us what difference it makes that the shoes exist. However, this meaning does not exhaust the shoes or the fields; the opaque resistance of things, their sheer uninterpreted givenness, can always return to the fore.[101]

Heidegger also mentions tools or equipment (*Zeug*) as beings that could shelter be-ing (70, 388–89). Perhaps an example is an ancient scoop used in the tea ceremony. Its singularity and irreplaceability contribute to the in-

101. Ibid., 13–16.

ceptive character of the ceremony. The ceremony partakes of urgency—not as frenzied fear, but as concentration that responds to the exigencies of a moment. In this moment, one renews one's attention to the natural and man-made worlds. Their import emerges anew. This event of emergence rests within the scoop, the cups, the clothing, the tea room, and even the surrounding earth.

Just another nostalgic myth? Maybe not. The tea ceremony is still practiced in Japan, and comparable moments may happen in every culture, in every life, whether they are traditional rites or spontaneous epiphanies. If we pick up a stone in our garden and find unfamiliar creatures beneath it, we may recognize for a moment that our home and our understanding of life are built on the unknown; the meaning of life and home may then emerge in its proper fragility. For Heidegger, of course, the event of appropriation is rarer than this. Still, we all encounter some inceptive moments when we get a glimpse of what it may be like to find be-ing in beings and experience the strife of earth and world.

As we have seen, Heidegger appeals to our indebtedness to the earth in order to combat transcendentalism (231, 239, 259, 448). We are not simply throwers—projectors of worlds—but are also thrown: our interpretations emerge from an opaque givenness of beings that we can never abolish. Beings assail us (315); they besiege us (481–82). This is not just to say that life is a challenge; the *sense* we make of things is also under attack by the things themselves. Their earthly dimension keeps returning to undercut the world that interprets them.

Heidegger's remark that *simultaneity* also involves the strife of earth and world (349) gives us the connection between sheltering and the question of empiricism and apriorism. The way to avoid both an a priori and an a posteriori conception of the being of beings is precisely through sheltering, which is the possibility of experiencing beings as involved in the strife of earth and world. Sheltering rules out an interpretation of being as an abstraction from particular beings, since the significance of beings as a whole—the world—always exceeds any particular being. But sheltering also rules out an interpretation of being as an invariable, a priori condition of the possibility of experience, since sheltering allows the earth, as well as the world, to make a difference to us; sheltering acknowledges the limits of significance, and thus makes room for a transformation of the world in response to the earth.[102] The difference things make to us is neither independent of, nor wholly dom-

---

102. Heidegger makes a more explicit connection to traditional disputes between empiricism and apriorism by remarking that earth and world are conceived metaphysically as "the sensible and insensible" (GA 65, 482). Empiricism would give priority to the former, apriorism to the latter; but Heidegger rethinks them and allows them to enter into simultaneous "strife."

inated by, our established patterns of meaning; things have the potential to reconfigure the very patterns of meaning within which they show up as significant.

None of this is automatic. Earth and world join battle only at moments of history; in fact, their struggle is the essence of history (96, 410). Whether history will happen, whether nature as earth will resist the world, has not yet been decided (91). "Steadfastness in the strife of earth and world" is a task for the future ones (62). So far, modernity has been incapable of recognizing the earth as such, of kindling its conflict with the world; machination is prevailing (277–78). Our mission, then, is to rescue the earth—and thus to renew the world, for a world that ignores the earth is a world grown stale and sterile (412). The first step is silence (34); we need to quiet the relentless chatter of articulation in order to listen to what we cannot articulate.

This delicate move is essential to entering being-there (483). For unless we let the earth challenge the world, there can be no "there"—and without a there, there can be no self (322). Selfhood is not a stable identity within a given system of meaning, but emerges only when one's own being, and being in general, come into question. By resisting the world, the earth can call being into question; being can then become a problem for us; be-ing and being-there can then take place—if the *gods* come into play. "The gods call the earth and in the call a world resounds, so that the call echoes as man's being-there" (510).

The Gods: The Ultimate Apocalypse

Heidegger's pronouncements on the gods in the *Contributions* have attracted more interest than any other theme, although—or because—they are even more cryptic than the rest of the book.[103] The introduction of "the passing

103. The most extensive study is Coriando's *Der letzte Gott als Anfang;* a brief version of her interpretation is Paola-Ludovica Coriando, "Zur Er-mittlung des Übergangs: Der Wesungsort des 'letzten Gottes' im seinsgeschichtlichen Denken," in Coriando, *"Herkunft aber bleibt stets Zukunft."* See also Jean-François Courtine, "Les traces et le passage du Dieu dans les *Beiträge zur Philosophie* de Martin Heidegger," *Archivio di Filosofia* 62:1–3 (1994): 519–38; Crownfield, "The Last God"; Françoise Dastur, "Le 'dieu extrême' de la phénoménologie: Husserl et Heidegger," *Archives de Philosophie* 63 (2000): 195–204; Esposito, "Die Geschichte des letzten Gottes"; Günter Figal, "Forgetfulness of God: Concerning the Center of Heidegger's *Contributions to Philosophy,"* in Scott et al., *Companion;* Günter Figal, "Last Gods: Hermeneutic Theology in Nietzsche and Heidegger," in Figal, *For a Philosophy of Freedom and Strife: Politics, Aesthetics, Metaphysics,* trans. Wayne Klein (Albany: State University of New York Press, 1998); Ángel E. Garrido-Maturano, "Las imposibilidades del Dios: Introducción al problema de Dios en los *Beiträge zur Philosophie* de Martin Heidegger," *Universitas Philosophica* 28 (June 1997): 63–91; Greisch, "The Eschatology of Being and the God of Time"; Jean Greisch, "La pauvreté du

of the final god" into the nexus of be-ing and being-there could hardly be predicted on the basis of *Being and Time*, which systematically relegates religious issues to the ontic level (see SZ 180 on sin, or SZ 248 on the afterlife). One might suppose, then, that the question of the final god is just an appendix to Heidegger's thought. But Heidegger claims that all the themes of the *Contributions* attempt "to say the same about the same" (82), and the few pages devoted primarily to the final god (part 7) are the climax of the *Contributions*. Heidegger forges close links between these thoughts and the other topics we have considered. His words on the gods can be understood only in conjunction with what he says about be-ing, beings, and being-there; they cannot be understood as a free-standing theology which may or may not be set beside an ontology and an anthropology. We must also try to understand them not as a present-indicative theory of the divine but as a future-subjunctive evocation of an event.

A quick and crude survey of Heidegger's sayings will prepare us for a more extended interpretation. (He speaks sometimes of "the god" or "the final god" in these passages, and sometimes of "the gods"; for now I will simplify by referring to "the gods.")

(a) The gods are not just a species of entity: they cannot be said to "be" (244, 263, 400, 437–38).

(b) The gods are not be-ing, either: they are subordinate to be-ing, or require it (6–7, 240, 243, 408–9, 413, 415, 438, 471).

(c) In turn, the essential happening of be-ing requires the gods (16, 27, 70, 228, 244).

'dernier Dieu' de Heidegger," in *Post-Theism: Reframing the Judeo-Christian Tradition*, ed. Henri A. Krop, Arie L. Molendijk, and Hent de Vries (Leuven: Peeters, 2000); Hans Hübner, "'Vom Ereignis' und vom Ereignis Gott: Ein theologischer Beitrag zu Martin Heideggers 'Beiträgen zur Philosophie,'" in Coriando, *"Herkunft aber bleibt stets Zukunft"*; Cristina Ionescu, "The Concept of the Last God in Heidegger's *Beiträge*: Hints towards an Understanding of the Gift of *Sein*," *Studia Phaenomenologica* 2, nos. 1–2 (2002): 59–95; Otto Pöggeler, "The Departure of the Final God," in *The Paths of Heidegger's Life and Thought*, 321–34; Jeff Owen Prudhomme, "The Passing-by of the Ultimate God: The Theological Assessment of Modernity in Heidegger's *Beiträge zur Philosophie*," *Journal of the American Academy of Religion* 61, no. 3 (fall 1993): 443–54; Umberto Regina, "I mortali e l'ultimo Dio nei *Beiträge zur Philosophie* di Martin Heidegger," in *Heidegger*, ed. Giorgio Penzo (Brescia: Morcelliana, 1990), and "L'ultimo Dio' di Martin Heidegger," in *Heidegger e la teologia*, ed. Hugo Ott and Giorgio Penzo (Brescia: Morcelliana, 1995); Schmidt, "On the Memory of Last Things"; Schürmann, *Broken Hegemonies*, 518, 593–94; Seidel, "Heidegger's Last God"; Stambaugh, *The Finitude of Being*, 139–43; Stenstad, "The Last God"; Ben Vedder, "Heidegger's Notion of the Last God and Revelation," *Archivio di Filosofia* 62, nos. 1–3 (1994): 553–64. For some broader recent studies of Heidegger's approach to god(s), see Laurence Paul Hemming, *Heidegger's Atheism: The Refusal of a Theological Voice* (Notre Dame: University of Notre Dame Press, 2002); Jeff Owen Prudhomme, *God and Being: Heidegger's Relation to Theology* (Atlantic Highlands, N.J.: Humanities Press, 1997); Frank Schalow, *Heidegger and the Quest for the Sacred: From Thought to the Sanctuary of Faith* (Dordrecht: Kluwer, 2001).

(d) Accordingly, the sheltering of be-ing in beings involves the gods (24, 35, 96, 308, 413).

(e) We need the gods: we must make room for the gods if we are to enter being-there (8, 18, 23, 52, 140, 230), and a people cannot become itself without its god (34, 398–99).

(f) But in turn, the gods need us: they require being-there in the form of grounders, creators, and thinkers (23, 417, 439).

Heidegger often sums up these connections by saying that be-ing or appropriation is "the between" for man and the gods (86–87, 428, 470, 476, 484); but he can also say that be-ing is the between for beings in general and the gods (62, 244), or that being-there is the between for man and the gods (28–29, 31). In short, it seems clear that even though be-ing, being-there, and the gods are distinct (26), Heidegger wants the gods to play a central part in the appropriating event in which be-ing, beings, and being-there come into their own.[104]

In what spirit should we take these claims? Is Heidegger constructing a theory of divinity, explaining what makes a god be a god? One might think so, since he uses expressions such as "the essence of god" (*das Gottwesen*, 406). Accordingly, Paola-Ludovica Coriando takes Heidegger to be interpreting the "*phenomenon* of the godly," or the "dimension in human existence" that enables the "possible fulfilled existentiell attestation" of a god. From this perspective, Heidegger's own expression "the gods" lends itself to "ontifying misunderstandings."[105] But Heidegger has good reason to speak of the gods and their "godding" in preference to "the godly." Heidegger's locution focuses on a particular, possible event instead of a universal *eidos*. By dropping *Being and Time*'s distinction between concrete existentiell realizations and general existential structures, Heidegger is affirming the priority of essential *happening* over invariant essences.[106]

104. These ideas are somewhat stabilized in *Besinnung* and *Die Geschichte des Seyns*, where Heidegger conceives of appropriation as the encounter of man and gods crossed with the strife of earth and world (e.g., GA 66, 15, 84, 307–8; GA 69, 27). The idea is already represented schematically in the *Contributions* (310). These passages are close to the postwar notion of the fourfold: see Ionescu, "The Concept of the Last God."

105. Coriando, *Der letzte Gott als Anfang*, 20 (cf. 177), 19. Similar interpretations are found in Figal, "Forgetfulness of God," 210; Friedrich-Wilhelm von Herrmann, "Die 'Beiträge zur Philosophie' als hermeneutischer Schlüssel zum Spätwerk Heideggers," in *Heidegger neu gelesen*, ed. Markus Happel (Würzburg: Königshausen and Neumann, 1997), 83; Pöggeler, *The Paths of Heidegger's Life and Thought*, 329; Prudhomme, "The Passing-By," 450; Schürmann, *Broken Hegemonies*, 518 (reading this "essentialism" as a retrograde aspect of Heidegger's thought of the last god that is countered by other tendencies). Even Schmidt's interpretation of the last god, which generally focuses on unique emergencies and future possibilities, ends up resorting to the "always already" ("On the Memory of Last Things," 102), as does Ionescu in "The Concept of the Last God," 92–94.

106. Derrida errs in suggesting that the *Contributions* are concerned with the "condition of possibility" of religion, whereas theologians are concerned with "singular, irreducible . . . events":

What is the alternative to philosophizing in the traditional fashion about the *eidos* of gods? Reiner Schürmann suggests the "counter-strategy" of reading the final god as Proteus—the multiple, unrepresentable, decentering god.[107] But this concept is arguably still metaphysical: Proteus is a being that *resists* form, and as such, he is still conceived *in terms of* form. Heidegger must be trying to think outside the duality of form and formlessness.[108] Schürmann also emphasizes expropriation without sufficiently acknowledging that, for Heidegger, expropriation is essential to the founding, gathering inception.

By giving Heidegger's nameless god a name, though, Schürmann raises another important possibility: rather than generalizing about gods, is Heidegger invoking some specific deity? He seems to be speaking of an individual god as distinctive as Zeus or Yahweh when he says, "This god will raise the simplest but most extreme opposites over his people, as the paths on which the people roams out beyond itself, in order to find its essence once again and to exhaust the moment of its history" (399). This is not just any god, but the god that belongs to a particular *Volk* and indicates the routes along which the people can meet its destiny.

However, Heidegger does not claim to know or have heard from such a god. There is only a "hint" that leaves room for either the "arrival" or the "flight" of the god (e.g., 24).[109] While Heidegger apparently craves the god's arrival, he does not claim to have discerned it. Instead, he is trying to establish a context in which the problem of the god can become urgent. True godlessness is not the absence of gods, but a state in which their flight or arrival makes no difference to us.[110] Even if we are unable to answer the question of gods, Heidegger wants the question to make a difference, and this may in fact be his main goal: "What if that domain of decision as a whole, flight or

---

"Conversazione," 7–8. However, Derrida's interpretation does work for *Being and Time*, as well as for some later essays: cf. "Letter on 'Humanism,'" in *Pathmarks*, 258, 267.

107. Schürmann, *Broken Hegemonies*, 518.

108. Cf. GA 65, 63–64 on the Greek concepts of the one and the many. Postmodern readings of Heidegger generally run the risk of merely inverting Greek hierarchies.

109. The uncertainty of hinting has generated dramatically different readings of Heidegger. For Heidegger as "religious fanatic" see Christopher Rickey, *Revolutionary Saints: Heidegger, National Socialism, and Antinomian Politics* (University Park, Pennsylvania: Pennsylvania State University Press, 2002), 273; for Heidegger's "holy atheism" see Hemming, *Heidegger's Atheism*, 290. For Hemming, this so-called atheism is "an openness, even a silent pointing, to who the God might be" (269). Similarly open-ended positions are expressed by Crownfield, "The Last God," 213; Schalow, *Heidegger and the Quest for the Sacred*, 20, 37, 50.

110. Cf. GA 39, 95. Richard Rorty expresses such a godlessness perfectly: "secularists are not saying that God does not exist, exactly; they feel unclear about what it would mean to affirm His existence, and thus about the point of denying it": *Consequences of Pragmatism* (Minneapolis: University of Minnesota Press, 1982), xiv.

arrival of the gods, were itself the end?" (405). In this sense, even "the most distant distance of the undecidability of the flight or the arrival of the gods" is a kind of "nearness of the god" (12).[111] This is why Heidegger constantly links the final god to the themes of decision and undecidability (18, 158, 230, 244, 382, 406). He warns us, however, not to think of decision anthropocentrically, in terms of our own choice or preference (87–88, 437); the decision about the gods is to take place in appropriation as a whole, an event in which we must participate but which we cannot direct. Instead of saying that the decision is ours, it would be better to say that the gods themselves are deciding about "their god" (239).

But this language, too, can be misleading, because it suggests a pantheon and a king of the gods. Heidegger's use of the plural "gods" is not meant as polytheism, and his use of *both* "the god" and "the gods" is deliberate. Metaphysical theology busies itself with the question of how many gods there are—one, many, or none (411); but Heidegger conjoins the gods with the "there are" itself. Authentic being-there is never concerned with counting the gods—or counting on them (293). Heidegger's plural "indicates the undecidedness of the being of the gods, whether of one or of many" (437).

Heidegger connects the gods to the fissure (27, 244)—so we might consider his attempt at nonmetaphysical thought about the gods in terms of the question of possibility. A traditional metaphysician would think of the essence of a being in terms of the possible ways in which the being can exist: the essence delimits the variations through which the being can pass while remaining the sort of being that it is, and the essence also establishes the *highest* possibility for the being, which defines what it would mean for it to actualize its nature most fully, and hence to be good. If man is essentially the rational animal, then all specifically human possibilities involve rationality, and we can become better human beings by making our rationality more actual. This thought pattern must be adjusted when it comes to God, since the supreme being cannot suffer from a disparity between possibility and actuality, essence and existence; however, metaphysical theology retains the underlying metaphysical concept of possibility. Possibility is an alternative way for a being to be present—an absent presence, as it were.

Being and Time already indicates that the possibilities of being-there cannot be captured by this metaphysical concept (SZ 143–44). My possibilities

---

111. Along these lines, Heidegger writes: the "harmonious natures," as one calls them, sometimes seem to embody the divine itself; but this illusion just covers up their lack of relation to the gods. In contrast, torn human beings, in whom the tearing runs through their essence, are opened up, so that this kind of opening holds ready an abyss into which the nearness and distance of the gods, and the restlessness of their undecidedness, can shine: "Überlegungen" XI, §37.

are not just alternative ways for me to be present; they direct my involvements in the world, making sense of who I am. They have everything to do with my being, even though they can never be reduced to a type of presence. Being-there appropriates the situation in which it finds itself in terms of ways in which it can be. Possibilities are thus fundamental to all understanding—of ourselves, of other beings, and of being (SZ §31, §68a). It can make a difference to us that there is something instead of nothing only if we are faced with possibility in this nonmetaphysical sense, which for convenience we can call *existential* possibility.

I suggest, then, that in the *Contributions* Heidegger is attempting to think of gods in terms of existential possibilities—on a grand scale that was only hinted at in *Being and Time* (SZ §74), involving an entire people. He is not theorizing about the essence of gods as the range of ways in which it is possible for gods to be present; he is thinking about the gods' "essential happening" in terms of the existential possibilities that inform a people's interpretation of itself and of the world around it. The gods bring to life the most important existential possibilities for a community—the "immeasurable possibilities" (411) that orient our concerns and establish the significance of everything.[112] These need not be dogmatic blinders that restrict us to one possible worldview; precisely as possibilities that illuminate the world, they must be open to a certain "trembling" (239, 244). These possibilities cannot be converted into pure actuality; they are *irreducibly* possible, so they remain open to question.[113] The gods would then serve as a vibrant center of our interests and interpretations, a re-ligion that would bind a community together and bind it back (*re-ligare*) to the world

112. Michael Lewis's interesting interpretation of the gods is only apparently at odds with mine. He proposes (citing little textual support) that the god is the "counter-essence of man" because "'god' is the name of those possibilities which are beyond the projection of man's understanding," such as earth and death. By letting us encounter our own finitude, the god enables the sense of beings to be given to us in a finite way: "God and Politics in Later Heidegger," 387–38. If Lewis is right, we can still say that the gods bring to life our existential possibilities: the gods themselves are not human projects, but they give sense to our projects precisely because they confront us with our limits.

113. Similarly, Figal interprets the uncertainty of the gods as enabling human freedom: "Forgetfulness of God," 201–8. As Esposito writes, "the future one does not call the dispersed people back into a presence that calls it together, but rather intimates that a people . . . can form itself only in the passing of a god who stays away": "Die Geschichte des letzten Gottes," 57. For a similar thought see De Carolis, "La possibilità della decisione," 184–85. Müller, in contrast, insists that Heidegger is preparing not just for a "possible godding," but for "a *fulfilled* godding": *Der Tod als Wandlungsmitte*, 310. The distinction is somewhat artificial, since as Müller himself points out, "godding" is a "self-withdrawing onrush" (328) or a "donation in passing" (343). Godding, then, can never become present in a completely "fulfilled" way. Still, Müller may be right in some sense to say (344) that Heidegger's "twilight" of the gods (GA 65, 411) is a dawn that points to a "day of the gods."

at large. The gods would matter to us by enabling *everything* to matter to us. There is no redemption here, no salvation or solution as dissolution (*Er-lösung*)—that would only be a degradation of man, an illusory escape; there is only a more intense engagement in our condition, an embrace and founding of the there (413).

We now need to make some sense of the phrase "the passing of the final god" (17, 27, 228, 331, 414). The word *final* (*letzter*) does not refer to the end of a series, or the cessation of a process (405, 411, 416).[114] What is final is not what has stopped or run down, but rather "the deepest inception" (405). "In . . . the hint [of the final god], be-ing itself arrives at its *ripeness*. Ripeness is readiness to become a fruit and a donation. Here what is *final* is essentially happening, the *essential end* that is demanded by the inception, not added on to it. Here the innermost finitude [*Endlichkeit*] of be-ing unveils itself" (410). The final god, then, is an "end" as a goal. This "end" is intrinsic to the existential possibilities of the first inception, which calls for the other inception. Existential possibilities become effective not by being converted into actualities, but by letting us respond creatively to our condition. The possibilities of the first inception become effective, in this sense, only when the other inception exposes the sources and limitations of the first.[115] The final god would become urgent at the juncture of metaphysics and postmetaphysics, at the moment when we leap into being-there, when "history up to now . . . must not come to an end [*verenden*], but must be brought to its end" (411)— not terminated, but opened to new horizons. In order to play a part in this ultimate moment, the final god must be "wholly other than the gods who have been" (403) (although "Das Ereignis" adds that they "all essentially happen with him"). Heidegger takes himself to be preparing for such a moment, rather than directly bringing it about or experiencing it himself (437); this moment is beyond the plans of an individual or a group, but requires the final god to "pass by."

The *Contributions* are not as forthcoming about the meaning of "passing" (*Vorbeigang*) as they are about "final." Hölderlin is the acknowledged source of much of Heidegger's conception of the gods (463), and in 1934–35, Heidegger draws on the poet to claim that "passing is the very way in which the

---

114. Heidegger might seem to imply the cessation of a process in at least one passage. The final god makes "being itself, appropriation as such, visible for the first time, and this illumination requires . . . the last [*letztmaligen*] sheltering of the truth in the altered form of beings" (GA 65, 70). *Letztmalig* can only mean "for the last time." I take this passage to express the conjunction of first and last that happens in an inception.

115. As Greisch puts it, Heidegger thinks "an eschatology of being which . . . is at the same time an archeology": "The Eschatology of Being and the God of Time," 37. On being as "eschatological," see Heidegger, "Anaximander's Saying," in *Off the Beaten Track*, 246; but cf. GA 66, 245.

gods are present."[116] Then there is a phrase from Nietzsche, the *Contribu-tions'* other main stylistic and conceptual source: "Zarathustra passed by me."[117] But the deeper source of these German passages is the Hebrew Bible. In Exodus 33:22 God "passes by" Moses in His glory, but Moses may not look on the divine face, for that would mean death. Similarly, in I Kings 19:11, God "passes by" Elijah accompanied by wind, earthquake, and fire. Yet God is not in the wind, earthquake, or fire; instead, He speaks in a quiet whisper afterwards. Both biblical passages stress our inability to behold God directly (compare the Greek myth of Zeus and Semele). The Lord manifests himself indirectly, for He exceeds what can be presented to us.[118] There is contact between man and God, but we can never represent or survey Him. Heidegger would surely agree. But this is not to imply that for Heidegger the god must be *infinite*—a Greek philosophical concept grafted onto He-brew monotheism. The god is as finite as be-ing.[119]

Like the biblical sources, Heidegger's "passing" indicates that our relation to the god is an event and advent, not a fixed structure. He calls on us to take a stand, but does not want our stance to deny historicity: the final god's "pass-ing demands a persistence [*Beständigung*] of beings, and hence of man in their midst—a persistence in which beings . . . withstand the passing—not by bringing it to a standstill but by letting it hold sway as a going" (413). As in earlier writings, Heidegger is appropriating the early Christian notion of the *kairos*, the crucial moment that decides one's relation to God.

It is up to us to prepare a momentous site for the passing of the god (264, 411), which confronts us as a decisive existential possibility. If this possibil-ity becomes effective, the question of the gods will give sense to our experi-

116. GA 39, 111. The occasion for Heidegger's claim is Hölderlin's line *So ist schnell vergäng-lich alles Himmlische.*

117. "Sils-Maria," a poem in the appendix to the second edition of the *Gay Science.* The whole discussion of the final god has a Nietzschean flavor: Heidegger accepts Nietzsche's claim that the Christian god is dead, and the possibility of being-there loosely resembles the possibility of the overman as an alternative to the last man. On the death of the Christian God, see GA 65, 118 and 411; for more on Christianity, cf. 24, 91, 139, 202, 237, 403, 416. For Nietzsche on the overman and the last man, see *Thus Spoke Zarathustra,* I, "Zarathustra's Prologue," §§3–5. The expression "final god" is used in *Zarathustra,* I, "On the Three Metamorphoses," but in what seems to be a non-Heideggerian sense. (Schelling also uses the expression, as a term for Christ: Seidel, "Heidegger's Last God," 89–93.)

118. For a similar interpretation of God's "passing" see Maimonides, *The Guide of the Perplexed* 1.21. On Heidegger's debt to the Hebrew Bible cf. Marlène Zarader, *La dette impensée: Heideg-ger et l'héritage hébraïque* (Paris: Seuil, 1990); Peter Eli Gordon, *Rosenzweig and Heidegger: Be-tween Judaism and German Philosophy* (Berkeley: University of California Press, 2003), 313–14.

119. "If God is powerful, then he is finite and in any case something other than what is thought in the vulgar representation of a God who can do anything and thus is degraded to an om-nipresent being": *Aristotle's Metaphysics Θ 1–3,* 135. Traditional "eternity" is also a degradation of the gods: GA 66, 253.

ences and activities. This moment of emergency and emergence will mark the inception of being-there, allowing us to respond to the way each thing shelters the import of what is.

We are ready to consider some of Heidegger's more puzzling claims about gods. First, the god and be-ing require each other: "the essential happening of [be-ing] grounds the sheltering and thus the creative preservation of the god, who always *gods through* [*durchgottet*] be-ing only in work and sacrifice, deed and thought" (262). Be-ing is urgent for gods (438): the god is manifest and meaningful only when be-ing is taking place. The god is sheltered by giving sense to our acts and experiences; this sheltering requires be-ing, as the granting of the import of what is.[120] Be-ing, in turn, requires the god: the god is an indispensable source of meaning. In the hint of the final god, appropriation can first be discerned (70). Be-ing cannot take place without the god, and the god cannot pass by without be-ing.[121]

So is there any difference between the two? As the self-concealing giver of the ultimate gift, be-ing obviously resembles God, and thinking of be-ing requires some nearly theological turns.[122] One might reply that be-ing, unlike a god, is not a person. Although Heidegger's language sometimes comes close to personifying be-ing, it remains a happening without will, action, or awareness—more like a wind than a whisper, insofar as a whisper presupposes an *intention* to communicate. A god, as usually conceived, has purposes and consciousness. A god cares about the world and humanity.

However, Heidegger nowhere assigns these personal attributes to his god or gods (although he does not rule them out either). The closest thing to a deliberate *action* that the god seems to perform is strange and disturbing: time-space is the "net" in which he hangs himself only to rip it (263).[123] The

120. The last god needs be-ing as "this space of encounter, this interval, in order to be able to visit man (*Dasein*) and so that *Dasein* may expose itself to the god": Greisch, "Les 'Contributions,'" 630.

121. Prudhomme is thus misleading when he objects to Heidegger's subordinating the gods to be-ing ("The Passing-by," 452–53). Be-ing is not higher than the gods, nor vice versa (GA 65, 438). Heidegger can even ask: "Why be-ing? Because the gods? Why the gods? Because be-ing?" (508). Ionescu makes the intriguing argument that the gods are essential to be-ing as *giving* because a pure gift, just like the passing of the final god, must be a unique, unpredictable event that cannot be fully possessed or controlled by its recipient: "The Concept of the Last God," 90–93. However, this close parallel between appropriation and the last god does not demonstrate an essential connection.

122. Kovacs clearly states the parallels: "grace in the theological sense is not a substance but an event, a relation of appropriation": "The Power of Essential Thinking," 50. Kovacs suggests that Heidegger may be in danger of "falling back into ontotheology" (51).

123. Heidegger also considered the milder image that the god "catches" himself in the net. The manuscript and typescript read *h/fängt*, with one initial letter over the other: Pöggeler, *The Paths of Heidegger's Life and Thought*, 349. For an interpretation of the passage see Müller, *Der Tod als Wandlungsmitte*, 344–48.

final god brings the emergency of be-ing to a head (410; cf. GA 66, 235). But is this the act of a living, willing, supreme being?

Not if we follow Heidegger's saying that the gods "'are' not at all" (244). A god is not a being, any more than be-ing itself is. But we should not say that gods are nonbeings (*unseiend*) either—this would simply be atheism, the ontic claim that there are no gods (263). The problem is that "all assertions about the 'being' and 'essence' of the gods not only say nothing about them . . . but simulate something objective by which all thinking is foiled, for it is immediately driven onto detours" (438). When we conceive of gods as be-ings, we tend to take it for granted that to be is to be a present object; a god then has to be explained as the most present of all objects. This is a meta-physical dead end that has nothing to do with "what is godlike about the god" (438). Following a certain negative theology, Heidegger refuses to subordi-nate the gods to any such preconceptions.[124] Instead, he wants the gods to play a part in be-ing itself—so they are not mere beings, not even supreme beings.

Heidegger makes these points only in vague terms; we will risk an illus-tration. A tribe celebrates the New Year with a day of dancing and feasting; on this day, they plant a tree in the center of their village and sacrifice a goat at the base of the tree. If we think of gods as beings, we will ask whether or how they are present in this ritual, and how the participants in the ritual rep-resent them. But if the gods are really at work here, they may be at work not as beings at all, but as sources of the *import* of beings: the day and the sacri-fice, the tree and the goat, make sense in terms of the gods. The meaning of things is permeated by the gods; the sacrifice does not reveal any god as a be-ing, but the gods allow the sacrifice to reveal *itself*, to make a difference to this tribe.[125] Thanks to the gods, the deeds and things of this day shelter the truth of be-ing. The tribe's gods allow it to be a people—a community that shares an understanding of what matters and why. Heidegger would add that

124. Cf. Crownfield, "The Last God," 218–19; David R. Law, "Negative Theology in Hei-degger's *Beiträge zur Philosophie*," *International Journal for Philosophy of Religion* 48, no. 3 (De-cember 2000): 139–56. Prudhomme rightly points out that Heidegger is trying to avoid the "metaphysical construction" of God as an entity "subsumed" under being; however, Prud-homme adds, Heidegger does not work out a satisfactory account of the relation of being and God: *God and Being*, 135. The best-known recent such account is Jean-Luc Marion, *God with-out Being*, trans. Thomas A. Carlson (Chicago: University of Chicago Press, 1991). But in my opinion, Marion's God is too abstract and remote to play a vital role in history, as Heidegger's "final god" would.

125. As Crownfield puts it, "gods are not extant but figures of remembrance and expectation . . . god occurs in narratives of claim and promise, and in [human] acts that venture to rely on the claim and promise": "The Last God," 214. In Regina's phrase, "*man and God enter into the semantification of being*," the arrival of sense by which the world is transfigured: "L'ultimo Dio,'" 344.

such an understanding keeps needing to be refreshed by those who are ready to be-there, the "grounders and creators" (23) who concern themselves not only with important things, but with import itself. These exceptional individuals maintain the gods as a vital and questionable force that continues to provide a community with existential possibilities.

Is this a satisfying account of the gods? Or does it destroy their independence from human beings by making them "wait" for us to leap into being-there (417)? The *Contributions* run the risk of reducing the gods to an aspect of the relation between be-ing and being-there. Could any people revere a god that they did not believe to be a being separate from them? The gods seem to become nothing but a totemic symbol—a dimension of import, but not anyone to whom anything could be important.[126] Heidegger could retort that when we insist that the gods "transcend" humanity, we presuppose a fixed sense of what it means to be human (25). But this argument is dubious, and it remains all too easy to interpret his gods as "an 'idea' or 'values' or a 'meaning,' the sort of thing one cannot live and die for" (25).

In this ultimate and most riddlesome strait of appropriation, we run up against questions that force us to think more critically about the *Contributions*. We are ready to ask where the paths begun in this text may lead us.

126. Hubert L. Dreyfus glosses Heidegger's "god" as "a new cultural paradigm that [would hold] up to us a new way of doing things": "Heidegger on the Connection between Nihilism, Art, Technology and Politics," in *The Cambridge Companion to Heidegger*, ed. Charles Guignon (Cambridge: Cambridge University Press, 1993), 310. No one can worship a cultural paradigm (once it is recognized as such), nor can a paradigm receive offerings or show mercy. Garrido-Maturano puts it trenchantly: "Is it possible to make music and dance before a God incapable of revealing himself by himself? . . . Is it possible to entrust our salvation to a God whom we ourselves must save?": "Las imposibilidades del Dios," 90–91. Here Garrido-Maturano deliberately echoes Heidegger's own criticisms of the God of metaphysics in "The Onto-theological Constitution of Metaphysics," in *Identity and Difference*, 72. For similar doubts see Greisch, "La pauvreté du 'dernier Dieu,'" 416–17; Law, "Negative Theology," 150–52.

4

Afterthoughts

The text *Contributions to Philosophy* is one of Heidegger's thought experiments.[1] One does not refute a thought experiment; one pursues it imaginatively and sees where it leads, without giving up one's critical awareness. It would be inappropriate to treat Heidegger's inquiry as nothing but a set of claims to be defended or attacked. Instead, we have to follow the paths it opens and decide as best we can which ones are promising, without assuming in advance that any are dead ends.

The *Contributions* point to the momentousness of truth—to the possibility of disclosure as an urgent event that takes its own place and time, making us its own and bringing us into our own. Truth in this sense would not be a universal or a set of propositions, but a happening that engages us as it opens our world. By cultivating styles of thinking and speaking that respect the momentousness of truth, Heidegger shows that this possibility does not simply cancel itself out or fall into the ineffable. For Heidegger, however, the event of appropriation is so singular that it can be thought only as another inception of Western history, a crisis that calls into question all that has come before. Such an event would transpose us into another, barely imaginable dimension, de-ranging us into being-there.

The radical singularity of *Ereignis* as thought in the *Contributions* brings

---

1. The expression is Theodore Kisiel's: "Heidegger's Apology," in Kisiel, *Heidegger's Way of Thought*, ed. Alfred Denker and Marion Heinz (New York and London: Continuum, 2002), 29. On the exploratory character of the *Contributions* cf. George Kovacs, "An Invitation to Think through and with Heidegger's *Beiträge zur Philosophie*," *Heidegger Studies* 12 (1996): 19–21; Kovacs, "The Leap," 40; Scott, "*Zuspiel* and *Entscheidung*," 161.

214

some problems with it. First, it tends to shift the topic of thought into the future in a way that threatens to turn this topic into an arbitrarily selected possibility. To put it bluntly: if the appropriation has not yet happened, and being-there differs from man, then on what basis can we say that the present *calls for* appropriation or *lacks* it? In order to experience the urgent need for appropriation, must we not have had some taste of appropriation itself? Of course, appropriation cannot be something ready-made that we simply observe and describe. It could, however, be a happening that takes place now, in and with our thinking of it. In fact, it often seems that Heidegger wants appropriation to work precisely this way, especially in his discussions of bethinking. There is a tension, then, between this approach and his deferral of appropriation to the apocalyptic "other inception." The apocalyptic impulse in the *Contributions* risks turning all its topics—appropriation, bethinking, being-there, be-ing—into remote possibilities that are invoked without justification.

I begin my critical reflections, then, with the future-subjunctive tonality of the *Contributions*. If being-there and appropriation are possibilities rather than actualities, how can we think about them and recommend them? What is the basis of this thinking, the source of its authority? Can there be a legitimate philosophy of possibility? The question of authoritative or desirable possibilities will bring us to the problem of goals. Heidegger both condemns the concept of goals as a symptom of Platonic metaphysics and insists that we must give humanity a new goal. Is there a way to resolve this contradiction? Heidegger's suspicion of goals involves a rejection of politics as we know it, and of liberal thought in particular; I will focus on his remarks on liberalism and suggest a defense. His attack on liberalism is part of a larger critique of the Enlightenment, and even of the entire Western tradition of seeking universal truths by way of reason. How fair is Heidegger's account of reason and its relation to a supposedly deeper "bethinking"? At this point it is appropriate to consider Plato, the champion of *logos* whom Heidegger blames for much of our oblivion of being. I will propose that *logos* in Plato is more flexible and inclusive than Heidegger assumes. Plato also alerts us to the need to return from the universal to the concrete. Ironically, the *Contributions*' rejection of truth as a universal remains largely on the universal, abstract level. Plato might suggest, in a line of thought that Heidegger disregards in his interpretation of Platonism, that what is lacking in the *Contributions* is a descent from the ultimate to the quotidian. We need to return from be-ing to beings, from the event of appropriation to that which *is*, finding connections between primordial time-space and ordinary, linear time. I will close, then, by sketching some ways in which the thinking of the *Contributions* might help us see the familiar in a new light.

A Philosophy of Possibility?

"What is most thought-provoking, is this—that we are still not thinking," says Heidegger in 1951. Why not? Because "what really must be thought keeps itself turned away from man since the beginning." He considers an obvious objection to his statement: "how can we have the least knowledge of something that withdraws from the beginning, how can we even give it a name? Whatever withdraws, refuses arrival. But—withdrawing is not nothing. Withdrawal is an event [*Entzug ist Ereignis*]."[2] And yet—how can we even recognize the withdrawal of what has never been given? How do we know that we need to think of it?

In the *Contributions*, with their invocation of an apocalyptic transformation, the problem of thinking the esoteric—perhaps the most difficult problem in the text—centers on the question of possibility.[3] We have already broached this issue in terms of "future-subjunctive" thinking, but we are now in a better position to come to grips with it, considering it both in terms of the very project of thinking of be-ing and in relation to the question of goals.

The problem is most obvious in regards to being-there; as we have seen, the *Contributions* tend to think of being-there as possible, not actual. *Being and Time* was "easily misunderstood" as claiming that being-there was simply the way of being of the given entity man (300). But man has never yet been historical; we have never attained the historicity of being-there (492, 454).[4] Being-there, then, is "the ground of a particular, future [way of] being human, not of 'Man' in himself"; it is "the *being* that distinguishes man *in his possibility*" (300–301).

Heidegger observes that any way of stating the relation between man and being-there can be misinterpreted if we are unwilling to engage in his question (301). This engagement is a leap into the unknown, the projection of a possibility—and being-there is precisely such a risk. It is a way of dwelling in which the being of beings becomes a problem, an emergency. Being-there

---

2. *What Is Called Thinking?* trans. J. Glenn Gray (New York: Harper and Row, 1968), 6–9. Compare Heidegger's statement that "things . . . have never yet been able to appear . . . as things": "The Thing," in *Poetry, Language, Thought*, 170–71. In "Das Ereignis," Heidegger writes that world history is happening without a world. Genuine thinking, worlding, and thinging all await the event of appropriation.

3. Umberto Regina sees the root of Heidegger's esotericism in the exigencies of thinking "an *other inception* that we have not yet reached": "Il problema antropologico nei *Beiträge zur Philosophie* di Martin Heidegger," *Fenomenologia e Società* 14, no. 2 (December 1991): 34.

4. Schmidt calls this "perhaps the strangest claim of the *Beiträge*": "On the Memory of Last Things," 97. It embodies the problem of the other inception's remaining in "abeyance": ibid., 93–94. In general, Schmidt's essay effectively evokes the difficulty and pathos of Heidegger's futural thinking.

is not merely questionable—it is itself a state of questioning. Being-there is a leap—and we cannot understand it unless we ourselves are leaping.

But even if we grant this point, the most charitable reading has to run into some difficult problems. If we have never been "there" at all, how can we leap into the possibility of being-there in the first place? In order to understand being-there, do we not already have to be-there to some degree?[5]

Because being-there plays a crucial role in the event of appropriation, this problem extends to all the central themes of the *Contributions*. For example, the decision about the gods is said to open "a completely other time-space for . . . the first grounded truth of be-ing, the event of appropriation" (405). How can we think of something completely other, much less perceive that it will provide a new, unprecedented ground? We must ask whether there is any basis for Heidegger's account of appropriation. Maybe, in trying to move beyond the present-indicative description of facts and essences for the sake of a future-subjunctive in-vention of be-ing, his thinking has sacrificed its authority.

We return to the question of a prophetic philosophy. Can there be such a thing, or does this text simply waver between prophecy and philosophy? Even if prophecy is not mere prediction or fortunetelling, it is primarily focused on possibilities. Can there be a philosophy of possibility? How does possibility become accessible? If it shows itself, it would seem that to some degree it is present and actual. Or if it is not a phenomenon at all, if it is completely hidden, then an evocation of it seems groundless. Does Heidegger have some basis for characterizing a future, unique event? If he does, is it still a future possibility—or is it an aspect of the present? Is it impossible, in the end, for philosophy to escape the present-indicative tonality? In grammatical terms, is the future tense built on the present?[6]

---

5. Cf. Alfons Grieder, "Essential Thinking: Reflections on Heidegger's *Beiträge zur Philosophie*," *Journal of the British Society for Phenomenology* 23, no. 3 (October 1992): 244; Neu, *Die Notwendigkeit der Gründung*, 174.

6. Dahlstrom argues that Heidegger, in the end, cannot elude a certain presence: "Every thematization, be it objectifying or not, continues to lay claim to the presence of its theme in a certain sense (not unlike a theme pervading a piece of music)": *Heidegger's Concept of Truth*, 445. Ruin puts it more paradoxically: "*Ereignis* is a concept through which Heidegger tries to think a presence beyond the present, and in doing so approaches the limits of the sayable and thinkable": *Enigmatic Origins*, 204. McNeill also brings out the paradox: "The occurrence of this event, of this *Ereignis*, is the extraordinary happening of that which has always already been and nevertheless has not yet been, but remains unforeseeable: the nonsimplicity of the originary future": *The Glance of the Eye*, 292. Greisch puts the problem trenchantly, quoting Heidegger's own critique of Plotinus a decade before the *Contributions*: "has Heidegger himself not 'departed from the phenomena' in order to deliver himself over totally to a speculation which could itself be misunderstood as a strange kind of 'theosophy'?": "The Eschatology of Being and the God of Time," 38. Perhaps unsurprisingly, Derrida joins those who doubt that Heidegger can think of

There are several avenues for a defense of Heidegger. First, one might insist that the only way to open the future is precisely to leap into it, without a present base to which to return. If we want a new possibility, then we cannot expect to find it right in front of us. One might *welcome* the otherness of the other inception: why not open ourselves to what exceeds every present and all presence, what is in no way a reproduction of the past? To view appropriation as a fulfillment of what is already present would assume a Platonic-Aristotelian ontology: we identify a present *eidos* and posit that things reach perfection if they bring this *eidos* to full presence. But would not appropriation, as the *giving* of the presence of the present, elude all such concepts? Maybe a venture into an ungrounded, even groundless future is the only way to escape from the oppressive tradition.

However, the doubts return if we ask for justifications. Why do we need to venture a new future? Why is this venture anything more than an arbitrary "leap of ontological 'faith'"?[7] Why should we be open to radical otherness and sheer possibility? Why should we reject Platonism, or think of the giving of presence in terms of appropriation? The answer "why not?" would be far too weak to bear the urgency with which Heidegger wants to invest his thoughts. In order to give a better answer, it seems that we have to point to something more than an other inception—not a present entity, perhaps, but some sort of phenomenon, something actual or evident. Unless a revolution is motivated by actual conditions, it leads not to a legitimate new regime but to an arbitrary tyranny.

Heidegger could answer that although no present phenomenon will demonstrate that we ought to carry out the leap, an experience of *emergency* can provide a deeper necessity than any argument (241–42, 328).[8] A truly free leap is not a choice, but the decisive recognition that one has already been decided in one's essence (GA 42, 267–68). What brings about this decidedness is emergency, which according to the *Contributions* is the truth of be-ing itself.

Yet the basic problem recurs, because the particular kind of urgency that Heidegger wants us to experience is the paradoxical urgency of the *lack* of ur-

---

a pure possibility: "the not-yet has already arrived, there is a necessarily past event that can announce the coming of the future. The future does not announce itself on its own, as pure future": "Conversazione," 11.

7. Greisch, "Les 'Contributions,'" 609.

8. Cf. *Basic Questions of Philosophy*, 125. Regina argues that our current experience of "emergency" provides the *Contributions* with their "phenomenological support" by pointing to the "necessary conditions for thinking the other inception as salvation": "Il problema antropologico," 33; cf. Regina, "I mortali e l'ultimo Dio," 168. But how can we perceive our condition as needy before we know what we need? An experience of the present as needing salvation seems to require a prior sense of what it means to be saved.

gency. How can the absence of emergency itself become an emergency? It would seem that the emergency of be-ing is supposed to emerge from thin air. Similarly, in the manuscript "Der Anklang," Heidegger interprets our contemporary expropriation as a sign of appropriation; he adds, however, that the sign can signify only if appropriation has already been displayed. We are back at the question of how to encounter the self-withdrawing, futural event of appropriation.

The "fundamental difficulty" here is that we are supposed to project an understanding of be-ing *as projection* (451). In other words, our projective interpretation of be-ing has been thrown or appropriated by be-ing (447), so it "is" itself the event of be-ing. Heidegger insists that the projection will be justified by what it projects (56): that is, it will connect to an appropriating event of be-ing greater than the projection itself. Yet this appropriation can be interpreted as such only retrospectively, only after we have taken the leap into the projection; it cannot be used as an advance justification of the leap itself.[9] Because the event of thinking the event is a projection of be-ing as projection, one could object that this move can be justified only on its own terms—and thus is supremely arbitrary.

It is tempting to cut this Gordian knot by reading "man has never yet *been* historical" (492) simply as meaning that we have never fully *understood* our own historicity. To say that being-there is the ground of a future way of being human (300) simply means that we have not yet sufficiently *acknowledged* that we are-there. Hermeneutic phenomenology will help us discover how we always already are.[10]

9. Rosales, "Übergang zum anderen Anfang," 80–83.

10. Kalary denies that being-there "is a task and a futural condition, something which humans must become," and argues that the account of being-there in the *Contributions* is fundamentally the same as the ontology of human being-there in *Being and Time:* "Hermeneutic Pre-conditions (Part Two)," 143. In order to make this case, he has to posit that when Heidegger speaks of changing man from the ground up, he refers exclusively to "the traditional understanding of man as *animal rationale*" (ibid., 149). Heidegger's language of revolutionary "de-rangement" (GA 65, 372) would then mean nothing but a new way of thinking about what we already essentially are. In a more convoluted exposition of the same view, Esposito writes that "the drastic claim that man has never yet been historical really means that man never will be able to be historical—insofar as he is 'human', that is, under his simply human aspect; [he is historical] only insofar as he is appropriated by the event of being itself." Yet this "'event' can never truly happen, by virtue of the simple fact that we always already are it": Esposito, *Heidegger,* 179, 214. Cf. Mario Ruggenini, "La questione dell'essere e il senso della 'Kehre,'" *Aut Aut* 248–49 (March–June 1992): 113. Neu's position is ambiguous: she denies that "future human being should be represented according to the vulgar conception of time, as what is not yet" (*Die Notwendigkeit der Gründung,* 179, cf. 188, 192); however, she holds that Heidegger is calling for "a new grounding of the human essence, in which another realm of history opens and man finds himself displaced" into being-there (179). Has this event already happened? It is hard not to conclude that being-there is not yet, vulgar though the idea may be. Beistegui's formulations are no less con-

But the reassuring moderation of this position comes at a high price: it eliminates the emergency of being. Believing that "we simply have being-there and securely subsist . . . would run contrary to the innermost essence of being-there."[11] In *Being and Time*, the "essence" of being-there was in effect whether we dealt authentically or inauthentically with our own being; in the *Contributions*, the "there" itself arises only if we are authentic, or "insistent." It is not as if we can be-there unawares; being-there is essentially in question, so we can be there only when an emergency impels us to ask *who* we are (51). The only alternative is "being-away" (323).[12] How can we think that we are "always already" there without draining be-ing and being-there of their urgency?

Similar questions are raised by Reiner Schürmann's intricate exploration of "the deferred *there*." He claims that the thought of being-there as a possibility is not really about a new stage of history that has not yet arrived—even though Heidegger himself does not always avoid this futural notion. Instead, Heidegger has noticed "a potential that is given now." In fact, appropriation and expropriation (which for Schürmann mean the institution and dissolution of hegemonic principles) have *always already* been part of our condition. Despite Schürmann's an-archism, he is willing to call appropriation-expropriation a "post-transcendental 'condition', post-hegemonic 'ultimate.'" Such ultimates are truths that we all already know, though we may not acknowledge them. As insightful as Schürmann's account of the human condition may be, it should be clear that here he is closer to the philosophical tradition than to the *Contributions*, where truth happens in a unique flash reserved for the few and the rare. By turning the singular event into a pattern of "singularization," Schürmann risks occluding its singularity.[13]

Could we say that what has not yet happened is the *full* event of appropriation, whereas appropriation in a more latent form is already in effect? Paola-Ludovica Coriando thus distinguishes between appropriation in "broader" and "narrower" senses. In the broader sense, appropriation is "the fundamental happening of being in all its epochs, which holds sway in a concealed and displaced way." This is a structure that always already pervades "every human comportment." In the narrower sense, appropriation is "the open es-

---

tradictory: being-there is "what man always and already is," yet it is "an altogether wholly different humanity" (*Truth and Genesis*, 132, 135; cf. 148–49).

11. Heidegger, "Das Sein (Ereignis)," 11. Cf. Müller, *Der Tod als Wandlungsmitte*, 111–17; Regina, "Il problema antropologico," 60, 70–72.

12. According to *The Fundamental Concepts of Metaphysics* (1929–30), "Only as long as we are-there can we be away at all" (65). But now that "*being*-there is only the *moment* and history, customary being-human [is] '*away' from* the withstanding of the there": GA 65, 323.

13. Schürmann, *Broken Hegemonies*, 558, 592, 534; cf. 532, 545, 553–74, 596, 601–2, 615–19, 621, 626.

sential happening of being in its truth, which is [yet] to be grounded." We can grasp "the structure of appropriation" (the broader sense) in an age when appropriation is not yet fully "ap-*propriating*" (the narrower sense). But, Coriando asks, is the possibility of full appropriation phenomenally attested, or is it merely a speculative construction? Her answer is that the experience of withdrawal or ex-propriation in the present age reveals the possibility of full appropriation by *hinting* at it.[14] A similar solution, as Joseph P. Fell argued over thirty years ago, is propounded by Heidegger himself in his postwar essays, where appropriation is not a "utopia" but "what has 'always already' ruled" without being fully revealed. Heidegger's thought does not plunge into sheer possibility, but "grounds 'the possible' in a new conception of the universal and necessary."[15]

However, the postwar *Ereignis* may not be the *Ereignis* of the *Contributions*. Do the *Contributions* ground the possible in the universal and necessary? When we look closely at the text, we find some inconsistencies. Despite his claim that we have never been historical, Heidegger sounds the alarm that "the beginning of the lack of history is already here" (100)—implying that we are and have been historical. Other passages claim, in accordance with Coriando's distinction, that appropriation or being-there is not yet "fully" happening or experienced (249, 299, 309). On one occasion, however, Heidegger warns us that this is a "formal" way of speaking (309). He probably hesitates because the distinction between partial and full appropriation runs the risk of becoming an "insight into essence" instead of a "*leap* into essential happening" (338). It seems to bring with it the traditional split between formal, a priori structures and concrete fulfillments of those structures. Coriando herself wishes to avoid empty generality, and affirms that be-ing happens only in unique historical moments; but when we abstract a universal from these moments, we run the risk of dehistoricizing be-ing.[16]

To gain a deeper understanding of the need for a leap into possibility, we have to recall the most inevitable dimension of be-ing's self-concealment. If be-ing is the giving of givenness, then be-ing itself cannot be given: it can-

---

14. Coriando, *Der letzte Gott als Anfang*, 47–52. For similar solutions see Beistegui, *Truth and Genesis*, 132–33; Neu, *Die Notwendigkeit der Gründung*, 115; Patt, "Martin Heidegger, *Beiträge zur Philosophie*," 409; Schürmann, *Broken Hegemonies*, 565, 569; Vallega-Neu, *Heidegger's "Contributions*," 43, 56, 88.

15. Fell, "Heidegger's Notion of Two Beginnings," 229, 234.

16. Coriando, *Der letzte Gott als Anfang*, 47, 62. Here I agree with Gianni Vattimo: "the eventuality of being . . . signifies that everything we see as a structure . . . is an event, an institution, a historical aperture of being. . . . the eventual character of being makes it impossible to view its own eventuality . . . as an archstructure valid for *all* possible history": *The Adventure of Difference: Philosophy after Nietzsche and Heidegger*, trans. Cyprian Blamires (Baltimore: Johns Hopkins University Press, 1993), 76, 78–79.

not appear as an available phenomenon, because it is the source of the meaning of appearing and availability themselves. For the very same reason, being-there cannot be given: it is the grounding and withstanding of the momentous site, not an item available within this site. Now: if be-ing and being-there cannot be given, why should we even try to think of them? We "should" only if givenness (the being of beings) becomes a *problem* for us. What draws us to the question of be-ing is the urgency that strikes us when we sense the contingency of the givenness into which we have been thrown. When we can no longer take the being of beings for granted, it reveals itself *as* granted—as contingent and calling for some ground. But this ground is an abyssal ground, a ground that can never be present. It cannot display itself except in the very experience of emergency—the experience of the coming-into-question of the being of beings. And this is precisely when we *receive* the being of beings by recognizing it as a gift. This is when be-ing happens.

Be-ing and being-there have never been present, and never can be present. They can take place only *as emergency,* and not as a given. All attempts to ascertain that appropriation has "always already" happened are doomed to fail—not because it could not have happened, but because if it happens, it happens only as a coming-into-question, and not as anything ascertainable. The question of whether appropriation has happened is strictly undecidable (488). It is not to be found—except by a leap into the *possibility* of questioning.[17]

One could object that appropriation *must* already have taken place, since we have already received the being of beings. But have we? We *possess* the being of beings: things are given to us in terms of a prior sense of givenness. But we can *receive* that givenness only in a moment when we experience it as problematic, as contingent. Has such a moment ever happened? I would suggest that it has, countless times, and that these inceptions have driven history—but this suggestion is not a *fact.* It is not a given, but a leap into a way of approaching givenness.

If this still seems all too strange, we should remember that *Being and Time*

---

17. In a subtle analysis of these issues, Massimo De Carolis argues that possibility as such requires the possibility of impossibility. (A possibility that was permanently guaranteed would not be a possibility at all, but a timeless actuality.) For the individual, the possibility of impossibility is one's own mortality. On the broader scale, it is the threat of the lack of urgency that shadows our age. Ironically, this shadow *enables* possibility and decision to take place. By experiencing our own situation as oscillating between the possibility and the impossibility of history and be-ing, Heidegger sets free a kind of thinking that stays with the possible itself, instead of reducing it to the actual. Heidegger can thus "*discover the greatest richness of the present within indecision itself*": De Carolis, "La possibilità della decisione," 184. The very danger of the present age harbors its saving power—not as a state of affairs that may someday become fully present and perfect, but as a trembling that allows us to experience being as irreducibly questionable.

itself is not so straightforward in its discovery of what is "always already" the case. All existential insight is based on the existentiell choice of one possibility over others (SZ 312–13)—so the entire project requires a leap. It is not simply present-indicative.

But *Being and Time*'s account of temporality can also help us moderate the extreme "futural" tendency in the *Contributions*. Time originates in the future, but the future necessarily draws on the past; together, the future and past open the present (SZ 329). Understanding is a projection of possibilities—ultimately, the projection of a possible way to be that addresses the question of one's own existence (SZ 336)—but this understanding must retrieve the past. Our interpretations have to pursue avenues that emerge from our previous familiarity with ourselves and our surroundings. We can then preserve the *Contributions*' future-subjunctive tonality while retaining a connection to who we already are. If we accept the projection of being-there that Heidegger proposes in *Being and Time*, then it is hardly fair to criticize the *Contributions* for projecting a possibility. Being-there and appropriation are futural because every way of understanding must be. We cannot first look at the world and then choose to explore a possibility; if we were not already exploring possibilities, we would not see anything at all.[18] (In this sense, no projection can be incorrect: 327.) But if the future must draw on the past, no possibility can be completely other, completely new. What makes a possibility original is not its independence from the past, but how deeply it retrieves the past. Authentic being-there takes over its own thrownness (SZ 325–26); it retrieves a possibility that has been handed down (SZ 383, 385). Similarly, the other inception is a retrieval of the first (55, 73, 185).[19] This means that being-there is a retrieval of humanity; be-ing as appropriation is a retrieval of being as presence. In projecting *Ereignis* we are not inventing a utopia ex nihilo, but in-venting an original way of seizing upon who we already are.

Does this mean that appropriation must already have happened? No— much less "always already." But we must at least have had experiences that can be taken as occasions or inspirations for the leap into appropriation. It is also possible to interpret those experiences as appropriations, but without thinking of appropriation as a permanent structure or necessary principle. Appropriation, then, would not be continuous, but would occur in intermittent, contingent emergencies that generate creative insights.

A philosophy of possibility may seem less strange now. Perhaps philosophy is essentially concerned with possibilities—because it is itself a possible way of finding possibilities in the past. Philosophy may necessarily be exper-

18. Cf. Greisch, "Les 'Contributions,'" 609, 617–18.
19. Cf. *Basic Questions of Philosophy*, 109, 171.

imental. But when philosophy *recommends* particular possibilities, the question of the legitimacy of its projections arises in a new way. What is the basis for this recommendation? How is the philosopher establishing goals? In regards to the *Contributions* these questions are especially difficult, because Heidegger both denounces the concept of a goal (*Ziel*) as a Platonic notion and uses the concept to characterize the heart of his own project.

Consider the list of either-or "decisions" presented in §44. Obviously Heidegger is hoping for one possibility over another: being-there instead of subjectivity, the clearing of self-concealment instead of correctness, and so on. But he does not want simply to impose a value or an ideal. The passing of the final god, for example, "is not an 'ideal condition'" (415). But then, why does Heidegger hope for it so passionately?

This problem is particularly acute in regards to being-there. Being-there is man in an "extension" (*Ausgriff,* 313) or "anticipation" (*Vorgriff,* 317); but how should we decide in which direction to extend ourselves? Why, of all the possibilities that lie open to human beings, does being-there have the "highest" rank (301)? Why should we be attuned to ourselves in such a way that we retrieve ourselves as being-there rather than as subjects, or rational animals, or *homo faber*? The retrieval will let us come into our own, Heidegger might say; but why is *this* possibility our own, why is it proper to us, why is it fitting? We "must" transform ourselves into being-there (242); we "must" be de-ranged into it (317); being-there "must" be grounded (387). This "must" cannot be an ahistorical, a priori necessity, for necessity emerges from emergency—a situated, historical need that may someday become urgent (45, 97). How, then, would the possibility of being-there emerge as the urgent one for us? When and why?

As we have seen, the essentialist answer is tempting: being-there is the truest interpretation of what we already are. We are failing to live up to our nature, and we must exist more naturally. Now we are back in the ambit of classical metaphysics; we need to look more closely, then, at Heidegger's critique of the classical notions of *idea* and *telos*, essence and goal. Section 110 presents an elaborate genealogy of the Platonic *idea* and its descendants. The *idea* of a thing is the distinctive way in which it presents itself (208–9). This is the thing's beingness, its *ousia*, what makes it be what it is. Plato suspects that *ousia* does not exhaust being; instead of discovering the event of *be-ing*, however, he proposes to go "beyond *ousia*" (*Republic* 509b) in the direction of the good (210, cf. 480). This fatal step initiates the Western tradition of idealism and ideals, all the way to Nietzsche's value-thinking (216; cf. 72, 138). But if Plato had been able to spot the real weakness in *ousia*, then instead of positing a hyper-abstract form of the good, he might have taken part in the unique, goalless happening in which the sense of being emerges.[20] An ideal or goal is too "petty and superfluous" (481) when it comes to this ultimate happening. For instance, the passing of the final god is too mysterious, unpredictable, and remote to be a goal (415). Treating be-ing as a goal would reduce it to an entity, albeit an ethereal entity such as an *idea* (477, cf. 267). Be-ing is not a fixed standard by which to evaluate beings; it is what appropriates beings "into the questionability of the decisions" (GA 66, 318). And no genuine decisions are possible as long as we are simply trying to decide between ideals; ideality itself as the *space* of decisions goes unquestioned (234).

Why, then, does Heidegger declare that we need to "give historical man a goal once again" (16)? Why is inceptive thinking "goal-setting thinking," establishing "the only and lonely goal of our history" (17)? One of Heidegger's complaints about his age is that there are no genuine goals (108, 443). The means—such as the preservation of the *Volk*—are mistaken for ends (99, 139, 319, 398). Real goals arise from "inception" (143), or from an "originary projection and leap" (305). What is the goal, then? We are to prepare a way of being human that can "gather the empowerment of be-ing into its essential happening in a unique moment of history" (430). The goal is care, or the grounding and preserving of the truth of be-ing (16), or the seeking of be-ing (17)—in short, being-there.

So are being-there and be-ing goals, or not? The easy answer would be that the *Contributions* are a transitional text in which Heidegger has not quite weaned himself away from metaphysical, goal-directed thinking. For example, the *Contributions* hope to "empower" time-space and be-ing (386, 430), whereas their immediate successor, *Besinnung*—the same text that declares, "We know no goals, we are simply a going" (GA 66, 9)—insists that be-ing lies beyond both power and powerlessness (GA 66, 83, 187–88). It could be that the craving for goals in the *Contributions* is a vestige of the tradition that culminates in the Nietzschean metaphysics of the will to power, whereas in his critique of goal-oriented thinking, Heidegger is starting to break free from this tradition.

This answer is less than satisfactory in two ways. First, it is too quick to view the *Contributions* as inconsistent, instead of trying to think through the apparent inconsistency on this text's own terms.[21] Second, the antipathy to

20. For some earlier, positive Heideggerian appropriations of Plato's "form of the good," cf. *Metaphysical Foundations of Logic*, 184–85, 219; *The Essence of Truth*, 77–80; GA 36/37, 199–200.
21. "Überlegungen" X, §52 is an extensive discussion of this issue that shows that Heidegger is well aware of the seeming inconsistency. Here he distinguishes between a superficial, humanist "having-no-need-for-goals" and a deeper "goallessness." He writes that although on occasion he may not be able to avoid calling the grounding of the truth of be-ing a "goal," here "goal"

action and decision that comes to the fore after the *Contributions*, culminating in the concept of *Gelassenheit*, has its own problems. In simple terms, it leaves us in a quiescent, contemplative state in which we simply wash our hands of all ethics and politics. This is admittedly too crude, and in order to do justice to the later texts we would have to investigate Heidegger's protestations that *Gelassenheit* is beyond the distinction between activity and passivity, that thinking is itself a form of action, and that he is practicing the ultimate "ethics."[22] Still, it would seem desirable to find some viable notion of goals, so that our thought can have some relevance to action as it is normally understood. In this regard, the *Contributions'* ambiguous use of the concept of goals is a virtue—it encourages us to think through the concept instead of simply discarding it.

One thought may resolve the inconsistency: "The goal is seeking itself, the seeking of be-ing. It happens, and is itself the deepest finding, if man becomes the preserver of the truth of be-ing. . . . The seeking is itself the goal. And that means that 'goals' are still too superficial and keep getting in the way of be-ing—and block what is necessary" (17–18).[23] To expand this thought: necessities emerge from the moment of emergency, not from our voluntary positing of goals. In the emergency, the being of beings becomes questionable; the problem of be-ing becomes our problem. Be-ing happens, as a question that can never be fully answered. The search for be-ing is at the same time its discovery, because being is intrinsically elusive and mysterious. To call this search a "goal" suggests that we are bound for some particular answer, some point of view on the problem; instead, what matters is becoming aware of the problem as such. Similarly, to say that we "must" attain being-there is not to force us into a particular possibility but to awaken us to possibility as such, to the questionability of who we are. The notion of seeking as a "goal" counters the ancient prejudice in favor of actuality over possibility: here there is no *telos* of coming into the presence of some insight, intuition, or object. The point is to become oneself through futural questioning (398). Why leap into this questionable possibility? In order to be someone.

As for whether this possibility fulfills human nature, we can give a qualified yes—as long as we realize that the essence of man cannot simply be "read off" from what is given. An *idea* of humanity is not there on the surface for

means something toward which man goes, but which throws him back, because as be-ing it is higher than the highest (i.e., any goal or final goal): it appropriates man to the abyss of the clearing as which be-ing essentially happens.

22. "Conversation on a Country Path," in *Discourse on Thinking*, 61; "Letter on 'Humanism,'" in *Pathmarks*, 239, 271. For an argument that the postwar Heidegger is not as divorced from action as he may seem, see Fried, *Heidegger's Polemos*, 84–86.

23. Cf. *Basic Questions of Philosophy*, 6–7; *The Essence of Truth*, 170–71.

us to absorb and repeat it—it requires a projection and a leap. To realize this, comments Heidegger, is already to overcome the *idea* (305). Essences become available only through a leap, and the ultimate leap is the leap into being-there. If being-there is a goal, it is not the sort of goal that fits a traditional *idea* because it is essentially open-ended and problematic; it is a question, not an answer.[24]

Where does this leave us as regards being-there's relevance to action? It might seem that if being-there is not a particular alternative but a general openness to be-ing, then it cannot be used as a critical tool for promoting or rejecting any particular ways of being. However, being-there might still have some critical force if certain ways of being can be shown to be closed to their own questionability. They may rest on assumptions about what we are without ever recognizing that our selfhood is open to question.

This is precisely how Heidegger criticizes modernity throughout part 2 of the *Contributions*. But instead of distinguishing better and worse options in our age, he tends to condemn it wholesale. All political and cultural alternatives are equally bad, since they are all oblivious to the possibility of being-there and the problem of be-ing.[25] Heidegger begins to develop this global critique in the *Contributions*, as he becomes increasingly disillusioned with National Socialism. By the outbreak of the war it is well established, and it persists for the rest of his life. Our next question is whether this critique is insightful or reductive. Rather than exploring all of Heidegger's polemics, we will focus on one revealing case—his attacks on liberalism, which prove to be connected to his general critique of the modern subject and modern science.

Liberalism and Modernity

The *Contributions* are charged with an urgency that has to be called political—they call for a revolution in German and Western being.[26] But instead of discussing specific political questions, the text focuses on the urgency of be-ing itself and on the lack of urgency that infects every aspect of modern

24. This approach to being-there is already central to *Being and Time:* the "essence" of being-there is its "existence," i.e., the fact that its own being is a problem for it (SZ 42).

25. As Schwan puts it, for Heidegger all ideologies are "encompassed and supported by the same subjectivity of the will to domination, creation, validation, self-assertion, and self-imposition": "Heidegger's *Beiträge zur Philosophie* and Politics," 76.

26. "The original and genuine relation to the inception is the revolutionary": *Basic Questions of Philosophy*, 35 (translation modified), cf. 39. But by the end of the 1930s, with Heidegger's growing distance from politics, he rejects the very concept of a "revolution" as no less superficial than conservatism: GA 69, 23; "Überlegungen" IX, §53.

life. Modernity, as viewed in the *Contributions*, is a time when monstrous quantity counts more than depth (135–37), the real is nothing but the usable (126), and the search for stimulating "experiences" has crowded out the possibility of creative self-transformation (129). It is easy enough to apply these thoughts to Europe in the 1930s—and maybe even easier to apply them to our time of resource processing, information processing, and the manic production and consumption of digital entertainment. The Heideggerian cultural critique has an undeniable power. But does it also obscure some critical political distinctions?

Most discussions of Heidegger's politics concentrate on his reasons for choosing National Socialism. The debate focuses on whether this choice was essentially connected to his philosophical thought, to what extent it was justified by his understanding (or misunderstanding) of Nazism, and whether he ever appropriately distanced himself from this choice. But we must also try to understand the choices that he did not make—among them, the choice of liberal democracy. The question of what Heidegger rejected, and why, is particularly important because although it can be argued that he was not, or ceased to be, a true fascist, it can hardly be argued that he ceased to be antiliberal.[27] Furthermore, while his search for an ideal Nazism is rarely condoned, his claim that actual Nazism is essentially the same as actual liberalism has gained extensive credence: in certain circles it has become a commonplace to hold that both fascism and liberalism are merely variants of an underlying subjectivism or "humanism."[28]

What does "liberalism" mean for Heidegger? He claims that liberalism focuses on "the 'I'" (52–53, 319); it also insists on individual freedom of opinion (38). It would seem, then, that "liberalism" for Heidegger (as for most political theorists today) refers to the Lockean tradition of defending individual liberties against governmental power. In rejecting "liberalism," then, he is

27. Cf. *What Is Called Thinking?* 67; "Only a God Can Save Us," trans. William J. Richardson, in *Heidegger: The Man and the Thinker*, ed. Thomas Sheehan (Chicago: Precedent, 1981), 55.

28. Luc Ferry and Alain Renaut document and critique the antihumanist vogue in France in *French Philosophy of the Sixties: An Essay on Anti-Humanism*, trans. Mary H. S. Cattani (Amherst: University of Massachusetts Press, 1990). For some instances of the Heideggerian analysis of fascism as humanism, see Philippe Lacoue-Labarthe, *Heidegger, Art, and Politics*, trans. Chris Turner (Cambridge, Mass.: Blackwell, 1990), 95; Schürmann, *Broken Hegemonies*, 611–12. Ferry and Renaut give further examples in their *Heidegger and Modernity*, trans. Franklin Philip (Chicago: University of Chicago Press, 1990), chap. 2. An American case is William V. Spanos's *Heidegger and Criticism: Retrieving the Cultural Politics of Deconstruction* (Minneapolis: University of Minnesota Press, 1993)—a book peppered with political analyses that depend on the Heideggerian concept of humanism. If Stephen Holmes is to be believed, the power of this concept extends far beyond avowed Heideggerians such as Spanos, for "Heidegger's influence on contemporary American antiliberals, though subterranean and indirect, is all-pervasive": "The Permanent Structure of Antiliberal Thought," in *Liberalism and the Moral Life*, ed. Nancy L. Rosenblum (Cambridge: Harvard University Press, 1989), 246.

rejecting the mode of political thought that focuses on individual rights—and, implicitly, the Weimar institutions that were designed to secure those rights. But "liberalism" means much more to him than a type of regime or a political theory: it is a comprehensive world view (24–25, 38), and it is exclusively on this level that he attacks it. He would probably agree with his contemporary Carl Schmitt's claim that "it is necessary to see liberalism as a coherent, all-embracing, metaphysical system."[29] Liberalism is a form of modern subjectivism (which we could just as well call objectivism). Subjectivism pictures the human situation in terms of the subject, the object, and a representational connection between the two. The subject is supposed to be in complete command of its own consciousness, perfectly self-present, or at least potentially so; the object is supposed to be a thing that occurs as present within a neutral space; finally, the subject is supposed to be capable of presenting itself with the object by re-presenting it, that is, by following some procedure that will yield the correct picture or account of the object and thus make the object available for manipulation. For Heidegger, then, the self-interpretation of liberalism in terms of political liberties is irrelevant to its essence, which is determined by the subjectivist distortion of human freedom that dominates all modern ideologies. He writes in 1940: "'Liberalism' . . . is just a particular permutation of the *libertas* whose essence unfolds as the history of modernity. . . . The history of subjectivity is the history of liberation for the new essence of freedom, in the sense of humanity's unconditional self-legislation" (GA 48, 213).[30]

As insightful as Heidegger's attack on subjectivist metaphysics may be, his dismissal of a political doctrine of individual liberties as a species of subjectivism should give us pause. Are the differences between liberal and illiberal political prescriptions as trivial as he implies? Is liberal politics in fact founded on subjectivist metaphysics? If it is, does this fact doom liberalism, or does it challenge us to seek a more adequate philosophical ground for liberal politics?

Consider some references to liberalism in the context of Heidegger's reflections on selfhood. The concept of "personality," whether it places spirit over body or vice versa, is merely subjectivism, which identifies reason with the ability to say "I." The (Nazi) attempt to ground personality on the body is just a crude "biological liberalism" (53).[31] Neither Nazism nor liberalism asks who we are; they shrink back before our own questionability. "This self-

---

29. Carl Schmitt, *Die geistesgeschichtliche Lage des heutigen Parlamentarismus*, 2d ed. (Berlin: Duncker and Humblot, 1926), 5.

30. This passage explains Heidegger's practice in the *Contributions* of putting "liberalism" within quotation marks (25, 38, 53, 319). On the "genuine concept of 'liberalism' [as] *self-determination*," cf. GA 46, 163.

31. Already in January 1934, Heidegger vigorously attacks the biologistic interpretation of National Socialism: GA 36/37, 209–13.

sureness is the innermost essence of 'liberalism', which for this very reason can apparently develop freely and devote itself to progress for all eternity" (53). The question of who we are is "*more dangerous*" than any controversy between self-satisfied, humanistic conceptions of human beings (54).

Heidegger tends to run all modern interpretations of humanity together—and the true danger here, we may suspect, is that crucial differences are being blurred. For instance, although at one point in this passage he resists the Nazi propaganda that equates Bolshevism and Judaism, he ends up associating Bolshevism with rationalistic egalitarianism, hence with Christianity, and hence eventually with Judaism. He then asks the ominous question, "What decisions become necessary on this basis?" (54). Possibly this means that Nazism needs to fight against Christianity no less than against its other enemies—and its own humanist tendencies.

These diverse ideologies supposedly share a complacency about human nature, a self-satisfaction that is oblivious to the possibility of being-there. To extrapolate from Heidegger's remarks: for Christianity, man is essentially the sinning creature; for Marxism, man is essentially the producer; for liberalism, man is essentially the individual ego, the "I" (cf. GA 38, 149). Liberalism focuses on "the faculty of being able to say 'I'" (53)—presumably because according to liberalism, I must have my rights and my freedom, as should every "I." But then the "I" is taken for granted as something immediately accessible—one knows who one is, what one wills, and what one believes. This concept of the self as self-presence misses the fact that presence in general depends on the historical emergence of meaning. For ideologies that are based on self-presence, we can do all sorts of things, achieve all sorts of things, but *who* we are remains certain and self-evident; consequently, the givenness of being itself remains unquestioned.

Elsewhere Heidegger criticizes the concept of transcendence that he claims is found in Christianity, Nazism, liberalism, and the notion of "cultural values." For all these ideologies, man is to be understood in terms of something that exceeds man; this higher entity shows human beings their place and assigns them their calling. But this higher entity is itself understood *in terms of man* (25). Perhaps Heidegger means that the higher entity is conceived as escaping all the limitations of individual human beings. For instance, God is conceived as nonmortal and nonsinful; the *Volk* is nonprivate, nonarbitrary, nonephemeral. Thus, there is an unquestioned self-interpretation of man at the basis of all these ideologies. Although it is difficult to say what the "transcendent" of liberalism would be—universal human rights?—Heidegger associates liberalism with the other ideologies because they all take the human essence to be predetermined.

This line of thought leads him to view the liberal position as no less authoritarian and totalizing than any other: "even in the 'liberal' world view there is still this arrogance, in that it demands that everyone should be allowed to have his own opinion. But arbitrariness is the slavery of the 'accidental'" (38). On this point, at least, Heidegger is hardly as anti-Platonist as he claims. His rejection of *doxa* and his contempt for political freedom are reminiscent of the classic attack on democracy in the *Republic* (557b–558c). Democratic regimes and souls are driven about capriciously by ignorant desires, without order or necessity (*Republic* 561d)—hence, their freedom is not true freedom.[32] According to this argument, demanding freedom of opinion turns out to be a way of imposing slavery: everyone is enslaved to the arbitrariness of his or her own beliefs.

Another passage again lumps liberalism together with Nazism while at the same time holding out hope for a deeper understanding of the *Volk*: "the people can never be a goal and purpose . . . such an opinion is just a 'folkish' extension of the 'liberal' thought of the 'I'" (319). Liberalism promotes the individual; Nazism promotes the people, which in this world view is nothing but a larger "I"—a willing, representing, power-seeking ego on the scale of an entire race (321; cf. GA 90, 67). In both cases, the essence of man is taken for granted as a form of subjectivity; what is lost is openness to be-ing.[33] However, Heidegger by no means abandons the idea of the people, but makes its essence reside in "a few" who are capable of creatively sheltering the truth of be-ing (319). Passages such as this give us a glimpse of how Heidegger's initial hopes for National Socialism were disappointed by its development. A "'total' world view" typically overlooks its own "concealed ground (e.g., the essence of the people)" (40). A "gathering of the people" in terms of "'world-historical' events" can possibly open "a way into the vicinity of decision"—"but with the highest danger at the same time of completely mistaking its domain" (98). The proper goal is not to maintain the people as one being among others, but to allow the people to become itself by attending to something far greater than itself—the truth of be-ing (99).

Humanism not only reduces being-there to a subject, but also reduces other beings to objects. The being of beings becomes usefulness for some subjectivity, be it the people or the individual (30). This manipulative relation to beings goes hand in hand with modern science. Heidegger accepts the Cartesian and Kantian characterization of modern science as privileging

---

32. Cf. Heidegger's attack on academic freedom as negative freedom (a favorite antiliberal trope) in his rectoral address: "The Self-Assertion of the German University," trans. William S. Lewis, in *The Heidegger Controversy: A Critical Reader*, ed. Richard Wolin (Cambridge: MIT Press, 1993), 34.

33. Cf. "The Age of the World Picture," in *The Question Concerning Technology and Other Essays*, 132–33, 152; GA 48, 212.

its own method and categories over all experience of its objects (*Discourse on Method*, part 2; *Critique of Pure Reason*, B xiii). Holding rigidly to its procedure, science can force beings to declare themselves one way or the other within preestablished parameters; this is known as experimentation and gathering data. The data can then be systematized and put to use. Heidegger does not claim that scientific results are incorrect; but by resisting all experience that might lead to a revision of its method, science narrows the meaning of being and encourages an impoverished relation to the world. Beings are treated as nothing but objects which can be mined as sources of information and exploited in the service of subjective will (§§76–77).[34]

Thus we see Heidegger associating liberalism (a form of subjectivism) with positivism (a form of objectivism). After explaining how in the modern age, the relation of thinking to beings is reduced to a relation between certitude and objects, he remarks that "the *lack* of strength for metaphysical thinking, in unison with the effective forces of the 19th century (liberalism—industrialization—technology) demands positivism" (181). The self-certainty of the subject leads to a conception of knowledge as the processing of useful information. The problem here, once again, is that a "subject" can become a *self* only by attending creatively to the event of be-ing that would happen at a level deeper than all true statements about beings.

Because science gives priority to its method over the being of what it studies, its results can be put to work in the interest of some subjectivity—be it the *Volk*, the dictatorship of the proletariat, or liberal democracy. Modern science yields correct and useful facts, but not genuine insights into entities' ways of being. (For instance, we might gather all sorts of zoological data, but fail to appreciate what it is to be an animal.) Scientific objectivism is thus subjectivist and manipulative—and manipulable. "Only a thoroughly modern (i.e., 'liberal') science can be '*völkisch* science'" (148). Nazi politicized science is essentially no different from American and Soviet science; none of it is open to "an essential transformation of knowing and truth" (149). Science is the same all over the world—not because it transcends subjectivity but because it provides universally reproducible means of forcing objects to conform to our subjective strictures.

Few today would deny some of the main points of Heidegger's critique: the "humanist" cult of progress has its dangers, and a brave new world of prosperity can conceal an insidious malaise. But must we follow him so far as to dismiss human rights as irrelevant, and to view both liberalism and fascism as manifestations of the oblivion of be-ing? Is it possible to articu-

---

34. Cf. Glazebrook, "The Role of the *Beiträge* in Heidegger's Critique of Science."

late a defense of liberalism that does justice to Heidegger's critique of subjectivism?[35]

First, it is to Heidegger's credit that he considers the metaphysical roots of liberal thought. Any attempt to dissociate liberal politics from the problem of being is an attempt to avoid some highly pertinent issues: the question, "Is a liberal regime good for human beings?" naturally leads to the question, "What is a human being?" and thus to the questions, "What is it to be?" and "How does being have a sense for us?" But has Heidegger correctly identified the only possible basis of liberal politics? Does liberalism rest on an understanding of being that is indissolubly bound up with a metaphysics of presence?

There is little room for doubt that classic liberal arguments have drawn on subjectivism in Heidegger's sense—a conception of the human being as a radically autonomous, representing, and willing subject—and on metaphysical individualism—a conception of the human being as a unit that is in principle isolable from other such units.[36] If human beings are not autonomous individuals—if they are, or ought to be, participants in a shared responsiveness to be-ing—it would follow that Lockean arguments for liberalism are invalid.

But maybe liberal political prescriptions can also be based on a more adequate conception of human beings. While the rise of liberalism as a political doctrine was certainly made possible by modern thought, it may be that this doctrine can be reconstructed without recourse to the subjectivist elements of modernity. What would a nonsubjectivist liberalism look like? Liberalism insists that government should make ample room for individual beliefs and choices, so liberals are committed to the ontological position that there are individuals who have beliefs and make choices. But this is not the same as a commitment to metaphysical individualism—a view of human beings as essentially asocial seats of absolute will and consciousness. The individualist core of liberalism is simply an acknowledgment that each human being is capable of *some* degree of control over his or her existence, so that there is a distinct difference between doing something voluntarily and being forced to do it, and between freely adopting a belief and conforming to an external dogma. It makes no sense to deny altogether that we make choices and have individual awareness. (Such a denial would invalidate itself by asking us to choose

---

35. For a fuller version of the argument that follows see Richard Polt, "Metaphysical Liberalism in Heidegger's *Beiträge zur Philosophie*," *Political Theory* 25, no. 5 (October 1997): 655–79.

36. Cf. Ian Shapiro, *The Evolution of Rights in Liberal Theory* (Cambridge: Cambridge University Press, 1986), 275. But Holmes argues that even Hobbes's and Locke's contract arguments are purely political, not ontological in nature, and that these thinkers did not mean to deny that individuals are necessarily embedded in social contexts: "The Permanent Structure of Antiliberal Thought," 237–39.

to adopt the view that there are no choices or views.) It does not seem impossible to develop meaningful concepts of individual will and consciousness that are not entangled in metaphysical individualism and can be incorporated into a liberal political theory. One thing we would need to do is show that although we always operate within a shared culture, we can, within limits, choose how we are going to appropriate this culture as individuals. In fact, *Being and Time* itself provides such an analysis of individual freedom.[37] Another example is the account of human agency presented by Charles Taylor, for whom, while "one cannot be a self on one's own," one can nevertheless take a stand of one's own within a shared "moral space."[38]

Overcoming individualism is not yet overcoming subjectivism. We have to consider the Heideggerian caveat that a community as well as an individual can be conceived subjectivistically, as an autonomous ego on the national scale. However, with the waning of the modern belief that an individual can be a self-sufficient source of meaning, there is reason to hope that the danger of communal subjectivism will also subside. If we can retain individual freedom while acknowledging our indebtedness to a community, then we can also retain it while acknowledging that this community itself is indebted to the event of be-ing. In fact, by weakening the notion that a culture or nation can serve as the final standard of meaning, we might promote the liberal idea that individuals should have some rights that protect them against oppression by the community.

If liberalism need not endorse the view that we are perfectly autonomous subjects, then it need not endorse the view that other beings are merely objects available for our representation and manipulation. This is not to deny that people under a liberal regime will often objectify beings; in fact, it is likely that this approach to the world is encouraged by the traditionally subjectivist background of liberal discourse and practice. Furthermore, it is certain that even if a nonsubjectivist understanding of liberalism became widespread, many people under a liberal regime would continue to behave subjectivistically—in fact, it is unclear how *any* political system could prevent such an attitude. But liberal liberty is not just the freedom to manipulate and exploit; it leaves individuals politically free to pursue selfish interests, to work for the welfare of larger groups, or to shelter be-ing in beings.

Why should the liberty to make one's own choices and express one's own opinions be guaranteed by a political system? Liberals can answer, first, that the exercise of free choice can lead to a life that is better than any life under

37. Jonathan Salem-Wiseman, "Heidegger's Dasein and the Liberal Conception of the Self," *Political Theory* 31, no. 4 (August 2003): 533–57.

38. Charles Taylor, *Sources of the Self: The Making of the Modern Identity* (Cambridge: Harvard University Press, 1989), 36, and chap. 2 in general.

a repressive regime: a person who has been denied the opportunity to act on his or her own choices is missing the integrity and responsibility that make a life fully human. Such responsibility need not be conceived in terms of subjectivistic self-domination; it can also be conceived in more Heideggerian terms of creative responsiveness. Liberals might also argue that although there are other virtues that are at least as desirable as any virtues that may flow from the opportunity to act on one's own choices, governments cannot be counted on to promote these nonliberal virtues, while they *can* leave room for liberties when regulated by a proper constitution. This argument rests on the observation that authorities are fallible, and cannot be trusted to use power benevolently and effectively to promote virtue. But this is the sort of humble political reality that Heidegger systematically ignores; he focuses on the metaphysical basis of political ideologies while completely disregarding actual institutions and policies, and their concrete effects on human beings.[39]

The liberal positions I have just outlined leave open the question of which human virtues should be developed, or what we are free *for*. But is this not what distinguishes liberalism from totalizing world views? Of all political orientations, liberalism seems to be the one that can best afford to accept the questionability of the human essence. Liberalism leaves room for the historical process of becoming ourselves by creatively appropriating meaning—the very process with which Heidegger was concerned. In practice, liberalism promotes possibility, even if its theorists have not yet sufficiently thought through the essential happening of possibility.

A full-scale post-Heideggerian reconstruction of liberalism would take much more work, but we can at least see now that Heidegger's indifference to the concrete effects of political institutions represents a significant gap in his thinking. It can be argued that this gap prevents him from being a political thinker at all.[40] For even though political philosophers should reflect on their understanding of human nature and of being itself, they also have to concern themselves with empirical generalizations about how people tend to act, and about which policies tend to work under certain kinds of circumstances. Crucial parts of political philosophy must be ontic. In this sense, Heidegger's critique of liberalism is not a specifically *political* critique: it is

39. Cf. Robert J. Dostal, "The Public and the People: Heidegger's Illiberal Politics," *Review of Metaphysics* 47, no. 3 (March 1994): 551–53.

40. This is not to deny that the *Contributions* make a "contribution to politics" on the ontological level: they explore the being of the *polis* (or *Volk*) and in this way provoke us to "think about our shared life": Schmidt, "Strategies for a Possible Reading," 42. The error would lie in mistaking an ontology of the *polis* for an ability to judge politics in its concretion. Cf. Jerry Weinberger, "Technology and the Problem of Liberal Democracy," in Melzer, *Technology in the Western Political Tradition*, 285. On Heidegger's inadequate "contributions to politics," cf. Schürmann, *Broken Hegemonies*, 522.

not about policy and practice, which are partially separable from ideology. When we look past policies and focus exclusively on the understanding of being that they presuppose, we fall into political irrelevance or worse: Heidegger was misled for a while into entrusting the task of fostering the virtue of authenticity to a political authority with absolute power. Even after his disillusionment with National Socialism, which is apparent in the *Contributions*, his blindness to the differences between fascism and liberalism permanently prevented him from squarely facing the evils that were specific to the Nazi regime.

Reason and *Logos*

I began this chapter by asking how we can think of and even embrace being-there and appropriation if they are only future possibilities, rather than aspects of what we already are. My answer was that they cannot be purely futural, but must be a retrieval of the given—a unique way of taking over who we are. This retrieval has a certain justification—though not an indubitable ground—because it is the *ultimate* leap, the leap that embraces the questionability of our own being and of being in general. To reject such a leap is to reject thoughtfulness and selfhood themselves. But the leap does not have to be deferred until the arrival of the other inception; maybe such leaps happen whenever we return to ourselves in a way that manages to challenge our received sense of being.

Because being-there and appropriation are essentially open-ended, they are goals that transcend any particular objectives. But Heidegger also wants to use them to criticize particular aspects of Western culture and politics that are supposedly oblivious to questioning. However, his criticism of liberalism, at least, is too broad and too theoretical; it ignores the gaps between theory and practice, between concepts and phenomena. The phenomenon of individual freedom is broader than the subjectivist interpretation of this phenomenon, just as the phenomenon of goals is broader than the Platonist interpretation of goals. Heidegger's revolutionary aspirations sometimes lead him to throw out the baby with the bathwater.

This does not mean that his criticisms are useless. For instance, it is healthy to expose liberalism to his critique in order to improve liberal theory. What other aspects of the tradition might be deepened or rediscovered by way of the *Contributions*?

We resolved the contradiction between Heidegger's critique of goals and his promotion of goals in part by seeing that a goal is not necessarily a Platonic *idea*, a fixed answer to the question of how to be. But then the tradition calls for closer scrutiny: if thinking about goals is not inevitably Platonic, then some of our tradition's ethical and political thought may well survive Heidegger's critique of Platonism. We might even ask: was Plato himself a Platonist?

One central current in Western ethics views the good life as essentially rational. This line of thought is especially important for us to consider, because the *Contributions* emphatically criticize reason. Reason identifies universals, formulates propositions, and links these propositions into logically ordered systems. Heidegger does not claim that we should stop doing such things, but he does claim that before any such activities can take place, beings as a whole need to be revealed in light of some sense of the being of beings. This sense can be given to us as a living problem only in an event of appropriation—which is not a universal but a unique, ungrounded happening. Thinking of this happening requires inceptive thinking or bethinking, which are not rational. It would seem that reason cannot bring us any nearer to being-there.

Does Heidegger do justice to reason and to its role in traditional ethical and political thought? Here I can only make a few suggestions. I begin by reconsidering the Enlightenment notion that reason's universality can help to lay the basis for liberal politics and an ethics of respect; then I turn to the role of *logos* in Plato's dialogues.

The Enlightenment's celebration of the universality of reason runs counter to Heidegger's thought, since he devotes himself to defending "one's own" against the universal. Instead of understanding finitude as a privation and limitation, he thinks of it as a rich gift that allows being to have a meaning. Thanks to the fact that we belong in a specific place and time and our existence is our own, be-ing can happen: the world can open for us as a field in which things belong together.

Heidegger's passion for belonging has its dangers. His support for National Socialism seems to have been an attempt to awaken a uniquely German way of belonging, and thus a uniquely German event of be-ing. His emphasis on finitude shades into particularism; in order to counter this tendency we might need to reintroduce a notion of universal principles and obligations.

His reply would be that precisely because reason is universal, or arbitrarily accessible to all, it conflicts with genuine freedom (62) and genuine truth (343). Reasoning belongs to everyone equally, and everyone is indifferent to it (65): it does not touch anyone intimately because it does not engage anyone in a unique, urgent event. What is rational is what is common and obvious (91)—not the fundamental happening of be-ing, which is reserved for the few and the rare because it itself is rare (122, 251).

But as Heribert Boeder has pointed out, Heidegger is attacking a "straw man" here.[41] Rational truths are *not* equally available to all. A mathematical proof, a product of pure reason, may be intelligible only to a handful of human beings—and only at rare moments of insight. The universality of rationally discovered truth is not to be confused with its popularity or its accessibility.

What *is* this universality? In the case of the advanced mathematical proof, the few who are able to follow it are brought face to face with certain necessary relations and patterns. The proof provides "universal" truths in the sense that those who can understand it are all compelled to see the same phenomenon. More broadly, whether reasoning is mathematical, physical, or political, its aim is to reveal the things themselves—even if this aim is achieved only for a minority.

There is another sense of the universality of reason that *is* a kind of accessibility for all. Although not everyone can go far in reasoning, every human being can begin to reason—otherwise, one is not human. Human beings are essentially capable of exploring and discussing what things are and why they are (and if we are going to resist the *Contributions'* tendency to make being-there purely futural, then surely this capacity should also be considered part of being-there). This means that a mathematician and a metalworker, or an American and a Japanese, have some common horizons and some ability to communicate. To say this is not to make everyone the same, but to insist on a certain openness to discussion that is part of the human condition. This capacity includes not only generalizing and proving, but also conversation, persuasion, and poetry—all are elements of reason in the broadest sense, which is tantamount to Heidegger's own concept of "discourse" in *Being and Time* (SZ §34).

If we accept this broad sense of reason, we may also be able to resurrect the Enlightenment claim that reason goes hand in hand with respect for other rational beings. The Kantian formulation of this idea is narrow: taking reason as the faculty of subsuming particulars under rules, Kant argues that the very attempt to find a universal rule for action implies the attempt to act in a way that is acceptable to all rational beings, and thus implies respect for these beings as ends in themselves. The problem here, from a Heideggerian standpoint, is that the activity of rule-finding is too specialized and derivative; it presupposes a prior openness to beings as such. If we adopt a broader concept of reason, however, we can reformulate and preserve Kant's insight: trying to act in an articulate, understanding way—a way that involves po-

---

41. Heribert Boeder, "Twilight of Modernity," in *Seditions: Heidegger and the Limit of Modernity*, trans. Marcus Brainard (Albany: State University of New York Press, 1997), 204.

tentially communicable insights—means respecting others with whom we may be capable of communicating. This ethic is conceived broadly enough that if one rejects it, one is rejecting a crucial part of humanity—and of being-there. One appealing feature of this rehabilitated Enlightenment ethic is its open-endedness. We do not have to restrict ourselves to a particular *idea* of human beings in order to recognize that we have the gift of reason, since this gift is flexible: it allows us to articulate countless ways in which we can be. The old saw that human beings are rational, if interpreted generously enough, fits the Heideggerian notion that being-there is essentially in question.

If we combined an ethic of respect for all rational beings with a Heideggerian respect for the event of be-ing, we might end up with a discourse that could drop the extrinsically esoteric features of the *Contributions* while retaining their appreciation for the intrinsically esoteric. We need not adopt the crabbed strangeness of the *Contributions* (or even heighten it, as the available English version does). We can reach out to our interlocutors instead of insisting that they must already have made their own way to our topic (8). Heidegger's style in this text discourages communication by making bald, gnomic pronouncements—but disclosure cannot thrive, cannot happen historically, without ongoing reasoning and communication.[42] Perhaps the very question of be-ing is a rational question: reason, in seeking grounds, leads us to the question of the ground of the meaning of givenness. However, reason does not require us to pretend that the truth is generally available and indefinitely reproducible; we can reason about the event of appropriation without presuming to represent it perfectly and while acknowledging that this event may require rare moments of insight.

Heidegger certainly would not be satisfied with this moderate neo-Enlightened position. Being-there, for him, is a radical break with the rational animal, the *zoon logon echon* as defined in the first inception (129). So we should turn briefly to Plato, whom Heidegger accuses of so much, to reexamine what *logos* means in his dialogues and why he introduces the fatal concept of the *idea*.

On his dying day, Socrates warns us against misology (*Phaedo* 89d–e). We may be tempted to hate reason because it seems to dissolve our dearest hopes—our desire for immortality, our will to be. Fighting misology, Socrates builds up his friends' confidence by contriving arguments for the immortality of the soul. Yet after his last argument and before his last myth, he warns that his "first hypotheses need to be examined more clearly" (107b).

---

42. Gadamer helpfully supplements Heidegger on this point: see Dostal, "The Experience of Truth for Gadamer and Heidegger."

And in fact, the final argument for immortality is specious. It proves that the soul is *athanatos*, "deathless" (105e)—but only in the sense that a soul is essentially alive as long as it exists, not in the sense that a soul can never cease to be. Reason fails to guarantee Socrates' survival. So why is Socrates still a friend of reason?

The answer may lie in the very uncertainty of the arguments, their need for further examination. Even if Socrates cannot examine them any more, his friends can, and we can. *Logos* links Socrates to the rest of humanity, or at least to those who are willing to engage in discourse. It is *logos* that is immortal—always open to further discussion and interpretation. *Logos* is never out of time.

What else is Plato teaching us by way of the failure of Socrates' last argument? The argument proceeds by way of essences: the essence of the soul, the essence of life and death. It rests on the hypothesis that there are essences, or forms (100b). Given this hypothesis, we can show that the soul is essentially alive. The problem is that the argument concerns essences only, timeless universals—and these universals do not address the question of whether one's *own* soul will survive after death. The atemporal *idea* falls short when it comes to the ultimate emergency, the most intimately urgent issue in our own, profoundly temporal lives.

If the forms are disconnected from life-and-death, temporal problems, why posit them at all? Socrates answers the question autobiographically, making it clear that the forms are his hypothesis, his projection (100a–b). (Heidegger claims that to recognize the need for a projection is to overcome the *idea* [305], but here Socrates freely admits that the forms are not simply "read off" from the given. They begin with a leap, rather than ending with one.) The hypothesis of the forms is second-best (99d). Socrates had hoped to discover a teleological explanation of the physical world, which would tell him why it is good that things are as they are (97c–d). Failing that, he resorted to a verbal and conceptual discussion of goodness, a discussion that treats the noble and the beautiful as if they had their being in a separate, invisible domain (99e). The purpose of this hypothesis is to make it possible to continue debating the question of the good life. In this way, even though the forms cannot satisfy our desires to see goodness in the physical world or to conquer death, they do have relevance to our lives, because they give us a way to reason together about our aspirations. The initial motive for the forms is ethical, not metaphysical.[43] It is absurd, then, for Heidegger to characterize

---

43. Heidegger calls Socrates the originator of metaphysics (GA 67, 89) without considering the ethical motives behind the hypothesis of the forms. For a more thorough elucidation of this hypothesis see Stanley Rosen, *The Question of Being: A Reversal of Heidegger* (New Haven: Yale

the very concept of a goal as a variant of the Platonic *idea* (216). Plato (if we may identify him with his character Socrates) posits the *idea* in order to think philosophically about ethical and political questions that are already current in Greek life. The concept of the *idea* does not create goals; it interprets the already given phenomenon of goals, and its interpretation is admittedly second best.

None of this means that we should become Platonists. We do not have to posit forms (either as Platonic separable beings or as Aristotelian species). Heidegger's critique of the *idea* still stands: the *idea* lures us away from the event of the emergence of the sense of givenness, because it eternalizes a current way in which the given presents itself to us. We do not have to adopt some narrow model of dialectical argumentation, either. What we can learn from Plato, however, is that rejecting the *idea* is not tantamount to rejecting all goals; it is just the rejection of one interpretation of goals. To wash our hands of all goals, to give up on the project of reasoning together about the good life, would be to fall back into the one-sidedness of pre-Socratic philosophy, which explained what *is* without helping us choose what ought to be. Possibly it is in this sense that Plato's form of the good lies "beyond being" (*Republic* 509b).

But if we reject the forms, what is left of Plato? Perhaps what is essential: a *desire* for truth and goodness without any fixed interpretation of what they are. We should remember that Socrates never tells us what the good is; in fact, he denies that he knows it. Although he has an opinion about the good, he is not willing to state it, because it falls short of knowledge and his companions would not understand it anyway (*Republic* 506b–e). At the heart of the *Republic*, then, is a mystery on which everything else depends: without knowledge of the good, we do not know what justice is, either in a city or in a soul, much less whether justice is good (506a). The central questions of the dialogue are never answered. But Socrates continues to insist that it *is* intrinsically good to have a just soul, and that a just soul is a soul led by *logos*. This is a circular declaration of faith more than a finished argument: we must have faith that reason can discover what is good, and that it is good for reason to lead us. Socrates stands as the exemplar of this examined life, despite (or because of) his knowledge that he knows nothing. He is good not because of his knowledge of the good, but because of his quest for it.

This idea parallels Heidegger's notion that the seeking of be-ing is itself the goal (17)—with the difference that Socrates' search is argumentative. He

---

University Press, 1993), 46–95. On Heidegger's general insensitivity to Platonic dialogues cf. Drew Hyland, *Finitude and Transcendence in the Platonic Dialogues* (Albany: State University of New York Press, 1995), chap. 6.

proceeds by way of dialectic. To be sure, he also draws on other elements of *logos* in the broader sense, such as myths, poetry, and rhetoric—but he always returns to *logos* as argument, never becoming misological. Does this make the Socratic search too narrow, too rationalistic? No, because Socrates is not a rationalist: he does not insist that the answers must be available to reason, or that life can be based purely on rationally discovered answers. Instead, he bases his life on the *search* for answers, placing his faith in *logos* as a capacity and orientation, not as a stockpile of truths.[44]

If Plato turns out to have an open-ended conception of human existence, then other thinkers in the tradition may also escape Heidegger's critique. Aristotle, for one, following in Plato's footsteps, claims that reason is the human function and the good life is the rational life; but he does not presume to dictate the particular decisions and discoveries that reason will make. "In a way, the soul is all things," because the mind is capable of turning in all directions and striving to understand everything (*De Anima* 431b21; cf. SZ 14). To be rational, then, is not to be locked into a particular mold.

The open-endedness of Plato's *logos* and the hypothetical status of the forms also allow us to interpret him from a Kantian standpoint, in the broad sense I sketched above. For Kant, what is essential in a good will is not some particular conception of a noumenal form of the good, or the possession of any objective certainty. What matters most of all is the very attempt to ask, "Why should I do this or that?" The question "why should I?"—the search for grounds of choice—is an assertion of reason and freedom. It includes a willingness to live by standards that can be articulated and defended, that are intelligible and acceptable to other rational beings. This willingness includes respect for others, even before we articulate any particular ideals or rules. Here is the *Grundlegung* of morality: reason is in itself already moral, because its desire for grounds involves respect for all who are capable of understanding those grounds. Maybe the Platonic positing of the forms, then, is also a moral ground-laying, even though we do not know the content of any of the forms. Maybe simply by encouraging people to have faith in reason and crave knowledge of the good, Socrates is promoting justice.

But for whom? Enlightenment universalism may seem to be a poor match for Plato, as it is hardly necessary to say that he is an elitist. What is sometimes overlooked, however, is Socrates' statement that *every* soul desires the good. When it comes to the good, no one wants opinion and appearances; we all seek knowledge of being (*Republic* 505d). What distinguishes philosophers is that they know that they do not yet possess such knowledge. Philosophers, then, are pursuing a goal that is universally human but which most

---

44. Compare Heidegger's thought that philosophy is a stance (*Haltung*) rather than a standpoint (*Halt*): GA 27, 376–90.

human beings think they have already attained. The rational quest for good-ness is universal because it lies dormant within every human being, and be-cause everyone can participate in *logos* to some extent. Reason is not, however, universal in the sense of providing a truth that is accessible to all, as Hei-degger claims. We can only hope that insight will flare up suddenly, after years of discussion between teacher and pupil (*Seventh Letter* 341c). Truth is a rare and unpredictable event.

A Kantian interpretation of Plato, which reduces the good to a good will, also runs the risk of formalism. Here we need to return to Plato himself, who recognizes our need for concrete experience. Consider the allegory of the cave: we are blinded not only by our exposure to the light, but also by our re-turn to the darkness (*Republic* 516e, 518a, 520c). Someone who clearly un-derstands the abstract forms can bungle concrete, practical matters in the physical world. The hypothesis of the forms enables us to articulate and dis-cuss goals, but the forms alone cannot determine how to act in accordance with those goals in a particular situation. We must learn both the ascent and the descent. Kant notoriously underestimates the difficulty of the descent.

Does Heidegger as well? Of course, Heidegger does not posit a separate in-telligible realm. He would insist that he is not thinking abstractly to begin with; he is thinking in and from the unique event of owning—the very opposite of disengaged, universalized, timeless, and placeless reflection. That is his intent, but does he succeed in avoiding abstraction in practice? The same nouns and verbs keep recurring in the *Contributions*, functioning as generalities. They point to an event that cannot be linked to any particular event, a time-space that seems separate from any particular time and space. Heidegger attacks the atemporal and abstract—but in an abstract way. Thinking the event of be-ing without beings is not the same as thinking about an abstract beingness, but it tends to have a similar effect. It leaves us unequipped to deal with what is (or in Heideggerian terms, to shelter the truth of be-ing in beings). To be sure, no argument or text can take the place of experience when it comes to dealing with beings. But *Being and Time*, with its respect for existentiell understanding, ac-knowledges this, whereas the *Contributions*, along with much of Heidegger's later work, seem to dismiss almost all human experience of particular beings as a blind reproduction of traditional prejudices. Western history is to be under-stood *only* in terms of the history of be-ing, which is to be worked out intel-lectually and textually. Material conditions, political circumstances, desire, chance—all the wealth of beings and our treatment of them—are irrelevant. Heidegger, not Plato, turns out to be the Platonist.[45]

---

45. "Although Heidegger insisted that essence for him is nothing metaphysical, nevertheless *how* Heidegger spoke of essence betrayed a kind of Platonism that is no less disengaged from concrete life" (and more disengaged than Plato himself, I would add): Lawrence Hatab, *Ethics*

Heidegger's attitude is surely too intellectual, too contemptuous of the descent to the cave. It also impoverishes our thinking itself. Despite his obsessive, hypnotic repetition of his interpretation of history, it remains a less-than-convincing myth with only a shadowy relevance to concrete situations. We can enrich the *Contributions'* thinking of be-ing, I propose, by tying it to experiences of particular beings, including ourselves.

From Beings to Be-ing and Back

The *Contributions* try to say how the event of be-ing happens. But *what* exactly happens in this event? Heidegger rejects the question, if it has any ontic intent. "What happens in the history of be-ing? . . . Nothing happens. But the nothing is be-ing. Nothing happens: appropriation ap-propriates" (GA 70, 171; cf. GA 6.2, 444). As much as we may appreciate the distinction between beings and be-ing, the vagueness of Heidegger's words is frustrating. *Ereignis* is the event of the founding of the there; but what does the there look like? Who lives there? What do they do? They shelter be-ing in beings—but in what ways? We find no answers in the *Contributions*, largely because the event of appropriation is reserved for the other inception.[46] Even though this inception will draw on the past, it is primarily futural—we can bethink it only in an intimation. The closest Heidegger comes to concretion is his dark portrait of the present as bereft of appropriation.

What if we broke with this mood and tried to find *Ereignis* within our experience as we know it? What if we could discover events of appropriation, inceptions, and emergency at work even within the ordinary, even in the realm of reproducibility? This is not to say that appropriation is "always already" happening; we do not have to turn appropriation into a universal or a transcendental. We can retain the distinction between customary experience and "the unaccustomed—happening once, happening this time" (463). Instead of restricting uniqueness to a single possible event, however, we can find uniqueness in many places (after all, multiplicity is not sameness).[47] Then we might discover that the there is here.

---

and Finitude: Heideggerian Contributions to Moral Philosophy (Lanham, Maryland: Rowman and Littlefield, 2000), 205. Cf. Caputo, *Demythologizing Heidegger,* chap. 6. Similarly, in an effort to preserve the phenomenological value of the *Contributions* and avoid sheer eschatological speculation, Neu argues that we need to set aside Heidegger's one-sided portrayal of the present age: *Die Notwendigkeit der Gründung,* 323–25.

46. Heidegger calls be-ing a darkly glowing forge, and asks: but where are the steady smiths who will hammer the truth of be-ing into beings in this forge? "Überlegungen" IX, §32.

47. Marion claims that even the "most banal" phenomena are essentially "events"—that is, they overflow our experience by being unpredictable, nonrepeatable, and never fully describable: *In Excess,* 34.

This will work only if we can connect be-ing to beings, the beings that we encounter now. As we have seen, Heidegger states programmatically that be-ing and beings must happen simultaneously and that be-ing must be sheltered in beings. But he provides no details on these connections, apparently because be-ing outranks beings (303, 428) and we must start to think be-ing by leaving beings aside (75–76). Some have argued that this very idea is absurd.[48] Heidegger himself sometimes seems uncertain about be-ing's (and being's) relation to beings.[49] But even if we grant the soundness of his basic approach, and concede that at least some straits of appropriation can be thought apart from beings, the promise of this thinking cannot be fulfilled unless we return to what *is*. As Heidegger himself says, the trick is to master the art of turning back to beings (452–53).[50] If "essential happening" is to be more than just a variation of the old, abstract "essence," it must help us discover "the multiplicity of *sheltering*" (275) and "the uniqueness and rank of each being" (66).

We may even need to challenge Heidegger's conviction that beings cannot ground be-ing. As I pointed out earlier, this conviction might be supported by the argument that scientific researchers take it for granted that beings are, and that their being has a certain meaning. Any scientific explanation of the origin of the meaning of being would presuppose such a meaning, and would thus fail. In order to pursue the question of be-ing we may have to sustain a sense of wonder at the givenness of beings and being—a wonder that is not scientific but philosophical. Givenness must remain questionable if we are to ask how it comes into question. But is it impossible for investigations of beings to sustain a wonder at givenness? The wonder usually remains in the background of scientific research (we speak of a scientist's "personal motivation" for science) or exists side by side with it (a person might have a "poetic" as well as a scientific appreciation of the world). Could

---

48. Rosen, *The Question of Being*, 119; Schwan, "Heidegger's *Beiträge zur Philosophie* and Politics," 81.

49. Notoriously, the postscript to the fourth edition (1943) of "What is Metaphysics?" claims, "although being essentially happens without beings, an entity never is without being." But the fifth edition (1949) revises this sentence to read, "that being never essentially happens without beings, that an entity never is without being" (GA 9, 306; cf. *Pathmarks*, 233). For interpretations see Max Müller, *Existenzphilosophie im geistigen Leben der Gegenwart* (Heidelberg: Kerle, 1949), 50; Walter Schulz, "Über den philosophiegeschichtlichen Ort Martin Heideggers," in *Heidegger: Perspektiven zur Deutung seines Werkes*, ed. Otto Pöggeler (Königstein: Athenäum, 1984), 118–19; Karl Löwith, *Martin Heidegger and European Nihilism*, trans. Gary Steiner (New York: Columbia University Press, 1995), 66–68; Richardson, *Heidegger*, 562–65. The picture is complicated by the statement in the *Contributions* that be-ing needs beings, but beings do not need be-ing (30).

50. Emad claims that "the experience of this returnership constitutes the backbone" of "Das Seyn" (part 8 of the published *Contributions*): "On 'Be-ing,'" 242. Perhaps so, but Heidegger does not express this experience in words that illuminate particular beings.

the wonder be *integrated* with the fact-finding? The results of this thinking could not be expressed purely mathematically—mathematics can measure and describe the given, but not wonder at its givenness. One would have to use living language in combination with precise vocabulary. Such efforts are typically thought of as "popular science," not pure research, but at their best they can convey more truth than their "pure" counterparts.

Perhaps by uniting scientific observation with a poetic sensibility, one could narrate the emergence of being from beings. Un-concealment might be an evolutionary process, a gradual dawning of truth from oblivion. "Chaos" theory, which attends to the emergence of nonlinear systems from simpler, linear systems, might be a useful tool in describing this process. We should not assume that complexity alone will "explain consciousness," or generate meaning; cosmic narratives must not slip being into beings by sleight of hand. Still, the attempt to find being emerging *from* beings is an important alternative to Heidegger's separation of be-ing (the event of emergence) from all beings. Such an attempt would not be new; it traces its pedigree to Schelling and includes Peirce, Whitehead, and Teilhard de Chardin.[51] The fact that this tradition sometimes appeals to New Age naiveté should not make us assume that it is fatally naive.

As a case in point, consider the problem of time-space. In the *Contributions*, as we saw, this is not meant as a formal concept (261), an a priori structure governing all experience, but as an element in the unique event of appropriation. Time-space is the momentous site where truth takes place. Once this site is founded, particular truths can be ascertained and the process of measuring beings can begin; formal, mathematical space and time are established. Heidegger's account of time-space parallels the general priority of be-ing over beings, truth over truths.

In the play of time-space, then, ordinary time and space would be opened. But if we say that time-space is the origin of linear time, we must explain what "origin" means. We cannot say that the event of time-space is chronologically earlier than linear time—we would then be placing time-space within linear time in order to establish the priority of time-space, which is incoherent. But if the "priority" here means that there is an essential structure that always underlies our experience of time and space, then we have given up radical eventuation and have returned to a present-indicative tonality, to the formal concepts of space and time that Heidegger was trying to avoid.

---

51. Beistegui's Deleuzian ontology is also promising here. Beistegui wishes to reintegrate man into nature because subjectivity is "not essentially different from the world it contemplates": *Truth and Genesis*, 20. The genesis of natural beings in themselves should in principle be relevant to the emergence of truth for us. However, I do not think Beistegui has done enough to explain the relation between these two "events."

Heidegger seems to be asking us to think of time-space as a happening, an event. But how can time itself take place? Would it not need a medium in which to happen? That medium, it seems, would be linear time—but then linear time would not derive from primordial time-space.[52] Maybe we can think of time itself as an event if we manage to distinguish the notion of event from the notion of change within the framework of a timeline. Heidegger thinks of the primordial event not primarily in terms of change, but in terms of the play of belonging and estrangement, uniqueness and reproducibility. But how would this primordial happening of time connect to the sequence of changes in linear time? Even if time-space cannot be understood in terms of this sequence, it must bear some relation to it. Even if time-space is more than change, it must involve change and must depend on earlier changes.[53]

We might approach this problem by reflecting on the conditions that must already be in place if time-space is to happen, and trying to narrate the emergence of time-space from linear time. Surely there are some prerequisites for time-space: humanlike animals must be alive, ready to enter being-there; these animals must have evolved.[54] To say this is not to reduce be-ing to the ontic, but to respect the role of beings in be-ing. We do not have to give up the priority of the event of appropriation in the order of meaning (it cannot be understood or explained on the basis of what it reveals) in order to acknowledge that this event has chronological antecedents.[55] As we saw, this project could also employ scientific research, if this research could be integrated with a poetic appreciation of be-ing.

---

52. Cf. D'Angelo, "'Svolta' e 'attimalità,'" 236; Grieder, "Essential Thinking," 246; Ionescu, "The Concept of the Last God," 90.

53. There are analogous problems in *Being and Time*: see Dreyfus, *Being-in-the-World*, 259; Polt, *Heidegger*, 106–9. Stambaugh claims that although questions like these are "the most natural questions in the world, [they are] still inappropriate, based on the conception of enduring objective presence": *The Finitude of Being*, 116. But if we simply abandon the questions, we easily fall into a quasi-Kantian dualism: on one hand, be-ing as a quasi-transcendental condition for presence; on the other hand, the quasi-empirical flow of beings from future to present to past. We have seen that Heidegger is trying to avoid this perspective by conceiving of be-ing and beings as "simultaneous." Stambaugh herself claims that for Heidegger, there is an "activity" of time (ibid., 119), and it seems that an activity must involve linear time. Schürmann claims that the *Contributions'* "originary time" is not the a priori condition of "empirical history" because the two are incommensurable and "out of sync": *Broken Hegemonies*, 595–96. But this solution (or nonsolution) disregards the themes of simultaneity and sheltering.

54. Stambaugh is right to say that for Heidegger, "time is in some sense *discontinuous*": *The Finitude of Being*, 134. The event of appropriation is not of the same order as what precedes it, so it can never be predicted. But this does not imply that nothing precedes the event.

55. This would be analogous to the German idealist project of "beginning" with self-consciousness (refusing to reduce it to empirical facts about objects) but drawing on the features of self-consciousness to reconstruct the process that must already have been at work in order to enable self-consciousness to arise.

In 1928 Heidegger felt the need for a similar thought experiment, which he called "metontology"; while respecting the special role of being-there as the interpreter of being, metontology would inquire into the ontic totality within which being-there comes forth and finds itself.[56] However, Heidegger never pursued this experiment, perhaps because he wanted to preserve the contingency and uniqueness of the event of be-ing. From a Husserlian perspective, it can be argued that the very notion of metontology is a confusion, a lapse of phenomenology into metaphysics.[57] But the temptation of this notion is at least worth taking seriously, because it expresses a healthy reluctance to accept an absolute separation between be-ing and beings.

A "metontological" narrative of the emergence of be-ing from beings is reserved for the future, if it is possible at all. However, we might also tie be-ing back to beings by bringing the *Contributions'* thoughts to bear on our more immediate existence. Could we draw on the straits of appropriation—such as inception, emergency, and owndom—to enrich our interpretations of experience? We might find, then, that events of appropriation happen countless times in our lives—though not at every time. We might find that every life is touched and sustained by inceptive moments, greater and lesser emergencies in which our own sense of being emerges into its own. As Benjamin puts it, the state of emergency is not the exception but the rule.[58] In order to recognize this plurality, we need to wean ourselves from the Heideggerian habit of tracing all meanings back to a single ground (albeit an "abyssal," noncausal ground), at the expense of the contrary movement of dispersion and multiplication. Yet the idea is not as un-Heideggerian as it may seem. "The Origin of the Work of Art" claims that whenever "art happens" there is an inception; "a thrust enters history and history either begins or resumes."[59] Inception is plural, then. Great art may be rare, but there are many moments that take part, to some degree, in the struggle between earth and world.

This approach would yield a plural conception of be-ing: significance takes place at many junctures in each individual life, in many lives, in many communities. There are multiple, sometimes competing, and perhaps incommensurable openings of sites, because there are many reinterpretive events. This is not sheer chaos, but there may be no supreme event of appropriation aside from these countless happenings.[60] Some reinterpretive events are par-

56. *The Metaphysical Foundations of Logic*, 156–57.

57. Crowell, "Metaphysics, Metontology, and the End of *Being and Time*."

58. Walter Benjamin, "Theses on the Philosophy of History," in *Illuminations*, trans. Harry Zohn (New York: Schocken, 1969), 257.

59. "The Origin of the Work of Art," in *Off the Beaten Track*, 49.

60. Heidegger seems to be moving in this direction in some passages in GA 70 that emphasize the plurality of inceptions and the "gaps" between them, together with the uniqueness of inception in each instance: GA 70, 37, 181, 187.

ticularly momentous; they are junctures that affect the entire subsequent course of our interpretations, or inceptions that open a new realm. Other reinterpretive events have relatively superficial effects, sending ripples through our existence that soon die back down, returning us to stable mirroring. When the surface of existence is calm, there are ordinary events of understanding, in which a settled meaning of being illuminates beings in a familiar way. There is a hierarchy, then, but none of these events is the master event, determining an entire era.

Reinterpretive events are also events of emergency. When one's interpretation of being comes into question, one experiences a crisis for which there are no rules. The crisis may be as minor as a moment of puzzlement, or it may plunge us into despair. In either case it calls for a decision, a resolution that may establish new rules and new concepts.

With these emergencies come appropriations. Until we face a crisis, we take our own for granted—our own home, language, body, customs, beliefs. We simply inhabit our network of ownness, with all its patterns of the proper and improper, the appropriate and the inappropriate, the apt and the inept. But this primordial habitation and habituation is not true owning; owning comes only when the own comes into question. We are then given an opportunity to recognize that we have been appropriated by our own and that we need to appropriate it ourselves, whether by affirming it or by transforming it. Then we can truly come into our own.

Examples of such moments are plentiful in literature, which, after all, is normally centered on emergencies—our problems and our attempts to resolve them. Consider one of the earliest evocations of existential anxiety, in Kierkegaard's *Repetition*: "One sticks a finger into the ground to smell what country one is in; I stick my finger into the world—it has no smell. Where am I? What does it mean to say: the world? What is the meaning of that word? Who tricked me into this whole thing and leaves me standing here? Who am I?"[61] The speaker's sense of his identity has been disrupted; he no longer knows his place. His being and the being of his surroundings have come into question. The experience is unnerving, but it can be the beginning of a new, deeper appropriation of self and world, as Don DeLillo suggests: "He picks up speed and seems to lose his gangliness, the slouchy funk of hormones and unbelonging and all the stammering things that seal his adolescence. He is just a running boy, a half-seen figure from the streets, but the way running reveals some clue to being, the way a runner bares himself to consciousness, this is how the dark-skinned kid seems to open to the world, how the bloodrush of a dozen strides brings him into eloquence."[62] "Unbe-

---

61. Kierkegaard, *Fear and Trembling; Repetition*, 200.
62. Don DeLillo, *Underworld* (New York: Scribner, 1998), 13.

longing" may be the prerequisite for a deeper belonging, an ability to in-vent oneself through decision, action, and articulation. Such inventions lend themselves to narrative—which Heidegger neglects in favor of poetry.

Events of appropriation occur repeatedly; there is no real learning or growth without them. They are probably most frequent in childhood, when natality—to borrow Arendt's term[63]—is constantly welling up within us: we keep giving birth to new ways of acting and thinking, and in this process we keep being reborn. The rarer but more dramatic emergencies happen in adolescence and at other formative turning points. At these points, tensions and unspoken issues in our lives burst out in reinterpretive events. We find new ways of being ourselves in our world.

Because these events involve choice and action, they may be an appropriate focus for an ethics and politics that are informed by Heidegger's thought. In this way, there may be an opening in the *Contributions* for a return to practical philosophy.[64] The *Contributions* stand between the decisionism that lurks in *Being and Time* and the quietism that hovers over the postwar works, where human life is shrouded in a pastoral mist. When we focus only on choice, we run the risk of exalting an arbitrary "will to will." When we focus only on indebtedness, we fall into a contemplative or even aesthetic point of view that is difficult to relate to action: we are simply supposed to "think," that is, appreciate the emergence of being. We need to combine an awareness of choice and responsibility with an acknowledgment of our indebtedness to events of emergence that we do not control. The *Contributions* try to steer between Scylla and Charybdis by overcoming the traces of subjectivism in *Being and Time* while still calling for decisions and goals.[65] The problem is that these decisions be-

---

63. Hannah Arendt, *The Human Condition*, 2nd ed. (Chicago: University of Chicago Press, 1998), 9. Schürmann also appropriates the concept: see *Broken Hegemonies*, 18–19, and Index of Terms, s.v. "natality." "In each new event there is a repetition of the proto-event of birth": Dastur, "Phenomenology of the Event," 186.

64. Salem-Wiseman argues that a Heideggerian understanding of a meaningful life as involving "crises" in which attachments come into question can support liberal theory: "Heidegger's Dasein," 536. María José Callejo Hernanz even suggests that the *Contributions* can be read in a Kantian spirit as specifying "certain conditions in the absence of which one cannot speak of praxis, for without them there is no room for decision—that is, conditions that are definitive of the intelligibility of actions as actions." These conditions include history (99), selfhood (100), and the gift of being (103). From this perspective, appropriation is not a mere fact, but a practically *"necessary construction"*: "Heidegger y la otra historia de Occidente: Notas kantianas para una lectura de los 'Beiträge zur Philosophie,'" *Anales del Seminario de Metafísica* 27 (1993): 99, 100, 103. Although Heidegger would surely reject this perspective as subjectivist, it has the merit of provoking us to reflect on the status of the *Contributions* as a philosophy of possibility, not a present-indicative metaphysics.

65. Other interpreters have noted this double character of the *Contributions*, but they generally see it as a defect rather than an advantage. According to Thomä, it amounts to a self-contradiction: *Die Zeit des Selbst*, 769–71, 774. Beistegui sees a similar tension between the pre-ontic

come too remote and rare. We need to use some of the *Contributions'* insights to help us think about more common choices; in the light of the *Contributions*, each significant choice can be seen as an event of emergency and appropriation.

But how could that bring us any closer to an ethics? It might seem that if every event of appropriation is, as Heidegger insists, self-concealing and unique, then any set of *articulated rules* for action would immediately exclude itself from such events. Ethics would be a derivative effort, a latecomer that could never attain the inceptive event. Unpredictability and uniqueness, the spices of action, are not included in ethical recipes.[66]

But ethics is not necessarily a set of rules; the heart of the Platonic ethics I sketched in the previous section is not a rule but the commitment to reason in the broadest sense, the *search* for communicable and defensible goals. That search does not exclude the possibility that truth may be granted at rare and unpredictable junctures that reason cannot bring about. In fact, by exploring its own limits, reason may bring us closer to recognizing the need for such moments. If we simply give up on reason, however, we run two risks. First, we may fail to draw on the unique moments by developing communication on their basis. Inceptions generate reproducibility; they call for articulation and representation, even if they themselves are unique. This means that we fail to do justice to inceptive moments if we leave them completely inarticulate, without letting them inspire new ways of communicating. The second risk is that we will mistake a communicable moment for a unique one. Our decisions may be more rational than we believe; the only way to tell is to try to communicate and articulate them as far as we can.

We could put this in terms borrowed from Kierkegaard: the ethical universal may sometimes be suspended for the sake of a unique, particular relation with the ultimate. At such moments an individual enters a condition that cannot be communicated directly, because all communication presupposes something universal, or at least shared.[67] But this does not mean that such an individual is indifferent to ethics. While striving to act ethically, the individual may sometimes be faced with a decision that exceeds ethics; but without

---

event of be-ing and the central role of man as an entity in this event, a tension he calls a "duplicity" (*Truth and Genesis*, 118, 123, 146) even though the two themes are "not incompatible" (140). Similarly, Schürmann reads the text as torn between "focalizing" and "dispersive" strategies: *Broken Hegemonies*, 517. This reading reflects Schürmann's unease with all active founding and creating; but as he himself says, the illusion does not consist in founding "the proper," but in doing so while "denying the withdrawal that alienates and expropriates" (589, cf. 611–12). Decisive action is not inappropriate, then, as long as it does not take itself as an absolute.

66. Thus, attacking Habermas, Schürmann complains that the principle of "consensus through discursive rationality, or through communicative action, can be posited only at the cost of denying the foreignness of the singular reference": *Broken Hegemonies*, 627.

67. Kierkegaard, *Fear and Trembling; Repetition*, 60.

the original striving there would be no "fear and trembling," no recognition of the excess, and no genuine encounter with the unique. Furthermore, it may be possible to communicate the unique indirectly, and such communication may be essential to setting others free for their own ultimate encounters.

In this way we may be able to preserve reason and ethics while understanding moments of decision as events of emergency and appropriation. Religious conversion is an excellent example (although Heidegger's insights are not exclusively religious). In such an event, one comes into a new relation with God (or the gods, or some other sacred source). There is a tendency for this relation to become codified and settle into "faith" in the sense of objective belief. But at the moment of conversion itself, what is certain is not the fact of God's existence or nonexistence, but the urgency of one's own need to establish a relation to the sacred. Faith, in this sense, is not knowledge or opinion about some fact, but a decision that enables us to take a stance regarding what is concealed and unconcealed. Although this decision is free, it is a response to an emergency, a *kairos* that comes upon one "as a thief in the night" (1 Thess. 5:2). The moment is neither arbitrary nor necessary, but urgent. It urges one to decide—not merely to choose between given options, but to leap out of indifference into the urgency of an either/or (cf. 101–2). This leaping is also a grounding—not the establishment of an unquestionable certainty, but the abyssal founding of a new way of being. The moment of conversion is thus an inception: it breaks into the ordinary sequence of events in order to establish an unfamiliar time-space. In this momentous site, one's own being and all being comes into question. In this event, one's own being emerges inceptively (one is "born again") just as the being of all beings becomes an issue in a fresh way. This is what Heidegger calls the "turn," the reciprocal happening of be-ing and being-there.

A religious conversion can hardly be complete unless it affects one's way of dwelling in the world. Be-ing must be sheltered in beings; such sheltering can take the form of religious rituals, writing, and art. It also needs to be incorporated into one's daily interactions with others: the conversion generates an ethics. While founded on a unique juncture that must ultimately remain mysterious, religious ethics can push toward the widest possible articulation and communication.

While religious conversions are some of the most dramatic events of appropriation, we could use much of the same language to characterize other events: decisions to marry or divorce, crises of conscience, encounters with birth and death, and lesser breakthroughs that provide the thrusts and turning points in our biographies.[68] In his early lectures, Heidegger explores just

68. Cf. Vallega-Neu, "Thinking in Decision," 248, 254.

these sorts of events (e.g., GA 58, 96–97; GA 60, 143–44). What insights might we gain if we returned to these topics armed with the rich thoughts of the *Contributions*?

As we think through these straits of human existence, we will need to engage in the types of thinking that the *Contributions* explore. First, bethinking: our thought needs to *be* the event that it is thinking. We cannot simply observe and describe moments of emergency; our thinking has to form part of these moments. In thinking about a religious conversion, for instance, we would need to undergo such a conversion. Any ready-made categorization—psychological, political, philosophical—would have to be discarded as inadequate. This does not mean giving up critical awareness, however. Most of the language used by recent converts is already derivative, a package of expressions that one "buys" along with the new religion. In contrast, bethinking the event of conversion would stay in the moment of crisis and would let words and thoughts emerge from this moment itself, drawing on it as an inexhaustible source. Since the moment is an emergency rather than a resolution, this attitude would avoid dogmatism and stay attuned to the question at the heart of the experience. Bethinking must pay attention to how a new constellation of meaning emerges in the moment, instead of merely describing beings as they appear once this constellation has been fixed. Instead of representing given beings, we must speak from the event in which they are given.

Similarly, thinking of an inception must be inceptive thinking. Such thinking is not a report on an occurrence, but helps to found a new time-space. An inception happens for the first and last time. Inceptive thinking springs from this happening and circles back to it, drawing on it as it explores the new realm that the happening has initiated. In this way, an inception generates reproducibility, a set of concepts that may illuminate many situations—yet it cannot be exhausted by this scheme. This is why our concepts need to be "incepts," subordinating universal representations to the fullness and particularity of the moment.

If we manage to think inceptively about our own lives, we will remedy some of the remoteness of the *Contributions*.[69] I suggested in chapter 2 that the poet experiences everything as if for the first time, while the philosopher experiences it as if for the last time. There is a certain philosophical finality that infects Heidegger, too, in his monolithic narrative about the West and

---

69. Modesto Berciano Villalibre makes an attractive suggestion along these lines: "Heidegger's self is always intended as concrete, historical existence. We could ask whether Heidegger always fulfills his intention. But maybe where it is best assured is precisely in the human being who happens in the event": "El evento (*Ereignis*) como concepto fundamental de la filosofía de Heidegger," pt. 2, *Logos* 18, no. 54 (September–December 1990): 83.

his insistence that inception is so rare and concealed. Despite his openness to the other inception, too much that is past and present ends up being sealed and finished in Heidegger's interpretation. Present-indicative thinking in the narrow sense—the arrangement of propositions about givens—fails to think of the event of giving. But when this event is displaced from the present altogether, becoming nothing but a future possibility, we fail to notice what is happening around and in us. We need to think more inceptively and more poetically about the present.

Thinking poetically is not fantasizing but matchmaking—arranging marriages between inherited words and inceptive moments. We have to draw on historical language as deeply as we can if we are to do justice to conversions, engagements, and other critical junctures. Most scientists and many philosophers seem to believe that truth requires severing the ties between things and historical language. Truth as unconcealment requires us, instead, to keep looking for new ways to tie our language to things—while never presuming that things can be articulated exhaustively.

We must appreciate not only given beings, but the *giving* of them *as* beings. Then the beings named are not simply taken for granted as more of the same—data, cases of "something." Instead, they come forth in their surprising uniqueness, in the wonder that beings are granted at all. The hope for a language of pure be-ing is chimerical; what *is* available is a way of speaking and thinking that interprets beings while cultivating and attending to their coming forth as beings, instead of nothing. Our thought runs the risk of sterility or silence unless it keeps returning to the wealth of beings themselves in order to appreciate the unique ways in which they are given. This is not to fall back into the mere inspection and labeling of what is present, but to practice the art of finding appropriate names, the names that not only identify beings, but also elicit the happening in which they become manifest as such.

These concluding afterthoughts have explored some beginnings—the first few steps of paths that lead out from the *Contributions* to our own thinking about our own world. If we go farther along these paths, we will need to draw on Heidegger's text with both respect and skepticism. It is a book saturated with emergency, drunk on apocalypse. But as the Persians did, according to Herodotus (1.133), we should make our decisions twice—once drunk and once sober. Heidegger chooses the time of tragedy, the time in which events are irreversible and unreproducible. But there is also the time of comedy, the time in which events are imitated, parodied, renewed, and undone. As Socrates argued at the end of one drunken night, an author should master both the tragic and the comic (*Symposium* 223d). Nonurgent moments have a comic dimension that is not devoid of truth and meaning. Sobriety—which is not humorlessness—requires us to remember these moments, too. If we can preserve our capacity for sobriety and humor while appropriating Heidegger's insights into emergency, then the legacy of the *Contributions to Philosophy* may be a thinking that cultivates one's own while preserving and even enhancing rational discourse and the ethics and politics that emerge from it.

Bibliography

**Volumes of Heidegger's *Gesamtausgabe,* published
in Frankfurt am Main by Vittorio Klostermann**

GA 1: *Frühe Schriften.* Edited by Friedrich-Wilhelm von Herrmann. 1978.

GA 6.2: *Nietzsche.* Edited by Brigitte Schillbach. 1997.

GA 9: *Wegmarken.* Edited by Friedrich-Wilhelm von Herrmann. 1976.

GA 13: *Aus der Erfahrung des Denkens.* Edited by Hermann Heidegger. 1983.

GA 16: *Reden und andere Zeugnisse eines Lebensweges 1910–1976.* Edited by Hermann
Heidegger. 2000.

GA 21: *Logik: Die Frage nach der Wahrheit.* Edited by Walter Biemel. 1976.

GA 22: *Grundbegriffe der antiken Philosophie.* Edited by Franz-Karl Blust. 1993.

GA 27: *Einleitung in die Philosophie.* Edited by Otto Saame and Ina Saame-Speidel.
1996.

GA 28: *Der deutsche Idealismus (Fichte, Schelling, Hegel) und die philosophische Problem-
lage der Gegenwart.* Edited by Claudius Strube. 1997.

GA 36/37: *Sein und Wahrheit.* Edited by Hartmut Tietjen. 2001.

GA 38: *Logik als die Frage nach dem Wesen der Sprache.* Edited by Günter Seubold.
1998.

GA 39: *Hölderlins Hymnen "Germanien" und "Der Rhein."* Edited by Susanne Ziegler.
1980.

GA 40: *Einführung in die Metaphysik.* Edited by Petra Jaeger. 1983.

GA 43: *Nietzsche: Der Wille zur Macht als Kunst.* Edited by Bernd Heimbüchel. 1985.

GA 44: *Nietzsches metaphysische Grundstellung im abendländischen Denken: Die ewige
Wiederkehr des Gleichen.* Edited by Marion Heinz. 1986.

GA 46: *Zur Auslegung von Nietzsches II. Unzeitgemäßer Betrachtung "Vom Nutzen und
Nachteil der Historie für das Leben."* Edited by Hans-Joachim Friedrich. 2003.

GA 48: *Nietzsche: Der europäische Nihilismus.* Edited by Petra Jaeger. 1986.

GA 49: *Die Metaphysik des deutschen Idealismus.* Edited by Günter Seubold. 1991.

GA 51: *Nietzsches Metaphysik/Einleitung in die Philosophie — Denken und Dichten.* Edited by Petra Jaeger. 1990.

GA 52: *Hölderlins Hymne "Andenken."* Edited by Curd Ochwadt. 1982.

GA 58: *Grundprobleme der Phänomenologie.* Edited by Hans-Helmuth Gander. 1992.

GA 65: *Beiträge zur Philosophie (Vom Ereignis).* Edited by Friedrich-Wilhelm von Herrmann. 2nd, rev. ed. 1994.

GA 66: *Besinnung.* Edited by Friedrich-Wilhelm von Herrmann. 1997.

GA 67: *Metaphysik und Nihilismus.* Edited by Hans-Joachim Friedrich. 1999.

GA 69: *Die Geschichte des Seyns.* Edited by Peter Trawny. 1998.

GA 70: *Über den Anfang.* Edited by Paola-Ludovika Coriando. 2005.

GA 77: *Feldweg-Gespräche.* Edited by Ingrid Schüßler. 1995.

GA 79: *Bremer und Freiburger Vorträge.* Edited by Petra Jaeger. 1994.

GA 87: *Nietzsche.* Edited by Peter von Ruckteschell. 2004.

GA 90: *Zu Ernst Jünger.* Edited by Peter Trawny. 2004.

Other Texts by Heidegger

"Der Anklang." Loyola University of Chicago Archives. Martin Heidegger-Barbara Fiand Manuscript Collection. Acc. No. 99–13. Box 5. Folder 4.

Aportes a la filosofía: Acerca del evento. Translated by Dina V. Picotti C. Buenos Aires: Editorial Almagesto and Editorial Biblos, 2003.

Aristotle's Metaphysics Θ 1–3: On the Essence and Actuality of Force. Translated by Walter Brogan and Peter Warnek. Bloomington: Indiana University Press, 1995.

"Art and Space." Translated by Charles Seibert. In *Rethinking Architecture: A Reader in Cultural Theory,* edited by Neil Leach. London: Routledge, 1997.

Basic Concepts. Translated by Gary E. Aylesworth. Bloomington: Indiana University Press, 1993.

Basic Questions of Philosophy: Selected "Problems" of "Logic." Translated by Richard Rojcewicz and André Schuwer. Bloomington: Indiana University Press, 1994.

The Basic Problems of Phenomenology. Translated by Albert Hofstadter. Bloomington: Indiana University Press, 1982.

"Beiträge zur Philosophie (Vom Ereignis)." Loyola University of Chicago Archives. Martin Heidegger-Barbara Fiand Manuscript Collection. Acc. No. 99–13. Box 2. Folders 1–2.

Contributions to Philosophy (From Enowning). Translated by Parvis Emad and Kenneth Maly. Bloomington: Indiana University Press, 1999.

Discourse on Thinking. Translated by John M. Anderson and E. Hans Freund. New York: Harper and Row, 1966.

Early Greek Thinking. Translated by David Farrell Krell and Frank A. Capuzzi. San Francisco: Harper and Row, 1975.

"Das Ereignis." Loyola University of Chicago Archives. Martin Heidegger-Barbara Fiand Manuscript Collection. Acc. No. 99–13. Box 4. Folders 1 and 2.

The Essence of Human Freedom: An Introduction to Philosophy. Translated by Ted Sadler. London: Continuum, 2002.

The Essence of Truth: On Plato's Cave Allegory and "Theaetetus." Translated by Ted Sadler. London: Continuum, 2002.

Four Seminars. Translated by Andrew Mitchell and François Raffoul. Bloomington: Indiana University Press, 2003.

"Die Frage nach dem Sein." *Heidegger Studies* 17 (2001): 9–16.

The Fundamental Concepts of Metaphysics: World, Finitude, Solitude. Translated by William McNeill and Nicholas Walker. Bloomington: Indiana University Press, 1995.

History of the Concept of Time: Prolegomena. Translated by Theodore Kisiel. Bloomington: Indiana University Press, 1985.

Identity and Difference. Translated by Joan Stambaugh. New York: Harper and Row, 1969.

Introduction to Metaphysics. Translated by Gregory Fried and Richard Polt. New Haven: Yale University Press, 2000.

Kant and the Problem of Metaphysics. Translated by Richard Taft. 5th ed. Bloomington: Indiana University Press, 1997.

Letter to Fritz Heidegger, June 26, 1948. Collection of Richard Polt.

Letters 1925–1975. By Hannah Arendt and Martin Heidegger. Edited by Ursula Ludz. Translated by Andrew Shields. Orlando: Harcourt, 2004.

"Martin Heidegger in Conversation." Translated by Lisa Harries. In *Martin Heidegger and National Socialism: Questions and Answers*, edited by Günter Neske and Emil Kettering. New York: Paragon House, 1990.

The Metaphysical Foundations of Logic. Translated by Michael Heim. Bloomington: Indiana University Press, 1984.

Nietzsche. Edited by David Farrell Krell. 4 vols. San Francisco: Harper and Row, 1979, 1984, 1987, 1982.

Off the Beaten Track. Edited and translated by Julian Young and Kenneth Haynes. Cambridge: Cambridge University Press, 2002.

On the Way to Language. Translated by Peter D. Hertz. San Francisco: Harper and Row, 1971.

On Time and Being. Translated by Joan Stambaugh. New York: Harper and Row, 1972.

"Only a God Can Save Us." Translated by William J. Richardson. In *Heidegger: The Man and the Thinker*, edited by Thomas Sheehan. Chicago: Precedent, 1981.

Pathmarks. Edited by William McNeill. Cambridge: Cambridge University Press, 1998.

Phenomenological Interpretation of Kant's "Critique of Pure Reason." Translated by Parvis Emad and Kenneth Maly. Bloomington: Indiana University Press, 1997.

Plato's "Sophist." Translated by Richard Rojcewicz and André Schuwer. Bloomington: Indiana University Press, 1997.

Poetry, Language, Thought. Translated by Albert Hofstadter. New York: Harper and Row, 1971.

The Question Concerning Technology and Other Essays. Translated by William Lovitt. New York: Harper and Row, 1977.

Schelling's Treatise on the Essence of Human Freedom. Translated by Joan Stambaugh. Athens: Ohio University Press, 1985.

"Das Sein (Ereignis)." *Heidegger Studies* 15 (1999): 9–14.

Sein und Zeit. 8th ed. Tübingen: Niemeyer, 1957.

"The Self-Assertion of the German University." Translated by William S. Lewis. In *The Heidegger Controversy: A Critical Reader,* edited by Richard Wolin. Cambridge: MIT Press, 1993.

Towards the Definition of Philosophy. Translated by Ted Sadler. London: Continuum, 2000.

"Überlegungen" VIII–XI. Loyola University of Chicago Archives. Martin Heidegger-Barbara Fiand Manuscript Collection. Acc. No. 99–13. Box 3. Folders 2–3.

"Die Unumgänglichkeit des Da-seins ('Die Not') und Die Kunst in ihrer Notwendigkeit (Die bewirkende Besinnung)." *Heidegger Studies* 8 (1992): 6–12.

"Das Wesen der Wahrheit: Zu 'Beiträge zur Philosophie.'" *Heidegger Studies* 18 (2002): 9–18.

What Is a Thing? Translated by W. B. Barton Jr. and Vera Deutsch. With an analysis by Eugene T. Gendlin. Chicago: Henry Regnery, 1967.

What Is Called Thinking? Translated by J. Glenn Gray. New York: Harper and Row, 1968.

Other Works

Ansell-Pearson, Keith. "The An-Economy of Time's Giving: Contributions to the Event of Heidegger." *Journal of the British Society for Phenomenology* 26, no. 3 (October 1995): 268–78.

Arendt, Hannah. *The Human Condition.* 2nd ed. Chicago: University of Chicago Press, 1998.

Aristotle. *Aristotle's Metaphysics.* Translated by Hippocrates G. Apostle. Grinnell, Iowa: Peripatetic Press, 1979.

Ayer, A. J. *Language, Truth and Logic.* New York: Dover, 1952.

——, ed. *Logical Positivism.* New York: The Free Press, 1959.

Babich, Babette, ed. *From Phenomenology to Thought, Errancy, and Desire: Essays in Honor of William J. Richardson, S.J.* Dordrecht: Kluwer, 1995.

——. "Heidegger against the Editors: Nietzsche, Science, and the *Beiträge* as Will to Power." *Philosophy Today* 47, no. 4 (winter 2003): 327–59.

Badiou, Alain. *Being and Event.* Translated by Oliver Feltham. London: Continuum, 2006.

——. *Manifesto for Philosophy.* Translated by Norman Madarasz. Albany: State University of New York Press, 1999.

Bambach, Charles. *Heidegger, Dilthey, and the Crisis of Historicism.* Ithaca: Cornell University Press, 1995.

Barash, Jeffrey Andrew. *Martin Heidegger and the Problem of Historical Meaning.* 2nd ed. New York: Fordham University Press, 2003.

Behler, Ernst. "The Nietzsche Image in Heidegger's *Beiträge, Contributions to Philosophy (On the Event)."* *International Studies in Philosophy* 27, no. 3 (1995): 85–94.

Beistegui, Miguel de. "Discussion: Response to Peter Warnek." *Research in Phenomenology* 33 (2003): 277–80.

——. *The New Heidegger.* London: Continuum, 2005.

——. "The Transformation of the Sense of *Dasein* in Heidegger's *Beiträge zur Philosophie (Vom Ereignis).*" *Research in Phenomenology* 33 (2003): 221–46.

——. *Truth and Genesis: Philosophy as Differential Ontology.* Bloomington: Indiana University Press, 2004.

Benjamin, Walter. "Theses on the Philosophy of History." In *Illuminations.* Edited by Hannah Arendt. Translated by Harry Zohn. New York: Schocken, 1969.

Bennington, Geoffrey. *Lyotard: Writing the Event.* New York: Columbia University Press, 1988.

Berciano Villalibre, Modesto. "El evento (Ereignis) como concepto fundamental de la filosofía de Heidegger." Pts. 1 and 2. *Logos* 18, no. 53 (May–August 1990): 29–45; no. 54 (September–December 1990): 69–84.

Bernstein, Richard J. *Beyond Objectivism and Relativism: Science, Hermeneutics, and Praxis.* Philadelphia: University of Pennsylvania Press, 1983.

Blackburn, Simon. "Enquivering." *The New Republic,* October 30, 2000, 43–48.

Blattner, William. *Heidegger's Temporal Idealism.* Cambridge: Cambridge University Press, 1999.

Bloch, Ernst. *The Principle of Hope.* Translated by Neville Plaice, Stephen Plaice, and Paul Night. Cambridge: MIT Press, 1986.

Boeder, Heribert. "Twilight of Modernity." In *Seditions: Heidegger and the Limit of Modernity.* Translated by Marcus Brainard. Albany: State University of New York Press, 1997.

Bohlen, Stephanie. "Von der Offenheit des Seins zur Offenbarung des Seyns: Heideggers Weg zum anderen Anfang des Denkens." *Archivio di Filosofia* 62, nos. 1–3 (1994): 539–52.

Borges, Jorge Luis. "Pierre Menard, Author of *Don Quixote.*" In *Fictions.* Translated by Anthony Kerrigan. New York: Calder, 1991.

Brogan, Walter. "The Community of Those Who Are Going to Die." In *Heidegger and Practical Philosophy,* edited by François Raffoul and David Pettigrew. Albany: State University of New York Press, 2002.

——. "Da-sein and the Leap of Being." In Scott et al., *Companion.*

Brown, Rita Mae. *Starting from Scratch: A Different Kind of Writers' Manual.* New York: Bantam, 1989.

Brutti, Vincenzo. "Ritrovare ente e divino nell'essere: una lettura dei *Beiträge zur Philosophie* di Heidegger." In *Passione dell'originario: Fenomenologia ed ermeneutica dell'esperienza religiosa: Studi in onore di Armando Rigobello,* edited by Emilio Baccarini. La Cultura 76. Rome: Studium, 2000.

Callejo Hernanz, María José. "Heidegger y la otra historia de Occidente: Notas kantianas para una lectura de los 'Beiträge zur Philosophie.'" *Anales del Seminario de Metafísica* 27 (1993): 59–109.

Caputo, John D. *Demythologizing Heidegger.* Bloomington: Indiana University Press, 1993.

Carman, Taylor. "Heidegger's Concept of Presence." *Inquiry* 38, no. 4 (December 1995): 431–53.

Carnap, Rudolf. "The Elimination of Metaphysics through Logical Analysis of Language." In Ayer, *Logical Positivism.*

Casey, Edward S. *Getting Back into Place: Toward a Renewed Understanding of the Place-World*. Bloomington: Indiana University Press, 1993.

Casper, Bernhard. "'Ereignis': Bemerkungen zu Franz Rosenzweig und Martin Heidegger." In *Jüdisches Denken in einer Welt ohne Gott: Festschrift für Stéphane Mosès*, edited by Jens Mattern. Berlin: Vorwerk, 2001.

Coriando, Paola-Ludovica, ed. *"Herkunft aber bleibt stets Zukunft": Martin Heidegger und die Gottesfrage*. Schriftenreihe der Martin-Heidegger-Gesellschaft 5. Frankfurt am Main: Vittorio Klostermann, 1998.

———. *Der letzte Gott als Anfang: Zur ab-gründigen Zeit-Räumlichkeit des Übergangs in Heideggers "Beiträge zur Philosophie (Vom Ereignis)."* Munich: Wilhelm Fink, 1998.

———. "Zur Er-mittlung des Übergangs: Der Wesungsort des 'letzten Gottes' im seinsgeschichtlichen Denken." In Coriando, *"Herkunft aber bleibt stets Zukunft."*

Courtine, Jean-François. "Les traces et le passage du Dieu dans les *Beiträge zur Philosophie* de Martin Heidegger." *Archivio di Filosofia* 62, nos. 1–3 (1994): 519–38.

Cover, Alessandra. "Essere e negatività nei 'Beiträge zur Philosophie' di M. Heidegger: Linee per uno sviluppo del problema dalle prime lezioni friburghesi alla *Abhandlung 'Hegel. 1. Die Negativität'* (1938/39, 1941)." *Verifiche* 22, nos. 3–4 (July–December 1993): 319–63.

Crowell, Steven Galt. "Metaphysics, Metontology, and the End of *Being and Time*." In *Husserl, Heidegger, and the Space of Meaning: Paths toward Transcendental Phenomenology*. Evanston: Northwestern University Press, 2001.

Crownfield, David. "The Last God." In Scott et al., *Companion*.

Dahlstrom, Daniel O. *Heidegger's Concept of Truth*. Cambridge: Cambridge University Press, 2000.

Dallmayr, Fred. "Heidegger on *Macht* and *Machenschaft*." *Continental Philosophy Review* 34 (2001): 247–67.

D'Angelo, Antonello. "'Svolta' e 'attimalità' in Heidegger: Alcune considerazioni sui 'Beiträge zur Philosophie' e su 'Die Kehre.'" *La Cultura* 30, no. 2 (August 1992): 217–46.

Dastur, Françoise. "The Critique of Anthropologism in Heidegger's Thought." In *Appropriating Heidegger*, ed. James E. Faulconer and Mark Wrathall. Cambridge: Cambridge University Press, 2000.

———. "Le 'dieu extrême' de la phénoménologie: Husserl et Heidegger." *Archives de Philosophie* 63 (2000): 195–204.

———. *Heidegger and the Question of Time*. Translated by François Raffoul and David Pettigrew. Amherst, N.Y.: Humanity Books, 1999.

———. "La pensée à venir: une phénoménologie de l'inapparent?" In *L'avenir de la philosophie est-il grec?* edited by Catherine Collobert. Saint-Laurent, Quebec: Fides, 2002.

———. "Phenomenology of the Event: Waiting and Surprise." *Hypatia* 15, no. 4 (fall 2000): 178–89.

de Boer, Karin. *Thinking in the Light of Time: Heidegger's Encounter with Hegel*. Albany: State University of New York Press, 2000.

De Carolis, Massimo. "La possibilità della decisione nei 'Beiträge.'" *Aut Aut* 248–49 (March–June 1992): 173–86.

Deleuze, Gilles. *The Fold: Leibniz and the Baroque*. Translated by Tom Conley. Minneapolis: University of Minnesota Press, 1993.

------. *The Logic of Sense.* Translated by Mark Lester with Charles Stivale. New York: Columbia University Press, 1990.

DeLillo, Don. *Underworld.* New York: Scribner, 1998.

Derrida, Jacques. "Freud and the Scene of Writing." In *Writing and Difference.* Translated by Alan Bass. Chicago: University of Chicago Press, 1978.

------. *Given Time: I, Counterfeit Money.* Translated by Peggy Kamuf. Chicago: University of Chicago Press, 1992.

------. *Of Grammatology.* Translated by Gayatri C. Spivak. Baltimore: Johns Hopkins University Press, 1976.

------. *Speech and Phenomena, and Other Essays on Husserl's Theory of Signs.* Translated by David B. Allison. Evanston: Northwestern University Press, 1973.

Derrida, Jacques, Charles Alunni, Maurizio Ferraris, Patricio Peñalver Gómez, Mario Ruggenini, Valerio Verra, and Vincenzo Vitiello. "Conversazione con Jacques Derrida." *Aut Aut* 248–49 (March–June 1992): 3–16.

Dostal, Robert J. "The Experience of Truth for Gadamer and Heidegger: Taking Time and Sudden Lightning." In *Hermeneutics and Truth,* edited by Brice R. Wachterhauser. Evanston: Northwestern University Press, 1994.

------. "The Public and the People: Heidegger's Illiberal Politics." *Review of Metaphysics* 47, no. 3 (March 1994): 517–55.

Dreon, Roberta. "La questione dell'*a priori* tra *Sein und Zeit* e i *Beiträge zur Philosophie (Vom Ereignis)* di Martin Heidegger." *Teoria* 8, no. 1 (1998): 19–40.

Dreyfus, Hubert L. *Being-in-the-World: A Commentary on Heidegger's "Being and Time," Division I.* Cambridge: MIT Press, 1991.

------. "Heidegger on the Connection between Nihilism, Art, Technology, and Politics." In *The Cambridge Companion to Heidegger,* edited by Charles Guignon (Cambridge: Cambridge University Press, 1993).

Dreyfus, Hubert L., and Mark A. Wrathall, eds. *A Companion to Heidegger.* Oxford: Blackwell, 2005.

Durigon, Albert Peter. "Heidegger and the Greeks: Hermeneutical-Philosophical Sketches of Ignorance, Blindness, and Not-Being in Heidegger's *Beiträge,* Plato, Plotinus, and Proclus." Ph.D. diss., Trinity College Dublin, 1998.

Elden, Stuart. "Taking the Measure of the *Beiträge:* Heidegger, National Socialism, and the Calculation of the Political." *European Journal of Political Theory* 2, no. 1 (January 2003): 35–56.

Emad, Parvis. "A Conversation with Friedrich-Wilhelm von Herrmann on Heidegger's 'Beitrage zur Philosophie.'" In *Phenomenology: Japanese and American Perspectives,* edited by Burt C. Hopkins. Dordrecht: Kluwer, 1999.

------. "The Echo of Being in *Beiträge zur Philosophie — Der Anklang:* Directives for its Interpretation." *Heidegger Studies* 7 (1991): 15–35.

------. "'Heidegger I,' 'Heidegger II,' and *Beiträge zur Philosophie (Vom Ereignis).*" In Babich, *From Phenomenology to Thought, Errancy, and Desire.*

------. "Mastery of Being and Coercive Force of Machination in Heidegger's *Beiträge zur Philosophie* and *Besinnung.*" In *Vom Rätsel des Begriffs: Festschrift für Friedrich-Wilhelm v. Herrmann zum 65. Geburtstag,* edited by Paola-Ludovika Coriando. Berlin: Duncker und Humblot, 1999.

------. "Nietzsche in Heideggers *Beiträge zur Philosophie.*" In *"Verwechselt mich vor Allem Nicht!": Heidegger und Nietzsche,* edited by Hans-Helmuth Gander. Schriftenreihe der Martin-Heidegger-Gesellschaft 3. Frankfurt am Main: Vittorio Kloster-mann, 1994.

——. "On 'Be-ing': The Last Part of *Contributions to Philosophy (From Enowning)*." In Scott et al., *Companion.*

——. "On the Inception of Being-Historical Thinking and its Unfolding as Mind-fulness." *Heidegger Studies* 16 (2000): 55–71.

——. "The Place of the Presocratics in Heidegger's *Beiträge zur Philosophie*." In *The Presocratics after Heidegger*, edited by David C. Jacobs. Albany: State University of New York Press, 1999.

——. "Thinking More Deeply into the Question of Translation: Essential Transla-tion and the Unfolding of Language." In *Reading Heidegger: Commemorations*, edited by John Sallis. Bloomington: Indiana University Press, 1993.

The Encyclopedia of Eastern Philosophy and Religion. Edited by Stephan Schuhmacher and Gert Woerner. Boston: Shambhala, 1994.

Esposito, Costantino. "Die Geschichte des letzten Gottes in Heideggers 'Beiträge zur Philosophie.'" *Heidegger Studies* 11 (1995): 33–60.

——. *Heidegger: Storia e fenomenologia del possibile.* Bari: Levante, 1992.

Fédier, François. "Traduire les *Beiträge zur Philosophie (Vom Ereignis)*." *Heidegger Stud-ies* 9 (1993): 15–33.

Fell, Joseph P. "Heidegger's Notion of Two Beginnings." *Review of Metaphysics* 25, no. 2 (December 1971): 213–37.

Ferraris, Maurizio. "Il sacrificio di Heidegger." *Aut Aut* 248–49 (March–June 1992): 121–52.

Ferry, Luc, and Alain Renaut. *French Philosophy of the Sixties: An Essay on Anti-Hu-manism.* Translated by Mary H. S. Cattani. Amherst: University of Massachusetts Press, 1990.

——. *Heidegger and Modernity.* Translated by Franklin Philip. Chicago: University of Chicago Press, 1990.

Figal, Günter. "Forgetfulness of God: Concerning the Center of Heidegger's *Contri-butions to Philosophy*." In Scott et al., *Companion.*

——. "Last Gods: Hermeneutic Theology in Nietzsche and Heidegger." In *For a Phi-losophy of Freedom and Strife: Politics, Aesthetics, Metaphysics.* Translated by Wayne Klein. Albany: State University of New York Press, 1998.

Fried, Gregory. *Heidegger's Polemos: From Being to Politics.* New Haven: Yale Univer-sity Press, 2000.

Friese, Heidrun. "Augen-Blicke." In *The Moment: Time and Rupture in Modern Thought*, edited by Heidrun Friese. Liverpool: Liverpool University Press, 2001.

Gander, Hans-Helmuth. "Grund- und Leitstimmungen in Heideggers *Beiträge zur Philosophie*." *Heidegger Studies* 10 (1994): 15–31.

——. "Sein—Zeit—Geschichte: Überlegungen im Anschluss an Heideggers *Bei-träge zur Philosophie*." In *Histoire et avenir: Conceptions hégélienne et posthégélienne de l'histoire*, edited by Ingeborg Schüßler and Alexandre Schild. Lausanne: Payot, 2000.

Garrido-Maturano, Ángel E. "Las imposibilidades del Dios: Introducción al prob-lema de Dios en los *Beiträge zur Philosophie* de Martin Heidegger." *Universitas Philo-sophica* 28 (June 1997): 63–91.

Gasché, Rodolphe. *The Tain of the Mirror: Derrida and the Philosophy of Reflection.* Cambridge: Harvard University Press, 1986.

Gebert, Sigbert. "'Für die Wenigen—Für die Seltenen': Heideggers Zeitdiagnose, Technikkritik und der 'andere Anfang.'" *Perspektiven der Philosophie* 30 (2004): 209-38.

Gedinat, Jürgen. "De l'un et de l'autre." *Heidegger Studies* 16 (2000): 73–86.

Glazebrook, Trish. "The Role of the *Beiträge* in Heidegger's Critique of Science." *Philosophy Today* 45, no. 1 (spring 2001): 24–32.

Gordon, Peter Eli. *Rosenzweig and Heidegger: Between Judaism and German Philosophy.* Berkeley: University of California Press, 2003.

Greisch, Jean. "The Eschatology of Being and the God of Time in Heidegger." *International Journal of Philosophical Studies* 4, no. 1 (March 1996): 17–42.

——. "Études heideggériennes: Les 'Contributions à la Philosophie (à partir de l'*Ereignis*)' de Martin Heidegger." *Revue des sciences philosophiques et théologiques* 73, no. 4 (October 1989): 605–32.

——. "La parole d'origine, l'origine de la parole: Logique et sigétique dans les *Beiträge zur Philosophie* de Martin Heidegger." *Rue Descartes* 1–2 (1991): 191–212.

——. "La pauvreté du 'dernier Dieu' de Heidegger." In *Post-Theism: Reframing the Judeo-Christian Tradition,* edited by Henri A. Krop, Arie L. Molendijk, and Hent de Vries. Leuven: Peeters, 2000.

Grieder, Alfons. "Essential Thinking: Reflections on Heidegger's *Beiträge zur Philosophie.*" *Journal of the British Society for Phenomenology* 23, no. 3 (October 1992): 240–51.

Grondin, Jean. "Prolegomena to an Understanding of Heidegger's Turn." Translated by Gail Soffer. *Graduate Faculty Philosophy Journal* 14, no. 2/15, no. 1 (1991): 85–108.

——. Review of Martin Heidegger, *Beiträge zur Philosophie* and *Vom Wesen der Wahrheit: Zu Platons Höhlengleichnis und Theätet. Archives De Philosophie* 53, no. 3 (July–September 1990): 521–23.

Guest, Gérard. "Aux confins de l'inapparent: l'extrême phénoménologie de Heidegger." *Existentia* 12 (2002): 113–41.

Guignon, Charles. "The History of Being." In Dreyfus and Wrathall, *A Companion to Heidegger.*

Haeffner, Gerd. "Heidegger über Zeit und Ewigkeit." *Theologie und Philosophie* 64 (1989): 481–517.

Harries, Karsten, and Christoph Jamme, eds. *Martin Heidegger: Politics, Art, and Technology.* New York: Holmes and Meier, 1994.

Hatab, Lawrence. *Ethics and Finitude: Heideggerian Contributions to Moral Philosophy.* Lanham, Md.: Rowman and Littlefield, 2000.

Hegel, Georg Wilhelm Friedrich. *Lectures on the Philosophy of Religion.* Edited by Peter C. Hodgson. Berkeley: University of California Press, 1985.

Held, Klaus. "Fundamental Moods and Heidegger's Critique of Contemporary Culture." In *Reading Heidegger: Commemorations,* edited by John Sallis. Bloomington: Indiana University Press, 1993.

Helting, Holger. "Heidegger und Meister Eckehart." In Coriando, *"Herkunft aber bleibt stets Zukunft."*

Hemming, Laurence Paul. *Heidegger's Atheism: The Refusal of a Theological Voice.* Notre Dame: University of Notre Dame Press, 2002.

Holmes, Stephen. "The Permanent Structure of Antiliberal Thought." In *Liberalism and the Moral Life*, edited by Nancy L. Rosenblum. Cambridge: Harvard University Press, 1989.

Hübner, Hans. "'Vom Ereignis' und vom Ereignis Gott: Ein theologischer Beitrag zu den 'Beiträgen zur Philosophie.'" In Coriando, *"Herkunft aber bleibt stets Zukunft."*

Husserl, Edmund. *Cartesian Meditations: An Introduction to Phenomenology.* Translated by Dorion Cairns. Dordrecht: Martinus Nijhoff, 1960.

——. *Logical Investigations.* Translated by A. J. Findlay. London: Routledge and Kegan Paul, 1970.

Hyland, Drew. *Finitude and Transcendence in the Platonic Dialogues.* Albany: State University of New York Press, 1995.

Ionescu, Cristina. "The Concept of the Last God in Heidegger's *Beiträge*: Hints towards an Understanding of the Gift of *Sein*." *Studia Phaenomenologica* 2, nos. 1–2 (2002): 59–95.

Janicaud, Dominique. "Back to a Monstrous Site: Reiner Schürmann's Reading of Heidegger's 'Beitrage.'" *Graduate Faculty Philosophy Journal* 19, no. 2/20, no. 1 (1997): 287–97.

Kalary, Thomas. "Hermeneutic Pre-conditions for Interpreting Heidegger: A Look at Recent Literature." Parts 1 and 2. *Heidegger Studies* 18 (2002): 159–80; 19 (2003): 129–57.

Kierkegaard, Søren. *Fear and Trembling; Repetition.* Edited and translated by Howard V. Hong and Edna H. Hong. Kierkegaard's Writings 6. Princeton: Princeton University Press, 1983.

——. *A Kierkegaard Anthology.* Edited by Robert Bretall. Princeton: Princeton University Press, 1946.

Kisiel, Theodore. "The Demise of *Being and Time*: 1927–1930." In *Heidegger's "Being and Time": Critical Essays*, edited by Richard Polt. Lanham, Md.: Rowman and Littlefield, 2005.

——. *The Genesis of Heidegger's "Being and Time."* Berkeley: University of California Press, 1993.

——. "Heidegger's Apology." In Theodore Kisiel, *Heidegger's Way of Thought*, edited by Alfred Denker and Marion Heinz. New York: Continuum, 2002.

——. "The Language of the Event: The Event of Language." In *Heidegger and the Path of Thinking*, edited by John Sallis. Pittsburgh: Duquesne University Press, 1970.

Kovacs, George. "An Invitation to Think through and with Heidegger's *Beiträge zur Philosophie*." *Heidegger Studies* 12 (1996): 17–36.

——. "The Leap (*der Sprung*) for Being in Heidegger's *Beiträge zur Philosophie (Vom Ereignis)*." *Man and World* 25, no. 1 (January 1992): 39–59.

——. "Philosophy as Primordial Science in Heidegger's Courses of 1919." In *Reading Heidegger from the Start: Essays in his Earliest Thought*, edited by Theodore Kisiel and John Van Buren. Albany: State University of New York Press, 1994.

——. "The Power of Essential Thinking in Heidegger's *Beiträge zur Philosophie (Vom Ereignis)*." In Babich, *From Phenomenology to Thought, Errancy, and Desire.*

Krell, David Farrell. "Contributions to Life." In *Heidegger toward the Turn: Essays on the Work of the 1930s,* edited by James Risser. Albany: State University of New York Press, 1999.

Lachterman, David R. *The Ethics of Geometry: A Genealogy of Modernity.* New York: Routledge, 1989.

Lacoue-Labarthe, Philippe. *Heidegger, Art, and Politics.* Translated by Chris Turner. Cambridge, Mass.: Blackwell, 1990.

Law, David R. "Negative Theology in Heidegger's *Beiträge zur Philosophie.*" *International Journal for Philosophy of Religion* 48, no. 3 (December 2000): 139–56.

Lee, Su-jeong. "Zeitkritik bei Heidegger." In *Vom Rätsel des Begriffs: Festschrift für Friedrich-Wilhelm v. Herrmann zum 65. Geburtstag,* edited by Paola-Ludovika Coriando. Berlin: Duncker und Humblot, 1999.

Lewis, Michael. "God and Politics in Later Heidegger." *Philosophy Today* 48, no. 4 (winter 2004): 385–98.

Lilly, Reginald. "The Topology of *Des Hégémonies brisées.*" *Research in Phenomenology* 28 (1998): 226–42.

Livingston, Paul. "Thinking and Being: Heidegger and Wittgenstein on Machination and Lived-Experience." *Inquiry* 46 (2003): 324–45.

Löwith, Karl. *Martin Heidegger and European Nihilism.* Edited by Richard Wolin. Translated by Gary Steiner. New York: Columbia University Press, 1995.

Maggini, Golfo. "Le 'style de l'homme à venir': Nietzsche dans les *Contributions à la Philosophie* de Martin Heidegger." *Symposium* 2, no. 2 (1998): 191–210.

Magris, Aldo. "I concetti fondamentali dei 'Beiträge' di Heidegger." *Annuario Filosofico* 8 (1992): 229–68.

Malpas, J. E. *Place and Experience: A Philosophical Topography.* Cambridge: Cambridge University Press, 1999.

Maly, Kenneth. "Imaging Hinting Showing Placing the Work of Art." In *Kunst und Technik: Gedächtnisschrift zum 100. Geburtstag von Martin Heidegger,* edited by Walter Biemel and Friedrich-Wilhelm von Herrmann. Frankfurt am Main: Vittorio Klostermann, 1989.

———. "Reticence and Resonance in the Work of Translating." In Babich, *From Phenomenology to Thought, Errancy, and Desire.*

———. "Soundings of *Beiträge zur Philosophie (Vom Ereignis).*" *Research in Phenomenology* 21 (1991): 169–81.

———. "Translating Heidegger's Works into English: The History and the Possibility." *Heidegger Studies* 16 (2000): 115–38.

———. "Turnings in Essential Swaying and the Leap." In Scott et al., *Companion.*

Marion, Jean-Luc. *God without Being.* Translated by Thomas A. Carlson. Chicago: University of Chicago Press, 1991.

———. *In Excess: Studies of Saturated Phenomena.* Translated by Robyn Horner and Vincent Berraud. New York: Fordham University Press, 2002.

———. *Reduction and Givenness: Investigations of Husserl, Heidegger, and Phenomenology.* Translated by Thomas A. Carlson. Evanston: Northwestern University Press, 1998.

Martínez Marzoa, Felipe. "A propósito de los 'Beiträge zur Philosophie' de Heidegger." *Daimon* 2 (1990): 241–46.

McNeill, William. *The Glance of the Eye: Heidegger and the Ends of Theory.* Albany: State University of New York Press, 1999.

———. "The Time of *Contributions to Philosophy.*" In Scott et al., *Companion.*

Müller, Christian. *Der Tod als Wandlungsmitte: Zur Frage nach Entscheidung, Tod und letztem Gott in Heideggers "Beiträgen zur Philosophie."* Berlin: Duncker und Humblot, 1999.

Müller, Max. *Existenzphilosophie im geistigen Leben der Gegenwart.* Heidelberg: Kerle, 1949.

Neu, Daniela. *Die Notwendigkeit der Gründung im Zeitalter der Dekonstruktion: Zur Gründung in Heideggers "Beiträgen zur Philosophie" unter Hinzuziehung der Derridaschen Dekonstruktion.* Berlin: Duncker and Humblot, 1997.

Olafson, Frederick A. "Heidegger on Presence: A Reply." *Inquiry* 39, nos. 3–4 (December 1996): 421–26.

Oudemans, Theodorus C. W. "Echoes from the Abyss? Philosophy and 'Geopolitics' in Heidegger's *Beiträge* and *Besinnung.*" *Existentia* 10 (2000): 69–88.

Panis, Daniel. "La Sigétique." *Heidegger Studies* 14 (1998): 111–27.

Pareyson, Luigi. "Heidegger: la libertà e il nulla." *Annuario filosofico* 5 (1989): 2–29.

Pascal, Blaise. *Pensées.* Translated by A. J. Krailsheimer. New York: Penguin, 1966.

Patt, Walter. *Formen des Anti-Platonismus bei Kant, Nietzsche und Heidegger.* Frankfurt am Main: Vittorio Klostermann, 1997.

———. "Martin Heidegger, *Beiträge zur Philosophie (Vom Ereignis).*" *Philosophisches Jahrbuch* 98 (1991): 403–9.

Pedersen, Paul Edward. "Martin Heidegger on the Homelessness of Modern Humanity and the Ultimate God." Ph.D. diss., Cornell University, 2001.

Pöggeler, Otto. "Being as Appropriation." Translated by R. H. Grimm. In *Martin Heidegger: Critical Assessments,* edited by Christopher Macann. Vol. 1. London: Routledge, 1992.

———. "'Historicity' in Heidegger's Late Work." Translated by J. N. Mohanty. *Southwestern Journal of Philosophy* 4 (1973): 53–72.

———. *Martin Heidegger's Path of Thinking.* Translated by Daniel Magurshak and Sigmund Barber. Atlantic Highlands, N.J.: Humanities Press, 1987.

———. *The Paths of Heidegger's Life and Thought.* Translated by John Bailiff. Atlantic Highlands, N.J.: Humanities Press, 1997.

Polt, Richard. "'Beiträge zur Philosophie (Vom Ereignis)'. Ein Sprung in die Wesung des Seyns." In *Heidegger-Handbuch: Leben — Werk — Wirkung,* edited by Dieter Thomä. Stuttgart: J. B. Metzler, 2003.

———. "*Ereignis.*" In Dreyfus and Wrathall, *A Companion to Heidegger.*

———. *Heidegger: An Introduction.* Ithaca: Cornell University Press, 1999.

———. "Heidegger's Topical Hermeneutics: The *Sophist* Lectures." *Journal of the British Society for Phenomenology* 37, no. 1 (1996): 53–76.

———. "Metaphysical Liberalism in Heidegger's *Beiträge zur Philosophie.*" *Political Theory* 25, no. 5 (October 1997): 655–79.

———. "Potentiality, Energy, and Sway: From Aristotelian to Modern to Postmodern Physics?" *Existentia* 11 (2001): 27–41.

———. "The Question of Nothing." In *A Companion to Heidegger's "Introduction to Metaphysics,"* edited by Richard Polt and Gregory Fried. New Haven: Yale University Press, 2001.

Prudhomme, Jeff Owen. *God and Being: Heidegger's Relation to Theology.* Atlantic Highlands, N.J.: Humanities Press, 1997.

———. "The Passing-by of the Ultimate God: The Theological Assessment of Modernity in Heidegger's *Beiträge zur Philosophie.*" *Journal of the American Academy of Religion* 61, no. 3 (fall 1993): 443–54.

Regina, Umberto. "I mortali e l'ultimo Dio nei *Beiträge zur Philosophie* di Martin Heidegger." In *Heidegger,* edited by Giorgio Penzo. Brescia: Morcelliana, 1990.

———. "Phenomenology and the Salvation of Truth: Heidegger's Shift in the *Beiträge zur Philosophie.*" In *Manifestations of Reason,* edited by Anna-Teresa Tymieniecka. Analecta Husserliana 40. Dordrecht: Kluwer, 1993.

———. "Il problema antropologico nei *Beiträge zur Philosophie* di Martin Heidegger." *Fenomenologia e Società* 14, no. 2 (December 1991): 29–73.

———. "L' 'ultimo Dio' di Martin Heidegger." In *Heidegger e la teologia,* edited by Hugo Ott and Giorgio Penzo. Brescia: Morcelliana, 1995.

Richardson, William J. "Dasein and the Ground of Negativity: A Note on the Fourth Movement in the *Beiträge*-Symphony." *Heidegger Studies* 9 (1993): 35–52.

———. *Heidegger: Through Phenomenology to Thought.* 4th ed. New York: Fordham University Press, 2003.

———. "Martin Heidegger." In Babich, *From Phenomenology to Thought, Errancy, and Desire.*

Rickey, Christopher. *Revolutionary Saints: Heidegger, National Socialism, and Antinomian Politics.* University Park: Pennsylvania State University Press, 2002.

Ricoeur, Paul. "Narrated Time." In *A Ricoeur Reader: Reflection and Imagination,* edited by Mario J. Valdés. Toronto: University of Toronto Press, 1991.

———. *Time and Narrative.* Translated by Kathleen McLaughlin and David Pellauer. 3 vols. Chicago: University of Chicago Press, 1984, 1985, 1988.

Rockmore, Tom. *On Heidegger's Nazism and Philosophy.* Berkeley: University of California Press, 1992.

Rölli, Marc, ed. *Ereignis auf Französisch: Von Bergson bis Deleuze.* Munich: Wilhelm Fink, 2004.

Romano, Claude. *L'événement et le monde.* Paris: Presses Universitaires de France, 1998.

Rorty, Richard. *Consequences of Pragmatism.* Minneapolis: University of Minnesota Press, 1982.

Rosales, Alberto. "Übergang zum anderen Anfang: Reflexionen zu Heideggers 'Beiträge zur Philosophie.'" *Recherches husserliennes* 3 (1995): 51–83.

Rosen, Stanley. *The Question of Being: A Reversal of Heidegger.* New Haven: Yale University Press, 1993.

Ruggenini, Mario. "La questione dell'essere e il senso della 'Kehre.'" *Aut Aut* 248–49 (March–June 1992): 93–119.

Ruin, Hans. "Contributions to Philosophy." In Dreyfus and Wrathall, *A Companion to Heidegger.*

———. *Enigmatic Origins: Tracing the Theme of Historicity through Heidegger's Works.* Stockholm: Almqvist and Wiksell, 1994.

———. "The Moment of Truth: *Augenblick* and *Ereignis* in Heidegger." *Epoché* 6, no. 1 (1998): 75–88.

Russell, Bertrand. "Logical Atomism." In Ayer, *Logical Positivism.*

Sacchi, Mario Enrique. *The Apocalypse of Being: The Esoteric Gnosis of Martin Heidegger.* Translated by Gabriel X. Martinez. South Bend, Ind.: St. Augustine's Press, 2002.

Safranski, Rüdiger. *Martin Heidegger: Between Good and Evil.* Translated by Ewald Osers. Cambridge: Harvard University Press, 1998.

Salem-Wiseman, Jonathan. "Heidegger's Dasein and the Liberal Conception of the Self." *Political Theory* 31, no. 4 (August 2003): 533–57.

Sallis, John. "Grounders of the Abyss." In Scott et al., *Companion.*

Schalow, Frank. "Decision, Dilemma, and Disposition: The Incarnatedness of Ethical Action; Heidegger and Ethics." *Existentia* 12 (2002): 241–51.

——. *Heidegger and the Quest for the Sacred: From Thought to the Sanctuary of Faith.* Dordrecht: Kluwer, 2001.

Schelling, F. W. J. *Bruno: Or On the Natural and the Divine Principle of Things.* Translated and edited by Michael G. Vater. Albany: State University of New York Press, 1984.

——. *On the History of Modern Philosophy.* Translated by Andrew Bowie. Cambridge: Cambridge University Press, 1994.

Schiano, Louis J. "The *Kehre* and Heidegger's *Beiträge zur Philosophie (Vom Ereignis)*." Ph.D. diss., Marquette University, 2001.

Schlick, Moritz. "Positivism and Realism." In Ayer, *Logical Positivism.*

Schmidt, Dennis. "On the Memory of Last Things." *Research in Phenomenology* 23 (1993): 92–104.

——. "Strategies for a Possible Reading." In Scott et al., *Companion.*

Schmitt, Carl. *Die geistesgeschichtliche Lage des heutigen Parlamentarismus.* 2nd ed. Berlin: Duncker und Humblot, 1926.

Schoenbohm, Susan. "Reading Heidegger's *Contributions to Philosophy.*" In Scott et al., *Companion.*

Schulz, Walter. "Über den philosophiegeschichtlichen Ort Martin Heideggers." In *Heidegger: Perspektiven zur Deutung seines Werkes,* edited by Otto Pöggeler. Königstein: Athenäum, 1984.

Schürmann, Reiner. *Broken Hegemonies.* Translated by Reginald Lilly. Bloomington: Indiana University Press, 2003.

——. "A Brutal Awakening to the Tragic Condition of Being: On Heidegger's *Beiträge zur Philosophie.*" In Harries and Jamme, *Martin Heidegger.*

——. *Heidegger on Being and Acting: From Principles to Anarchy.* Bloomington: Indiana University Press, 1987.

——. "Riveted to a Monstrous Site." In *The Heidegger Case: On Philosophy and Politics,* edited by Joseph Margolis and Tom Rockmore. Philadelphia: Temple University Press, 1992.

——. "Technicity, Topology, Tragedy: Heidegger on 'That Which Saves' in the Global Reach." In *Technology in the Western Political Tradition,* edited by Arthur M. Melzer, Jerry Weinberger, and M. Richard Zinman. Ithaca: Cornell University Press, 1993.

——. "Ultimate Double Binds." In *Heidegger Toward the Turn: Essays on the Work of the 1930s,* edited by James Risser. Albany: State University of New York Press, 1999.

Schwan, Alexander. "Heidegger's *Beiträge zur Philosophie* and Politics." Translated by Elizabeth Brient. In Harries and Jamme, *Martin Heidegger.*

Scott, Charles E. "Introduction." In Scott et al., *Companion.*

——. *The Lives of Things.* Bloomington: Indiana University Press, 2002.

——. "Seyn's Physicality." *Existentia* 10 (2000): 21–27.

——. "*Zuspiel* and *Entscheidung:* A Reading of Sections 81–82 in *Die Beiträge zur Philosophie.*" *Philosophy Today* 41 (1997), Supplement: 161–67.

Scott, Charles E., Susan M. Schoenbohm, Daniela Vallega-Neu, and Alejandro Vallega, eds. *Companion to Heidegger's "Contributions to Philosophy."* Bloomington: Indiana University Press, 2001.

Seidel, George. "Heidegger's Last God and the Schelling Connection." *Laval Théologique et Philosophique* 55, no. 1 (February 1999): 85–98.

——. "A Key to Heidegger's *Beiträge.*" *Gregorianum* 76, no. 2 (1995): 363–72.

——. "Musing with Kierkegaard: Heidegger's *Besinnung.*" *Continental Philosophy Review* 34, no. 4 (December 2001): 403–18.

Shapiro, Ian. *The Evolution of Rights in Liberal Theory.* Cambridge: Cambridge University Press, 1986.

Sheehan, Thomas. "Dasein." In Dreyfus and Wrathall, *A Companion to Heidegger.*

——. "*Kehre* and *Ereignis:* A Prolegomenon to *Introduction to Metaphysics.*" In *A Companion to Heidegger's "Introduction to Metaphysics,"* edited by Richard Polt and Gregory Fried. New Haven: Yale University Press, 2001.

——. "A Paradigm Shift in Heidegger Research." *Continental Philosophy Review* 34 (2001): 183–202.

Shin, Sang-Hie. *Wahrheitsfrage und Kehre Martin Heideggers. Die Frage nach der Wahrheit in der Fundamentalontologie und im Ereignis-Denken.* Würzburg: Königshausen und Neumann, 1993.

Sinn, Dieter. *Ereignis und Nirwana: Heidegger — Buddhismus — Mythos — Mystik; Zur Archäotypik des Denkens.* Bonn: Bouvier, 1991.

Spanos, William V. *Heidegger and Criticism: Retrieving the Cultural Politics of Deconstruction.* Minneapolis: University of Minnesota Press, 1993.

Stambaugh, Joan. *The Finitude of Being.* Albany: State University of New York Press, 1992.

Stenstad, Gail. "*Auseinandersetzung* in the Thinking of Be-ing." *Existentia* 10 (2000): 1–10.

——. "The Last God—A Reading." *Research in Phenomenology* 23 (1993): 172–84.

Strauss, Leo. *Persecution and the Art of Writing.* Westport, Conn.: Greenwood Press, 1973.

Strube, Claudius. *Das Mysterium der Moderne: Heideggers Stellung zur gewandelten Seins- und Gottesfrage.* Munich: Wilhelm Fink, 1994.

Taylor, Charles. *Sources of the Self: The Making of the Modern Identity.* Cambridge: Harvard University Press, 1989.

Tertulian, Nicolas. "The History of Being and Political Revolution: Reflections on a Posthumous Work of Heidegger." In *The Heidegger Case: On Philosophy and Politics,* edited by Tom Rockmore and Joseph Margolis. Philadelphia: Temple University Press, 1992.

——. "Qui a peur du débat?" *Les Temps Modernes* 45, no. 529 (August–September 1990): 214–40.

Thomä, Dieter. *Die Zeit des Selbst und die Zeit danach: Zur Kritik der Textgeschichte Martin Heideggers 1910–1976.* Frankfurt: Suhrkamp, 1990.

Thomson, Iain. "The Philosophical Fugue: Understanding the Structure and Goal of Heidegger's *Beiträge*." *Journal of the British Society for Phenomenology* 34, no. 1 (January 2003): 59–73.

Trawny, Peter. *Martin Heideggers Phänomenologie der Welt*. Freiburg: Karl Alber, 1995.

Tugendhat, Ernst. *Der Wahrheitsbegriff bei Husserl und Heidegger*. 2nd ed. Berlin: de Gruyter, 1970.

Vallega, Alejandro. "'Beyng-Historical Thinking' in *Contributions to Philosophy*." In Scott et al., *Companion*.

Vallega-Neu, Daniela. *The Bodily Dimension in Thinking*. Albany: State University of New York Press, 2005.

——. "Discussion: Human Responsibility (A Reply to Peter Warnek)." *Research in Phenomenology* 33, no. 1 (September 2003): 281–83.

——. *Heidegger's "Contributions to Philosophy": An Introduction*. Bloomington: Indiana University Press, 2003.

——. "Poietic Saying." In Scott et al., *Companion*.

——. "Thinking in Decision." *Research in Phenomenology* 33, no. 1 (September 2003): 247–63.

Van Buren, John. *The Young Heidegger: Rumor of the Hidden King*. Bloomington: Indiana University Press, 1994.

Vattimo, Gianni. *The Adventure of Difference: Philosophy after Nietzsche and Heidegger*. Translated by Cyprian Blamires. Baltimore: Johns Hopkins University Press, 1993.

Vedder, Ben. "Heidegger's Notion of the Last God and Revelation." *Archivio di Filosofia* 62, nos. 1–3 (1994): 553–64.

Vietta, Silvio. *Heideggers Kritik am Nationalsozialismus und an der Technik*. Tübingen: Niemeyer, 1989.

Vitiello, Vincenzo. "Seyn als Wesung: Heidegger e il nichilismo." *Aut Aut* 248–49 (March–June 1992): 75–92.

von Herrmann, Friedrich-Wilhelm. "Die 'Beiträge zur Philosophie' als hermeneutischer Schlüssel zum Spätwerk Heideggers." In *Heidegger neu gelesen*, edited by Markus Happel. Würzburg: Königshausen and Neumann, 1997.

——. "Besinnung als seinsgeschichtliches Denken." *Heidegger Studies* 16 (2000): 37–53.

——. "*Contributions to Philosophy* and Enowning-Historical Thinking." In Scott et al., *Companion*.

——. "Technology, Politics, and Art in Heidegger's *Beiträge zur Philosophie*." Translated by Parvis Emad and Karsten Harries. In Harries and Jamme, *Martin Heidegger*.

——. "Wahrheit—Zeit—Raum." In *Die Frage nach der Wahrheit*, edited by Ewald Richter. Schriftenreihe der Martin-Heidegger-Gesellschaft 4. Frankfurt am Main: Vittorio Klostermann, 1997.

——. "Way and Method: Hermeneutic Phenomenology in Thinking the History of Being." Translated by Parvis Emad. In *Martin Heidegger: Critical Assessments*, edited by Christopher Macann. Vol. 1. London: Routledge, 1992.

——. *Wege ins Ereignis: Zu Heideggers "Beiträgen zur Philosophie"*. Frankfurt am Main: Vittorio Klostermann, 1994.

Wansing, Rudolf. "Im Denken erfahren: Ereignis und Geschichte bei Heidegger." In Rölli, *Ereignis auf Französisch*.

Weinberger, Jerry. "Technology and the Problem of Liberal Democracy." In *Technology in the Western Political Tradition*, edited by Arthur M. Melzer, Jerry Weinberger, and M. Richard Zinman. Ithaca: Cornell University Press, 1993.

Wood, David. *Thinking after Heidegger*. Cambridge, UK: Polity, 2002.

Wood, Robert E. "The Fugal Lines of Heidegger's *Beiträge*." *Existentia* 11, nos. 3–4 (2001): 253–66.

Zarader, Marlène. *La dette impensée: Heidegger et l'héritage hébraïque*. Paris: Seuil, 1990.

Zimmerman, Michael. "For a New Beginning?" *Times Literary Supplement*, 16–22 March 1990, 295.

Index

CPSIA information can be obtained
at www.ICGtesting.com
Printed in the USA
LVOW12s1748030117
519590LV00003B/213/P

9 780801 479236